Dr. Oswalt provides a daily
Old Testament, sometimes f
the truth of that passage to c
the issue. Read this book eacı.
truth that bring the Scripture passages to life in our culture and our daily
activities. I commend it to you.

Mark D. Taylor, Chairman of the Board
Tyndale House Ministries

This wonderful resource from Dr. Oswalt will take you deeper in your
knowledge of scripture, theological knowledge, and—most importantly—
your walk with Jesus. Oswalt is not only a masterful, Spirit-filled interpreter
of scripture but also has an unmatched ability to map the deep truths of
scripture onto the spiritual life in the most practical ways. This devotional
will be a priceless resource for the church.

Matt Ayars, President
Wesley Biblical Seminary

What a refreshing change! As you would expect from Dr. Oswalt, these
daily entries are not trite pick-me-ups. They are deep reflections, taking
you into the heart of a holy and loving God as revealed in his Word, leading
you to bow in awe and worship. I'm sure the Holy Spirit will use each day's
insights to draw you near and hold you close in wonder, love, and praise.

Linda Adams, Bishop
Free Methodist Church USA

JOHN N. OSWALT

WHEN *Morning* GILDS THE SKIES

*To Kent & Talena
from Vic & Cindy
Christmas 2023*

A Collection of Devotional Thoughts

JOHN N. OSWALT

WHEN

Morning

GILDS THE SKIES

A Collection of Devotional Thoughts

Francis Asbury Press

Wilmore, Kentucky

Copyright © 2023 John N. Oswalt. All rights reserved. No part of this book may be photocopied, scanned, emailed, placed on the Internet, or otherwise reproduced or transmitted in any form or by any means, electronic or mechanical, or used in any information storage and retrieval system per United States copyright law unless expressly consented to by the copyright holder in writing.

Cover design by D. Curtis Hale.

Published by The Francis Asbury Society
ISBN 978-0-915143-58-0
Printed in the United States of America

To order this book, go to www.francisasburysociety.com or contact:
PO Box 7
Wilmore, KY 40390–0007
859–858–4222
800–530–5673
fas@francisasburysociety.com

Unless otherwise indicated, all Scripture quotations are from the Holy Bible, New Living Translation, copyright © 1996, 2004, 2015 by Tyndale House Foundation. Used by permission of Tyndale House Publishers, Inc., Carol Stream, Illinois 60188. All rights reserved.

Scripture quotations marked "ESV" are from The Holy Bible, English Standard Version. ESV® Text Edition: 2016. Copyright © 2001 by Crossway Bibles, a publishing ministry of Good News Publishers.

Scripture quotations marked "KJV" are taken from the Holy Bible, King James Version (Public Domain).

Scripture quotations marked "NIV" are taken from the Holy Bible, New International Version®, NIV® Copyright ©1973, 1978, 1984, 2011 by Biblica, Inc.® Used by permission. All rights reserved worldwide.

Scripture quotations marked "NRSV" are taken from the New Revised Standard Version Bible: Anglicised Edition, copyright © 1989, 1995 the Division of Christian Education of the National Council of the Churches of Christ in the United States of America. Used by permission. All rights reserved.

Scripture quotations marked "NASB" are taken from the New American Standard Bible 1995 (NASB1995), New American Standard Bible®, Copyright © 1960, 1971, 1977, 1995 by The Lockman Foundation. All rights reserved.

*To all my students across the years
whose eagerness to learn the Word
has kept me on my knees*

WHEN MORNING GILDS THE SKIES

*(German hymn, translated by Edward Caswell
and Robert Seymour Bridges)*

*When morning gilds the skies
My heart awaking cries
May Jesus Christ be praised
Alike at work and prayer
To Jesus I repair
May Jesus Christ be praised*

*Does sadness fill my mind?
A solace here I find
May Jesus Christ be praised
Or fades my earthly bliss
My comfort still is this
May Jesus Christ be praised*

*The night becomes as day
When from the heart we say
May Jesus Christ be praised
The powers of darkness fear
When this sweet song they hear
May Jesus Christ be praised*

*Ye nations of mankind
In this your concord find
May Jesus Christ be praised
Let all the earth around
Ring joyous with the sound
May Jesus Christ be praised*

*Be this while life is mine
My canticle divine
May Jesus Christ be praised
Be this the eternal song
Through all the ages long
May Jesus Christ be praised*

ACKNOWLEDGEMENTS

Several people have made contributions to this work without which it would have probably never seen the light of day.

First, is my friend Dr. Ron Smith who suggested to me now nearly ten years ago that I should undertake it.

Then there is Mrs. Peggy Allender. I asked her if she would be willing to listen to my recorded sermons and Bible studies that were collected in the Francis Asbury Society archives and extract segments that might be rewritten for this purpose. She graciously agreed to do it, and I have laughingly, but thankfully, said to many that Peggy is the only person in the world who has listened to all my sermons and lectures. Thank you, Peggy!

Next is my son Peter, who created a website for me and suggested that I publish a weekly devotional thought on it.

When Peter's life got too complicated for him to continue as webmaster, my good friend Marvin Rayborn took over and has faithfully posted these thoughts weekly for over six years.

Then, just as we were coming up to number 365, Mary Hamilton reported to me that she had collected all of the devotions and organized them in the order of their biblical quotations and asked if I would have any use for the manuscript! I certainly did! It has made getting the material ready for publication much easier than it would have been otherwise.

Finally, I must thank Dr. Vic Reasoner and Ms. Jennie Lovell of the Francis Asbury Press, both for taking on the project and for shepherding it through to completion.

Thanks to all of you! I get the credit, but you did the work.

A NEW SONG

Oh sing to the LORD a new song, for he has done marvelous things!
His right hand and his holy arm have worked salvation for him. The
LORD has made known his salvation; he has revealed his righteousness
in the sight of the nations. He has remembered his steadfast love
and faithfulness to the house of Israel. All the ends of the earth
have seen the salvation of our God. (Psalm 98:1–3 ESV)

It seems likely that Psalms 90 through 106, sometimes designated as the
fourth book of the psalms, were collected together with the Babylonian
exile in mind; whether they were written during that time (586–539 BC)
is another question. They particularly stress that Yahweh is the King, a
thought that would be very appropriate with the apparent dissolution of
the Davidic royal dynasty. This divine kingship is a cause for overflowing
joy throughout these psalms. But there is another thought that appears in
these songs. That is the one seen here and also in the first verse of Psalm 96.
This is the idea of a "new song" (see also Psalms 33:3, 40:3, 144:9, 149:1).
What does that mean? Why a new song? A clue to the answer to the
question is found in Isaiah 43, where, following a contest between Yahweh
and the Babylonian idols, Yahweh announces that he is going to do a "new
thing" (v 19). The point is that the idols, being simply personifications of
this world's endlessly cycling forces, can never do anything new. They
must simply repeat what they have always done. So, it is not really a new
day, or a new year; it is simply a "rerun." But for followers of Yahweh, that
is not true! He, standing outside the universe, having made the universe,
can do things that have never happened before. Even though no one had
ever gone home from exile before, Yahweh says he can do it. Sing a new
song! He is not shackled neither by our situation nor by our limitations.
He can transform us!

A *Wall Street Journal* article (December 21, 2017) tells the story of
"the napalm girl," who is shown in the famous photo as a naked, screaming
child running toward the camera with flames at her back. In the article she
tells of the agony and hurt, but then of the way Christ has healed her and
made her whole—a new thing!

It is not for you and me at the dawn of a new year to dictate to God
what new thing he must do for us. But what we can do is to step into the
unknown with joyous anticipation for the ways in which our "new-making"
Father can take whatever comes to us, whether it be grief, or frustration,
or a dead-end, and transform it into joy, into fruitfulness, into endless
possibility. "Behold, I make all things new" (Rev 21:5).

January 2

FREEDOM OR BONDAGE

"But the LORD God warned him, "You may freely eat the fruit of every tree in the garden—except the tree of the knowledge of good and evil. If you eat its fruit, you will surely die." . . . "You won't die!" the serpent replied to the woman. God knows that your eyes will be opened as soon as you eat it, and you will be like God, knowing both good and evil." (Genesis 2:16–17, 3:4–5)

Current attitudes in the United States demonstrate how little we are removed from the profoundly simple words of Genesis 2 and 3. What has happened—and is happening—among us is an increasingly extreme expression of the doctrine of human freedom cut loose from the restraints of revelation. This doctrine of freedom says that humans are free to do anything they wish so long as it does not hurt someone else. And "hurt someone else" is construed very narrowly. For instance, whether the action is destructive of the society by destroying some essential element in society, such as the family, is only allowed into the discussion to be dismissed as silly. What this means is that we are each absolutely free to determine the terms of our own existence, and indeed, the nature of reality itself. We determine our gender; we determine what a family consists of; we determine how sexuality is to be expressed, etc. This is, of course, exactly what Genesis 2 and 3 say we cannot do. God, the Creator, has determined what is right and wrong for us. The first step to wisdom is to recognize and accept this truth. When our first mother and father insisted on determining right and wrong for themselves, all the evil that now infects our world came into being. Interestingly, this biblical truth that all our "rights" have been given to us by God and must be exercised within the constraints he built into his creation is implied in the U.S. Declaration of Independence. That document says "The Creator has endowed us with certain rights . . . ." (Notice "you may freely eat"?) In other words, we only have a right to freedom because the Creator gave it. Remove the Creator and his constraints, as we have tried to do, and where is freedom? It is gone and we are left with bondage, a truth our society is demonstrating every day, with people in bondage to drugs, rage, possessions, sexuality, power, etc. So, for all our vaunted intelligence, we refuse to take the very first step to wisdom: there is a God, and you are not him.

January 3

TWO RIVERS INTO ONE

"At last!" the man exclaimed. "This one is bone from my bone, and flesh from my flesh! She will be called 'woman,' because she was taken from 'man.'" This explains why a man leaves his father and mother and is joined to his wife, and the two are united into one. Now the man and his wife were both naked, but they felt no shame. (Genesis 2:23–25)

But "God made them male and female" from the beginning of creation. "This explains why a man leaves his father and mother and is joined to his wife, and the two are united into one." Since they are no longer two but one, let no one split apart what God has joined together. (Mark 10:6–9)

Near where Karen and I live in Kentucky, the Dix and Kentucky rivers join. Both are flowing in deep gorges and there is an overlook making it possible to look down on the junction. The Kentucky River is typically a tan color from the burden of silt it is carrying. The Dix River, on the other hand, having just come over a tall dam a mile or so upstream, and having dropped its silt to the bottom of Herrington Lake behind the dam, is a deep, clear green. Looking down on the two waters as they come together, the difference is marked. For several hundred yards, they flow side by side with a sharp line between them, green Dix water on the south side, tan Kentucky water on the north. As they approach the crossing of a great railroad trestle, the line of demarcation grows less and less clear, and if you look on the other side of the trestle, there is no distinction at all, but the color of the combined water is subtly different. This is an apt metaphor for marriage. Once it was "John" and "Karen" (you can guess which was muddy and which was clear!). Now it is "Jokahrnen." This is what God intended. We find our true self in giving it away to another. And that is why Satan hates marriage so. Poor deluded spirit. He thinks that the only way to find himself is in protecting that self from all comers. He does not know that his identity is a gift, a gift that can only be opened when it is given back to the Giver and away to others, especially another. I am now a different, better, truer person than I was, and that is true whether Karen is physically with me or not. We have become one. It is truly "Jokahrnen." To God be the glory.

January 4

SELF-CONSCIOUSNESS

At that moment their eyes were opened, and they suddenly felt shame at their nakedness. So they sewed fig leaves together to cover themselves. . . . "Who told you that you were naked?" the LORD God asked. "Have you eaten from the tree whose fruit I commanded you not to eat?" (Genesis 3:7, 11)

Have you ever thought about that? Why didn't Adam and Eve know they were naked before they disobeyed God, and why did they know it after they disobeyed him? I can't prove it, but I think I know the answer. Before they disobeyed God, their lives were completely in his hands and as a result they were completely un-self-conscious. Some people say, "Oh, this is just a myth to explain our change from childhood to puberty." No, I think it is the other way around. Our change from childhood to puberty mirrors what happened to our first mother and father. Furthermore, I think this is what Jesus meant when he said that we must all become as little children if we want to enter the kingdom of God (see Mark 10:15).

What am I saying? I am saying that when Adam saw Eve, he wasn't thinking of himself at all; he was just looking at the most gorgeous creature on earth. It was the same with Eve. When she looked at Adam, all she saw was a luscious hunk. But what happened when they decided they could not trust their Father to give them what they needed, that they were going to have to supply their needs for themselves? Now, when Adam looked at Eve, all he saw was Adam reflected in Eve's eyes, and it was the same for Eve. They no longer saw each other. Now, all they saw was themselves, and what they saw was shameful in its limitations and its inadequacy.

Ever since that day, we, their children, have walked through life with a mirror fastened in our hands. Of course, in this life since that day, we will never be free of self-consciousness, and it is not by any means all bad. But, oh, for the freedom not to have to worry about what others are thinking and saying about us or whether we are getting all we deserve (of course not—thank God!). To be focused—and other-focused—is exactly what 100% surrender offers us, the chance to get ourselves off our hands and onto his.

January 5
COMING HOME: PART ONE

When the cool evening breezes were blowing, the man and his
wife heard the LORD God walking about in the garden. So they
hid from the LORD God among the trees. Then the LORD God
called to the man, "Where are you?" (Genesis 3:8–9)

The longer I teach the Bible, the more impressed I am by its fundamental
unity. What is it about? It is about God coming home. From beginning
to end, that's what it is about. In Genesis 3:8–9 it is apparent that God
had been completely at home with Adam and Eve. When he walked in
the garden in the cool of the evening, he was surprised that the two of
them did not come dancing around him as they had previously, as children
with their father. But they had become unclean, and they knew it. If they
dared to allow the Clean One to embrace them, they would be struck dead
on the spot. So, they had to leave their home, the garden, and he had to
leave his home, their hearts. The Devil was sure he had won. But God
was determined to come home—and he has! This is what you see in the
book of Exodus. What was getting them out of Egypt and giving them his
instructions for life all about? The Tabernacle! It was about God being
able to come down off the mountain and take up residence right in their
midst—without frying them alive! What is the story of Israel's experience
about, from Joshua through the Judges and the Kingdom and the Exile
through the Return? There is a theme that keeps cropping up in all sorts
of ways: the house of God! Located, destroyed, built, rebuilt, destroyed,
and rebuilt. Then there is the mysterious picture in the last chapters of
Ezekiel of that perfect temple to come. Through it all, woven in, is "the
house of David." First referenced in the Old Testament in 1 Samuel 20:16,
"the house of David" is mentioned 804 times in 92 verses. What do the
two houses have to do with each other? Well, in a word—everything! God
is going to come home!

COMING HOME: PART TWO

Together, we are his house, built on the foundation of the apostles
and the prophets. And the cornerstone is Christ Jesus himself. We
are carefully joined together in him, becoming a holy temple for the
Lord. Through him you also are being made part of this dwelling where
God lives by his Spirit. (Ephesians 2:20–22 Author's translation)

The house of David and the house of God have everything to do with
each other. Throughout Israel's history, the house of God is a golden
thread running through, often tarnished, but then re-gilded. Alongside it
is the house of David. The house of God is the symbol of what God wants,
and the house of David is the means. The house of our hearts, like the
temple, is precious to God, but as the temple was so often, our hearts are
filthy—God can't live there. What is to be done?

The Son, David's and Yahweh's, would pour out his blood to cleanse
God's house—the house of David. This is such a key point. Too much of
popular evangelical theology misses it. "Why did Jesus die?" they ask. "Oh,
it was to clear our judicial record," is the response. What's the problem
with that? Well, it's not wrong, but it suggests that clearing a record,
expunging our guilt, is the sum total of salvation. That *is* wrong. Salvation,
as the Apostle John makes clear (see John 15) is to live in God (abide in
him) and for him to live in (abide in) us. I like "abide" better than all the
contemporary translations because it has that flavor of "settle down"–
be at home.

Paul understood salvation in this same way. Read the Ephesians
passage again. Does it make the hair on the back of your neck stand up?
It should! "A holy temple for the Lord," a "dwelling where God lives by his
Spirit." Me? Yes, me. You? Yes, you. This is why he wants us to know how
wide and long and high and deep Jesus's love is (see Eph 3:18). That's the
blueprint of his house—you, and me!

What do we see at the end of the story? "Look, God's home is now
among his people! He will live with them, and they will be his people. God
himself will be with them" (Rev 21:3). "I saw no temple in the city, for
the Lord God Almighty and the Lamb are its temple" (Rev 21:22). God
at home in us; we at home in him. That's the Bible—beginning to end—
coming home.

January 7

CAIN AND ABEL

"Why are you so angry?" the LORD asked Cain. "Why do you look so dejected? You will be accepted if you do what is right. But if you refuse to do what is right, then watch out! Sin is crouching at the door, eager to control you. But you must subdue it and be its master." (Genesis 4:6–7)

What was it that killed Abel? It was resentment. Cain had had a good idea of giving a present to God. His little brother copied him and for reasons that are not explained, Abel's gift was accepted, and Cain's was not. We can hear Cain saying what we have all said at one time or another, "It's not fair!" And our mothers have responded, "Honey, life's not fair." Well, it's true. There is much about life that just doesn't seem right. In this instance, we can guess that Abel's offering was accepted because it involved blood. There is no remission of sin apart from the shedding of blood, the Scripture says, and the biggest, orangest pumpkin in the world can't die for what I have done. I don't think either Cain or Abel understood that. It was supposed to be a teaching moment. But Cain couldn't get it. All he knew was that from his point of view, his little brother had gotten what he should have had.

Here is the moment for you and me. Something has happened to us that should not have, at least by our estimate. What will we do with it? God says to us as he said to Cain, "Let it go. Hang onto it, and sin will be in your living room. It's at the door now, but you don't have to let it in." "But it's not right," we say. Alright, so it wasn't. Will hugging our hurt to our breast make it right? No! In fact, Jesus has already taken that hurt—all the hurts—into himself. Why should you keep on carrying it when he already has? Offer your resentment up to God as a stinking whole burnt offering. Amazingly, it will smell good to him. If you won't, here is the bad news. At a minimum, that resentment will corrode your soul, eating up your joy and corrupting whatever is clean in you. But worse, much worse, it can build to the point where you cannot contain it anymore, and it will burst out in murder. Oh, maybe not physical murder, like Cain, but murder just the same. Resentment kills. It kills families, it kills businesses, and it kills churches. Sin is crouching at your door and mine, but by the grace of Christ and the power of the Holy Spirit, we can be its master. Praise God!

January 8

RESENTMENT

You will be accepted if you do what is right. But if you refuse to do
what is right, then watch out! Sin is crouching at the door, eager to
control you. But you must subdue it and be its master. (Genesis 4:7)

Many of us live with hidden resentments. Things have been done to us, said to us, said about us, and we are twisted-up inside. So, what do we do about it? In some situations, very healthy ones, we can address the injustice or the wrong and get it straightened out. But in many situations, that is just not possible. Think about Cain and Abel. Cain had the idea to give God an offering and Abel, little brother, copied him. But Abel's offering was accepted and Cain's was rejected! It's not fair! What did Cain do? He hugged his resentment to his heart until it boiled over into murder. Our resentments might not go that far, but the results inside of us can be as deadly.

Where did Cain fail to master the sin that was crouching at his door? He had three opportunities, and he muffed them. First, he could have chosen praise over self-pity. He could have thanked God for showing him what an acceptable sacrifice is. Instead, he clutched to himself that feeling that he had been unfairly treated. In every unfair situation there is something for which to praise God, to get your focus off of poor you.

Second, Cain could have chosen prayer over self-absorption. I was once eaten up over something nasty and uncalled-for that had been said to me. I was totally focused on my own pain. I asked God to take my resentment away. God had the nerve to ask me to pray for the other fellow! I didn't like it, but I did, and I found my whole attitude changed as I found compassion for a man whose life must have been so hard.

Finally, Cain could have chosen presentation over self-justification. We love the feeling of having been right. But God asks us to surrender the whole situation to him, including our feelings of having been wronged. But wait! If I just let it go, what will I have left? As long as I hold onto it, I will have the satisfaction of knowing they were wrong and I was right. Just give it up to God and forgive them? What will I have left? Freedom? Health? Hope? Yes.

January 9

IT BROKE HIS HEART

The LORD observed the extent of human wickedness on the earth, and
he saw that everything they thought or imagined was consistently
and totally evil. So the LORD was sorry he had ever made them and
put them on the earth. It broke his heart." (Genesis 6:5–6)

I confess I was shocked when I read those words, "It broke his heart." I
guess I was primed to read something like, "It made him furious." So,
I went to the Hebrew to check if the New Living Translation translators
had been a little loose. But no, they got it exactly right. The noun is indeed
"heart" and the dictionary says the verb means "to hurt, to pain, to grieve,"
and the form used in this verse suggests doing something again and again.
So "broke his heart" catches the point precisely.

What is that point? We can hurt God! Does our sin anger him? Of
course. There are plenty of places in the Bible where we are told that—
and well it should. He made us for something better than sinfulness. This
passage tells us something deeper about God. He made us for love! He
made us to walk with him in unbroken, fruitful fellowship. But we have
turned and slapped him in the face, and he is heart-broken. This phrase
tells us about a God who cares, a God who is fully personal. Could The
Force in the "Star Wars" movies ever be heart-broken? Of course not!
But Yahweh is not The Force! If we ever doubted that, just look at Jesus
mournfully asking if the Twelve are going to desert him like everyone else
had. That is God speaking!

But there is another side to this thought: if we can break his heart,
we can also delight him. Think of that! When you gladly say yes to his
invitation to walk with him, and to walk as he walks, in love, can you feel
his arm around your shoulder and see his smile? When the road gets steep
and you're out of breath and your calves ache but you hang on to his hand
and keep pushing, do you feel the joy pulsing through that strong hand?
Oh, brothers and sisters, let's make his heart glad!

ROCKS OR GRASS?

Finally Abram said to Lot, "Let's not allow this conflict to come between us
or our herdsmen. After all, we are close relatives! The whole countryside
is open to you. Take your choice of any section of the land you want,
and we will separate. If you want the land to the left, then I'll take the
land on the right. If you prefer the land on the right, then I'll go to the
left." Lot took a long look at the fertile plains of the Jordan Valley in
the direction of Zoar. The whole area was well watered everywhere,
like the garden of the LORD or the beautiful land of Egypt. (This was
before the LORD destroyed Sodom and Gomorrah.) Lot chose for himself
the whole Jordan Valley to the east of them. (Genesis 13:8–11a)

What happens to you when you really learn to trust God, when you
know he is for you, when you know that he is really out for your
best? You stop being a grasper, a person whose eye is always on "the main
chance." That's what happened to Abraham. He had come to the land God
had promised to him and his family. Then, afraid of a famine, he had left
it and gone to the good land of Egypt. There, afraid for his life, he had
persuaded his wife to deceive the Pharaoh and lie about her relationship
to her husband. When the Pharaoh learned about the deception, he not
only did not kill Abraham, he sent him away wealthy! I can imagine him
saying to Sarah on the way back to Canaan, "I think we have met a god we
can trust."

It was in that light then, as God continued to bless Abraham and Lot,
and their flocks continued to grow, and they needed to separate, that
Abraham could allow Lot to choose. Now think about that. Abraham is
the sheik, the head of the clan. He has absolute power over everybody in
the clan. He could easily say to Lot, "Here, *boy,* you're going to take the
poorest land, *and like it.*" Instead, as they stood there on the rocky central
ridge, looking down on the rich green of the Jordan Valley, Abraham said
to Lot, "My boy, you choose where you would like to go." It did not take
ten seconds for Lot to choose the grass in the valley. Who wouldn't? What
was going on? Why did Abraham do that? He did it because he trusted
God. Abraham knew that if he ended up with the rocks he could trust God
to take care of him. Better rocks from God's hands than grass that we have
grabbed for ourselves. From the rest of the story, we know that indeed the
rocks were better than the grass. But Abraham didn't know that as Lot
headed away down the hill. What he did know was that whatever comes
from God's hand is best. Have you learned that, really learned it? Do you
trust him?

January 11

BE PERFECT

When Abram was ninety years old and nine, the LORD appeared
to Abram, and said unto him, I am the Almighty God; walk
before me, and be thou perfect.'" (Genesis 17:1 KJV)

What does God want? He wants to walk with us. This is what
Genesis 17:1 tells us. Thirteen years had elapsed between the end of
chapter sixteen and the beginning of chapter seventeen. Thirteen years in
which there is no report of any interchange between Yahweh and Abraham.
If indeed there was none, what a relief this encounter must have been to
Abraham. It was not all over; God had not abandoned him. What does God
say? "Walk in my presence and be all you were meant to be." Is that what
it says, you say? Well, not precisely. What it says is "be thou perfect," but
I didn't think you would want to hear that. The NIV says "be blameless,"
which to our Reformation-conditioned ears says "be forensically innocent
while living in sin." But that is not what *tammîm* connotes. It means to
be whole, complete. A "perfect" lamb was not necessarily a show lamb,
but it was one that was a whole lamb, all that a lamb was supposed to be.
So, what was Yahweh saying? He was saying that if Abraham would enter
into an ongoing relationship with him, he, Yahweh, would see to it that
Abraham would become all that a human could be reasonably expected to
be. Wow!

When Morning Gilds the Skies

January 12

STANDING IN THE GAP: PART ONE

Abraham approached him and said, "Will you sweep away both the righteous and the wicked? Suppose you find fifty righteous people living there in the city—will you still sweep it away and not spare it for their sakes? Surely you wouldn't do such a thing, destroying the righteous along with the wicked. Why, you would be treating the righteous and the wicked exactly the same! Surely you wouldn't do that! Should not the Judge of all the earth do what is right?" And the LORD replied, "If I find fifty righteous people in Sodom, I will spare the entire city for their sake." Then Abraham spoke again. "Since I have begun, let me speak further to my LORD, even though I am but dust and ashes." (Genesis 18:23–27)

One of the many remarkable things in the Bible is the significance of a single individual. For us in individualist America that is not such a big thing. But in the ancient world where individuals mattered not at all, it is a very big thing. God says to them and to us, *you* can make a difference.

How? There are at least three different ways that the Bible identifies. The first is in prayer. Now if you understand how prayer works, please let me know. I like what Archbishop Temple is supposed to have said, "I do not understand prayer. I only know that when I pray for my friends, happy coincidences happen to them that do not happen when I don't pray for them." Yes. We do not change God when we pray, but we can change the course of history. When Yahweh's two companions went on, Yahweh stayed behind because he wanted to talk to Abraham and invite him to pray for the righteous people who lived in Sodom. If there were enough, God would spare that entire wicked city for them. But how many is enough? By staying behind, he was inviting Abraham to wrestle with him over that question. It was also a teaching time for Abraham. How big is God's mercy? When Abraham stopped at ten, I wonder if Yahweh was a little disappointed. If he had gone on down to five, maybe Yahweh would have counted the four of Lot's family and rounded it up to five, and saved the whole place. The point is this: does the fate of a family, or a church, or a city, or a nation depend on you—on your conversations with God? It very well may. Even if you think you are dust and ashes!

STANDING IN THE GAP: PART TWO

And I sought for a man among them who should build up the
wall and stand in the breach before me for the land, that I should
not destroy it, but I found none." (Ezekiel 22:30 ESV)

He saw that there was no man, and wondered that there was
no one to intercede; then his own arm brought him salvation,
and his righteousness upheld him. (Isaiah 59:16 ESV)

I mentioned in Part One that there are at least three ways that the Bible envisions standing in the gap. The first that we talked about is prayer. As we bear the burdens of others, we stand in the gap for them.

The second way is the one mentioned in Ezekiel 22:30. The prophet envisions the people of Israel as a walled city. It is under attack by the enemy. In Ezekiel's day there were basically two means of breaking down a city wall: a battering ram, or undermining (tunneling underneath and setting a fire in the tunnel so that the wall above would collapse). If the wall collapsed for either reason, then the defenders could only rush troops into the gap and hope to hold off the enemy until temporary repairs could be made. The believer who lives a life of integrity and love is standing in the gap when a culture begins to fall apart. As with Sodom, if God can find anybody like that, the whole "city" can escape destruction.

The third way is described in the Isaiah 59:16. Here we have substitution, where we are willing to take the punishment that is due to another. We stand in the gap for them, laying down our lives for their sake. As Paul says, that is incredibly rare (Rom 5:7). Maybe we would do it for a family member or a bosom friend, but who would do it for someone who had offended and insulted them? Yet that is exactly what Jesus did, asking the Father to be merciful to us because we really did not know what we were doing. Here is the most truly Christlike life of all, offering ourselves in the place of others.

January 14

HE WAS LIMPING

The sun was rising as Jacob left Peniel, and he was limping
because of the injury to his hip. (Genesis 32:31)

Up until that night beside the Jabbok River, Jacob had been able to get anything he wanted. Sometimes he had had to work around the obstacles, as with Rachel, but in the end he had gotten it all. Now it looked like he was going to do it again. To be sure, he was definitely in a tight spot. He had been on his way back to Canaan with all the family and wealth he had acquired during his twenty years in Syria. Maybe he thought that his brother Esau would have forgotten how Jacob had cheated him, but now the word had come that Esau was coming to meet him with 400 armed men. Jacob, forever looking out for himself, had put his family and his flocks and herds between himself and Esau, and now he was left alone to wrestle with the man who was clearly God.

Mr. Tough Guy Jacob appeared to be winning. He was going to force God to bless him. Foolish thought! God simply reached out and touched Jacob's hip, throwing it out of joint. In that moment Jacob saw all his dreams of making God do his will go glimmering. All he could do was cling to God and beg for the divine blessing that he now knew he could not do without. But this is something our gracious God longs to do, and he gave it freely. Then what? Jacob went out *limping* to meet his enemy brother. Wasn't that cruel of God? If he was going to bless Jacob, why didn't he heal him? I don't think it was cruel at all. The rest of his life I think Jacob blessed God for the reminder with every step: I can't, but God can; I can't, but God can. That is the understanding every one of us must come to, especially those of us who have always been successful: I can't, but God can. If God has given you some reminder of your weakness (as he did Jacob—and Paul [see 2 Cor 12:9]), don't pity yourself, but thank God for it. You can't, but he can!

Converted from the World

Then Jacob said to his household and all who were with him, "Put away the foreign gods that are among you, purify yourselves, and change your garments. Then let us arise and go up to Bethel; and I will make an altar there to God . . . ." . . . And God said to him, "Your name is Jacob; your name shall not be called Jacob anymore, but Israel shall be your name." So He called his name Israel. (Genesis 35:2–3, 10 NKJV)

E. Stanley Jones describes a conversation in *Christ and Human Sufferings* that has been simplified into this popular saying: "Everyone needs to be converted *to Christ* in their twenties, and they need to be converted *from the world* in their forties." A great illustration of this is found in the Jacob narrative. For many years I saw his spiritual journey as culminating when he wrestled with the man as recorded in Genesis 32. There, he came to a full surrender of himself. However, reading something by the great British preacher F. B. Meyer showed me I was wrong. Jacob was on his way home to Hebron upon God's instruction to do so (see Gen 31:13). What happened after the wrestling incident and then his meeting with Esau? He did not go to Hebron, but crossed the Jordan and settled in Shechem, "in the land of Canaan," to the extent of buying land there, paying the kind of exorbitant prices that the Canaanites required of immigrants (see Gen 33:18–19). He did build an altar there, but his family still worshipped "foreign gods." Somehow the change that had been predicted ("your name will be Israel") in chapter 32 had not taken effect. It was because Jacob thought that he could have God and the world.

It was only after his daughter had been raped by the Canaanite prince and his sons had slaughtered the Canaanites in revenge, making Jacob's name "stink," that Jacob heard (could hear?) God's call to return to Bethel, the place where Jacob had had his first encounter with God. Somehow, he finally realized that God's call is an exclusive one. He will never be content with "God and . . ."—which is what our idolatrous spirits always crave. It was only after that renunciation of Canaan and his return to his "first love" at Bethel that he truly became "Israel."

"The world" will manifest itself in differing forms for each of us, but it will always involve us in compromise of some sort. It will always be something, or someone, we have to have, something we cannot give up. Left to itself, it will make Bethel an alien place and Peniel a nostalgic memory. Give up the foreign gods, go back to Bethel, build an altar there, and allow conversion to go to the depths of your soul.

January 16

SIN AGAINST GOD

But he refused and said to his master's wife, "Behold, because of me my master has no concern about anything in the house, and he has put everything that he has in my charge. He is not greater in this house than I am, nor has he kept back anything from me except you, because you are his wife. How then can I do this great wickedness and sin against God?" (Genesis 39:8–9 ESV)

That last sentence in this passage always catches my attention; it seems so illogical. The wife of Joseph's Egyptian master is attempting to seduce Joseph. In response, Joseph tells how his master trusts Joseph with everything he owns. Logic dictates that Joseph's next statement should be, "How can I sin against my master by betraying such trust?" But he says, "How can I sin against God?" What? How did God get into the conversation? It's not the logical response. Ah, but it is profoundly logical when we ask about the foundation of social ethics. Potiphar trusts Joseph. So what? If Potiphar is stupid enough to trust him, and if Joseph has reason to think he can get away with the betrayal, why shouldn't he? He could come up with a hundred good reasons to do it, not the least of which is the unfairness of his slavery. Who says betrayal of trust is wrong, anyway? In a godless world, the only ethic is survival of the fittest and devil take the hindmost.

Yet in a world created on purpose in love by a God who shows us that in his world trust is the foundation of all relationships, the betrayal of trust is to deny the way the world is made; it is a *sin*. In short, Joseph's reasoning is exactly right; a betrayal of Potiphar's trust is wrong for one reason: *because God says so!* Many years later, David shows us the same reasoning when he cries, "Against you [God] and you only have I sinned." What? Didn't he sin a little bit against Bathsheba? And what about poor, dead Uriah, whose body is rotting out on the battlefield? Didn't he sin more than a little bit against him? Yes, by all means, David did sin against them. But *the reason* those acts were sinful was because there is a God who is even greater than a king, and he says that what King David did was wrong. Take God out of the picture, and who says that what I want to do is wrong? Certainly not you! But if I know the God of the Bible—the Trustworthy One—then you don't have to tell me what's right and wrong. I know.

ANOTHER SPIRIT

So Pharaoh asked his officials, "Can we find anyone else like this man so obviously filled with the spirit of God?" (Genesis 41:38)

I said to him, "Belteshazzar, chief of the magicians, I know that the spirit of the holy gods is in you and that no mystery is too great for you to solve. Now tell me what my dream means." (Daniel 4:9)

It is interesting that the earliest recognition of the Holy Spirit at work in a person is in the book of Genesis and it comes out of the mouth of a pagan king. Do you remember? That king is the Egyptian Pharaoh. He has just seen this young Hebrew man, Joseph, come out of an Egyptian dungeon that had been only the bottom rung of some thirteen years of reverses, where all of his obedience to God has gotten him into deeper and deeper holes. Yet Joseph is not bitter against his Egyptian persecutor. He is not cynical, not sarcastic, not arrogant; he does not even take credit for his ability to interpret dreams. After he has interpreted the dream, what does he do? Does he hug the bad news of the seven years of famine to his breast, thinking, "Good, they're going to get what is coming to them!"? No, he does not. Instead, he volunteers some good sound advice about storing up grain from the good years in preparation for the bad ones. It is no wonder that Pharaoh says, "Can we find such another in whom is the spirit of God?" That's a pagan king talking, but that pagan recognizes that there is another spirit than the old human spirit at work in the life of Joseph.

Hundreds of years later, there is another situation that is remarkably similar. Here it is the Judean captive, Daniel, who tells the dream of his captor, the Babylonian monarch: Nebuchadnezzar. Once again, the pagan king recognizes a different spirit at work. Here there is not a breath of the vindictive, the vengeful, or the self-serving that so often characterizes the human spirit. Here there is compassion, understanding, and a sincere desire to help. That is a different spirit indeed. Could such a spirit characterize you and me in our dealings with one another? Yes, indeed. The same Spirit who filled Joseph and Daniel is now the present possession of every one of us who has accepted the sacrifice of Christ on our behalf. It is only a question of turning him loose.

January 17

SALVATION

Then he blessed Joseph and said, "May the God before whom my
grandfather Abraham and my father, Isaac, walked—the God who has been
my shepherd all my life, to this very day, the Angel who has redeemed
me from all harm—may he bless these boys." (Genesis 48:15–16a)

Jacob is an old man in Egypt. The man who had thought he had to
deceive his father to get a blessing had come to understand that God
is the only true source of blessing. Out of that understanding the deceiver
had become the devoted and had himself become a means of blessing:
to Pharaoh (see Gen 47:7), to his grandsons (see Gen 48:15–16), and to
his sons (see Gen 49:28). What he says in the blessing of his grandsons
is beautiful. This is truly the meaning of salvation. We are invited to a
life-long walk with God, a God who is the Good Shepherd, one whom
the vulnerable sheep know they can trust with their lives. I see the sheep
walking down the path on which the shepherd has set them, every so often
looking back to be sure he is still there and that this is the path on which
they are to be walking. At certain points he calls, and they look back to see
him pointing to the right or the left with his staff and they turn that way.
This is how Abraham and Isaac, and now, though it took awhile, Jacob too,
had learned to live. As the Psalmist says, we are the sheep of his pasture.
Bless his name!

Unfortunately, sheep are prone to trouble. They can get going in one
direction in a mass and be impervious to the shepherd's direction. They lie
down in a low place and cannot get up again. They single-mindedly pursue
one clump of grass after the next until they suddenly realize they don't
know where they are and panic. So Jacob says that his God has not only
been the shepherd who guided him but also the "Angel" who redeemed
him when he got into trouble. Why "Angel"? Perhaps it is a reference to
the man with whom he wrestled for blessing as reported in Genesis 32,
but I think he uses "Angel" to talk about God's direct intervention in our
situation. He is not far away calling out instructions; rather, he is right in
amongst us, pulling us out of the hole, getting us back on the path, beating
off the lion, holding us close to still the hammering heart. In short, Jesus if
our Shepherd, our Angel. This is what it means to be saved.

January 18

HOLY TO THE LORD

Even before he made the world, God loved us and chose us in
Christ to be holy and without fault in his eyes. (Ephesians 1:4)

What is God's goal for human life? It is holiness and completion.
That is what Ephesians 1:4 tells us, and that is in confirmation of
Genesis 17:1, where God says to Abram, "Walk before me and be complete"*
(ESV). It is interesting to see how that thought is developed in the Bible. It
really starts with the revelation to Moses that God is so holy that the very
dirt where he appears is holy (see Ex 3:5) and confirmed again to Joshua
(see Josh 5:15). It then is fleshed out in Exodus 19:5–6, where God says
Israel will be a holy nation. The point here is that whatever belongs to God
takes on his exclusive character. That is emphasized by the gold medallion
on the front of the High Priest's turban on which was inscribed "Holy to
the LORD" (Ex 28:36). This is a key point. Holy does not mean "set apart,"
with no ethical implications, as you sometimes hear said. Holy means
partaking of the character of what you have been dedicated to. For Yahweh
that character is good, true, right, just, pure, and unfailing love. That is
God's goal for all of us, not just the priests. You get a clue to that at the
end of the Old Testament. Zechariah tells us that in the last day, even the
cooking pots will be holy, and the horses' harness bells will be inscribed
with "Holy to the LORD" (see Zech 14:20). Joel 3:17 says "Jerusalem will
be holy forever." Yahweh means for everything and especially everybody
to be his alone, sharing his character. This thought is sealed by the very
last words in the Bible: "The grace of the Lord Jesus be with all the holy
people" (Rev 22:21; see NLT and NRSV). That's the goal. God wants us
to be like him; he wants us to share his character. He began in the most
general and representative ways and brought it down to all people through
his gracious provision in Jesus.

---

* The typical modern translation of the Greek and Hebrew words for "wholeness"
or "completion" is "blameless." This might give the impression that while
something is quite defective, it is still considered to be without blame. That
impression is quite false.

January 19

HEART-HARDENING

And the LORD said to Moses, "When you go back to Egypt, see that you do before Pharaoh all the miracles that I have put in your power. But I will harden his heart, so that he will not let the people go." (Exodus 4:21 ESV)

Many people are troubled by the final sentence of this passage. It sounds as though God has taken away Pharaoh's ability to choose. Well, in a way that's true, but not in the way we tend to think. Consider for a moment. Did God arbitrarily make Pharaoh incapable of doing things he would be otherwise inclined to do? No. Pharaoh was not a nice person who would normally do kind things that would benefit others. He was a tyrant who, knowing that he was God, did only what pleased himself. Would he be naturally inclined to let his slave labor force go if asked nicely? Of course not! Would he be easily persuaded to recognize that there was a God greater than he, that in fact he was not a god at all? Never! This was who he was; these attitudes defined him. So, what is this about God hardening his heart? Why was Pharaoh this way? It was because he had made a succession of choices over a lifetime that finally left him with no capacity to make any other choices. Rudyard Kipling said it this way, "What you do when you don't have to determines what you will be when you cannot help it." God has made the world, and us, in this way: our choices determine our choices. It is in that sense, and that sense only, that God hardened Pharaoh's heart. That is how he is hardening your heart, and mine. What choices are you making today that will make it impossible for you to choose anything else tomorrow? Are you choosing God and his way at all costs? If you are, that choice will get easier and easier as time goes on. God is "hardening" your heart for what is right and true. Or are you choosing the broad, smooth way of the world? If you are, then there will come a day when you simply cannot choose the narrow, rugged road to God and his best.

January 20
YOUR GOD

You have seen what I did to the Egyptians. You know how I carried
you on eagles' wings and brought you to myself. (Exodus 19:4)

Do not bring shame on my holy name, for I will display my
holiness among the people of Israel. I am the LORD who makes
you holy. It was I who rescued you from the land of Egypt, that
I might be your God. I am the LORD. (Leviticus 22:32–33)

Why did God bring his people out of Egypt? I suspect most people
would say it was for two reasons: he wanted to deliver them from
Egyptian bondage, and he wanted to bring them into the Promised Land.
But look what the two verses above say: *he wanted to bring them to
himself so that he could be their God!* What an amazing thought. Many
people describe religion as man's search for God. We are trying to figure
out how to get him on our side, so we can use him to make our lives go a
little better. That is exactly backwards as far as the Bible is concerned. God
is looking for us, trying to get us on his side. He wants us in his arms, to
be his friends.

This is what salvation is about. Does God want to deliver us from the
guilt and power of sin? Absolutely! But why? Because it prevents us from
fellowship with him. Does he want to give us the promise of eternal life?
Of course! But why? Because that will be the completion of that life in
his arms that began here. Heaven will not be sitting on a cloud playing
a harp. It will be perfect union with your Creator. Don't miss this: the
infinite, eternal God, who needs nothing, wants to be your God, to belong
to you. What incredible condescension! And why? Because he made us for
fellowship with himself. He likes you; he wants to "hang out" with you. To
be saved is to be in that sweet relationship with him. So, are you saved?

January 21

A ROYAL PRIESTHOOD

"Now if you will obey me and keep my covenant, you will be my own special treasure from among all the peoples on earth; for all the earth belongs to me. And you will be my kingdom of priests, my holy nation." This is the message you must give to the people of Israel. (Exodus 19:5–6)

"But you are not like that [i.e., stumbling over Christ], for you are a chosen people. You are royal priests, a holy nation, God's very own possession. As a result, you can show others the goodness of God, for he called you out of the darkness into his wonderful light. (1 Peter 2:9)

At the very outset, at the foot of Mt. Sinai, when Yahweh was preparing his people to receive and accept his covenant, he gave them a vision of what he wanted for them, and indeed, for all his people forever, as Peter recognized. That vision involved a status, a character, and a function. First, they would be his "special possession," a phrase that speaks of the way he views each of us who hear his voice and give our hearts to him. We are dear to him, like an engagement ring to a bride; something to be treasured and protected and delighted in. Don't ever forget that; you are not his employee, or worse, his tool. In all his world, you are priceless to him, not because you are useful, but because you *are*.

Besides a precious status, Yahweh envisioned a particular character. That character reflects his character. Who is he? He is the transcendent Sovereign of eternity, the holy king. To belong exclusively to him, the holy king, means to share his distinctive character: God's people act like he acts as his royal emissaries in the world. But are we only emissaries? No, we are much more than that; our function is to be his royal priests. What does that mean? What is a priest, particularly in the biblical context? It is to be a mediator, a go-between, someone who brings sinful people to a righteous but forgiving God, and someone who brings a forgiving but righteous God to sinful people. We are to be windows through whom the world can see God as he really is and through whom the life-giving rays of heaven's Son can shine into darkened lives. For much of its history, Israel only remembered the first of the three parts of the vision. May we, as those who have not stumbled over Christ, not make the same mistake.

January 22

NO ONE CAN SEE MY FACE

Thus the LORD used to speak to Moses face to face, as a
man speaks to his friend. (Exodus 33:11a ESV)

And he said, "I will make all my goodness pass before you and will proclaim
before you my name 'The LORD.' And I will be gracious to whom I will be
gracious, and will show mercy on whom I will show mercy. But," he said, "you
cannot see my face, for man shall not see me and live." (Exodus 33:19–20 ESV)

These two passages seem contradictory, don't they? In Exodus 33:11,
Moses and Yahweh are face to face, yet in the Exodus 33 verses,
Yahweh says no one can see his face and live. What's going on? Actually,
there are two different experiences being described. Exodus 33:19–20
is describing a sensory experience, the act of seeing. That is simply not
possible with the transcendent God. The pagans had no difficulty in seeing
their gods; they had reproduced them in human form. But whenever the
Bible reports a vision of God, it is fascinating how the human language
breaks down. The seventy elders had a meal with God and it is said they
saw him (see Ex 24:9–11). But the only description of what they saw
was that the pavement under his feet was like heaven for blueness! The
pavement was as far as words could go. In the same way, when Isaiah saw
God, his description could go no farther than the hem of God's robe. And
when Ezekiel is describing his vision of Yahweh, he can only say, "It was a
reflection of a reflection" (Ezek 1:26–28). As creatures we cannot look on
the transcendent Creator.

So what is this about Moses speaking to God "face to face" in
Exodus 33:11? That is a spiritual experience. Yahweh desperately wants
to speak with us, to communicate with us, in an experience of intimate
fellowship. He wants us to know him, for that is the source of our life.
We cannot see him, but we can be face to face with him in heart-to-heart
communication. That is what Exodus 34:1–7 is about: Moses could only
see God's back (and notice that there is not one word of description of the
divine back), but he could hear God's heart. Don't ask for some visionary
experience. If he gives one, fine and good; but what each of us should be
asking for is to be brought to the place where we are face to face with him.

January 23
WHAT IT IS ALL ABOUT

And he said, "My presence will go with you, and I will give you rest."
And he said to him, "If your presence will not go with me, do not
bring us up from here. For how shall it be known that I have found
favor in your sight, I and your people? Is it not in your going with
us, so that we are distinct, I and your people, from every other
people on the face of the earth?" (Exodus 33:14–16 ESV)

What is salvation, biblically speaking? What does it mean to be saved? Or lost? The longer I study the Bible the more I am convinced that the Bible and the cross and salvation are all about *the presence of God*. To understand that we have to go back to the very beginning, to the Garden of Eden. What made the experience of Adam and Eve in the garden an experience of bliss? It was the presence of God. What was special about the "cool of the evening?" It was about their Father coming. He had made them for fellowship with him and he must have had tears running down his face as he watched them leave the Garden when sin entered their lives. The rest of the entire Bible is about God beating Satan and coming home. That's what it's about—God wanting to share his presence with us. God wasn't content to just live *with* his people, he wanted to live *in* them. God's people are his temple. From the beginning he has intended to return to that kind of fellowship that Adam and Eve knew in the garden. That's why Jesus came to die on the cross—so that he could live within us. He died to save us from our sins, but it doesn't stop there; it begins there. He came in order that the presence of God might be real in your life and in mine. He came to share the glory of God. "Christ in you, the hope of glory" (Col 1:27 ESV). If God is not present in your life and mine in a real sense, then we have missed what it's all about. We have missed those centuries of patriarchs and prophets and apostles. We've missed it. What it was all about was that *God could come home*. Is he at home in your life? Or do you just know the doctrine and not the reality? The greatest blessing of being a Christian is to be able to experience the presence of God in your life. Don't miss it.

January 24

I KNOW YOU BY NAME

And the LORD said to Moses, "I will do the very thing you have asked, because I am pleased with you and I know you by name." (Exodus 33:17 NIV)

At one time I was reading devotionally in 1 Chronicles, and as I read each day, I looked for something in the chapter that particularly spoke to me. The chapter for one particular day (chapter three) was nothing but names, and very strange names at that (e.g., Nogah, Nepheg, and Japhia). As I came to the end, I thought to myself, "Well, so much for that! There's nothing in there that says a thing." On the one hand, I understood why those names were important to the Chronicler. He was establishing the continuity between those desperate people who had come back from captivity in Babylon with their whole history back to Abraham, and beyond him to Adam. Yes, he is saying, despite that awful tragedy, we can still know ourselves to be the people of God.

But, on the other hand, I thought, why does it matter to God? Why put those interminable lists into the canon of Scripture for all the rest of us to read down through the ages? Then I heard a whisper, "I know you by name," and it dawned on me that God likes rehearsing all those names. They were people whom he knew—and knows. We are not just momentary bubbles on the surface of an endless ocean, here for a moment and then gone without a trace. No, each one of us is *known* in the fathomless mind of God. There will never be another one of us, and God delights in knowing each Tom, Dick, and Harry with everything that makes us who we are, talents and foibles alike. Do you feel like a cog in a machine, or a cipher on a page? Don't! God delights to know you by name and will do so through all eternity. He can never forget you; your name is written on his heart.

January 25

SHOW ME YOUR GLORY

Moses responded, "Then show me your glorious presence." The
LORD replied, "I will make all my goodness pass before you, and I will
call out my name, Yahweh, before you." (Exodus 33:18–19a)

Many times what we want from God and what God intends to give us
are two different things. Moses had just come through the horrifying
experience of the Golden Calf. It had looked as though Yahweh was not
going to personally accompany Moses and the people to the Promised
Land. But Moses had told Yahweh that they did not want the land if they
could not have him. And Yahweh had told Moses that he, Moses, was very
special to him. That encouraged Moses to ask for what many of us want:
an unforgettable experience of God's presence. He wanted to see God's
"glory." God's answer is very instructive. He says he will show Moses his
"goodness." What's the difference? A lot! Seeing God's glory is for ourselves.
But God wants to go far beyond that. He wants us to know his character.
He wants us to know who I AM really is. And it worked in Moses's case.
God did give Moses an experience of his presence: he was permitted to
see God's back. But as amazing and as awe-inspiring as that must have
been, that was not what grabbed his attention, because we have not one
word of description of the vision. What did seize hold of his mind and
heart was words, the message he heard Yahweh speak (see Ex 34:6–7).
He heard of God's compassion and tenderness, his patience and unfailing
love, his intention always to forgive—shocking ideas in the ancient world
and still pretty shocking today. Does God want you to have inexpressible
experiences of his presence? Of course he does. But much, much more
than that he wants you to know him, to know his character so deeply as
he speaks to you through his revealed word that it changes the way you
behave forever. You want to see his glory? He wants to speak with you of
his goodness.

January 26

THE WRITTEN WORD

Then the LORD said to Moses, "Write down all these
instructions, for they represent the terms of the covenant I
am making with you and with Israel." (Exodus 34:27)

The voice said to me, "Son of man, eat what I am giving you—eat this
scroll! Then go and give its message to the people of Israel." So I opened
my mouth, and he fed me the scroll. "Fill your stomach with this," he said.
And when I ate it, it tasted as sweet as honey in my mouth. (Ezekiel 3:1–3)

We live in a day of instant communication, when it is possible to think something foolish, put it in digital form, and hit Send all in a moment—and then, a moment later, bitterly regret it. But it is now "out there" and however much we may disavow it, there it is. That is what was going on with the ancient covenants. The kings who made them with subject peoples required that the covenant be written down and a copy be kept in the principal temple and read aloud regularly. Either party might have said about spoken words, "Oh, I didn't really mean that." But once the words were in permanent form, there they were, and neither side could escape the consequences of denying them. That is why God required his Word to be written. It stands as a fact, a fact that cannot be overlooked or dismissed. It is to this writing that we must return again and again. This is what God has committed himself to and what we commit ourselves to when we receive his offer of salvation by faith in Christ. When we forget it, or never know it, we have no foundation for our house of faith and like the houses of the first two little pigs, that house can be blown over by the first puff from the Big Bad Wolf's lungs. But if like Ezekiel, we have taken that written truth into our very selves, our house is built of brick on a solid foundation, and the Wolf doesn't stand a chance. Where is the Word in your life? Is it your daily food? Is it a snack from time to time? Is it gathering dust on a back shelf of the pantry? It is more important than any physical food you will ever eat? Devour the Word, the written Word of God!

January 27

THE SACRIFICIAL SYSTEM

And the LORD spoke to Moses, saying, "Speak to the people of Israel, saying, If anyone sins unintentionally in any of the LORD's commandments about things not to be done, and does any one of them . . . . And the priest shall make atonement for him for the sin which he has committed, and he shall be forgiven." (Leviticus 4:1–2, 35b ESV)

The location of the sacrificial system in the flow of the material in Exodus and Leviticus is very important. That location gives us a much deeper understanding of what sacrifice is about and how we should think about it. Now, we rightly understand that the sacrifice of Jesus, "the Lamb slain from the foundation of the world" (Rev 13:8 KJV) is the means by which God can extend his grace to us and deliver us into a saving relationship with himself. That was as much true of the Old Testament believer as it is for us. They did not understand how God's grace was available to them; we are privileged to know.

The danger is that we view that sacrifice mechanically—even magically. The blood of Jesus is interposed between me and an angry God, and then everything is okay. But that is not what the system laid out in Leviticus 1–9 teaches us. The Israelites were delivered from bondage in Egypt by grace alone. They neither earned it nor deserved it. It was available to them because Jesus Christ has given himself. They did not have to do a thing to make it happen except to obey the command: believe me and come out.

Why did God deliver them? To make them like himself. The method for that was the covenant he invited them to enter with himself (see Ex 19–24). Why did he do that? Because he wanted to live in them (see Ex 25–40). How is it possible for the absolutely holy God to live in people who sincerely intend to be in covenant with him but will ignorantly and unintentionally fall short of his absolute holiness? That is what the sacrificial system was for! It was not for people who expect to sin intentionally every day but then "plead the blood." It was not for escaping their willful sins and going to heaven anyway. It was for those who were joyfully and sincerely seeking to keep his covenant. This is why the sacrificial system follows the covenant and the tabernacle. God has made it possible for those who want to be in covenant and to live in him to be fallible and yet not be destroyed by his holiness. This is what John is speaking of in 1 John 2:1. Expect not to sin; live in the glory of his presence. But if it comes to your attention that in some way you have sinned without intending to, don't despair, we have an Advocate! Praise his name!

BOUNDARIES

I am the LORD your God. You shall not do as they do in the land of Egypt, where you lived, and you shall not do as they do in the land of Canaan, to which I am bringing you. You shall not walk in their statutes. You shall follow my rules and keep my statutes and walk in them. I am the LORD your God. You shall therefore keep my statutes and my rules; if a person does them, he shall live by them: I am the LORD. (Leviticus 18:2b–5 ESV)

W e often think that paganism is something primitive and ancient. Actually, that is not the case. The common denominator among all worldviews rightly called "pagan" is the insistence that this psycho-socio-physical cosmos is all there is to reality and that everything in it is continuous with everything else in it. Thus, at the heart of paganism is the conviction that there are no boundaries between the spiritual, the human, and the natural realms. What paganism says is, "I am ultimate and nobody tells me what to do with my life!" It says there are no boundaries between me and another man, between me and my daughter, between me and an animal—no boundaries.

God says, "There is a boundary between me and the creation and if you believe that, you will accept the boundaries I have placed in the world, especially those related to your sexual relationships." God designed us to find our fullest humanity in the sexual embrace between two sexually differentiated lifetime-committed individuals. That is not some stray, rural, unsophisticated idea, as is sometimes suggested. Neither is it an antique religious demand designed to oppress people who, through no fault of their own, have "different" desires. It is at the very heart of what it is to believe that Yahweh is God. He made us, and he is not us. So, it becomes imperative to guard our minds, our souls, and our eyes in this sexually saturated culture. We have abandoned God's boundaries, and we are immersed in a swamp of adultery, incest, bestiality, and homosexuality. God simply says, "Don't do it." If he does not change our desires, then he will give us the strength and courage to be masters over them. But don't try to deny his boundaries.

January 29

GOD'S PLAN

Moreover, I will make My dwelling among you and My soul will
not reject you. I will also walk among you and be your God,
and you shall be My people." (Leviticus 26:11–12 NASB)

The structure of the book of Exodus is not accidental. It tells us what God's plan is for us. It begins with deliverance from bondage by means of a gracious revelation of himself. That is what the plagues are about: showing who God is. That is what God has done for us in Christ. He has revealed his grace and truth (faithfulness) to us and delivered us. Then he invites his delivered people into a mutual covenant with him. If we will covenant to live in certain ways, he covenants to care for us and bless us. But what are those "certain ways"? They are behaviors that please him. And why do they please him? It is because they reflect his character. Is there something more than deliverance? Oh, yes! He saves us so that we may share his character, which is called holy (because it is the character of the Holy One).

The book of Exodus does not end when the covenant is sealed (see ch 24). What follows? Sixteen of the most boring chapters in the Bible. First of all we have instructions about how to build a beautiful worship center (see Ex 25–31). Then after a three-chapter interlude, we repeat those same instructions, but this time as a report of how they built the thing (see Ex 35–40)! Why the repetition? Because of that interlude. The people knew what they needed: the presence of God in their lives. But they thought they could do it their way and made a god for themselves (see Ex 32). That never works. God made us; we don't make God. Finally, they got the point (see Ex 33–34). Do it the way God said, not their way.

So what's the point? The goal of salvation is God's presence in our lives, right in the middle, as the Tabernacle was right in the middle of the camp. How is that presence possible? When we share his character. Holy behavior is not an end in itself. We are to live this way so that the Holy God can inhabit us. Is his presence a reality in your life? If not, is it possible that you have never allowed him to make your behavior like his?

BLESSING?

The LORD bless you and keep you; the LORD make his face to shine upon you and be gracious to you; the LORD lift up his countenance upon you and give you peace. (Numbers 6:24–26 ESV)

What is it to be blessed? Too easily we take a totally pagan attitude: it is when we have all the pleasure, comfort, possessions, and security we want. No, it is when God is in control of your life, giving you exactly what he knows you need. When he is present in your life, fulfilling his promises for you, you are blessed. Now, the good news is that he is able to bless you in spite of all human failings and in spite of the unpredictability of this natural world. In fact, he will work *through* these things to achieve his promises.

That takes us straight to Jesus. Jesus redeemed the world *through* human evil. In many ways, Joseph is the precursor of Jesus. Joseph's story tells us how God uses human evil to bring about blessing. Underneath the story is the looming famine. Can God keep his promises to Abraham that he would bless him and give him a huge family? Yes, but how? Through Joseph being sold into slavery by jealous brothers? Through Joseph being thrown into jail because of the lies of a seductress whom he rightly rejected? Through being left in jail for an extra two years because the fellow he helped forgot him? Blessing? Yes, because Joseph never gave up on God. How easily that could have happened during those long thirteen years. If it had, God would still have kept his promises, but he would have had to do it through someone else.

God is at work in your life, too. Don't assume that everything has to work right or God's not working. Don't assume that everybody has to treat you right or God's not working. Don't assume that natural disasters only befall bad people or God's not working. God is at work in everything and sometimes his working is most wonderfully seen in the most disastrous situations. If God is reigning in your heart, you are blessed with the greatest blessing of all. Don't give up on him. He's not giving up on you.

January 31

UNBELIEF = REBELLION

[Joshua and Caleb] said to all the people of Israel, "The land we traveled through and explored is a wonderful land! And if the LORD is pleased with us, he will bring us safely into that land and give it to us. It is a rich land flowing with milk and honey. Do not rebel against the LORD, and don't be afraid of the people of the land. They are only helpless prey to us! They have no protection, but the LORD is with us! Don't be afraid of them!" (Numbers 14:7–9)

What a moment it was! Everything that the people of Israel had been preparing for nearly two years was on the moment of coming true. But wait—it was going to be hard! In some ways, up to this point everything had been handed to them. God had delivered them from Pharaoh's armies without their doing anything. He had provided water and food, protection and care. So perhaps they had been lulled into thinking Canaan would be like that too—they could just walk in. But no—there was going to be opposition, and maybe, just maybe, suffering.

It is that way for us: coming into a saving relationship with Jesus is easy, relatively speaking. Yes, we need to pick up and leave our Egypts in response to his call, but he has done all the "heavy lifting." As the great Baptist preacher F. B. Meyer says, it is the walking out of that decision that is hard. The outlook is beautiful: a single heart, a surrendered will, victory over temptation. But there are giants in the way, giants that are going to fight us tooth and nail. This is the hour of crisis. Do we believe? *Can* Yahweh take us in? *Can* he do the things in us that his Word promises? *Can* he give us power to defeat the biggest giants in our lives? Well—yes— theoretically. We believe he *could*, but we're not going to give him the chance to prove it (and maybe fail). Maybe *he* could, but *we* can't (and that means that he can't either).

Joshua and Caleb scream at us across the years, "Don't rebel!" What? We're not rebelling, we just don't choose to accept his invitation. No, they tell us. Going into Canaan is not just an invitation, although it certainly is that. It is much more than an invitation; it is a command. And if you and I do not believe in his wisdom and power enough to go forward on his command, we are not merely unbelieving, we are in rebellion.

Where is Yahweh calling you forward today? Are there giants in the way? Of course! When have there not been? But they have no defense, and our God is able! Go!

February 1

OBEDIENCE

And I heard the voice of the LORD saying, "Whom shall I send, and who will go for us?" Then I said, "Here I am! Send me." (Isaiah 6:8 ESV)

Obedience has taken a "very bad rap" among us. Personally, I think this is one of the signal victories of the Enemy. Almost instinctively, we think of "obedience" as something a beaten-down peon must do at the demand of his all-powerful Sovereign or suffer some very serious consequences. How sad! This false idea is the result of a false idea of God and of our relationship to him. Yes, he is the all-powerful King. But, at the same time, he is the gracious Savior. The powerful hand extended toward us has our name written on it in blood! Do I want only to do the minimum so that I can escape the wrath of the King, or do I want to do everything I can to express my undying gratitude to the One has delivered me from eternal death? This was the response of Isaiah in the passage quoted above. He knew himself to be simply dissolved because he was filthy in the presence of the Clean. Yet here he is not only alive but cleansed of all the filth of his sin.

Oh, Yahweh, I want to do anything you want! Obedience is a glad response to the grace of God. I *want* to share the nature of my Savior. Does my behavior lift God up to a place of singular honor, glory, and wonder, or does my behavior suggest he is cold, distant taskmaster? *Our behavior reflects our relationship to God.* And our whole life is our religion. Our lives cannot be compartmentalized so that we say, "Just this part is my religion." When every day we joyfully live out the love, the patience, the ethical purity, and the integrity of God, doing so in glad response to his request (not demand) of us, *that* is our religion.

February 2

ALL OF YOU

And now, Israel, what does the LORD your God require of you, but to
fear the LORD your God, to walk in all his ways, to love him, to serve
the LORD your God with all your heart and with all your soul, and
to keep the commandments and statutes of the LORD, which I am
commanding you today for your good? (Deuteronomy 10:12–13 ESV)

What does God want from us? It's pretty simple—he wants *us*! He
wants our whole heart, our whole soul. Your heart is the core of
your being. It's the place where you make decisions, the place where you
think, where your affections shape what you do. He wants your thoughts
as they shape your behavior and your will. He wants a style of life, a way
of living; he wants your *walk*. He wants to shape the whole way you and
I live.

What does your walk look like? Does he have your whole heart? What
shapes the walk of the person whose whole heart, whose whole decision-
making apparatus, whose whole thought process, whose whole pattern of
choices belongs to God? What will be the evidence that God has gotten
your whole heart? By the way you *obey* him and the way you *serve* him. If
he has my whole heart and thus my whole being, I will want to be about
his work. If he wanted to confront evil in the world, then I should want
to confront evil. If he gave himself away for the lost, the outcast, and the
broken, then I will want to give myself away for them. If he loved the
stranger, the one who doesn't belong, the one on the outside, then I will
love them. If Jesus has my whole heart, then I will be obedient to him, and
my walk will be shaped by his life, and his life is a life of service.

Does God have a right to ask you for your whole heart? You'd better
believe it! He made you, he chose you, he loves you, and he died for you.
He will never be satisfied with anything less than all of us. What does God
want of you? Just you, but he does want all of you. Could I have ever been
satisfied with part of Karen's love? Never! Neither can Jesus be satisfied
with anything less than all of you.

February 3

ALL ABOUT LOVE

Love the LORD your God and keep his requirements, his decrees,
his laws and his commands always. (Deuteronomy 11:1 NIV)

When we think of the Ten Commandments, we often think in terms of negatives ("You shall not..."). But actually, the commandments are about love. They are establishing boundaries outside of which love will not go. Once you set the boundaries then everything within the boundaries is free. So, when God says, "Don't commit adultery," he is leaving us free within those wide boundaries to practice married love. So, it is because I love Karen that I will not break my promises to her. It is because you love God so much that nothing else will take the place of God in your life. It is because you love him that his name, his reputation, is priceless to you. You love him so much you'll be glad to take one day a week and say, "Lord, this is the evidence that all my days are yours." You'll love people so much that you'll gladly honor that couple who gave you life. You'll love people so much that you'll cherish and *respect* their possessions. You'll love people so much that you'll cherish their life, their reputation. You'll love God and humanity so much that you'll never think that your real life consists only of your possessions.

God is love and love is holiness—that selfless, purifying, consuming fire that touches all our relationships so that we are clean in them. We obey as an expression of holy love. Anything less than that is not obedience.

February 4

BACK TO THE BOOK

Fix these words of mine in your hearts and minds; tie them as symbols on your hands and bind them on your foreheads. Teach them to your children, talking about them when you sit at home and when you walk along the road, when you lie down and when you get up. (Deuteronomy 11:18–19 NIV)

I once heard that when the makers of the films "Chariots of Fire" and "The Mission" went to the Hollywood moguls and asked them to promote these films, the answer was, "We have decided we will never consciously promote anything that makes Christianity look good. Christianity has done too much evil to the world already." I do not know that that report is correct, but it certainly could be—couldn't it?—given the present culture.

Where once Christianity was the norm in America, accorded a measure of respect and authority, that is definitely no longer the case. We now find ourselves in the position of Christians in many other places in the world where Christians are in the minority—and sometimes a despised minority. So we ask, "How do we live in a society that is increasingly hostile to us, in a society in which we find ourselves constantly having to justify our existence?" The answer is not to pull our heads inside our shells and wait for the end. The answer is: Back to the Book! Why is that? Because the Bible is the Word of God, the revelation of his nature and of the one he wants to share with us.

At the heart of the Christian faith is this resounding truth: there is a God, and he has spoken! He has shown us the way to life, life eternal, and he has written it in a Book. In the words of John Wesley, "Oh give me that book!" What was it that made America a Christian nation? The Book. Many of our ancestors had only one book, the Bible. So it provided much of the furniture of the American mind. We thought in its categories, we imagined in its images, we dreamed in its stories. You and I need to recapture that in our own lives and in our families. There our beliefs will be grounded, there our morals will be shaped, there we will be nerved to stand with Daniel; Shadrach, Meshach, and Abednego; and Esther. There we will have our eyes lifted from the sordid lures of materialism. There we will be armed for whatever battles our Father calls us to. Back to the Book! If you are not reading and studying it now, then today resolve to start. Tomorrow is too late.

February 5

IN HIS HAND

Surely, it is you who love the people; all the holy ones are
in your hand. At your feet they all bow down, and from
you receive instruction. (Deuteronomy 33:3 NIV)

I give them eternal life, and they shall never perish; no one
can snatch them out of my hand. (John 10:28 NIV)

Deuteronomy 33:3 is very difficult to understand in the Hebrew. The NIV probably has the sense of it correctly, but the text actually says something like this: "Indeed, a lover of peoples, his holy ones are in your hand; they [meaning uncertain] to your feet; he lifts up from your [meaning uncertain]." Apart from the rest of the verse, I want to focus on that phrase "the holy ones are in your hand," a passage that may well have been in Jesus's mind when he spoke the words recorded in John 10:28. What a thought! Held in our Father's hand. The picture may be more graphic than that. This is the only occurrence in the Old Testament of the word here translated "love." In Arabic this root has the connotation of "embrace." So the sense may be: "You embrace us, holding us in your arms." Thank God!

One of the struggles that many people have is whether we can know that we will spend eternity in heaven. There are those who, on the basis of a statement like that of John 10:28, insist that "once saved, always saved." But that misses the whole understanding that salvation is much more than a legal position; it is a developing dynamic relationship that must be nurtured.

On the other hand, there are those who live with constant uncertainty, wondering whether they really are a believer or not, fearing that if they were to commit a sin and die before repenting of it, they would spend eternity in hell. Too often, persons like this really feel that it is their good behavior that earns them a place in heaven.

The thought contained in these two verses tells us that, as is often the case, the truth is between the two extremes. Our eternal destiny is dependent on one thing only: our faith relationship to Jesus, and that relationship is not dependent upon our ability to hold on to him, but his ability to hold onto us. To be sure, we never surrender our ability to insist that he let us go, and if our settled patterns of behavior show that we don't want him but only what we think he can do for us, we do take ourselves out of his arms. But just as long as we want to stay there and show it by our choices, nothing can break his hold. Praise his name!

CLOTHING

But the Spirit of the LORD clothed Gideon, and he sounded the trumpet, and the Abiezrites were called out to follow him. (Judges 6:34 ESV)

Since God chose you to be the holy people he loves, you must clothe yourselves with tenderhearted mercy, kindness, humility, gentleness, and patience. Make allowance for each other's faults, and forgive anyone who offends you. Remember, the Lord forgave you, so you must forgive others. Above all, clothe yourselves with love, which binds us all together in perfect harmony. (Colossians 3:12–14)

What an interesting thought: the Spirit *clothed* Gideon. The Spirit did not take over Gideon, erasing Gideon's personality. Neither did the Spirit simply use Gideon as a tool. It was still Gideon underneath, with all his uniqueness, but it was the Spirit empowering him, enabling him, enhancing him. The old saying is: "Clothes make the man." Whether that is true as a general statement or not, it was certainly true in this case. It was Gideon acting, but a Gideon who was able to be and do more—much more!—than he could have ever done without these "clothes" on. In the language of today, this is "so God." Our God does not want to wipe out our individuality; he does not want to erase our personality. He made us in all our uniqueness, and he glories in what he has made. What he wants to do is to set each of us free to be all we were meant to be, to allow us to be at our best. That's what the Spirit does when we allow him to clothe us.

Now look at what St. Paul does with this idea in his letter to the Colossian Christians. He wants us to put on the new clothes that Christ bought for us on Calvary. He does not use the language of the Spirit here, as he does in Galatians 5:22 and Romans 8:13–17, but there can be no doubt that it is the same thought. When we allow the Holy Spirit to clothe us, he frees us from our neurotic concern for ourselves and sets us free to use the awesome power of our unique personhood to bless others.

What clothes are you wearing today? Are they the grungy rags of your self-doubt and your self-inflation that you have to cling to, or are they the shining suits and dresses of Jesus, freeing you to give yourself away in blessing?

February 7

LOSING GOD

She said, "The Philistines are upon you, Samson!" And he awoke from his sleep and said, "I will go out as at other times and shake myself free." But he did not know that the LORD had departed from him. (Judges 16:20 NASB)

How do you lose God? That seems crazy, like losing the Empire State Building. Actually, it is not hard at all. We find a great example in the Old Testament character Samson. If you remember, he was designated as a champion to deliver his people from the oppression of their neighbors, the Philistines. He had great strength as a gift from God, and that gift was symbolized by his uncut hair. The day came when, as the verse above says, he went out not knowing that God was not with him. He had lost God.

How did it happen? There were three easy steps. First, he catered to his weakness, which in his case was women—enemy women! He went from one Philistine woman to another. Do you know your weakness? Are you guarding against it?

Second, he made no recorded effort to stay close to God, the source of his strength. He clearly took his strength for granted. He had always been strong, and as far as he was concerned, always would be. What about you? Are you spiritually strong now? It is a gift. Are you cultivating your relationship to the Giver?

Third, he allowed his enemy-lover closer and closer to the source of his strength. Here again we see his fundamental error: he did not really believe his strength was a gift. If he had, he never would have allowed Delilah near his hair. But inch by inch, he let her come closer and closer, until finally he was shorn, and God was gone.

This story is not about hair. It is about a relationship with God. Will you guard it with your life? You must, for it *is* your life. God won't let go of you easily, but he will let go, if you insist. As in a marriage: persistently neglect it, and one day some other relationship will be more important than it, and the marriage will be gone. Whatever you do, don't lose God!

WHERE IS THE GLORY?

Now [Eli's] daughter-in-law, the wife of Phinehas, was pregnant, about to give birth. And when she heard the news that the ark of God was captured, and that her father-in-law and her husband were dead, she bowed and gave birth, for her pains came upon her. And about the time of her death the women attending her said to her, "Do not be afraid, for you have borne a son." But she did not answer or pay attention. And she named the child Ichabod, saying, "The glory has departed from Israel!" because the ark of God had been captured and because of her father-in-law and her husband. (1 Samuel 4:19–21 ESV)

The name "Ichabod" means "Where is the glory?" In Hebrew *kabod* "glory" has a meaning that is contrary to the connotation of "glory" in English. To us "glory" is something beautiful and wonderful but without substance, like the glory of a sunset. While we have it, it is stunning and absorbing, but we know that it will not last. That is not the sense of the Hebrew word. It connotes lasting significance, a weightiness and importance that comes from significant achievements. Thus, when Isaiah 6:4 says that Yahweh's glory fills the earth, it is saying that when we look at nature, we ought to see the unchanging reality of the Creator. What was the ark of the covenant? It was the sign that the unchanging God had entered into a covenant with Israel that he would not break. This gave Israel a significance, a glory, different from any other nation on earth. It gave Israel a reality that could not be shaken. Now the ark was gone, and with it the glory that made Israel what it was. Jesus said he came to share the glory of God with us (see John 17:22). As partakers of the New Covenant, we have a glory that must make us different from a world that is caught up in all the latest fads, here today and gone tomorrow. All the polls tell us that there is no significant difference between the values of the church and the values of the world. Where is the glory?

Christ has come to make us real, solid, dependable people who can be counted on—counted on to keep their promises, counted on to give when the giving is costly, counted on to be there when everybody else has run off after some new thing, counted on to do what is right whether anyone is watching or not. None of this is possible in the long haul unless the Glory—the reality of Jesus—is in us. Where is the glory in your life and mine? Is it there?

February 9

GIVE US A KING

Finally, all the elders of Israel met at Ramah to discuss the matter with Samuel. "Look," they told him, "you are now old, and your sons are not like you. Give us a king to judge us like all the other nations have." Samuel was displeased with their request and went to the LORD for guidance. "Do everything they say to you," the LORD replied, "for they are rejecting me, not you. They don't want me to be their king any longer." (1 Samuel 8:4–7)

The Hebrew people were frightened. It was a new day. No longer was it warlords who ruled for a time and then disappeared. Now the Philistines had settled on the Mediterranean coast with their new iron weapons, and it was clear that they intended to occupy Canaan for the long term. Furthermore, it seemed clear that the old system was failing them: Samuel was not long for this world, and his sons were not fit to follow him. Who was going to be their "judge," their deliverer? They could not stand the idea of dependence on God while waiting for an anointed leader of his choosing. In their fear they demanded the kind of despotic leader the world knew: a king.

Was that a good choice? Not really. In very few cases does a human being have the character to hold absolute power lightly. So, Samuel told them just what kind of oppression they had to look forward to in the kings they had demanded (see 1 Sam 8). That did not take a lot of prophetic acumen; he had only to point to the world around. Yet they insisted: fear always clouds judgment.

Samuel was absolutely right, as any perusal of the books of Kings makes amply clear. Even the best kings usually ended their reigns under some sort of a cloud caused by an abuse of power or of faulty judgment. So, is this what we have to look forward to when we decide to give people power out of fear? Well, yes.

Thank God, that is not the end of the story. If the people demanded a king, which was not God's ideal plan, then God would use that very demand to identify and shape the true deliverer. Who would he be? The Messiah, that is, the anointed King. As the people groaned under a long succession of failed human kings, they began to wonder if God could ever give them a true King, one who would care more for them than for himself. Sure enough, that day came, although certainly not in the way they anticipated. God is always faithful, but he is also always creative.

So, for us, if we act out of our fear, demanding a human deliverer of our own making, we may expect to reap long, hard results of that foolish action. But, praise be to God, he can transform even the results of our folly into unimaginable good. We only need to have the fortitude to stay the course in faith, love, and integrity—and probably suffering—while we wait to see how God will use it all for the ultimate blessing of the world.

February 10

SAUL

And Samuel said, "Though you are little in your own eyes,
are you not the head of the tribes of Israel? The LORD
anointed you king over Israel." (1 Samuel 15:17 ESV)

Have you ever given much thought to the sins of Saul? What was it that cost him the kingdom? His sins are described in 1 Samuel 13–15. He tried to play the part of the priest; he made a foolish oath; and he would not obey God and sacrifice to him everything the Amalekites had. What's so bad about those? To understand it, you have to recognize the thing all three have in common. They were all about Saul's image. In the first case, the soldiers were leaving him and he could not attack unless an offering had been made. In the second, he wanted to make sure nobody stopped to eat until the enemies who had humiliated him were destroyed. And in the third, he was afraid his troops would turn on him if he did not let them keep the best of the spoils.

Saul was 6'4 and handsome. Did he have a towering ego convinced that the world revolved around him? I don't think so. What we actually see in Saul is a devouring inferiority complex. Inside that tall, impressive shell was a little man constantly thinking, "Do they like me? How am I doing? What are they saying?" That's where his consuming jealousy of David came from. At the end, he was never able to get Saul off Saul's hands. He was a dejected, rejected, abandoned man trying to keep his floundering ship afloat.

Saul's sins were sins of the spirit. They are the sins that grow out of an *un*-surrendered spirit, a spirit that can never quite give itself away to God, a spirit consumed with its own reputation and not God's, a spirit never really set free—that's the way of great loss. Have you given yourself away? Are you free?

February 11

WHICH TRAIL?

Now, therefore, the sword will never depart from your
house, because you despised me and took the wife of Uriah
the Hittite to be your own. (2 Samuel 12:10 NIV)

Once, while reading in 2 Samuel, I was struck by the trail of death that extends outward from 2 Samuel 11, where David violated Bathsheba and had her husband killed. It starts with the crown prince, Amnon. The narrator does not tell us that Amnon justified violating his half-sister Tamar on the basis of what his father had done, but the juxtaposition of the two events surely invites us to make the connection. Surprisingly, David does nothing about this; the result of his own guilt over what he had done? So Absalom, Tamar's brother and Amnon's half-brother, engineers Amnon's death at a party. According to the text, David is actually glad about this, but of course he cannot countenance bloody treachery in his own house, so he must refuse to be reconciled with Absalom in any meaningful way. That leads Absalom to revolt, and the life of David itself is threatened.

Ahithophel, David's most gifted counselor, sides with Absalom, but when he recognizes that one of David's other counselors, Hushai, is secretly working against him for David and that Hushai's counsel is being accepted, Ahithophel commits suicide. The trail of death.

Ahithophel's counsel would have led to the capture of David alone, but that having failed, Absalom must lead his army against David's, resulting in many more deaths, finally even Absalom's. But the trail has not ended yet. Because of the revolt, the country has become divided, with Judah becoming separated from the other tribes of Israel. David, unable to forgive his faithful general Joab for having brutally killed Absalom, offers the generalship to Amasa, a Judean, if he will bring the Judean army under David's control. Joab, unwilling to accept such a demotion, kills Amasa. The trail of death.

I remind you of this gruesome story for one reason: you and I can start a trail. It can be a trail that leads from life to life, or it can be a trail that leads from death to death. Did David have any idea what trail he was starting that afternoon when he stole his neighbor's wife? No, he did not. He thought it was just a moment of stolen pleasure with no consequences. But that one sin splashed a widening smear of blood across David's life and the lives of all those around him. Don't think your sudden little choices have no consequences. They do. What will be the result of your choices today? Life, or death?

February 12

WHAT ARE YOU MAKING OF YOURSELF?

So the king sent for Shimei and demanded, "Didn't I make you swear by the LORD and warn you not to go anywhere else or you would surely die? And you replied, 'The sentence is fair; I will do as you say.' Then why haven't you kept your oath to the LORD and obeyed my command?" (1 Kings 2:42–43)

In 1 Kings 2, three men die. One of them is Joab, the general who had murdered two of his rivals in cold blood. The other two, Adonijah and Shimei, didn't have to die. What happened? Each of them succumbed to what he had made of himself.

Adonijah's attempt to make himself king had failed. David had chosen Solomon to succeed him, following Yahweh's direction. Now Solomon had magnanimously extended amnesty to Adonijah, but Adonijah played the fool. David, Adonijah's father, had not taught him to discipline himself (see 1 Kings 1:4). As a result, Adonijah had made himself self-indulgent, doing whatever he wanted, whenever he wanted. So, with incredible lack of foresight, Adonijah asked that David's de facto concubine, Abishag, be given him. As Solomon said, "Next, he'll be asking for the kingdom," and Adonijah died.

What about Shimei? When David was fleeing Absalom, Shimei let himself go in a fury of contempt against David, screaming curses, throwing rocks, etc. (see 2 Sam 16:13). Then when David was returning after Absalom's death, Shimei was right at the front to welcome David back (see 2 Sam 19:16). What do we see? Another man who did not think. In this case, it was impetuosity. If it occurred to him, he did it. David forgave him, but he told Solomon to keep an eye on him. So, Solomon told Shimei to stay in Jerusalem or die. What happened? A couple of Shimei's slaves ran away. What did Shimei do? He took off right after them. Bad choice.

Both these men destroyed themselves, one through thoughtless self-indulgence, the other through thoughtless impetuosity. This is what they had made of themselves through years of self-serving choices. What are you and I making of ourselves? What grooves are we wearing in our souls that one day we will not be able to get out of? Thank God, he can redeem us and transform us, but it will not happen without our active cooperation. What are you making of yourself today?

February 13

UNTIL IT'S OVER

In Solomon's old age, [his wives] turned his heart to worship other gods instead of being completely faithful to the LORD his God, as his father, David, had been. Solomon worshiped Ashtoreth, the goddess of the Sidonians, and Molech, the detestable god of the Ammonites. In this way, Solomon did what was evil in the LORD's sight; he refused to follow the LORD completely, as his father, David, had done. (1 Kings 11:4–6)

However you look at it, Solomon's story ends badly. After all his accomplishments, after all his glory, to have these things said about him—they are his epitaph. What a tragedy! It makes me think of the words of the famous baseball player, Yogi Berra: "It ain't over till it's over." How easy it is for those of us who are older to think that now that we have reached the sunset years, we can sort of coast. It is not true! Our enemy remains the implacable roaring lion whose unchanging goal is to destroy us. He does not "back off" as we come nearer to the end of the earthly road. He is just as eager to destroy us in our last days as in our first. Regular examination of our motives, commitments, and behavior is just as necessary in the twilight as it was in the dawn.

That brings us to another thought. Solomon's story is not merely about failure at the end. That final failure was the fatal flowering of something that had been planted years before. First Kings 1–2 tells us how Solomon became king and how his rule was firmly established. Then 1 Kings 3:2–15 tells the beautiful story of his humbly asking God for wisdom to rule God's people and of God's gracious response. What about 1 Kings 3:1? It is almost an aside, as though the narrator is saying, "Oh, by the way . . . ." By placing it here at the very beginning of the story of Solomon's accomplishments, the narrator is subtly saying that his "by the way" has deadly implications. The little verse says that Solomon married an Egyptian princess. What a coup! What an honor! What a great statement about the surrounding world's recognition of Solomon's significance at the very outset of his career. Yet it was something that had been forbidden by God. It was just a little thing, only worth a single verse. But it was not a little thing. It set a course in Solomon's life that was to prove deadly in the end.

In the days before paved highways, when roads were simply muddy tracks, deep ruts would form. It is said that somewhere on the plains was a sign saying, "Choose your ruts carefully, you'll be in them for the next 40 miles." What seemingly unimportant little choices are you making today that will hold you in iron and perhaps even write your epitaph years from now?

SUFFERING WITH CONFIDENCE

And if children, then heirs—heirs of God and fellow heirs
with Christ, provided we suffer with him in order that we
may also be glorified with him. (Romans 8:17 ESV)

And while he was still speaking with them, the messenger came
down to him and said, "This trouble is from the LORD! Why
should I wait for the LORD any longer?" (2 Kings 6:33 ESV)

But they who wait for the LORD shall renew their strength; they
shall mount up with wings like eagles; they shall run and not be
weary; they shall walk and not faint. (Isaiah 40:31 ESV)

King Joram of Israel was what the Apostle James calls "a double-minded man" (James 1:8). That is, part of him wanted God's way in his life, but part of him wanted his own way. Joram and his people were suffering because their enemies were besieging them. So how does a double-minded man react when suffering comes?*

In Joram's case, he saw every bad thing that happened to him as a sign that God was out to get him. He'd been asking God to get him out of this mess and God was not paying off. So that was that. No more trusting (the meaning of "wait") God for him. In fact, he decided to kill God's prophet because he was evidently in "cahoots" with Yahweh to make Joram suffer.

Alternatively, how do "single-minded" persons react when suffering comes? We know that God is *always for* us. We know that God has permitted this suffering and that, having permitted it, he is going to accomplish a good purpose for us if we will not give up our trust in him. We may have to "wait" a long time, but however long it takes, we know that *nothing* can separate us from his love. That confidence is one of the signal blessings of having allowed the Holy Spirit to make us one for God.

---

* Suffering *will* come. The health and wealth folks are simply wrong. Paul says
that we are heirs of God *provided we suffer with Christ* (see Rom 8:17).

When Morning Gilds the Skies

February 15

A BOOK OF ILLUSTRATIONS

As she came in, the king was talking with Gehazi, the servant of the man of God. The king had just said, "Tell me some stories about the great things Elisha has done." And Gehazi was telling the king about the time Elisha had brought a boy back to life. At that very moment, the mother of the boy walked in to make her appeal to the king about her house and land. "Look, my lord the king!" Gehazi exclaimed. "Here is the woman now, and this is her son—the very one Elisha brought back to life!" "Is this true?" the king asked her. And she told him the story. So he directed one of his officials to see that everything she had lost was restored to her, including the value of any crops that had been harvested during her absence. (2 Kings 8:4–6)

When people find out that I teach the Old Testament, they often say to me, "I just don't understand the Old Testament." My response is, "I'm not surprised." Unlike any other of the world's religious books, this book is written to a specific people in a specific time in a specific place. That means that in order to really understand what is being said, we need to know something about those people, places, and times, and that takes a little work. Get a study Bible, like the New International Version (NIV), or English Standard Version (ESV), or New Living Translation (NLT), and *read* it.

That being said, let me ask, how many of the great Bible stories come from the Old Testament? Most of them! Why is that? It's because God had put his truth into a life setting. We understand things, we remember things, when they are in a life context, a life setting. And that's what God has done in the Old Testament. God has put himself and his truth into our life. He has "fleshed" (incarnated) himself!

So, you see, the Incarnation didn't start with Jesus; rather, it culminated with him. The process starts in the Old Testament. God so much wants us to understand his truth that he puts it into a specific time, a specific place, a specific people. He wants us to *know* him, to know his truths, and so he has put it into an illustration, a huge 39-book illustration; God incarnating himself in our life. The whole Bible is built on the principle that God has stepped into people's lives and shown himself in their experience so that they can recognize who he is, what he's like, and what he wants with us. Thank God he has done that. Study the Old Testament; it will repay you in a fuller, deeper, more robust faith.

February 16

WHAT LASTS?

In the fifteenth year of Amaziah the son of Joash, king of Judah,
Jeroboam the son of Joash, king of Israel, began to reign in Samaria,
and he reigned forty-one years. And he did what was evil in the sight
of the LORD. He did not depart from all the sins of Jeroboam the son
of Nebat, which he made Israel to sin. (2 Kings 14:23–24 ESV)

There was a plaque in our house when I was growing up that said, "Only what's done for Christ will last." Substitute the word "God" for "Christ," and that truth applies to the past as well. Nowhere is that more clearly seen than in the Bible's summary of the reign of Jeroboam ben Joash (Jeroboam II), king of Israel, the northern kingdom. He began to reign about 793 BC and ruled until 753 BC. From all the evidence, he was a very effective king, humanly speaking. The empire of Assyria, which had been quite rapacious during the previous century, had backed off (the influence of Jonah?), and Jeroboam had moved to restore and even expand Israel's territory (see 2 Kgs 14:25). Evidently, his reign was a highly prosperous time for Israel, maybe approaching the times of Solomon (see the comments in Amos, who prophesied at this time).

Yet what does the Bible say about Jeroboam's forty-year reign? Seven verses! Beyond verse 25 and the statement that what Israel was enjoying was by the grace of God (vv 26–27), there is nothing more except the standard statements about the records of his reign and his death announcement (vv 28–29). What is this? Seven verses for forty years?

Will that be the heavenly record of my life, of yours? Humanly speaking, Jeroboam II was a great king, but from God's point of view, none of those achievements mattered in the end, because none of them were done with the end of pleasing God. All of them were rendered worthless because he did not do the main thing, namely turning his people away from the idolatry that Jeroboam's namesake, Jeroboam I, had instituted many years before (see 1 Kgs 12:28–32). May this not be true for us. Instead of being worth-less, let our lives be worth-y. Perhaps your accomplishments or mine will never make the history books, but let them be worthy of pages and pages in the Lamb's Book of Life. Live for Jesus!

February 17

LITTLE THINGS

Then King Ahaz went to Damascus to meet Tiglath-Pileser king of Assyria.
He saw an altar in Damascus and sent to Uriah the priest a sketch of the
altar, with detailed plans for its construction. . . . As for the bronze altar that
stood before the LORD, he brought it from the front of the temple—from
between the new altar and the temple of the LORD—and put it on the north
side of the new altar. . . . He took away the Sabbath canopy that had been
built at the temple and removed the royal entryway outside the temple of
the LORD, in deference to the king of Assyria. (2 Kings 16:10, 14, 18 NIV)

Demas, because he loved this world, has deserted me and
has gone to Thessalonica. (2 Timothy 4:10a NIV)

In 2 Kings 16:10–18 we read of some apparently insignificant changes
that King Ahaz made in the temple furnishings and structure. On the
surface they don't seem that important and the Bible nowhere says he
should not have. But in the context, it is clear that they are indicators
of much deeper issues. These changes did not come from Yahweh. Ahaz
made them because he was concerned to gain the favor of Tiglath-Pileser,
the Assyrian king to whom he had sold himself: If something about the
worship of Yahweh could be changed to get and keep that favor—change it!

It can be the same in our lives. An acquaintance who had been part
of a small group of conservative Christian graduate students at a major
university told me, "Whenever one of our number began to smoke a pipe,
we knew his doctrine of Scripture was changing." Is there a necessary
connection between pipe-smoking and one's doctrine of Scripture? Of
course not. Can one smoke a pipe and have a high view of Scripture? Of
course. But the point is still valid. If, because of one's view of Scripture, one
has maintained a certain lifestyle, and then one changes the lifestyle, what
is the reason? Surely, it may be because one's *interpretation* of Scripture
has changed; in which case the change may be entirely justified. But it is
also possible that the change is the result of a lessening of one's *reverence*
for Scripture and, more importantly, for the God of Scripture. In this case,
the small change is diagnostic of a far deeper, and more important, change.
The love of God is being pushed aside by the love of what the apostles call
"the world" (see 2 Tim 4:10; 1 John 2:15–17). That was what happened to
Ahaz, and it can happen to us.

WORTHLESS: PART ONE

They rejected his decrees and the covenant he had made with
their ancestors and the statutes he had warned them to keep.
They followed worthless idols and themselves became worthless.
They imitated the nations around them although the LORD had
ordered them, "Do not do as they do." (2 Kings 17:15 NIV)

One of the recurring statements in the Old Testament is that if you worship idols you make yourself worthless. Worthless? Yes, worthless. How does that work? Well, on the surface it is fairly simple. The idols are worthless because they cannot do anything. It may appear that they can, but they really can't. So, if you stake your life on them, your life is not going to accomplish anything. You spend your life trying to manipulate those things to do something they can't, and in the process waste your life.

Okay, but what does that have to do with us? Here is where the truth goes beneath the surface. What is at the heart of idol worship? It is the idea that we can manipulate the forces of this world to guarantee our comfort, pleasure, and security through the acquisition of power. In other words, our needs are primary, and the fulfillment of those needs depends on our ability to fulfill them. Do you see what that means? It means that I am supreme in my life. I have made God in my image. Today, we in the West don't make human figures and call them gods, but we might as well. We worship passion, power, and acquisition just as fervently as any ancient ever did.

Do you see what that means? The so-called gods are just an amplification of humanity. Humanity is all there is, "there ain't no more" (excuse the bad grammar). But if that is true, then life is meaningless. We came from nowhere, and when they close the casket, we go nowhere. Life is a bad joke. There is no meaning, and our search for meaning is silly. So, what are we to do? Modern philosophy says we each have to manufacture meaning for ourselves. That doesn't work, as the raising suicide rate tells us.

So, what? I'll answer that in Part Two.

WORTHLESS: PART TWO

I have given them the glory that you gave me, that they may be one as we are one—I in them and you in me—so that they may be brought to complete unity. Then the world will know that you sent me and have loved them even as you have loved me. "Father, I want those you have given me to be with me where I am, and to see my glory, the glory you have given me because you loved me before the creation of the world." (John 17:22–24 NIV)

In Part One, I pointed out that the worship of this world—making this world ultimate—only results in making us worthless. If this chance-driven cosmos is all there is, then all existence, including ours, is meaningless. So, is there no hope? There is a lot of hope in our Christian faith, but we have to be a little careful on that front. Sometimes faith is presented in such a way that it actually makes us feel more worthless. Who are you? You're a miserable, guilty sinner, totally depraved, unable to do anything good. Is that true? Yes, it is. But we *must not* stop there! Who are you in Christ? That is the question.

As I have said, "glory" in the Bible connotes "reality" or "significance." Yahweh's glory is his inescapable reality. In that light, look at Jesus's astonishing words in the passage above. He has given *us* the same glory that the Father has given him! What can that possibly mean? Well, it means a lot more that we can open up here, but let me say this much: how much are you worth to God? You are worth the life of his Son. He gave his life for you, and he did so in order to put in you the reality of God: his love, his power, his truth, the very things Jesus shares with him. He wants us to "see" (experience) that reality. When we do, the world will see it too.

Worship this world—and yourself in it—and you become nothing. Lay down your right to be God in your own life and allow your Creator to be your Lord through the death and resurrection of Christ, and you will go from being a vapor (vanity) to sharing the very reality and significance of the Creator himself.

February 20

THAT THEY MAY KNOW

And Hezekiah prayed before the LORD and said: "O LORD, the God of Israel, enthroned above the cherubim, you are the God, you alone, of all the kingdoms of the earth; you have made heaven and earth. Incline your ear, O LORD, and hear; open your eyes, O LORD, and see; and hear the words of Sennacherib, which he has sent to mock the living God. Truly, O LORD, the kings of Assyria have laid waste the nations and their lands and have cast their gods into the fire, for they were not gods, but the work of men's hands, wood and stone. Therefore, they were destroyed. So now, O LORD our God, save us, please, from his hand, that all the kingdoms of the earth may know that you, O LORD, are God alone." (2 Kings 19:15–19 ESV)

This brief prayer is one of the great ones in the Bible, prayed in the middle of a great crisis. Sennacherib, the Assyrian emperor, the successor to nearly 200 years of Assyrian conquest, was at the gates. Virtually the whole ancient Near Eastern world was at his feet. Only one rich region remained: Egypt. He was on the verge of taking that, but one small irritation remains: Judah. He had conquered all but Judah's capital, Jerusalem.

Sennacherib had sent one of his officers to demand that the people force Hezekiah to surrender, and then he had followed up with a letter in which he showed how foolish it was for Hezekiah to think that Yahweh could deliver Jerusalem from Assyrian devastation. Think of all the gods the Assyrian kings had proven helpless. Why would Hezekiah think that Yahweh was one degree different?

Well, the simple answer, as Hezekiah knew, and Sennacherib did not, is that Yahweh is in *every* degree different from the gods. They are part of the world, but he *made* the world. He is the *living* God, and they were not gods at all but simply the creations of human minds and hands. Of course, the Assyrians had destroyed those gods. Why wouldn't they?

So why should Yahweh deliver Jerusalem from Sennacherib's hands? Here, apart from the true understanding of Yahweh that the prayer portrays is what makes the prayer great. Hezekiah could have said that he and his people deserved it because they had been faithful to Yahweh. Or, he could have said that Yahweh needed these people to declare his name. Instead, he asked for deliverance *so that the world might know who Yahweh really is.* The scholars fall all over themselves to find some naturalistic explanation for why Sennacherib did not attack Jerusalem and precipitately left that part of the world never to return. But it was because Yahweh heard Hezekiah's prayer! Why should God deliver you and me?

February 21

KINGS AND QUEENS OF THE EARTH

God created man in his own image, in the image of God he created him; male and female he created them. God blessed them; and God said to them, "Be fruitful and multiply, and fill the earth, and subdue it; and rule over the fish of the sea and over the birds of the sky and over every living thing that moves on the earth." (Genesis 1:27–28 NASB)

So God created human beings in his own image. In the image of God he created them; male and female he created them. Then God blessed them and said, "Be fruitful and multiply. Fill the earth and govern it. Reign over the fish in the sea, the birds in the sky, and all the animals that scurry along the ground." (Genesis 1:27–28)

I wonder if you realize how important you are to God? Paganism, based on observation of the world, says that we really are quite unimportant in the grand scheme of things. Stand outside on a clear night, look up, and tell yourself that you really matter in the face of all that. A TV program has spoken of "non-human animals." Do you see what is being very intentionally implied? We are just another kind of animal, not essentially different from all the rest. To all this, the Bible speaks a resounding "NO!" It is there in the very first chapter. God is not in our image; we are in his. What does that mean? It means that unlike everything else in the universe, we alone are self-conscious *persons*, as he is. And God made this world for us to inhabit. Can you believe it? That is what the Book tells us. God did not make a chaos; rather, he constructed an orderly universe *for us, being like him, to inhabit!* (see Isa 45:18).

Hugh Ross, an astronomer and cosmologist, has shown that if just one of forty different variables had not occurred in the first instant after the Big Bang, life would not be possible. Just one! You and I are that important to our Father. Beyond that, he made his world so that it could not reach its full potential without you and me. That is what that sometimes-maligned statement in Genesis 1:28 means. We are given "dominion" over the earth. What does that mean in a biblical context? Does it mean we have a right, as it were, to carve our initials in the furniture of the world, to stomp it down? It does not. Biblically speaking, to have dominion over something is to care for it, to cultivate it, to bring it to its full potential. So, rather than our being simply chips floating aimlessly here and there on a cosmic sea, we are the lords and ladies before whom the universe comes bowing, looking to us to achieve all the glorious possibilities the Creator has crammed into it. (A trumpet flourish, please!)

February 22

REPENTANCE

Before [Josiah] there was no king like him, who turned to the LORD with all his heart and with all his soul and with all his might, according to all the Law of Moses, nor did any like him arise after him. Still the LORD did not turn from the burning of his great wrath, by which his anger was kindled against Judah, because of all the provocations with which Manasseh had provoked him. And the LORD said, "I will remove Judah also out of my sight, as I have removed Israel, and I will cast off this city that I have chosen, Jerusalem, and the house of which I said, My name shall be there." (2 Kings 23:25–27 ESV)

Many commentators are very troubled by this passage. They do not understand why Yahweh held onto the bad behavior of Manasseh and did not credit the good behavior of Josiah. They say things like, "God never gives up his freedom to do what he wants, but if he is free to judge, he is also free to extend grace." But that is the result of not looking at the text closely enough. Look at what Josiah does when he hears the awful truth about how Israel has broken her covenant (see 2 Kgs 22:11–23:3). He instantly tears his clothes and asks for God's word on whether the consequences are reversible or not. He learns that they are not, but that doesn't matter: he commits himself to the covenant and immediately sets out to obey it with everything in him.

What do the people do when they hear the Word? Nothing! No weeping; no tearing the clothes; nothing. We are only told that when Josiah publicly committed himself, they "stood up" for the covenant, whatever that means (NIV "pledged themselves" is highly interpretive). The truth is that Josiah repented and the people went along with him but never changed their own attitudes and behavior. There was no national repentance. The attitudes and behaviors that Manasseh had cemented in them were still there. That is clearly seen when the instant Josiah died all the old idolatries and injustices were right back with a vengeance.

Repentance is not merely a matter of making some changes, some "improvements." Repentance, as it was for Josiah, is a matter of total renovation, of a complete turnaround. If the people had been cut to the heart as Josiah was, and had they been as repulsed by sin as he was and rejected them as he did, the sins of Manasseh would have been forgiven. But in fact, far from repenting of those sins, they secretly embraced them and would not give them up. When God punished them, he was not exercising some inexplicable "freedom." He was simply being just.

February 23

KNOW YAHWEH

And you, Solomon my son, know the God of your father and serve
him with a whole heart and with a willing mind [an eager self],
for the LORD searches all hearts and understands every plan and
thought. If you seek him, he will be found by you, but if you forsake
him, he will cast you off forever. (1 Chronicles 28:9 ESV)

David is giving Solomon his final instructions. What a moment! After all the preparations for the temple that Solomon is to build, after all the thought about the kind of worship that will take place in the temple, after a lifetime of living, what do you want to say to your son to prepare him for what lies ahead of him?

What would *you* say? What kind of detailed instructions would you give? I dare to suggest it might be a lot more complicated than this but also maybe a lot less penetrating. What did David say? "Know Yahweh!" Is that it? Is that all? Yes, that's it and that's all. In the end, all of life comes down to this.

Now, of course, if there is no God, no great I AM, then indeed there are a lot of other things that you could spend your life's energy doing. But if there is a Person who is both beyond the stars, and present in the tiniest atomic fragment, a Person upon whom our lives depend, a Person who has given his life for us, then yes, to be on the stretch for an intimate personal acquaintance with that Person is the most important thing in the world. Just as he loves to probe into the inner recesses of your being, he invites you to probe into his [notice that "searches" above is the same verb that is translated "seek" a few words later—he "seeks" us and calls us to "seek" him].

God invites us to view him as the young lover views his beloved: the most fascinating subject in the world. That's the way God sees us—can you believe it?—and that's the way he wants us to see him. Do you know him? Are you eager to know him and know him more fully? If not, why not? What else will matter when they close the casket lid? The tragedy of Solomon's life is that he was so involved with "knowing" a lot of women that he forgot about knowing Yahweh. Oh, don't let that, or something similar, be your tragedy. Know Yahweh!

February 24

THE HOUSE OF GOD: PART ONE

This is what King Cyrus of Persia says: "The LORD, the God of heaven, has given me all the kingdoms of the earth. He has appointed me to build him a Temple at Jerusalem, which is in Judah. Any of you who are his people may go there for this task. And may the LORD your God be with you!" (2 Chronicles 36:23)

This is the last verse in the Old Testament. "Wait a minute," you will say, "Malachi 4:6 is the last verse." Yes, it is in the English order, which is borrowed from the Greek order. But in the Hebrew order of books, Chronicles is the last book, and this is the last verse. Is that intentional? I think so. The books of Chronicles are about the history of Israel in the light of the worship of Yahweh, especially temple worship. Temple worship is important to God. Think about the book of Exodus. What is the climax? Sixteen chapters having to do with the Tabernacle! Then what about Leviticus? Worship in the Tabernacle. Samuel? Worship in the Tabernacle, and then the loss of the Ark and ensuing religious chaos. What about Kings? The building of the Temple (see 1 Kgs 5–8); the periodic rebuilding of the Temple after neglect (see 2 Kgs 12, 22); and the destruction of the Temple as Judah heads into exile (see 2 Kgs 25). Ezekiel? The concluding eight chapters focus on a glorious new Temple. And then, of course, there is this final verse in the Book.

What's going on? It is this: the Tabernacle/Temple represents the heart of biblical theology. This heart is expressed in two ways. The first is this: The eternal, transcendent (holy) Creator, the one self-existent Being in the Universe, from whom all other existence derives, wants to live in intimate fellowship with his human creatures! He does not want to live in isolation on the mountain; he wants to reside right in the midst of us.

But that's not enough! God is not a building and cannot be contained in a building. He is a Person; so, he has come in Jesus Christ to be *with* us. This is what Jesus meant when he said, "If you destroy *this temple* I will raise it up in three days" (see John 2:19). *He* is the temple in our midst. But the truth is even better: we are invited to live in him, in the temple (see John 15:7).

February 25

THE HOUSE OF GOD: PART TWO

Consequently, you are no longer foreigners and strangers, but fellow citizens with God's people and also members of his household, built on the foundation of the apostles and prophets, with Christ Jesus himself as the chief cornerstone. In him the whole building is joined together and rises to become a holy temple in the Lord. And in him you too are being built together to become a dwelling in which God lives by his Spirit. (Ephesians 2:19–22 NIV)

[That you] may have power, together with all the Lord's holy people, to grasp how wide and long and high and deep is the love of Christ, and to know this love that surpasses knowledge—that you may be filled to the measure of all the fullness of God. (Ephesians 3:18–19 NIV)

In Part One, I said that the Tabernacle/Temple is so prominent in the Old Testament because it represents the two ideas that are at the center of biblical theology: God intends to live *with* us, but even more than that, he intends for us to live *in him*. He has accomplished this in the Incarnation, Crucifixion, Resurrection, and Ascension of Jesus Christ, the true Temple. But there is another side to this second idea: he intends to live *in us*. Yes, in one way, Jesus is the ultimate temple of God, but in another, as Paul correctly understood, *we* are the intended temple. God wants to live his life in us and through us! What a thought! It is no wonder that Paul becomes almost lyrical as he thinks about the dimensions of the building that could contain the fullness of the love of God. But that is what God has been intending since he closed the gates to the Garden of Eden: he wants to come home and fill us with himself.

So, again, we come to John 15. Is it that we live in him or that he lives in us? It is not either-or but both-and. Jesus is the image of God (see Col 1:15) and we are made in the image of God (see Gen 1:27). We live in God, and God lives in us. What is the result? A river flows out of the Temple that can turn even the Dead Sea sweet (see Ezek 47:1–8 and John 7:37–39). Are you living in the Temple? Are you the temple of the Holy, Living God?

67

February 26

THE MOCKERY OF OUR ENEMIES

After thinking it over, I spoke out against these nobles and officials. I told them, "You are hurting your own relatives by charging interest when they borrow money!" Then I called a public meeting to deal with the problem. At the meeting I said to them, "We are doing all we can to redeem our Jewish relatives who have had to sell themselves to pagan foreigners, but you are selling them back into slavery again. How often must we redeem them?" And they had nothing to say in their defense. Then I pressed further, "What you are doing is not right! Should you not walk in the fear of our God in order to avoid being mocked by enemy nations?" (Nehemiah 5:7–9)

Mocked by enemy nations? What was happening? I suggest that it was something like this: The wealthy were gaining more and more control over the land by forcing the poor to mortgage their property to them to guarantee their loans. Evidently the interest rates were ruinous, with the result that the poor were losing their land—land that actually had been a gift from God. The rich clearly were not conducting their lives in awe and reverence for God and his commandments (i.e., no fear of God). In fact they were acting just like their pagan neighbors. The result was mockery from the enemy neighbors. It was probably along these lines: "Oh, you hypocrites! You say your God is the only God because he is different from all the rest and expects a different kind of living from his people. Oh, yeah? Well, then why are you living just like us? You don't really believe in your so-called God. He is just a convenient crutch you use when it's to your advantage."

The application to us is pretty obvious, isn't it? If we claim that Jesus is the only Savior and buttress our claims with statements that he can give new life and new living to people he saves, then our lives had better give concrete evidence of that new life. To paraphrase Nehemiah, "Shouldn't we be determined to show the life of Christ in everything we do so that the enemies of the gospel will have no grounds to mock him or us?"

February 27

A CLEAN HEART

Later I went to visit Shemaiah son of Delaiah and grandson of Mehetabel, who was confined to his home. He said, "Let us meet together inside the Temple of God and bolt the doors shut. Your enemies are coming to kill you tonight." But I replied, "Should someone in my position run from danger? Should someone in my position enter the Temple to save his life? No, I won't do it!" I realized that God had not spoken to him, but that he had uttered this prophecy against me because Tobiah and Sanballat had hired him. They were hoping to intimidate me and make me sin. Then they would be able to accuse and discredit me. (Nehemiah 6:10–13)

What does it take to make a good leader? A clean heart. What are we talking about? We are talking about having the core of your life wholly given over to God. He is the only source of cleanness. If there is any taint of me there, me that needs to be seen, me that needs to be successful, me that needs to be prominent, me that needs to protect myself, my heart is not clean. But if it is wholly his, then it is clean, and people can trust me. Then I can act for their good, not mine. Then I can act decisively, not worrying about appearances.

If you are seasoned, salted, and grounded in prayer, and can say, "As best I know, this is what I'm called to do, and I'll do it, and do it with gladness, and then I'll leave the results to God," that's a good place to be able to live. But you can't do it if your heart is divided. Does that mean the person with a clean heart will never fail? Of course not! We're human. Yet failure won't destroy us. We won't be consumed by it because our heart is clean.

We live with a lot of gray areas in our lives today, and we may need to spend time on our faces before God saying, "What is the moral right in this situation?" Still, there are many other times when the matter is perfectly clear and the only issue is, "Am I going to *stand up* for what is right?" When we surrender our lives to God, it simplifies life tremendously, because our decisions and our actions are already determined.

February 28

THE JOY OF THE LORD

And Nehemiah continued, "Go and celebrate with a feast of rich foods and sweet drinks, and share gifts of food with people who have nothing prepared. This is a sacred day before our Lord. Don't be dejected and sad, for the joy of the LORD is your strength!" (Nehemiah 8:10)

I made an interesting discovery recently: the Hebrew language has at least ten different terms for singing joyfully! That is pretty surprising not only because of the large number but also because, frankly, most of us do not think of the Old Testament as a really joyful book. Oh yes, it has happier places, like this verse from Nehemiah, but so much of it seems so grim. Yahweh seems to have such high standards, and the people he chose for himself seem to fall short of those standards so much of the time—with really bad results. Yet these are the people who have to come up with ten different ways to express joy.

In modern language, we might ask, "what's up with that?" It is actually captured in this verse. The people had gone into captivity because of their sins, but God had, against all the odds, brought them home again! Unfortunately, after the first flurry of excitement, they had sort of subsided into a sloppy, half-pagan way of living again, not even bothering to rebuild the walls of Jerusalem. After almost a hundred years, Nehemiah the governor, and Ezra the scribe/priest (and maybe Malachi, the prophet) have come to them, gotten them "off square one," gotten the walls rebuilt, and have reintroduced them to their divine instruction manual, the Torah.

When the people hear what they are supposed to be like, what they could have been, they start wailing. There they are, standing in the rain with tears pouring down their faces. "No," the leaders cry, "this is a day for joy." Joy? Today? Why? It is because of the incredible grace of God! That is the thing that keeps washing over us in the Old Testament:

1. The grace that he ever chose us.
2. The grace that he wants to commit himself to us in a covenant.
3. The grace that he has revealed his way—and ours—to us in that covenant.
4. The grace that when we have sinned it all away, he brings us home again.
5. The grace that, when we have done it all over again, he won't give up on us.

GRACE, GRACE, God's GRACE! That is cause for shouts of joy!

When Morning Gilds the Skies

February 29

FAITH UNDER FIRE

But he knows the way that I take; when he has tested
me, I will come forth as gold. (Job 23:10 NIV)

Dr. Nick (first name) was one of the only endocrinologists in the
country of Romania, but during Communist times there was a fifteen-
hundred-member church without a pastor, and the Holy Spirit said, "Nick,
you are the man." Now that constituted a problem, because he had no state
license to be a pastor. Still, the church and the Spirit were insistent, so for
three years he left medicine and preached, never sleeping in the same bed
two nights in a row. After three years someone informed on Dr. Nick, so
the secret police called him in and interrogated him for ten hours straight.
At the end of that time, they said, "Alright, you can go, but stop preaching."
Nick said, "Thank you, gentlemen. Thank you for making me the happiest
man in the world." They said, "What?!" He said, "Let me preach a little
sermon to you. My Bible tells me: blessed are you when all men persecute
you falsely for my name's sake. Blessed means happy, and you have just
proven to me today that I am a real Christian, because you have been
persecuting me for ten hours. I am a happy man. Thank you! Good night!"
He was out the door while they were still dumbstruck.

That isn't usually the way we see it, is it? Usually when testing and
trials come to us, we say, "God, what did I ever do to you? I don't deserve
this." Peter says, "Don't be surprised if present testing comes, its purpose
is that when your faith is tested by fire, it may be found to the praise and
honor and glory of Jesus Christ when he comes" (see 1 Pet 1:6–7, 4:12).
There is no pure metal without refining. You don't just find pure gold. It
is mixed through rock. So, the first thing that happens is that the gold-
bearing rock is sent to the crusher. Then, it is sent to the fire "so that
the proven genuineness of your faith—of greater worth than gold, which
perishes even though refined by fire—may result in praise, glory and honor
when Jesus Christ is revealed" (1 Pet 1:7).

How badly do we want our faith to shine purely when Jesus is revealed?
Badly enough to say, "Turn up the flame, God, turn it up"? That is what
biblical faith is all about. If you believe because everything goes well, what
does that prove? It is when you believe in spite of the difficulties, in spite
of the trouble, in fact, because of the difficulty, that your faith comes forth
like gold.

March 1

HAPPY OR BLESSED?—PART ONE

Blessed is the man who walks not in the counsel of the wicked,
nor stands in the way of sinners, nor sits in the seat of scoffers;
but his delight is in the law [*torah*] of the LORD, and on his law
[*torah*] he meditates day and night. (Psalm 1:1–2 ESV)

Blessed are all who take refuge in him. (Psalm 2:12b ESV)

What is it to be blessed? Is it to be happy? No, it is not, for happiness is fleeting like every other emotion. Being blessed is a real condition that exists apart from any emotion. To be blessed is to receive good and favorable things, most especially the ultimate good, that life-giving fellowship with our Maker both now and forevermore. The two passages above give us the ultimate basis for being blessed. They occur at the beginning of Psalm 1 and the end of Psalm 2. Many commentators believe these two psalms are intended to act as the introduction to the entire collection of psalms. The "book-end" effect resulting from beginning the first with blessing and ending the second in the same way supports that idea. So, what are the two bases for blessing? First, if we are to experience all the good things our Creator wants to give to us, we must not only be familiar with God's instruction manual for life, his Torah, his Word, we must take delight in knowing it and doing it. Our Designer has given us the manual for experiencing life at its best. Why are we surprised when, having ignored it, our lives fall apart?

March 2

HAPPY OR BLESSED?—PART TWO

Blessed is the man who walks not in the counsel of the wicked,
nor stands in the way of sinners, nor sits in the seat of scoffers;
but his delight is in the law [*torah*] of the LORD, and on his law
[*torah*] he meditates day and night. (Psalm 1:1–2 ESV)

Kiss the Son, lest he be angry, and you perish in the way, for his wrath is
quickly kindled. Blessed are all who take refuge in him. (Psalm 2:12 ESV)

In Part One, we talked about the first basis for being in a blessed condition. It is to know and delight in God's instruction manual, his *Torah*. Alongside that one is a second. It is introduced in Psalm 2. This principle is a proper relationship to Yahweh's anointed king, his Messiah.

Why don't we instinctively turn to God's Word for guidance for living and instead turn to the wicked, the sinners, and the scoffers? It is because of the fundamental strain of rebellion found in all of Adam and Eve's children. *We* will be kings of our lives. But that way is not the way of blessing; it is the way of disaster, as humans have proven ever since the events recorded in the third chapter of Genesis.

So, if we are to be blessed, what must happen, according to Psalm 2? We must recognize our rebellious character, and recognizing it, turn from it by willingly allowing another King, God's Chosen, to take control of us. Notice how the verse ends. It takes us beyond mere submission to the King, who is justly angry at our rebellion, and instead invites us to crawl up into his arms and take refuge in that gracious love revealed in his Cross. There is blessing. Can we be blessed and unhappy at the same time? Of course!

All of us experience circumstances that are unpleasant and grievous. To put a mask of happiness on our faces in such occasions is simply to live a lie. But if we have been delighting to live in God's instructions and are hiding in the arms of Jesus, we are blessed, because we have resources in his Word and his presence to meet those circumstances and triumph through them.

March 3

Thoughts on a Centipede

What are humans that you pay any attention to them
at all? (Psalm 8:4 author's translation)

I sat in my study, looked at a miniscule centipede wandering across the floor, and wondered, "What is it thinking?" Then I thought how great the gap was between it and me, its brain and mine, and suddenly I was thinking about God and me. "Is this a tiny glimpse into the infinite gap between you and me?" What would it cost me to become a centipede? What did it cost the Second Person of the Trinity to become one of us? What did he have to give up? It was neither merely his rightful glory nor merely some of his attributes. No, if you will permit me to say it crudely, it was his "hugeness," his immensity in every direction, to be condensed down to a tiny-ness in every dimension, condensed much farther down than it would be for me to be condensed down into the form of a centipede.

There is this, however, a "this" that must not be overlooked: the centipede and I are two different orders of being. Jesus and we are not different orders. *We are made in the very image of God.* We are of the same order as God! So Jesus did not need to cross some uncrossable boundary of being. But he did have to undergo an almost infinite diminishment of the capacities of that being. What amazing condescension! Why did he—why would he—do it?

I think of the little boy sitting on a curb watching a crowd of ants hard at work in a crack in the curbing. Clearly, they had a colony inside, and they were industriously expanding it out through the crack. Then the boy heard a noise and looked up. A few hundred yards up the street a city maintenance crew was flushing out the fire hydrants, and a tidal wave of water was coming down the gutter. As quickly as he could the little boy picked up ants and put them up on the sidewalk. But the instant he let them go they scurried back down. More frantically he worked, but it was no use, he could only pick up his feet as the water rushed by and carried all the ants away. The boy thought for a moment and then said, "I guess the only way I could have saved them was to become an ant myself." Yes, that's what Jesus did, and in a far more profound way than this little illustration can portray. He became one of us.

March 4

I WILL PRAISE YOU

O LORD, how long will you forget me? Forever? How long will you look the other way? How long must I struggle with anguish in my soul, with sorrow in my heart every day? How long will my enemy have the upper hand? . . . But I trust in your unfailing love. I will rejoice because you have rescued me. I will sing to the LORD because he is good to me." (Psalm 13:1–2, 5–6)

About half of the psalms in the Bible are in the form of a lament. This form has four characteristic features: direct address to God (e.g., "O my Lord"), complaint (e.g., "why have you forsaken me?"), petition (e.g., "come quickly to my aid"), and a vow of praise in the future ("I will praise you in the great congregation."). There is a very profound truth in this form, as seen in Psalm 13. That truth is that complaint and faith are not mutually exclusive. Too often, we have been taught that if you have "real faith," you will always "look on the bright side" and will never allow circumstances to "get you down." So, when you face real difficulties, if you become down and depressed and feel as though God has turned his back on you, the obvious conclusion is that you have lost your faith in him. Too often the result of this kind of thinking is that we try to deny what we are really feeling and to pretend to something that is not so. That is not faith; it is only pretense!

These seventy-five or more psalms give us permission to be real. To be subject to emotional highs and lows, to be affected negatively by negative circumstances, is simply part of the human condition. To be honest about them is not necessarily a sign of a lack of faith. It is simply to tell God what he already knows, believing that he is big enough to accept it!

Yet if the psalmists are conscious of the reality of what they are going through and their feelings about that, they are equally certain that God is going to respond to their cries and that the day will come when they will be able to tell everyone what a great God he truly is. There is not a hint of emotional blackmail here. There is no "if you answer my prayer, then I will give praise to you." Praise is simply a certainty. Although it is not true in all cases, in many psalms this vow is stated with completed action verbs. We don't have such a verb form in English, so we must put it in the future tense. For the psalmist the praise is already given. It is a "done deal."

This is faith: the confidence that in spite of the reality of feelings of abandonment and rejection by God, of inexplicable and undeserved pain, he who has proved himself faithful in the past is still at work, and praise for his wonderful grace is a foregone conclusion.

March 5

WHAT IS THE BIBLE?

Yahweh's instructions are perfect; they revive the soul. Yahweh's decrees can be trusted; they make simpletons wise. Yahweh's precepts are right; they bring joy to the heart. Yahweh's commands are pure; they make it possible to see clearly. Obeying Yahweh leaves you forever clean. His regulations are completely true and right. They are more desirable than the finest gold, sweeter than the sweetest honey. They are a warning to us, but also a reward if we obey them. (Psalm 19:7–11 author's translation)

A newspaper religion columnist recently counseled his readers to stop arguing that some behavior was right or wrong on the basis of biblical statements. He said that there are too many differing opinions about the Bible and that if one's opponent did not accept the authority of the Bible, it was a pointless argument. He suggested that Christians should confine their appeals to the Bible to conversations within the church.

While it is certainly true that trying to convince a secular-humanist about something on the basis of the Bible is a fruitless task, when the writer calls for confining biblical discussion to the church, he betrays a sad misunderstanding of the issues. For twenty centuries Christians have known the Bible to be a revelation, a "word," from the sole Creator and Redeemer of the universe, Yahweh. Thus, we find in it the nature of reality and the terms of human existence as the Designer intended. The whole problem of the human race—sin—is that we have been determined to define those terms and the reality behind them for ourselves. You don't have to go farther than Genesis 3 to see that happening, and it has been happening ever since.

If the Bible is indeed the Word of God—and twenty centuries of evidence points to that—then Christians must explain their ethical choices to the world on the basis of the Bible. Why are we convinced that adultery is wrong? Because of its evil social consequences? Yes, but much more so, and more simply, because the Creator of the universe says he did not make us to do that. Will that convince a worldling not to commit adultery? Probably not, but neither dare we address the issue simply on their terms. We believe what we believe and act as we do because the Bible is the Creator's instruction manual. If it is anything less than that, for instance, simply a group of writings that a certain faith group has collected for their guidance, then we hardly need to talk about it in our little social club, the church. What we need to do is to disband the whole misguided organization and get on with our meaningless lives. But, thank God, the Bible is not simply the creation of Israel or the church. It is the Word of God, and we can stake our lives on it. Does it need interpretation? Of course it does. But its truth is much clearer and more penetrating than its detractors, who desperately do not want to obey it, will ever admit.

March 6

JOY

You have given him his heart's desire, and have not withheld the request of
his lips. For you meet him with rich blessings; you set a crown of fine gold
on his head. He asked you for life; you gave it to him—length of days forever
and ever. His glory is great through your help; splendor and majesty you
bestow on him. You bestow on him blessings forever; you make him glad
with the joy of your presence. For [he] trusts in the LORD, and through the
steadfast love of the Most High he shall not be moved. (Psalm 21:2–7 NRSV)

I am thinking today of one of the two most formative people in my life,
one who has passed from this life, Dennis F. Kinlaw (1921–2017), and of
some of the things he taught me. Of all the hundreds of things, it is difficult
to isolate one, but at this moment at least, I do think I can. He taught me
that living God's life is not one of unremitting effort, but one of joy. It is not
meant to be an attempt to climb up a slippery slope to get to God. Rather it
is to walk through a succession of doors into ever wider vistas. Holiness is
not a series of impossible demands but an incredible invitation into all we
were ever meant to be. Is effort involved? Of course, nothing worth doing
is ever easy. But it is not a grim, teeth-gritting slog. It is the wondering
"yes" when he tells you to raise your sails in a dead calm. It is the daring
"yes" when you are marooned on a cliff, and he shows you that tiny crack in
the cliff above your head that is just big enough for you to jam your fingers
into and pull yourself up. It is the reluctant "yes" when he says "That way
there be dragons." It is to know that if at some point you say "no," he is
not done with you but will open up another way. It is to live in wondering
joy that in the arms of God you have found yourself. It is to live life as an
expression of joy and gratitude and wonder. For holiness is nothing other
than to be set free in a wholesome awe of God, a sincere love of God and
others, and a glad self-forgetfulness.

March 7

CART-TRACKS OF RIGHTEOUSNESS

He renews my strength. He guides me along right paths,
bringing honor to his name. (Psalm 23:3)

Then you will understand what is right and just and
fair—every good path. (Proverbs 2:9 NIV)

I will teach you wisdom's ways and lead you in straight paths. (Proverbs 4:11)

There are several Hebrew words connoting "way," or "path," and among them is the one used in the well-known and well-loved Psalm 23:3 (see also Prov 2:9 and 4:11). Among all the words used for the idea, the one that appears in the passages above is perhaps the most specific. It denotes the track made by a wheeled vehicle. Thus, it is clearly marked, relatively hard and smooth, and not as crooked as some animal paths might be. I suspect that the reason the term is used in Psalm 23 (it is not very common in the Old Testament) is because sheep have to be kept out of soft ground. Their small hooves, bearing a good deal of weight, can easily sink into soft soil, and then the animal is in trouble.

Fortunately for us, God's "cart-tracks" are clear, firm, and easily discerned. We do not need to be afraid of getting mired down in the soft ground of relativism. He has shown us what he made us for and how we are to live, and such living brings incredible honor to his name, because it shows how good he is. Too often we spend too much time trying to figure out God's particular will in this situation or that and forget to pay attention to the vast spread of his general will that he has displayed so clearly in his Word. His way is right and straight and good, and it is a well-marked cart-track. Let's not miss it.

March 8

FACE TO FACE

The one thing I ask of the LORD—the thing I seek most—is to live in the house of the LORD all the days of my life . . . . My heart has heard you say, "Come and talk with me." And my heart responds, "LORD, I am coming." (Psalm 27:4, 8)

Although I have read Psalm 27 many times, something struck me in a new way in my most recent reading of it. I thought, "This psalm is about relationship with God." The opening words make it clear: "Yahweh is my light and my salvation." It does not say, "Yahweh gives me light and saves me." It is not about what he does for me but who he, in himself, is to me and for me. I think then of Jesus's words, "I am the way, the truth, the life" (John 14:6). These are all in him: get him, and you get them; don't get him, and you don't get them. It's all about personal relationship. But I mustn't seek a relationship with God through Christ in order to get these things. They are all byproducts of the main thing—knowing him! That's what we see in this psalm. Does David want deliverance and protection? Of course! Does he look to his God for them? Yes, but look at the underlying theme: I don't want to live on my own with a little help from God in the rough places. I want to live in his very house. I want to experience his presence. I want to have conversation with him (the NLT rendering of verse eight captures well the sense of the Hebrew "Your face will I seek."). On the other side of the coin, what would be ultimate loss? It would be for God to turn his face from me, to turn his back on me (see Ps 27:9). But that will never happen so long as there breathes in us one desire to be his. "Even if my father and mother abandon me, [Yahweh] will hold me close" (Ps 27:10). What a thought! To be held in his arms, to gaze into his face, to hear his whisper in our inmost ear. That is salvation!

March 9

THE PRESENCE OF GOD

You have said, "Seek my face." My heart says to you,
"Your face, LORD, do I seek." (Psalm 27:8 ESV)

God clearly wants to be known in a personal ongoing relationship, and that is what we, his creatures, desperately need. So God invites us to "seek his face." That is how his divine presence is expressed in the Old Testament. There is no Hebrew word for "presence;" it is always "face." So, the so-called Aaronic benediction asks that his face may shine upon us (see Num 6:26).

But what are the prerequisites for that to happen? How can we continually see his smiling face in our lives? The first thing we must decide is whether we actually want God's presence, or if what we really want is what he can do for us, in short, his presents. All too many Christians have settled for that bargain. All too many have said, "If I can just get the presents, if I can just get what God offers, if I can just get the deal, that will be enough. If I can't have his presence, well that's too bad."

That's what the story of Abraham and Isaac is all about. Abraham had the present—his son, Isaac. God asked him to choose which one he had to have. Abraham chose God. Presents come and go, but God's presence is the one thing we cannot afford to lose. The same was true for Moses. God told him he could have the Promised Land, but he could not have God there. Moses responded that if he could only have God's presence by staying in the desert, he would stay in the desert.

The tragedy is that for many of us the presents are what we think we cannot live without. The first prerequisite for the presence of God is to decide what you really want, what you are really willing to sell your soul for. Is it the presents? If it is, then in the end you will have gotten dust and ashes. Sell your soul for the presence of God, his face, and you will have found eternal life. Life forever!

March 10

THE FEAR OF THE LORD

Come, my children, and listen to me, and I will teach you to fear the
LORD. Does anyone want to live a life that is long and prosperous? Then
keep your tongue from speaking evil and your lips from telling lies! Turn
away from evil and do good. Search for peace, and work to maintain it.
The eyes of the LORD watch over those who do right; his ears are open
to their cries for help. But the LORD turns his face against those who do
evil; he will erase their memory from the earth. (Psalm 34:11–16)

Many Christians struggle with the concept of "the fear of the LORD."
We think of a Scripture like 1 John 4:18 that tells us there is no fear
in love, and we wonder if "the fear of the LORD" is really some outmoded
Old Testament context. After all, God is love. But no, the fear of the Lord
is not just an Old Testament idea. Remember that it was Jesus who said,
"Do not fear those who kill the body but cannot kill the soul. Rather fear
him [God] who can destroy both soul and body in hell" (Matt 10:28 ESV).

So, what are we talking about? First of all, it is not some nameless
dread, that unclean terror of an arbitrary tyrant who is going to step on
me if I get out of line. That is not the kind of fear John is talking about.
He is saying that if we have come to know the love of God living in us and
shining out of us, we know we belong to God and don't have to live in dread
that God is just waiting for a chance to "get us."

Now we know what it *isn't*, but what *is* "the fear of the LORD"? The
passage above is very helpful. The fear of the Lord is a way of living, a way
that is shaped by wholesome awe of the One, Living God. It is to shape
your life in the knowledge that the Creator has made us to live in certain
ways, ways that if we follow will result in whole, productive, secure lives.
By the same token it is to know that if we don't live in those ways, we are
headed straight for a brick wall—the brick wall of God's unchanging truth.
This is why Proverbs 1:7 says, "The fear of the LORD is the beginning of
knowledge." To live as if there was no God and that you are not accountable
for what you do with your life is really, really dumb.

So, the fear of the Lord is a bit like looking up into a clear night sky.
It is that awe-filled understanding that he is God, I am his creature, and
all that I do is finally judged in terms of the way he has made the world to
function. The fear of the Lord is a way of life that takes into account the
fact that he is God and it is he with whom I finally have to do.

March 11
WHY HERE?

I waited patiently for the LORD to help me, and he turned to me and heard my cry. He lifted me out of the pit of despair, out of the mud and the mire. He set my feet on solid ground and steadied me as I walked along. He has given me a new song to sing, a hymn of praise to our God. Many will see what he has done and be amazed. They will put their trust in the LORD. (Psalm 40:1–3)

In February 2023, there was an outpouring of the Holy Spirit that was manifested particularly in Hughes Auditorium on the campus of Asbury University—the ninth of such events to be recorded in Asbury's 133-year history. The event raises two questions: why here and why now? There are two answers: we don't know and this is the way God reveals himself.

Why did God choose Jerusalem? We don't know, but he did. Why? Because the true God, the God of the Bible, reveals himself not in the timeless cycles of nature, which come from nowhere and go nowhere, but in unique places, times, and persons in human history. This is what distinguishes the Bible from the myths. The myths speak about "everyman" in timeless events occurring in places that don't exist. So real people in real places in real time are without value. You only matter to the extent that you somehow correspond to some ideal of humanity. Wrong! You matter! God has chosen to put his very image in you.

The world that God made on purpose matters. Is God revealed in the sunrise? Of course he is. But, oh, so much more is he revealed in a unique man like Abraham, in a unique place like Jerusalem, and in a unique time like 4 BC–29 AD. But in this way, he says every person, every place, every time is important. Rather than everything being dissolved into the ideal, everything is sanctified by the actual. We can only say "thank you."

> *Thank you for breaking in upon us and for a few days allowing us to soar like the eagles. Because of that we can now run the marathons of our days and not be worn out, and we can walk on long dusty roads and not quit. You have baptized the ordinary with yourself and with your blood have washed away the filthiness that we had come to accept as normal.*

That is revival.

March 12

THERE IS A RIVER

God is our refuge and strength, a very present help in trouble. Therefore we will not fear though the earth gives way, though the mountains be moved into the heart of the sea, though its waters roar and foam, though the mountains tremble at its swelling. There is a river whose streams make glad the city of God, the holy habitation of the Most High. God is in the midst of her; she shall not be moved; God will help her when morning dawns. (Psalm 46:1–5 ESV)

There is a device in the theater called a "scrim." A scrim is a curtain of cheesecloth hung across the stage opening. Something is painted on the scrim fitting the story of the play; perhaps a landscape, the exterior of a house, or whatever. When the play begins, the house lights are shining on the scrim and the stage lights are out. The scrim appears to be a hard surface. But as the action continues, the stage manager begins to dim the house lights and raise the stage lights. At some point the audience begins to see dimly that something is going on behind the scrim. Finally, when the stage is fully lit and the house lights are completely out, the scrim is virtually invisible. When the audience is engrossed in the action, the scrim is swiftly and silently raised, and most are not even aware of its going.

That is somewhat like what the Psalmist is saying. In the night an earthquake comes; the seemingly solid mountains are like Jell-O, quivering and sliding into a tsunami that comes roaring onto the shore. All our comfortable certainties are sliding away! What to do? Is that chaos reality? Yes, to some extent, the Psalmist says, but it is a scrim. Behind the raging sea and the slip-sliding mountains, there is a deeper, truer reality: a mighty River majestically and quietly flowing through the city. "God is our refuge and our strength."

In 2020 and 2021 we experienced a worldwide epidemic. Was that virus and all the grief it brought about reality? Of course it was. But it is not *all* there is to reality. Behind all this "standeth God within the shadows, keeping watch above his own."* We can look through the chaos, indeed we *must* look through the chaos to the mighty River who is the true reality. We do not know either how long the night will last or what it may cost us in the end. But we do know that through the night, he will carry us quietly along, and that when the morning comes, he will be seen in all his unending glory—and we will know that he is for us. Keep the faith!

---

* James Russell Lowell (1819–1891), "The Present Crisis" (public domain).

When Morning Gilds the Skies

March 13

UNCLEAN

Scrub me with hyssop, and I shall be clean; wash me, and I shall
be whiter than snow. (Psalm 51:7 author's translation)

It's all over for me! I am done for, because I am a man with unclean lips and
I live in the midst of a people with unclean lips, and I have seen the King,
Yahweh of Heaven's Armies with my own eyes. (Isaiah 6:5 author's translation)

When we compare Psalm 51 and Isaiah 6, we see an interesting—and even an arresting—similarity. It is the concept of "uncleanness." Isaiah does not say that his lips are finite, mortal, or temporal but that they are unclean. Likewise, David is clearly oppressed by a sense of pervasive uncleanness. He wants God to take a hyssop branch, the Israelite version of a scrub brush, to him and make him clean. He goes so far as to ask Yahweh to "create" a clean heart in him.

Clearly, these men had a remarkable understanding of the impact of sin in a life. Doing what is contrary to God's will and purposes, whether in action or speech, has an intrinsic effect on the one doing it—and not merely an extrinsic one. It changes our condition and not merely our circumstances.

What is the idea here? What is uncleanness? It is to attend a party where the men are in tuxedos and the women in formal gowns and be dressed in greasy, sweaty overalls. It is to walk into a hospital with manure on your boots. It is to go into a sickroom carrying the COVID virus. When we sin, we are changed, and we can no more exist in the presence of God than a pig can fly. That is what Isaiah knew, and it is what David knew. Sin is not a little peccadillo, a minor mistake, a "slip-up," or an "oopsie." It is filth in the presence of the eternally clean. Thus, to coddle it, to make a place for it, to excuse it, is not merely an error; it is a tragedy. Think of the heroic efforts around the world to confront COVID. Can the contagion that is killing us eternally be treated any less seriously? No!

To be sure, it is God who must cauterize those unclean lips; it is he who must make that stinking heart like the driven snow. But will we believe him to do it? Or will we expect to arrive at the wedding supper of the Lamb dressed in filthy rags, claiming that it is alright because a certain legal transaction has taken place? The legal transaction, dealing with the circumstance, is necessary, but it is not enough; our condition must be changed too: our words and our actions have to be made clean.

March 14

A Clean Heart

Create in me a clean heart, O God. (Psalm 51:10a)

Anything you eat passes through the stomach and then goes into the sewer. But the words you speak come from the heart—that's what defiles you. For from the heart come evil thoughts, murder, adultery, all sexual immorality, theft, lying, and slander. These are what defile you. Eating with unwashed hands will never defile you. (Matthew 15:17–20)

What is going on with the obsession with clean and unclean, especially in Leviticus 10–15? In paganism, there are unclean spirits in the world that we have to protect ourselves against or our rituals won't work. That is not the case in the Bible. There is only one Spirit—Yahweh. So, what is unclean? It is whatever does not belong to Yahweh or reflect his character and is thus unholy.

Nadab and Abihu, Aaron's sons, did not get the point of Leviticus 1–9 in which God is saying that his holiness is a danger to us and that we need to live in his way or that holiness, that cleanness, will destroy us. These two fellows thought he was just God, so why get too worried about doing things his way. Well, if the priests hadn't gotten the point, it was for sure the people hadn't. What to do? Give them a whole series of object lessons to drive home the point: whatever belongs to God is clean, and whatever does not is unclean. Furthermore, there is a radical difference between the two. Living any way but his way will defile you and what is defiled cannot exist in his presence.

So, what is that clean heart that David understands has to be "created" (made brand new)? An unclean heart is one that is not wholly God's and out of which comes thoughts and behaviors that are contrary to his character. David recognized that as the root of his problem. He was not made unclean by eating pork. That was an object lesson. As Jesus was to say later, it is not what goes into your mouth that makes you unclean; it is what comes out. So, what's a clean heart? One that is absolutely, irrevocably God's. And that only happens if we believe God to do it for us. Have you ever believed God to do that for you?

March 15

DAVID

Do not banish me from your presence, and don't take your
Holy Spirit from me. Restore to me the joy of your salvation
and make me willing to obey you. (Psalm 51:11–12)

What about the sins of David: adultery, lying, judicial murder? When Saul's sins are compared with these, Saul's don't seem that important. Yet Saul lost the kingdom, and David was granted an eternal dynasty. What's going on? Now don't misunderstand me! David's sins were tragic. I am in no way condoning them, excusing them, or recommending them! They poisoned his reign to the end of his days. But I want to say this: Saul's sins were those of an unsurrendered spirit, whereas David's sins were sins of the flesh. We rather instinctively think of the sins of the flesh as worse, but they aren't necessarily. It is pride, envy, jealousy, and covetousness that are the most destructive of all. For David, as with all of us, his weaknesses were the opposite side of his strengths. Because David had thrown himself on God at an early age, he was remarkably free of himself. He was not second-guessing himself all the time, wondering what people were thinking of him. This is why his troops were so fantastically loyal to him. Saul would never have committed adultery with Bathsheba because he would have been worrying about what somebody else would think. David was free of that need to think about himself. On the positive side, it made David able to be decisive, but decisive can become impulsive, which is what happened here.

How can it be said that David was a man after God's own heart? There is a world of difference between a lapse and a settled way of living. We can see the difference in David's response and Saul's. When Saul was confronted with his sin, his only thought was that he might lose face in front of his people (see 1 Sam 15:30). When David was confronted, his thought was that he might lose God! His cry was, "Don't take your Holy Spirit from me" (Ps 51:11).

So what shall we say? That it is better to commit sins of the flesh than sins of the spirit? Never! Don't sin! But this is to be said: surrender your spirit to the Lord and be free of yourself. Then stay so close to the Spirit that your strengths will never become your weaknesses.

March 16

ETERNAL INSECURITY

Cast your burden on the LORD, and he will sustain you; he will
never permit the righteous to be moved. (Psalm 55:22 ESV)

Sometimes those of us of a Wesleyan-Arminian persuasion give a wrong
impression. In our attempts to combat the "sinning religion" that
results from an unthinking adoption of the concept of "eternal security,"
we too easily seem to be promoting "eternal insecurity." That is, we seem
to imply that our relationship with God depends on the care with which
we live our lives. Unless one keeps oneself from any sin whatsoever, he
or she is lost. That is not the case. Yes, as John says, we must "abide in
Christ" (John 15:7). Yes, we must, empowered by the Holy Spirit, live lives
that constantly display the qualities of Christ. But our ongoing, saving
relationship with him is not a matter of our holding on to a greased rope
while he shakes it from above.

It is Jesus who holds us (see John 10:28); as Psalm 55:22 says, Yahweh
will not allow us to be shaken loose from him and our commitment to him.
Marriage is a wonderful illustration of this truth. I am absolutely secure in
Karen's love. Because of that, I try to be the best husband I can. But if I fall
short of that ideal sometimes (and I do), I have no fear whatever that she is
going to kick me out. Is it impossible for me to get out of this relationship?
Oh, no, it is possible. If I am stupid enough to trample on Karen's love,
doing things she hates, carousing with other women, and finally saying,
"I don't want you anymore," she may continue to love me, but precisely
because of that love, she will open her hand and let me go. It is the same
with Jesus: we are held securely in his love, regardless of occasional
shortcomings, just so long as our loving behavior shows we want *him* (and
not just what he can do for us—like eternal bliss). So, brother, sister, be
secure! You are his, and just as long as you want to be his, you *are* his.

March 17

FEARING AND TRUSTING

In God, whose word I praise, in God I trust; I am not afraid;
what can flesh do to me? . . . In God, whose word I praise, in the
LORD, whose word I praise, in God I trust; I am not afraid. What
can a mere mortal do to me? (Psalm 56:4, 10–11 NRSV)

It is interesting how often fear of others drives our choices. We are afraid of what others may think of us or of what they might do to us, and so we compromise our truest values and justify behavior that we would condemn in others. But it is simply because we have succumbed to our fears, fears that often prove completely unfounded. David knew something about that. In his case, his fear of Saul was completely founded. The man was out to kill him. And now it appeared that the people of Judah were turning against him and would turn him over to Saul if they could. What to do? Whether it was a good idea or not, he chose an extreme expedient: fly to Judah's enemies, the Philistines. Now those Philistines are debating what to do with him. He says two fundamentally important things: he is going to trust God's word to him, and he is not going to be ruled by fear. He says each of those things twice, and his terminology in the fear statements is interesting. He calls humans "flesh" and "dust" and he asks what flesh and dust can do to him? That perspective can be life-changing.

God's Word is ours: his word of honor, his word in Scripture, his eternal Word in Christ. Somehow or other, even in this extreme crisis, David knew God was going to keep his "Word" of life to him. Did David have an intimation of eternal life here? I think he did. In any case, he was not going to let a piece of meat or a cloud of dust keep him from living out the truth, because God has given him his Word. Can the same be true for you and me? Why not?

March 18

GOD IS FOR US

Then my enemies will turn back in the day when I call.
This I know, that God is for me. (Psalm 56:9 ESV)

David, worn down by Saul's dogged pursuit of him and his own people's, the Judean's, persistent betrayal of him to Saul, has finally fled to the Philistines, Judah's mortal enemies. Now he waits, perhaps in a prison cell, to see what they will do to him. Here is a man who has suffered terrible disillusionment. Everything he has ever believed about humanity is in ruins. They want to devour him, they twist his words, their promises are worthless, there seems to be nothing good in humans of any sort. But underneath that disillusionment is a singing assurance: God is for us. That Person whose clothing is the universe, that Spirit who is existence itself, is on our side. This being so, what can a little piece of meat ("flesh," Ps 56:4), a cloud of dust ("man," Ps 56:11), do to us?

In the midst of his trouble and despair, David has not lost his perspective. If Yahweh, the great I AM, is for us, we don't need to be afraid of anything. But how can David say that? He says it because of the Word. God is not silent; he has spoken. He had made promises to Abraham, and Jacob, and Moses, and he had kept those promises—every one.

Now, to us he has given his best promise and fulfillment: the Word, Jesus. Don't doubt it: God is for you and me, whatever the circumstances may be. That being so, what does David do? He trusts Yahweh. The cell door is still closed. The debating voices still rise and fall. But David trusts God. He knows that, whatever the outcome, God will lead David out in triumph. Are you disillusioned, in trouble? Don't lose your perspective. God is for you; his Word guarantees it. So, walk forward in confidence, trusting him, knowing that whatever happens, you will be the victor.

March 19

GOD IS WITH US

All this took place to fulfill what the Lord had spoken by the prophet: "Behold, the virgin shall conceive and bear a son, and they shall call his name Immanuel" (which means, God with us). (Matthew 1:22–23 ESV)

King Ahaz of Judah was terrified. His two northern neighbors were attacking Judah, intending to get rid of Ahaz and put their own man on the throne. Isaiah showed up and told Ahaz not to worry because Yahweh had everything under control. All Ahaz had to do was to trust God. Then Isaiah told the king that Yahweh would give him a sign that Ahaz could stand on: a little boy named "God with us" would be born.

We're not told what Ahaz's response was, but I think it might have been, "Is that all? I don't need a baby. I need a monster-man!" But there it is: a baby named "God with us."

First of all, what does that name even mean? It means that somehow, some way, God—the eternal, transcendent God—wants to share our lives. He wants to come alongside us in joy, in sorrow, in trouble, in excitement. He does not want to live in the lonely isolation of his holiness, watching us from far off. He wants to walk hand in hand with each of us. You are not alone.

Second, a baby? Yes. Here is where Isaiah was probably speaking more than he knew. Is God's being with us just a metaphor, a figure of speech, or is it a fact? It is a fact. God has found a way to enter into our human experience, and he has taken our humanness right from the outset. Like us, he entered the world as a baby. God knows every human experience, from birth to death, intimately, personally. There is nothing you can go through that he has not. You are not alone. He is with you. Walk into today with that confidence.

March 20

THE LIE

These wicked people are born sinners; even from birth they
have lied and gone their own way. (Psalm 58:3)

Indeed, I was born guilty, a sinner when my mother conceived
me. You desire truth in the inward being; therefore teach
me wisdom in my secret heart. (Psalm 51:5–6 NRSV)

Several years ago it dawned on me in a bolt of revelation: we never had to teach our children to lie! Now maybe your children were different, but with ours, getting them to tell the truth was the problem. What is going on? The passages above suggest that lying is inbred and is, in fact, the heart of what sin is. What does that mean? Why do we lie? We lie in order to try to make reality conform to what we think is our best interest. Why doesn't reality often do so? That's a topic for another time. For now there is something in us which insists that there is no reality (truth) outside of ourselves. We are the arbiters of reality. One has only to look at our society to see that principle run amok. For instance, if I wish to be a woman, then I can make myself so. The folly of this approach is everywhere evident. Drive your car into a brick wall going 100 miles an hour and tell me that no damage will result. Not even Obi-Wan-Kenobi can prevent that! Reality (truth) demands that we conform to it and conduct our lives in full respect of it. But fallen humans insist that "I and my desires are the only reality." This is to tragically "miss the target" (to sin), for God's target for us is to have truth (reality) at the core of our being. What is that truth? There is a God, and you're not him!

Here is the problem: I want to rule my life. "Sins" spring from this, but merely dealing with them is not enough. The *sin*, the lie, at the core is what has to be dealt a death-blow. Truth must replace the lie. Has it for you?

March 21
O THAT YOU WOULD LISTEN!

Listen to me, O my people, while I give you stern warnings.
O Israel, if you would only listen to me!" (Psalm 81:8)

Psalm 81 seems frighteningly appropriate for America in these days. What does it say? "Praise Yahweh who has saved you—don't go after some alien god!" What is the issue? Who will we turn to—trust—to defeat our enemies and fill our mouths? That is the basic issue of life: protect me from what would hurt me and provide for my wants. Who will do that? Our very own God who has already delivered us from bondage? Well, no, because he forthrightly tells us that we will have to submit to a "light" yoke and an "easy" burden (see Matt 11:28–30). Light or not, easy or not, we don't want yokes or burdens! We would rather be seduced by lying gods who tell us that with them we can have our own way at no cost to us at all. Liars all! That road, one on which Yahweh will regretfully let us go, is the road of progressive enslavement to our way—the way of our desires—until in the end, like Pharaoh, we cannot do anything different even if we should want to (which is very unlikely anyway). Oh, that we would listen! Yahweh alone can deliver us from those enemies, our true enemies, that would enslave us. He alone can fill our mouths with good things. He is calling. Is it too late for America to listen? Perhaps so, but it is not too late for you and me. Listen!

March 22

THE WRATH OF GOD

Who considers the power of your anger? Your wrath is as great as the
fear that is due you. So teach us to count our days that we may gain a
wise heart. Turn, O LORD! How long? Have compassion on your servants!
Satisfy us in the morning with your steadfast love, so that we may rejoice
and be glad all our days. Make us glad as many days as you have afflicted
us, and for as many years as we have seen evil. (Psalm 90:11–15 NRSV)

Many people are troubled by the wrath of God. They ask how such
anger, especially as seen in the Old Testament, can be consistent
with the love of God. There are several things we need to say at the outset:

- Don't dismiss this as some outdated Old Testament idea. The
doctrine of Hell is a New Testament teaching, coming first from
the mouth of Jesus (no fewer than seven times in the Gospels!).

- God is love but he gets angry. That is a vital distinction. His love is
who he is, while his anger is a temporary emotion.

- His anger is not primarily for himself and what has been done to
him. His anger is over the violation of his creation standards and
for what we are doing to ourselves in that violation.

- God is a person, and if he can experience affection, as he does, he
can also experience anger. They are two sides of the same coin.
You can't have one and not the other. But God's love is not merely
affection. It is the conscious and joyful choosing of the best for
another person at whatever cost to oneself.

A man has a beautiful and intelligent teenaged daughter. She is the
light of his life, but she is hanging out with a bunch of low-lifes who are
into alcohol, drugs, and group sex. When he tries to tell her that she is
ruining her life and heading for an early grave, she says, "Dad, you don't
love me," and flounces out. What is his reaction? He's angry! Why? Because
he doesn't love her? No, precisely because he *does*!

It is the same with God. For a thousand years the Hebrew people,
excellent examples of the rest of us, thumbed their noses at the God who
had saved them from Egypt and given them the land of Canaan, choosing
to live in defiance of his life-giving covenant. He is not supposed to get
angry about that?

March 23

WINGS: PART ONE

Whoever dwells in the shelter of the Most High will abide under
the shadow of the Almighty. . . . He will cover you with his pinions.
He will shelter you with his wings. His faithful promises are your
armor and shield." (Psalm 91:1, 4 author's translation)

I have seen a hen and her chicks pecking about a barnyard when suddenly
a shadow passed over the sun, and the hen gave a squawk and spread
out her wings. The chicks quickly gathered under those wings, which
closed down around them. A few minutes later one yellow head popped
out between the wing and the breast and from that point was ready to take
on the world.

This image is what William Cushing (1823–1902) was thinking of
when he wrote the hymn "Under His Wings" (see below). Cushing had
been a gifted preacher, but at age fifty lost his voice. What to do? During
the remaining years of his life, he wrote more than six hundred hymns. He
knew what it was to be under God's protecting wings. He knew that God
would die—indeed has died—to deliver his own from death to life.

Do you need those wings to be spread over you today? Don't be afraid
of the shadows, dive under his wings. They are spread for you.

Under His wings I am safely abiding;
though the night deepens and tempests are wild.
Still I can trust Him—I know He will keep me;
He has redeemed me and I am His child.

(Refrain:) Under His wings, under His wings,
who from His love can sever?
Under His wings my soul shall abide, safely abide forever.

Under His wings—what a refuge in sorrow!
How the heart yearningly turns to His rest
Often when earth has no balm for my healing,
There I find comfort, and there I am blest. (Refrain)

Under His wings—oh, what precious enjoyment!
There will I hide till life's trials are o'er;
Sheltered, protected, no evil can harm me;
resting in Jesus I'm safe evermore. (Refrain)

March 24

WINGS: PART TWO

You have seen what I did to the Egyptians. You know how I carried
you on eagles' wings and brought you to myself. (Exodus 19:4)

Like an eagle that rouses her chicks and hovers over her
young, so he spread his wings to take them up and carried
them safely on his pinions. (Deuteronomy 32:11)

Imagine this: high up on a cliffside there is what looks like an ungainly pile of sticks. If we could get above it and look down on it, we would realize that it is an eagle's aerie and that there are several chicks in it. They are clearly hungry, hopping around the nest squawking. Where is their mother with food? One of them, bigger than the rest, hops up on the edge of the nest, balancing precariously, scanning the sky, craning his head this way and that. Suddenly, the mother swoops down with a rabbit held in her talons, but as she comes by, she almost casually taps the eaglet with her wing, and he goes tumbling off into space. He falls through the air, flailing about, flapping his stubby wings, crying in fright. What was the mother thinking? Did she hate him, want to kill him? At the last moment, when it seems he must crash on the rocks below, here she comes, effortlessly sweeping under him, and he plops onto her back, gazing about with terrified wonder as she soars up and up, finally tipping him off into the nest. How many times more must that happen until finally the little one gets the idea and realizes he too can fly?

Have you felt pushed off the nest? Have you wondered what in the world God is doing, treating you in such a cavalier and thoughtless way? Does he hate you? No, he does not. But so long as we are safely in the nest, demanding that he meet our needs, impatient with his slowness, we will never learn that he is absolutely trustworthy. We will never come to the place where we can dare for him and receive wonders from him that are beyond our imaginings.

The Hebrews in Egypt were in the nest, crying out for God to do something for them. When he pushed them out of the nest into the Sinai Desert, they had to learn to trust him. So do we. Are you ready to fly?

March 25

WINGS: PART THREE

Fear and trembling overwhelm me, and I can't stop shaking. Oh, that I had wings like a dove; then I would fly away and rest! I would fly far away to the quiet of the wilderness. (Psalm 55:5–7)

But those who trust in the LORD will find new strength. They will soar high on wings like eagles. They will run and not grow weary. They will walk and not faint. (Isaiah 40:31)

When the dragon realized that he had been thrown down to the earth, he pursued the woman who had given birth to the male child. But she was given two wings like those of a great eagle so she could fly to the place prepared for her in the wilderness. There she would be cared for and protected from the dragon for a time, times, and half a time. (Revelation 12:13–14)

There are wings under which we can take refuge, and there are wings that come underneath us and carry us when we are helplessly falling. But there are also wings given us to soar above and away from whatever is oppressing us. In Psalm 55, it is the effects of betrayal by a close friend that David needs to be delivered from. In Isaiah 40, the Judean captives needed to persevere through the Babylonian exile and dare to believe the promises of a return. In Revelation, the woman (the Church?) needs to escape from the dragon who seeks to devour her. In the first case, David wishes for wings, and in the second and third, wings are given.

Paul said that every test that we may face is common to everybody, and that God will make a way of escape (see 1 Cor 10:13). Wings! He protects us as chicks, carries us as fledglings, and delights to soar with us over and above everything that threatens us. As his Spirit soared over the empty cosmos, so he delights to work in us and gives us the grace and power to rise above everything that would drag us down. This is the power that enabled Jesus to face rejection, injustice, and even death, and at the end of it all, to breathe, "Forgive them, for they don't know what they are doing" (Luke 23:34). That, dear friends, is to soar, and it is our birthright!

March 26
WALK IN MY HOUSE

I will sing of steadfast love and justice; to you, O LORD, I will make music.
I will ponder the way that is blameless. Oh when will you come to me? I
will walk with integrity of heart within my house. (Psalm 101:1–2 ESV)

This psalm is a powerful statement of David's personal commitments. I
suspect "house" here has two connotations. The first is the literal one:
his home. The second is a metaphorical one: his inward self. The two are
intimately related. David is going to guard his own behavior in his own
home with great care. The terms used here are ones we have encountered
before: "steadfast love" is *hesed* and "justice" is *mishpat* (God's pattern
for life), while "blameless" and "integrity" come from the same root: *tmm*,
which means "whole, complete, unblemished." The King James Version
regularly translates it "perfect." A life that is marked by *tmm* is one that is
single-mindedly reflective of God's pattern for life, his *mishpat*, a pattern
governed by self-giving love.

In short, David is saying that he is going to give careful attention to
cultivating within himself the nature, the character, and the standards of
God. He recognizes that if that is ever to happen, it will only be because
God comes in his divine power and enables it. When that happens it will
transform his behavior in his most intimate relations.

How often our godly behavior is for "public consumption," whereas
at home we are irritable, sarcastic, impatient, and demanding. That ought
not to be! With those who are closest to us, the evidence of our Christian
transformation ought to be most apparent. Here we ought to be most
compassionate, forgiving, and "long-suffering." Here the proof of God's
work in our lives ought to be most evident. The great tragedy of David's life
was that once he failed in this resolution. He did not walk with integrity of
heart in his own house. Let that never be said of us.

March 27

GOD'S PROVISION

For his unfailing love toward those who fear him is as great as the height
of the heavens above the earth. He has removed our sins as far from
us as the east is from the west. The LORD is like a father to his children,
tender and compassionate to those who fear him. For he knows how
weak we are; he remembers we are only dust. (Psalm 103:11–14)

Earlier, I pointed out that the instructions for the sacrificial system
come only at the beginning of Leviticus, after the deliverance from
Egypt, the sealing of the covenant, and the directions for the building of
the Tabernacle. I said that this placement was designed to show that we do
not get into a relationship with God by manipulating him in some magical
fashion. Rather, it is God who brings us to himself only because of his
own grace. This placement of the sacrificial system says something more.
Exodus is unmistakably clear: to be in a saved condition is to be living the
life of God in covenant obedience. We are joyfully walking with our Father.
But just as sacrificial love made it possible to be in this relationship,
sacrificial love makes it possible to remain there. God did not give the
system of sacrifices for those who wanted to sin and still get to heaven.
That becomes strikingly clear when we discover that the whole system
was for unintended sins. If you sinned intentionally, as David understood,
there was no prescribed sacrifice for that. It had to be dealt with on a case-
by-case basis.

Yahweh's sacrificial forgiveness is for those who want to live with him
and yet in human weakness and ignorance will necessarily fall short of
perfect performance. As the psalmist says, he knows our weaknesses and
has made a means whereby these need not forever separate us from him.

Bottom line: you and I may never use the blood of Christ as a fire
escape, allowing us to do what we want and get away with it. Neither may
we ever suppose it simply gives God Jesus-colored glasses so that he never
sees the real character of our lives. Rather, blood-bought and blood-sealed,
we may walk with him in unblemished fellowship secure in the knowledge
that if in ignorance or weakness we unintentionally fall short in some way,
there is grace, grace for all.

March 28

DEATH: FRIEND OR FOE

Precious in the sight of the LORD is the death of his saints. (Psalm 116:15 ESV)

Should Christians welcome death as the vehicle to get us from "this vile world" into the courts of heaven? St. Francis spoke words to that effect. Sometimes this verse is used in that way. It seems to say that God is especially gratified when someone dies in the faith.

In fact, the psalmist is saying the opposite. He is saying that the death of a saint is terribly costly to God. That is what "precious" meant for the writers of the King James Version in 1611. Like all the ancient Israelites, the psalmist sees death as something terribly wrong. He had been about to die: "The snares of death encompassed me . . ." (Ps 116:3 ESV). But "you have delivered my soul from death" (Ps 116:8 ESV).

We can imagine King Hezekiah saying these words after his near-death experience. So when the psalmist says, "The death of his saints is very costly to the LORD," he is saying that God does not want anyone to die. How true that is! God made us for life, a life that would begin in this world and move without decay, dissolution, and pain directly into the world to come. But Sin has intervened and brought with it the great obscenity of all existence—Death.

This is why Jesus agonized so in the Garden. He who was Life Incarnate was about to bear all the Death(s) of this broken world. This is not to deny the reality of eternal life. But the death we now die is not the way God planned for us to transition from this life to the next. Death as we now know it, and as Christ experienced it, is a dark blot on the world, and God hates it. So, if you weep uncontrollably when a sainted loved one dies, know this: God is weeping too. The death of his saints is horribly costly to him—as costly as the Cross.

March 29

How Close?

How blessed are those whose way is blameless,
Who walk in the law of the LORD.
How blessed are those who comply with His testimonies,
Who seek Him with all *their* heart. (Psalm 119:1–2 NASB)

In my years of ministry I have often been asked, although not always in these exact words, "as a Christian, how far from Jesus can I live?" What a strange question. And yet, maybe not, for it betrays a certain understanding of salvation. Salvation is about avoiding deserved punishment and receiving undeserved blessing. So, what is the minimum I have to do to get the blessing—eternal life?

This is like some students I have had. They ask me, "Prof, what is the minimum I have to do to pass this course?" What are they saying? They are saying that the goal is passing the course. "So, how many of your (boring) lectures can I skip? Do I have to read all three of those, long, hard textbooks? What is the minimum number of sources I have to cite in the research paper?" But suppose passing the course is not the goal? Suppose the goal is to gain a mastery of the material, to become genuinely educated in this subject? Oh, the joy of that student, the one who says, "Prof, I am really excited about this subject. Can you suggest some extra reading I could do? Could I drop in from time to time to ask some questions about your lectures? I want to be sure I understand what you are saying." I have to restrain myself from breaking some of that student's ribs with a massive bearhug! That's what it is with Jesus. The goal is not eternal life! The goal is to know—really know, in the sense of becoming like—Jesus. Eternal life is a by-product, just like passing the course is a by-product.

We were made to be Christ-like, holy and blameless—without a defect (see Eph 1:4). So, the question is not how far from Jesus can I live, but how close to him! It is not how little time can I spend with him, but how much! It is not how little do I have to know about him, but how much can I know! What's your goal? Heaven or Jesus? "How blessed . . . are those who seek him with all their heart."

March 30

I LOVE YOUR LAW

I will always obey your law, for ever and ever. I will walk about in
freedom, for I have sought out your precepts. I will speak of your
statutes before kings and will not be put to shame, for I delight in your
commands because I love them. I reach out for your commands, which
I love, that I may meditate on your decrees. (Psalm 119:44–48 NIV)

When we read Psalm 119:44–48 and then remember that the Apostle
Paul says Christ has redeemed us from the curse of the law (see
Gal 3:13), we do a doubletake. What's going on? What is going on is not
either/or but two sides of a single coin. Is God's instruction manual for
life (that's what *torah*, which the English Bible translates "law," means—
instruction) a bad thing. Never! Thank God he has shown us how he
designed us humans to function. That's why the psalmist can say he can
walk about in freedom. The *torah* is a blessing!

But Paul says it's a curse! What he is describing is the result of having
misunderstood what the *torah* is for. If we think that *torah*-keeping can
make us acceptable to God, as the Pharisees did, we have got it backwards,
and our persistent inability to keep the *torah* will indeed curse us. Nobody
can be good enough for God except one man—Jesus. Every one of us, from
Abraham on, comes to God by grace alone.

Look at all of Paul's letters. What is Paul calling his new Christian
disciples to do? He is calling them, now that they are Christ-followers, to
live according to *torah*! Stop stealing, stop lying, stop committing adultery,
etc. Why? To make themselves acceptable to God? Of course not! That is
where the Galatians went off-track. No, Paul wants them to live that way
because this is the life of Christ that is now, praise God, being reproduced
in us by the Holy Spirit if we will just surrender to him.

The good news of the gospel is that because Christ has cleansed the
temple of our hearts, the Holy Spirit has moved in with the marvelous
power to make God's *torah* no longer an impossible demand but all that
the psalmist dreamed of: our delight, our liberation, our testimony, our life.

March 31

MISSED CHANCES

My heart is set on keeping your decrees to the very end. (Psalm 119:112 NIV)

Someone says, "Suppose your Christian faith is a delusion. Suppose you close your eyes for the last time and that's all there is. Think of all you will have missed because you stuck to all those stupid rules." Missed? Yes, I will have missed making a fool of myself in a drunken stupor at a party. Or worse, killing someone while driving with one too many drinks under my belt. Missed? Yes, missed sexually abusing my children or having sex with twenty or thirty women other than my wife in an increasingly frantic attempt to prove my manhood. Missed? Yes, missed abandoning my wife and children because "that's just not fun." Missed? Yes, missed living a lonely, self-absorbed life on a private island in the Bahamas with illegal millions sequestered in an off-shore account. Missed? Yes, missed dropping $100,000 on the slots at Vegas. Missed? Yes, missed shuttling between luxury apartments and mansions all bought with money I had cheated my business partners out of.

Do you know what? Because of Jesus I have missed ruining these few short years given to me. Thank God! Because of Jesus I have had a satisfying, fulfilling career with a wonderful woman who has loved me unreservedly all these years. Because of Jesus, she and I have three whole, optimistic, confident children who are raising children like themselves. Because of Jesus, I am healthy and well. Because of Jesus, I can look back not with regrets but with overflowing gratitude. It is these realities that convince me that, indeed, this faith is not a delusion, and that when I close my eyes for the last time on this earth, it will be to open them to an eternity of joy. *Even if that were not so, following the instructions for living found in the Bible would still be the smartest thing a person could do.* So, with the psalmist affirm, "My heart is set on keeping your decrees to the very end!"

April 1

ON SACRIFICING CHILDREN

Children are a gift from the LORD; they are a reward from him. Children
born to a young man are like arrows in a warrior's hands. How joyful
is the man whose quiver is full of them! He will not be put to shame
when he confronts his accusers at the city gates. (Psalm 127:3–5)

They have committed both adultery and murder—adultery by worshiping idols
and murder by burning as sacrifices the children they bore to me. Furthermore,
they have defiled my Temple and violated my Sabbath day! On the very day
that they sacrificed their children to their idols, they boldly came into my
Temple to worship! They came in and defiled my house. (Ezekiel 23:37–39)

When we read the Ezekiel passage printed above we are rightly
horrified. How could those people do such things? Thank God we
have gotten beyond that stage in the development of human culture. Or
have we? We have to understand what was going on there. Humans are
fragile and needy. If we don't get what we want and need, life is pretty
grim. Beyond the bare necessities for physical life, what do we want?
Possessions, pleasure, power and position (see 1 John 2:16). How do we
get them? Well, life is pretty simple when you get right down to it: you get
what you pay for. Those folks personified life forces as gods, and sold their
kids to those forces in order to satisfy their desires.

Are we different? I am afraid not. How many men and women
have sacrificed their children in order to serve the gods of money and
position? How many of us have sacrificed our children on the altar of our
pleasure? How many of us have dolled our little girls up as though they
were prostitutes or forced our little boys into sports in order to satisfy
our thwarted desires? How many of us have sacrificed our children on
the altar of our desire to be great parents and to be appreciated by our
children? How many of us have sacrificed our children to the gods of this
world because we were unwilling to accept the hard work involved in being
trustees of heaven's gift? Before we are too harsh on those people of long
ago and far away, perhaps we need to take a look in the mirror and fall on
our faces.

When Morning Gilds the Skies

April 2

SEARCH ME

O LORD, you have examined my heart and know everything about me. . . .
I can never escape from your Spirit! I can never get away from your
presence! . . . Search me, O God, and know my heart; test me and know
my anxious thoughts. Point out anything in me that offends you and
lead me along the path of everlasting life. (Psalm 139:1, 7, 23–24)

While not all commentators agree with me, I am convinced that in the first twelve verses of Psalm 139, the psalmist is uncomfortable with God's intrusion into his life. There is no place he can go to get away from this God who is everywhere. It is just too much. A person needs to be able to get away and hide in the privacy of his own thoughts sometimes, he says. But there God is, knowing what he is going to think before he thinks it. The opening direct address, typical of psalms of lament, gives the psalm an intimacy and directness: you search me and know me [whether I like it or not—and I don't!].

Yet, when we come to the end of the psalm, the writer is *asking* God to search him and know him, the very same words as verse one. What has happened to account for the shift? Two things have happened, I think. The first is that he has remembered that Yahweh is his Creator, his Author (see vv 13–18). We are characters in a story that Yahweh is telling. Just as characters in a story only have their existence in the mind of the author, so we exist only in the mind of Yahweh. That being so, "Don't stop thinking about me!" What a relief then to wake up and know that he is still here—and I am too!

The other thing that happened is found in verses 19–22. The psalmist is now completely in God's corner. If he is dependent on God for his existence, he is going to be totally dependent. Because this God hates evil, he is going to hate it too, and especially those who do it. In fact, he cannot imagine how God can put up with those people; he ought to wipe them out. Oh, wait. What if I am one of those people? Suppose there is something lurking inside of me that might one day make me his enemy. Oh, no, not that! Search me and know me. Like a doctor doing a physical examination, do a spiritual examination on me. I am your man, your woman, living in your thought. Don't let anything cut me loose from you!

April 3

EXALT CHRIST

Let them praise the name of the LORD, for his name is exalted; his splendor is above the earth and the heavens. (Psalm 148:13 NIV)

I eagerly expect and hope that I will in no way be ashamed, but will have sufficient courage so that now as always Christ will be exalted in my body, whether in life or by death. (Philippians 1:20 NIV)

Therefore, as the Scriptures say, "If you want to boast, boast only about the LORD." (1 Corinthians 1:31)

One of the greatest dangers for the Christian who is seeking to live a holy life is the temptation to make that kind of living an end in itself. That is, the focus comes to be on our achievement (or lack of thereof!) as a holy person. That is deadly. Satan does not really care how he gets us to focus on ourselves. The result is a morbid introspection on the one hand and an arrogant self-righteousness on the other, with every other kind of aberration in between.

So what is the solution? It is to exalt Jesus. The holy life is not an "it," but a "him." It is about walking with God through Jesus by the Holy Spirit, about knowing him, pleasing him, glorifying him. Let us not exalt an experience, but Jesus; let us not exalt this ideal behavior, or that, but Jesus. The holy life is a by-product of a holy relationship. When we are in love with him, wanting him to be glorified in every part of our life, then life like his, a holy life, just naturally flows out of us.

The Christian life is about Jesus! He is our hope, he is our redemption, he is our sanctification, he is our joy. If we focus on him, and glorify him, we can't go wrong. There is one glory in the Christian life: Christ in you (see Col 1:27). Let us not exalt an experience. Let us not exalt this ideal or that ideal. Let us exalt Christ, who graciously plants his own sweet character in us through the Holy Spirit!

April 4

SIN IS AN ABOMINATION

And he said to me, "Son of man, do you see what they are
doing, the great abominations that the house of Israel are
committing here, to drive me far from my sanctuary? But you
will see still greater abominations." (Ezekiel 8:6 ESV)

For twenty-five years Ezekiel had trained to be a priest in the temple of God in Jerusalem. Then five years before he would have entered priestly service, he had been carried away to unclean Babylon as a hostage. We can imagine how he must have been pining for what might have been back in that beautiful, holy temple back home.

Through the Holy Spirit, God gave him a horrifying vision of what was actually going on back there in the Temple. They were committing "abominations." What is an abomination? It is that which is disgusting to God because it is contrary to the nature of his creation. Sin is an abomination to God, and it is so because it is flying in the face of the way he made us. He made us to be submissive to him, and when we are proud and arrogant, it is an abomination. He made us to find our glory in him, and when we find our glory in ourselves and in our world, it is an abomination. He made us to forget ourselves in concern for one another. Sin is an abomination.

One of the tragedies of our day is that we have become desensitized to the abominable character of sin. We watch television, and we see a murder a minute: "Another murder, oh well, that's life." We see all the evils: "Oh, they're having an affair. Oh, well." We see all of the sins and lose our capacity to be disgusted, horrified, and grieved by the sin around us. Through television, we invited the enemy into our homes. I'm not saying that we all need to get rid of our TV sets, but if it's in our homes, we'd better guard it exceedingly carefully. We need to gain a sense of horror at the sin around us. Sin is a heart condition before it is anything else, and the Holy Spirit asks us whether there is an abomination in the temple of our hearts.

April 5

THE KINGDOM IS AT HAND

Let Israel be glad in his Maker; let the children of Zion
rejoice in their King! (Psalm 149:2 ESV)

Have you ever wondered at the content of the message Jesus preached and the one he told his disciples to preach? I have. I have wondered about it because it seems so simple and indeterminate:

- "The time promised by God has come at last!" he announced. "The Kingdom of God is near! Repent of your sins and believe the Good News!" (Mark 1:15)

- "Go and announce that the Kingdom of Heaven is near." (Matt 10:7).

Is that it? What "Good News"? Today we say that the Good News, the gospel, is that Jesus has died for your sins. But clearly that had not happened yet when Jesus and the disciples were preaching. So what were he, and they, talking about? What were those people to believe?

I suggest the Good News they were to believe was that the kingdom promises were about to be fulfilled. And that belief should make them repent of the way they had been living and get ready for the rule of God— his kingdom—to break loose in their lives. What were the promises? What needed to happen for God to truly rule? What needs to happen in your life and mine for him to rule?

What needs to happen is the fulfillment of the promises of Ezekiel 36:24–27. God promises to deliver us from the consequences of our sins—our hell. Next, he promises to cleanse us from both the results and the practice of idolatry—trying to get this world to satisfy our needs. Then, he promises to smash our stubborn hearts and give us tender, pliable hearts. Finally, he promises that he will put his Spirit within us to make all that possible.

I think Jesus—and the disciples—were saying that this whole package that the Jews had longed for was about to be unwrapped. The Kingdom has come! God can rule in our lives without a rival and without a limit. Christ's blood can cleanse the temple of our hearts, and the Holy Spirit can come home.

Are you experiencing God's rule in your heart? Has he broken you of your idolatry? Is your heart tender to the slightest whisper of his will? Repent of unbelief and believe the Good News! Jesus has done everything necessary for God to rule in your life. Is he?

April 6

TRUST

Trust in the LORD with all your heart; and lean not on your
own understanding. In all your ways, acknowledge him, and
he shall direct your paths. (Proverbs 3:5–6 KJV)

Trust is at the very heart of any relation with Yahweh. There is no other
basis for relationship with him. That is because of his nature. He is not
a part of his creation; he is utterly other than anything that he has spoken
into existence. That means he is utterly beyond human control. We have
no power over him whatsoever. So, we must believe that he is good, and
believing that, cast ourselves upon him. If we will not do that, there is
nothing he can do for us.

But that alternative is frightening. It means we surrender the supply of
our needs into his hands, not knowing if he will supply them or not. Even
worse, it means that we surrender the direction of our lives into his hands,
not knowing if he may lead us into a dead end.

Now, if we will listen to the testimony of those who have gone before
us, he *is* good, and he *is* reliable, or "true" (see Ps 100). They tell us that
he does supply our needs (if not always our desires) and that he leads his
people to places of rest, refreshment, and restoration (see Ps 23). He can
be trusted. As we do trust—and discover that Yahweh is trustworthy—it
becomes easier to trust him further, but the sense of risk is never taken
away. Will he be there this time?

This is why idolatry is always hovering on the fringes of our lives.
Idolatry is the attempt to avoid the necessity of trust. We believe that
we can manipulate the forces of this cosmos to make ourselves secure,
comfortable, and powerful, and *not to have to trust*. But this is exactly why
idolatry, ancient or modern, is so reprehensible. It puts us "in the driver's
seat," in control, the place we were never meant to be. Only the I AM,
the basis of existence, can be there, and any attempt by creatures, dying
creatures, to sit there can only result in disaster (see Isa 14:4–21).

April 7

ACCURATE SCALES

The LORD detests the use of dishonest scales, but he
delights in accurate weights. (Proverbs 11:1)

Perhaps, like me, after the excesses of a good meal, you would like
inaccurate scales—though only on the low side, of course. Yahweh will
have none of that. By my calculations, his disgust with inaccurate scales
is referred to no fewer than eight times.* In today's vernacular, what's up
with that?

I think there are two points being made—a philosophical one and
a personal one—and both of them relate directly to our day. On the
philosophical side, he is saying that he has made the world according to
certain standards, and those standards cannot be altered. Whether we call
them shekels, ounces, or grams, what I weigh is what I weigh, and I cannot
alter that fact by changing the standard. Most of us will accept that fact
when it comes to the physical world. It is only when those standards begin
to impinge on what we conceive to be our self-interest, when it becomes
personal, that the shoe begins to pinch. For example, my grain business is
not making as much money as I wish. So what do I do? I have a set of scales
with which I weigh the grain I buy and sell. I have a set of weights, and I
put the grain on one side and the weight on the other to determine just how
much I am buying and selling. But I actually have two sets of weights: one
for buying and one for selling. So, I pay you for a bushel, but it's actually
a bushel and a quarter. And you pay me for a bushel, but you actually
received three quarters of a bushel. Hey, it's just business! So what?

God hates the self-interest that makes us say his standards are always
up for re-negotiation according to what we think is right for us. To be a
Christian is to say, "Father, your Word tells me how you made the world
to work, I here surrender my self-interest into your hands, believing that
you can care for me better than I can care for myself. I will live by your
standards, not my self-serving ones."

---

* See Lev 19:36; Prov 11:1, 16:11, 20:23; Ezek 45:10; Hos 12:7;
  Amos 8:5; Mic 6:11.

When Morning Gilds the Skies

April 8

PLANS

We can make our own plans, but the LORD gives the right answer. People may be pure in their own eyes, but the LORD examines their motives. Commit your actions to the LORD, and your plans will succeed. (Proverbs 16:1–3)

As we look at our lives, it is perfectly normal to make plans. In fact, the Bible tells us to do so, and we are condemned if we do not do so. But here is the issue: whose plans? If we do not take account of the fact that there is a great Transcendent Person upon whose existence the whole universe depends, we will certainly plan wrongly. We will plan as though the future were ours to shape for our benefit alone. That is what the Assyrians had done as they crashed their way across the ancient Near East. But Yahweh said it was not Assyria's plans but his that would shape Assyria's future (see Isa 14:24–27). In the same way, the wise men of Egypt, that Grand Dame of ancient cultures, thought that they could plot out their nation's direction. Yet, in fact, they knew nothing of Yahweh's purposes for Egypt (see Isa 19:12), and being ignorant of that, their plans were chaff.

So, should we just sit on our hands and see how the Father unfolds things? Oh no. Here is the beauty of the relationship God has planned for us. He wants us to take responsibility and to act responsibly, but always with him and his purposes in view. We must also be aware of his infinite creativity and his capacity to shape things differently as new circumstances arise. General Dwight Eisenhower is supposed to have said, "You must plan, but you must also remember that as soon as the battle starts, all your plans are out the window."

Yes, let's plan, but let our plans reflect God's great purposes for our lives. Plan to serve him, to please him, to grow more into his likeness, and then, as those plans unfold, let's keep our eyes on him for all the ways he will reshape and redefine our plans in wonderful ways we could never have imagined in advance.

April 9

THE RELIGION OF DESIRE

Just as Death and Destruction are never satisfied, so
human desire is never satisfied. (Proverbs 27:20)

LORD, we show our trust in you by obeying your laws; our
heart's desire is to glorify your name. (Isaiah 26:8)

A book published in 2020, *Is Europe Christian?* by Olivier Roy (Oxford University Press), examines modern Europe's present cultural foundations and arrives at a profound and disturbing answer. The author, a French political scientist, argues that as recently as the 40s and 50s, those leaders who were shaping the European Union grounded their vision in profoundly Christian ideas. But in the 60s and 70s in Europe and America all that changed radically. The Christian vision was replaced with another in which the desires of the individual became the basis of all ethics and all political legitimacy. What humans desire they have an inalienable right, and even duty, to do. Roy says this is a genuine revolution in civilization, one that is now complete and essentially irresistible, but one whose ultimate implications no one yet comprehends. He goes on to say that nothing could be farther from traditional Christian ideas.

These insights are profoundly true. The Bible tells us that desire is tyrannical and that Jesus has come to set us free from that tyranny. Our enemy whispers that if we can just do whatever we want, we will be free. But that is a lie. Our real desire is for God, and to attempt to satisfy that desire with anything else is futile. We rightly understand that to live with him, we must give up our right to ourselves, something we don't want to do. So we rush from one desire to another, more and more frantically attempting to find anything that will truly satisfy, not realizing that nothing we desire apart from him can satisfy—or was meant to satisfy. Roy calls this "the religion of desire," and says it is impossible to build a sustainable social order out of a collection of individuals ruled by desire.

This calls us to a personal inventory. You and I live in the middle of this revolution; how deeply has it affected us? How much am I ruled by desire for possessions, pleasure, comfort, security? Do I say that I have surrendered my all to Christ when in fact my desires rule me, making it essentially impossible to deny myself for the sake of others—or for the Christian cause? "Am I a soldier of the Cross, a follower of the Lamb . . .?"* Or am I really a devotee of the religion of desire?

---

* Hymn lyrics by Isaac Watts (1721).

April 10

COME AWAY, MY BELOVED

The fig trees are forming young fruit, and the fragrant
grapevines are blossoming. Rise up, my darling! Come
away with me, my fair one! (Song of Songs 2:13)

Believers from earliest times have struggled with the Song of Songs (or Song of Solomon). What's it doing in the Bible? After all, it's composed of some pretty explicit love poems. The Jewish people and the early Church solved the problem by interpreting the book as an allegory of God's love for his people. The reason they did so was because they accepted the idea that there is a deep gap between the physical and the spiritual. Something so blatantly physical as human love does not have in it spiritual meaning.

I want to suggest that the division between the physical and the spiritual is not a biblical idea. In fact, God never intended the spiritual and the physical to be separated. This is why we believe in bodily resurrection. What does that mean for Song of Songs? It means that human love is not a *symbol* of divine love; human love is an *expression* of divine love! Why do we find members of the opposite sex so desirable? Because God, who is love, made the world that way. He made us to find our truest selves in giving ourselves away to another who is like us, and yet not like us. When we surrender our deepest selves, body, soul, and spirit to the beloved we are participating in what C. S. Lewis called "The Great Dance." When I call my beloved to come away with me, God smiles. Human love and divine love are part of a single continuum. They are two expressions of a single thing.

So is Song of Songs about human love? Absolutely. But it is about human love as an expression of divine love. God made us to love one another because he is love, and the degree to which we really give ourselves away in a selfless desire to please and care for that only beloved is one of the measures of our knowledge of the love of God. Human love is not by any means the totality of divine love, but it is a part of it and is intended to lead us to its consummation in God.

AT THE CROSS

"Come now, let's settle this," says the LORD. "Though your sins are like scarlet, I will make them as white as snow. Though they are red like crimson, I will make them as white as wool." (Isaiah 1:18)

There is a scene in the movie *Ben Hur* that I will never forget. This once, Hollywood got it right. It is raining, and Jesus is hanging on the cross; the soldier stabs him in the side with his spear; the blood comes rushing out, streaming down his legs, down the cross and onto the ground. There it stains a trickle of water; that stained trickle joins a larger trickle, which it stains in turn; that larger trickle flows into a brook that is stained, and so on into larger and larger streams. We, the viewers, are left to imagine all the oceans of the world stained red. So it is. Since that day 2,000 years ago, the very blood of God has flowed to every part of the world, from the top of Everest to the bottom of the Marianas Trench, from the North Pole to the South, from one side of the International Date Line back around to the other side again. "Oh, the blood of Jesus, oh, the blood of Jesus. It washes white as snow!"*

Lady Macbeth looked at her hands, perfectly clean but in her mind dripping with Duncan's blood, and screamed, "Out, damned spot!" But then she says that nothing can ever make those hands clean again. But she was wrong! In the theater, if you want to make a red surface white, you put a red lens over a light and shine it on that surface. It will appear white. So it is with the blood of God. Only here, it is not mere appearance. Pour that blood over the crimsoned surface of our lives, and "I will make them as white as wool." Do you know that, really know it? It's true, true for you! Oh, the blood of Jesus!

---

* Hymn lyrics, author unknown.

April 12

ISAIAH'S MISSIONARY MANDATE

People from many nations will come and say, "Come, let us go up to the mountain of the LORD, to the house of Jacob's God. There he will teach us his ways, and we will walk in his paths." For the LORD's teaching will go out from Zion; his word will go out from Jerusalem. (Isaiah 2:3)

All humanity will come to worship me from week to week and from month to month. (Isaiah 66:23)

More than any other Old Testament book, and more than many New Testament books, the book of Isaiah makes it clear that God's heart is for the world. As the passages quoted above show, this thought is at both the beginning and the end of the book, and it is also found at many places in between. God will save the Israelite people in order that the world might be saved. To be sure, God—and Christ with him—is sharply focused on the saving work on the Cross to be carried out in the context of Israel. Jesus will not allow anything to distract him from that goal, as his encounter with the Sidonian woman made clear (see Matt 15:21–28). He was not going to be sidetracked into attempting to heal the world's illnesses before he dealt with the world's sins. But the *final* goal of the Father through Christ and the Holy Spirit is to reconcile the world to himself, and Isaiah knew that.

This must be the case for us too. A salvation that is focused on "me and mine" and getting "us all" to heaven is both short-sighted and wrong. God is doing his work in "us" for "them." Just as the heart of God is turned away from himself and toward his creatures, so our hearts must be turned toward those around us who have not heard. Moreover, we must pay attention to the evidence of our lives. The nations ought to be saying, as they observe us, "We want to know their God. We want to walk like that." God forbid that they say, "Boy, I don't want to have anything to do with those people."

April 13

SEEING GOD

It was in the year King Uzziah died that I saw the LORD. He was sitting on a lofty throne, and the train of his robe filled the Temple. (Isaiah 6:1)

Many things could have gotten Isaiah's attention. He had watched the original "evil empire," Assyria, fix its borders six miles north of Jerusalem and carry three quarters of Israel's people into captivity. He had watched as God brought his man to the throne of Judah, a man who brought about a revival to the people of Judah. He had watched as Assyria had stripped Judah almost to the bone and had then, in turn, been humbled by the mighty power of God. All of these, especially the revival, could have claimed a lot of space in his book. But they do not.

Why? I suggest it was because of what had really captured Isaiah's attention. What was that? It was God. The most important thing that can happen to any one of us is to see God, an earth-shaking, life-changing vision of God. Isaiah's whole life was changed when he saw God.

We have got to see God as well. We've got to see him in a way that's going to blow apart the boxes we try to keep him in and focus our attention on him. I think it is in this light that Isaiah does not give a lot of attention to the revival that occurred in Hezekiah's (and Isaiah's) time. He was not so much interested in the outward manifestations of an apparent turn to God. He wanted the reality of God himself.

It is very easy for us to get distracted. We focus on what the wind has done and forget to pay attention to the wind itself. That seems to be what happened in Judah, because after Hezekiah died, his son Manasseh was able to lead the people astray very easily. Many of them had settled for the manifestations and had missed the reality. So when the manifestations disappeared, as they will, nothing remained behind. It appears that Isaiah recognized this misplaced focus and so did not give the phenomenon as much attention as we might expect.

What about you and me? Is our focus on the Person himself or is it on his work? Are you intent on seeing God or are you only looking at the evidences of his passing. Look for God!

April 14

THE FINAL SURRENDER

Then I heard the voice of the LORD saying, "Whom shall I send, and who will go for us?" And I said, "Here am I; send me!" And he said, "Go and say to this people: 'Keep listening, but do not comprehend; keep looking, but do not understand.' Make the mind of this people dull, and stop their ears, and shut their eyes, so that they may not look with their eyes, and listen with their ears, and comprehend with their minds, and turn and be healed." Then I said, "How long, O LORD?" And he said: "Until cities lie waste without inhabitant, and houses without people, and the land is utterly desolate." (Isaiah 6:8–11 NRSV)

Isaiah's vision was finally one of surrender, and that surrender was of his own success. What a temptation it must have been to preach a smooth, palatable message, to which some might have turned in a superficial way. But if he had, the truth that needed to be inscripturated would never have gotten preached. And two hundred years later, when people were crying out to God in an agony of repentance, they would never have had that truth to turn to and say, "Ah, there is hope for even people like us." The call to Isaiah in his own lifetime was to preach a compassionate, whole, burning word, but one that God knew would not turn that generation to himself.

The call of the servant of God is not to be successful but to be faithful. That does not mean that you and I have the right to preach harsh, mean, little words and when people don't respond, to say, "Well, they are just turning their backs on God." No, it does not give us that right, but neither does it give us the right to try to wash away the power of his truth by making it more palatable to a generation that, because of its previous choices, will not hear.

What is the antidote for our rebellion, yours and mine? It is a vision of our need, a vision of the Holy God, a vision of our ruined, unclean selves, a vision of redemption, a vision of obedience, and most of all, because rebellion is the problem, a vision of surrender, surrender of our own success.

April 15

THE RATIONALITY OF BIBLICAL FAITH: PART ONE

The head of Ephraim is Samaria, and the head of Samaria is the son of
Remaliah. If you do not stand firm in faith, you shall not stand at all.
Again the LORD spoke to Ahaz, saying, "Ask a sign of the LORD your God;
let it be deep as Sheol or high as heaven." But Ahaz said, "I will not
ask, and I will not put the LORD to the test." (Isaiah 7:9–12 NRSV)

In the Hebrew of the first sentence in the passage above, there is a word
play whose force is difficult to convey in English. The same word is
used in two different forms that give it slightly different connotations. It
is something like, "If you will not make firm (in trust), you cannot be firm
(in the face of your enemies)." The Hebrew term used is one that connotes
reliability, and nouns formed from it include "truth" and "faithfulness."
The opponents of Christian faith often equate "faith" with mere wishful
thinking. Even Christian thinkers have compared it to jumping over the
rail of a speeding ocean liner on a dark night in the expectation that we will
be caught. That is not faith, but lunacy!

No, the Hebrew concept conveys something else. It is to put confidence
in the reliability, the "truth" of someone. That is the whole thrust of the
Bible: God has made some incredible promises, and then he has fulfilled
them. In other words, if we believe his promises, which is what biblical faith
is, there are very good reasons for doing so. As F. B. Meyer says, "Although
our faith is sometimes more than rational, it is never irrational."*

Jesus told his followers before the fact that he would rise from the
dead. Then he did so, as a matter of fact. To believe in resurrection is more
than rational, but the evidence we have been given for our faith is perfectly
rational. This is true throughout the Scripture. We are not called to blind
faith, but to confidently put our trust in God, to risk everything for him,
because he has proven himself "true" again and again.

---

* *Our Daily Homily*, vol 4 (Grand Rapids: Zondervan, 1951), 78.

April 16

THE RATIONALITY OF BIBLICAL FAITH: PART TWO

He will use every kind of evil deception to fool those on their way to destruction, because they refuse to love and accept the truth that would save them. So God will cause them to be greatly deceived, and they will believe these lies. Then they will be condemned for enjoying evil rather than believing the truth. (2 Thessalonians 2:10–12)

I have said that, biblically speaking, "to have faith in" is to believe the truth about something and to act accordingly. It is not wishful thinking, and it is not a "leap into the dark." In his book *He Is There, and He Is Not Silent*, Francis Shaeffer has a fine illustration of this point. He imagines a climber in the Alps who has not kept careful track of his time and is high up on a narrow ledge in the late afternoon when he is suddenly engulfed in clouds. He cannot see forward or back and knows only that there is a bottomless chasm on his left and a sheer cliff on his right. He cannot stay where he is, for with the falling nighttime temperatures, he will be dead of exposure before morning. Suddenly, a voice comes out of the fog, telling him that if he will lower himself over the side of the ledge and let go, he will only fall a few feet and will land on a lower ledge where there is a cave in which he can shelter. If he does hang off the edge of that ledge and let go, that is not faith, but foolishness. But suppose the climber calls out to the voice, and learns that the speaker is the foremost guide in that area, that he is just across that gulf and knows the area perfectly, being able to tell the climber some of the features on that path where he is. Now if the climber does hang off the edge of that cliff, he will still feel nothing but air beneath his feet. But when he lets go, that will be faith in the true biblical sense; more than rational, but not irrational.

April 17

GOD WITH US: GOOD NEWS?

Therefore, the LORD will overwhelm them with a mighty flood from the Euphrates River—the king of Assyria and all his glory. This flood will overflow all its channels and sweep into Judah until it is chin deep. It will spread its wings, submerging your land from one end to the other, O Immanuel. (Isaiah 8:7–8)

Immanuel—God with us! Good news, right? Well, it depends. It is good news if you are willing to be with him. But suppose, like King Ahaz, you are not willing for that to be the case. Ahaz was unwilling to take the risk of trusting Yahweh alone in the face of his two enemies from the North. So he chose to put his trust in the worst enemy of all, Assyria. Isaiah told Ahaz he had made a bad choice.

The fact is, God is with us, like it or not, whether we want it or not. If we accept the fact and build our lives on it, it is the best news there is. But if we try to live as though it were not true, we are going to find ourselves stumbling over it the rest of our lives. For whatever we trust in place of God will one day turn on us, and God will not be preventing it but will be bringing it on. He is like a factor on one side of an equation. If you don't take account of him on the other side of the equation, the equation will never balance.

So the question for you and for me is, what am I going to do about God's presence in my world? Am I going to take it into account and find joy, solace, protection, direction, and power from him, or am I going to try to live as though he were not everywhere present and keep finding big empty holes in the life I have constructed? Make no mistake, God is with you.

April 18

WHOM SHALL WE DREAD?

The LORD has given me a strong warning not to think like everyone else does. He said, "Don't call everything a conspiracy, like they do, and don't live in dread of what frightens them. Make the LORD of Heaven's Armies holy in your life. He is the one you should fear. He is the one who should make you tremble." (Isaiah 8:11–13)

We live in times of dread. On every hand, it seems new causes for anxiety sprout up around us: the economy, the world situation, earthquakes, leadership crises in our nation, and the collapse of character. How should we as Christians respond to times like these?

First of all, we need to remember that we aren't the first people to live in troubled times. This passage of Scripture is addressed to people in that kind of situation. The question is how to respond to a frightening situation. Unfortunately, too often we think it is "them," some backroom conspiracy that we have no control over, and we live in nameless dread. God says, "Stop that. You don't know—and can't know—what's really going on. Let it go. Stop worrying about it."

What should we do? We should practice what we preach. We say God is sovereign; we say he is all-powerful; we say he is altogether loving. So, let's live that way. To fear God is to order your life as if he were the ultimate destiny of our souls—which he is! If we say God is holy—the only transcendent Lord—and then live as if he does not control the world, we lie. To sanctify him is to let him be God. Don't dread conspiracies; dread displeasing the Holy One.

We are called to be those in whom the light of the holy, self-revealing, self-giving God shines forth with power. His light shines because we daily surrender ourselves to that holiness, saturate ourselves in that revelation, and open ourselves to that light that will one day banish night forevermore: God, the holy, the revealing, the light. He shall be our sanctuary, and we have nothing to dread.

April 19

DON'T CALL IT A CONSPIRACY: PART ONE

Don't call everything a conspiracy, like they do, and don't live in dread of what frightens them. Make the LORD of Heaven's Armies holy in your life. He is the one you should fear. He is the one who should make you tremble. He will keep you safe. But to Israel and Judah he will be a stone that makes people stumble, a rock that makes them fall. And for the people of Jerusalem he will be a trap and a snare. (Isaiah 8:12–14)

As you look at world and national events, do you ever feel helpless? Do you ever feel that there are things going on behind closed doors that could have incredible effects on all of us, things we don't even know about, much less have control over? That is exactly the way the people of Judah felt in 735 BC. Mighty Assyria was threatening, and closer at hand, their two neighbors, Israel and Syria, were planning to conquer Judah and put their own king on the throne. Everybody was conspiring against poor Judah. What to do?

Yahweh's prescription to Isaiah was devastatingly simple. Stop it! Get your focus off all that stuff and get it on God! If you think history is in the hands of the conspirators, then you really don't think God is holy. You don't think he is the One who stands outside of time and space and works in it all to accomplish his good purposes. Focus on him and your relationship with him and he will be a safe place for you. That does not mean that in his providence no bad stuff can happen to us and our nation. But it does mean that, whatever happens to you and me, we can know he is in control and that he holds our lives securely. If we won't do that, we will be constantly falling over him. He is inescapable, and we will either run with him or we will run into him. He is reality; if we leave him out of our plans and thinking, we have missed the key factor in life. So, he will either be our sanctuary, or he will be our stumbling block. The choice is ours.

In the middle of uncertain and frightening times we can live with confidence and courage, doing what we know is right and true in our own realms of influence, or we can flit back and forth, ruled by fear and dread, doing nothing constructive. The choice is ours. Let's make him holy in our thinking and in our behavior.

DON'T CALL IT A CONSPIRACY: PART TWO

Don't call everything a conspiracy, like they do, and don't live in dread of what frightens them. Make the LORD of Heaven's Armies holy in your life. He is the one you should fear. He is the one who should make you tremble. He will keep you safe. But to Israel and Judah he will be a stone that makes people stumble, a rock that makes them fall. And for the people of Jerusalem he will be a trap and a snare. (Isaiah 8:12–14)

Last week I happened onto what is apparently a very popular survivalist radio talk show. The host explained with great intensity how the Covid-19 virus had been created by the Chinese Communists (as well as a secret vaccine to protect themselves after allowing several thousand to die) so that they could destroy the U.S. economy and prepare for a one-world government. Who knew? He did, evidently.

Thinking about that, my mind went to the above passage. Judah was being attacked by its two northern neighbors, Israel and Syria, with a goal of deposing the Davidic king and putting their own man on the Judean throne. Isaiah 7:2 says the hearts of the king and his people were shaking like trees in a windstorm. We can see them wringing their hands and hear them saying, "It's a conspiracy! What are we going to do?!"

I don't know whether the Covid-19 virus was produced in a conspiracy, although I sincerely doubt it, but I see a lot of frantic people feeling helpless and that history is out of control, just as the Judeans did. What is Yahweh's prescription to them and to us? It is, "Get your priorities right!"

Who is the Holy One? Who is the I AM of Heaven's Armies? The "Chicoms"? A rampant virus? No! Shall our lives be dictated by the dread of mere creatures? Never! Shall we let the fear of those things govern our outlook? Not at all! Our approach to life must be dictated, governed, by the reality that there is one God who rules and overrules in all things. (By the way, that last sentence is what is meant by "the fear of God"; it is not living in constant anxiety that if I happen to look cross-eyed at God, he is going to hit me.)

If we make God our focus, knowing he, the transcendent Holy One, is in control of all things, then we can live in confidence, in the sanctuary of his power and his love. If we forget that, leaving him out of the equation of our lives, then we will be in turmoil because we are actually stumbling over him in our self-imposed darkness. Let's not forget him; let's live in the light.

April 21

A BABY FOR HEAVEN'S SAKE

For a child has been born for us, a son given to us; authority rests
upon his shoulders; and he is named Wonderful Counselor, Mighty
God, Everlasting Father, Prince of Peace. (Isaiah 9:6 NRSV)

What is God's answer to the oppression, the cruelty, the brutality, and the loss of this world? A baby, for heaven's sake! Yes! A baby, for heaven's sake. That was God's answer to Abraham and Sarah in their homelessness and the shame of their childlessness. It was his answer to the Judean king Ahaz, who was faced with the aggressive power of both Israel and Syria ranged against him and behind them the even more ominous power of the empire of Assyria. And it was his answer to Judea, under the boot of mighty Rome. A baby? Yes, a baby. But why?

Of all things weak, a baby is the weakest. What is God saying? He is saying that his power is not to be more oppressive than the oppressor, nor to be more cruel than the cruel, nor more brutal than the brute. Rather, his power is the ability to absorb all the brutality, all the cruelty, indeed, all the evil of this tragic world and to give back love. That is power.

If we respond to evil power by attempting to become more evil, there will always be someone more evil and more powerful. But if, by the grace of Christ, no one has the power to make us hate them; that is, if we have the power to love in every circumstance, that is power. Is such a response weakness? Yes—from the world's perspective, but it is a power that the world cannot produce in and of itself. It is the power to break the cycle of evil in my family, my community, and my world.

April 22

THE ANGER OF GOD

In that day you will sing: "I will praise you, O LORD! You were
angry with me, but your anger keeps turning away, and instead
you encourage me." (Isaiah 12:1 author's translation)

As an Old Testament teacher, I am asked over and over again, it seems, about the wrath of God in the Old Testament. I am asked often enough that I have to keep from becoming exasperated. I know it is a sincere question, and I know it is motivated by a lot of Old Testament data. At the same time, I have the feeling that it springs from a pretty shallow reading of the text. It seems to me that a reading of the Old Testament text with an eye to what is really being said goes far toward answering the question.

To put the answer in a nutshell, it is this: God *gets* angry, but he *is* love. John's affirmation: "God is love" (1 John 4:8) is merely capturing what the Old Testament makes very clear. Think about this: In about 1400 BC the Hebrew people swore in blood to keep their loving Deliverer's simple covenantal expectations: don't worship other gods and don't infringe on other people's God-given prerogatives. They immediately broke this covenant and then continued to break it for another 1,000 years, *all the time blaming God for not blessing them!* What is God supposed to do? Say, "tut, tut"? Would you get angry with people like that? Of course, you would!

So what did God do? He forgave them, and forgave them, and forgave them, and forgave them! Even when their sin had finally mounted so high that the land spit them out into captivity, did God wipe his hands of them? No, he took them back to himself, looking forward to the blood of Christ. Is that a God of wrath? No, he is a God of love. So the Psalmist cries out, "Oh, give thanks to the LORD, for He is good! For *His mercy [love] endures forever*" (Ps 106:1 NKJV, emphasis added). In another place he says, "For his anger lasts only a moment, but his favor lasts a lifetime! Weeping may last through the night, but joy comes with the morning" (Ps 30:5).

So is there a lot of divine anger in the Old Testament? Yes, about a thousand years' worth. But that is not surprising. What is surprising is the ten thousand times ten thousand years of unfailing love that perseveres through and beyond that anger.

April 23

DEATH

In the place of the dead there is excitement over your arrival. The spirits of world leaders and mighty kings long dead stand up to see you. With one voice they all cry out, "Now you are as weak as we are! Your might and power were buried with you. The sound of the harp in your palace has ceased. Now maggots are your sheet and worms your blanket." (Isaiah 14:9–11)

What is the final mockery of all human pride? Death. Adolph Hitler died. Joseph Stalin died. Pol Pot died. In the background behind every tyrant who stands up and says, "I rule the world, bow down to me, you worms," is the grim reaper saying, "You fool. You think you are God? Tell me that out of the grave."

For me, one of the most vivid illustrations of this is in a movie called *Duel*. In it a man (Dennis Weaver) driving a car has accidentally cut off a large tractor-trailer truck, but he drives on and forgets about it. Suddenly there is a tremendous crash on the rear of his car. He looks in the rearview mirror and sees only a huge radiator grill, and then he is hit again. He tries to speed up, but the truck is more powerful than the old car Weaver is driving. He tries everything he can think of to get away, sometimes gaining ground going upgrade, but then losing it on the downgrades. The chase goes on and on through a number of hair-raising episodes. Finally, at the top of a long grade, there is a gravel side road, and he whips off on it, clearly hoping the truck is far enough behind not to have seen him turn. But as he drives up the road, he despairs to see the truck behind again. He is driving wildly and barely makes it through an s-curve on the edge of a cliff. As he straightens up from the skid, he looks in the mirror and sees the truck miss the curve and go over the edge of the cliff. Weaver slowly coasts to a stop, and we can see him wondering if somehow the awful thing is going to come back up over the edge. It does not. He gets out and slowly walks back to the spot. He gingerly looks over, and there is the wreckage far below. He sits down on the edge, and a hysterical giggle escapes him. He tosses a pebble over, and the sound of breaking glass comes back. Death.

Often we think of Death as the enemy, but it also the friend of all the world's oppressed, all those beaten down by monstrous human pride. Every one of us must take it into account. What have we done with our lives? Will we be mourned, or will our disappearance from the earth occasion a shuddering sigh of relief?

YAHWEH OF HEAVEN'S ARMIES HAS SPOKEN

I have a plan for the whole earth, a hand of judgment upon all the nations. The LORD of Heaven's Armies has spoken—who can change his plans? When his hand is raised, who can stop him? (Isaiah 14:26–27)

In Isaiah 14, the phrase "Yahweh of Heaven's Armies" appears four times between verses 22 and 27. In all four cases it is said that he speaks or has spoken. First, he speaks judgment on Babylon and then on Assyria, two nations that had intended to absorb and thus eliminate the people of God. That was never going to happen. Why not? Because I AM, the only self-existent being in the universe, the one who has all the power that flung the host of stars, heaven's armies, across the skies has said differently. He is not merely The Force, silent and unaccountable. He is the Person, who has plans and purposes and has communicated them to the world, most wonderfully in the Word, who came to us in Bethlehem.

What does this mean? It means we do not have to wring our hands over the collapse of our political systems, the disappearance of civil discourse, the destruction of public morality, or the rise of autocratic nationalism around the world. Yahweh of Heaven's Armies has spoken his Word over it all. His announced plans will be accomplished now just as surely as they were more than 2,600 years ago.

> *Then pealed the bells more loud and deep,*
> *God is not dead nor doth he sleep.*
> *The wrong shall fail, the right prevail with*
> *peace on earth, good will to men.**

Yahweh's plans and purposes may not accord with our wishes and desires, but they will be accomplished, and his intentions for the ultimate salvation of his creation will be carried out.

---

* Henry Wadsworth Longfellow (1807–1882), "I Heard the Bells on Christmas Day."

April 25
SHALOM: WHOLENESS

You will keep in perfect peace all who trust in you, all whose
thoughts are fixed on you! Trust in the LORD always, for
the LORD GOD is the eternal Rock. (Isaiah 26:3–4)

George* was a graduate student at a prestigious eastern university. He
had finished his coursework and had been diligently working on his
doctoral dissertation for two years when disaster struck. His supervisor
was denied tenure and, as a result, was terminated from the faculty. What
to do? George canvassed the other faculty members in his department to
see if anyone else would take him on with his almost-complete project. No
one would. Finally, one faculty member said he would supervise George,
but only with a completely new project. So, as George said, "I put two years
of my life on the shelf and started over." After about a year of work on the
new project, the faculty supervisor was giving George a ride home. When
they stopped in front of George's apartment, just as George was about to
get out of the car, the supervisor, a man of a non-Christian faith, said,
"George, I wanted to ask you a question. I have been watching you for this
last year. If I were in your shoes, I would be a very angry man. I would be
angry at the university, at the rest of the faculty, at my new supervisor who
demanded a new project; I would be angry at the world. But you're not
angry. Does that have anything to do with your Christian faith?" For the
next hour and a half George was able to tell his supervisor how a settled
trust in God through Jesus Christ means that God can put all the pieces of
our lives together (the meaning of the Hebrew *shalom*) and give us what
the world can never give—inner serenity, even in the midst of calamity and
misfortune.

---

* Not his real name.

April 26
PERFECT PEACE?

You will make that person completely whole whose imagination is anchored in you, because he or she trusts in you. Trust in Yahweh always, because Yah, Yahweh, is an everlasting Rock. (Isaiah 26:3–4 author's translation)

On this Spring morning, with the feel of rain in the air, I fell to thinking about my grandfather and what he might have been doing on a morning like this 120 years ago. Perhaps he would have been husking corn to feed to the pigs and chickens, the same thing his father and grandfather would have been doing for a century before him. So little change, and now—"Change on every hand I see!" At our institution, expensive electronic equipment that was "state of the art" fifteen years ago is now virtually useless and must be replaced. I wonder about the replacements— what will their life expectancy be?

We are not the only ones in the history of the world to face upheaval and change. The ancient Judeans were surrounded on every hand by enemies, not least the voracious Assyrians who would take as "tribute" everything the Judeans owned and then deport many of them a thousand miles from home. What is Isaiah's word to them? "Don't let your imagination run off with you! Focus your attention on that God who has given his personal name—I AM—to you. If you will make him the center around which all your life revolves, he will knit all the disparate threads of your life into a single skein. He is the Rock that will breast the flood, in whose shade you can shelter from the sun, upon which you can climb when the Enemy threatens."

But wait a minute! What did I do with the KJV's "perfect peace" in my translation above? Well, it's not bad, but it just doesn't go far enough. When Yahweh puts us together there *is* an inner serenity ("peace") despite outside upheaval, but that serenity is a byproduct of an inner wholeness (which is the base idea of *shalom*) that is the result of allowing our Almighty Friend Yah to focus everything in our lives on him. That oneness is the foundation of the serenity, and it is a continuing reality even when the serenity is not so serene! Here's the bottom line: we can have so intimate a relationship with the Great Creator that we can call him by his pet name. Yah, and with our wild imaginations all focused on him, we can become whole persons. Saved.

April 27

THE REBEL SIGH

Your own ears will hear him. Right behind you a voice will say, "This is the way you should go," whether to the right or to the left. (Isaiah 30:21)

In the great hymn "Spirt of God, Descend Upon My Heart," there is a line that caught my attention recently: "To catch the rising doubt, the *rebel sigh* . . ." (italics mine). "The rebel sigh"—what a thought. It's not an outright refusal, not a defiant fist, just a sigh, a sigh that says, "Oh no, here we go again," or perhaps, "Dear God, what impossible thing are you going to ask now?"

I had the unmatched privilege of being one of the twelve editors who created the New Living Translation. What a wonderful opportunity to spend entire days with eleven other highly-trained men who loved God and loved his Word and were passionate to connect that Word and people. We might spend an hour debating how best to communicate the meaning of a Hebrew or Greek phrase in English. Highly-trained meant we each had strong opinions and convictions, and sometimes the debates were intense (but, I must say, never rancorous). Finally, in cases where there was "a division in the house," it would come to a vote. After one such vote, the Chair, beside whom I happened to be sitting, looked at me and said, "What's wrong, John?" I replied, "I didn't say anything." He said, "No, but you sighed." We had been together too long!

Is that what it is when God asks me and you to do something? We don't say anything, we just sigh. Does that hurt God? I think it does. He wants something in me and you that leaps up and says, "Sure! Why not?! He wants us to be that well-trained horse, which, feeling the rein laid on its neck, turns that way instantly. He wants to only have to whisper, and we move to do what he says, not with a rebel sigh, but with glad abandon.

> *Teach me to feel that you are always nigh;*
> *teach me the struggles of the soul to bear,*
> *to check the rising doubt, the rebel sigh;*
> *teach me the patience of unanswered prayer.*
>
> *Teach me to love you as your angels love,*
> *one holy passion filling all my frame:*
> *the kindling of the heaven-descended Dove;*
> *my heart an altar, and your love the flame.*
> *(George Croly, 1854)*

April 28

PILGRIMS: PART ONE

Peter, an apostle of Jesus Christ, to the pilgrims of the Dispersion in Pontus, Galatia, Cappadocia, Asia, and Bythinia, elect according to the foreknowledge of God the Father, in sanctification of the Spirit, for obedience and sprinkling of the blood of Jesus Christ: Grace to you and peace be multiplied. (1 Peter 1:1–2 NKJV)

Most modern English versions of the Bible call the people to whom Peter is writing "exiles," but I like the word the New King James Version translators chose: "pilgrims." Whether exiles or pilgrims, one point is the same: we are not at home in this land where we are living. But "pilgrims" suggests that not only are we not at home here but also that we are headed somewhere else. This is certainly true of us Christians: we are pilgrims on our way home. That's what John Bunyan captured so well in his classic *Pilgrim's Progress*.

I'd like to think with you about some characteristics of pilgrims: They travel light. People on a journey can't carry a lot of stuff. One of the things we don't have to carry is the heavy baggage of reputation. There is no limit to what God can do with you if you don't care who gets the credit. You don't have to succeed if you're a pilgrim, all you have to do is follow. It doesn't matter what "they" think of you, it doesn't matter how you look, because you have gotten yourself off your hands. Possessions? They only slow you down and get in the way. You're going to have to shed them all at the river anyway. So be free, be free of all that stuff because you only have one concern and that's the prize, the goal.

Pilgrims live for the long term and therefore they can live the short term to the full. Does that sound strange? It isn't. If today is all we have, then today can make us or break us. If you are a pilgrim, you are looking to the end of the road, at the light shining there. If today is good, that's great. If today is bad, that's OK. The only question is, "Does it get me closer home?" That means you're free. That means that today can be enjoyed because it doesn't have its hooks in you. Come on, pilgrims, let's go home.

April 29

PILGRIMS: PART TWO

And the ransomed of the LORD shall return and come to Zion with singing;
everlasting joy shall be upon their heads; they shall obtain gladness
and joy, and sorrow and sighing shall flee away. (Isaiah 35:10 ESV)

We said in Part One that pilgrims travel light, letting neither reputation nor possessions weigh them down. We also said that for pilgrims, the long view prevents the short view from capturing them and obscuring their vision. Here are a couple of more things about pilgrims.

Pilgrims have very little investment in the structure of this world. Structures, whether physical or institutional, can nail our feet to the floor. There was a man who had invested his life in becoming a bishop of his church. He had done everything right, climbing up the next rung of the ladder at just the right time. Everything was perfectly planned and perfectly carried out. But on the day when he should have reached the top rung, someone else was chosen. That day he left his wallet and his watch on the seat of his car and walked down the railroad tracks to meet an oncoming train. He had given his soul to the pursuit of a soap bubble.

Pilgrims have a contagious enthusiasm. One of the things that fueled America's westward expansion was that kind of enthusiasm. Historians speak of whole villages in rocky New England being almost depopulated because someone in the town caught the vision of those western lands with topsoil six feet deep, just waiting for a man and a plow. His excitement fired that of others, and in short order almost the whole town was on the road.

Oh, but friends, we're not talking about topsoil, we're talking about The Celestial City—"Jerusalem the Golden, with milk and honey blest, beneath whose contemplation sink heart and voice oppressed."* Can you see that holy highway? Can you hear those ahead of us singing? Come on, pilgrims, let's go! What about it? Is your pack too heavy? Has the short term blinded you to the long term? Have you invested so much in the structures of this world that your feet are dragging? Has your enthusiasm waned? Oh, lift your eyes! Can you see it there? It's the City! Come on! What is there here that could possibly compare with that? Let's go!

---

* Hymn lyrics by Bernard of Cluny (trans. by J. M. Neale), ca. 1145.

When Morning Gilds the Skies

April 30

ENCOURAGEMENT FROM THE BENCH

"Comfort, comfort my people," says your God. "Speak tenderly to Jerusalem.
Tell her that her sad days are gone and her sins are pardoned." (Isaiah 40:1–2a)

I am extremely uncoordinated. The only sport in my high school was basketball and there was no point in my even trying out for that team. But we had a church league and they needed bodies so they wouldn't have to forfeit a game, so anybody could play on those teams, even me. I'll never forget one particular day. Because I was the slowest person to get down the court to the other end, I was actually behind the guards of the other team. They didn't know I was back there, so when one passed the ball to the other, I just ran forward and grabbed it. This was it—my chance! So I turned around and started lumbering for the basket. As I went, I heard people yelling, "Pass it off." No way! I was going to do it. So I went in for the easiest layup—and missed it. I heard their groans and I knew what they were thinking, "You dummy. We knew you couldn't do it."

Is that God when we miss the easy lay-ups of life? Is God saying, "You fool, I told you, you couldn't do that." No! No! When you go sneaking back to the bench so low you have to look up to see the worms, it's God who puts his arm around your shoulders and says, "Hey, there will be other games. I'm on your side." That's our God. That's what he said to the Judeans whose sins had landed them in exile far from home, and that's what he says to us. It is the Accuser who says, "You're no good, a failure." It's our Father who speaks tenderly (lit. "speaks to the heart"), telling us how special we are in his eyes and how much confidence he has in us.

May 1

YOU ARE MY WITNESSES

"First I predicted your rescue, then I saved you and proclaimed it to the world. No foreign god has ever done this. You are witnesses that I am the only God," says the LORD. (Isaiah 43:12)

But you will receive power when the Holy Spirit has come upon you, and you will be my witnesses in Jerusalem and in all Judea and Samaria, and to the end of the earth. (Acts 1:8 ESV)

Through Isaiah, God is predicting the time when the people of Judah will be in captivity in Babylon. He says they will be living evidence that he is God when he saves them from that captivity, having predicted it in advance. No other god has ever made such specific predictions, he says. And no other god could do something that had never happened before: taking a people home from captivity. Simply by being delivered they will be God's living evidence—his witnesses in the court of the universe.

Jesus, quoting Isaiah, was making the same point. The apostles and their followers were going to be the living evidence that Jesus was the promised Messiah, the Son of God come in the flesh. Here it was not deliverance from Babylon that had been predicted but that God would come to his people to deliver them from the condemnation of their sin and to write his *torah*—his instructions for life—on their hearts.

That's who we are supposed to be: witnesses, living evidence that Jesus Christ can save to the uttermost—from guilt, from temper, from addiction, from self-serving, from everything that would destroy us. The Greek word translated "witness" is *marturos*. Yes, "martyr." To be a witness is not so much to talk about Jesus's saving power as to be the hard evidence of that power, even to the point of imprisonment and death, as many of our brothers and sisters are doing right now and as we need to be ready to do in the not-too-distant future. "You are my evidence in the court of the universe."

May 2

FIND US FAITHFUL

See, the LORD GOD comes with might, and his arm rules for him; his reward is with him, and his recompense before him. (Isaiah 40:10 NRSV)

The LORD has made proclamation to the ends of the earth: "Say to Daughter Zion, 'See, your Savior comes! See, his reward is with him, and his recompense accompanies him.'" (Isaiah 62:11 NIV)

These words, some of them duplicates, were probably intended for the Judean exiles in Babylon (Isa 40:10) and then for those who returned from exile (Isa 62:11). But they raise questions: "Reward" for what? "Recompense" for what? Are they being rewarded and repaid for having gone into exile? But they richly deserved that. Moses had told them more than 800 years earlier that this is what would happen to them if they broke the covenant, yet they had done it repeatedly throughout that whole time. God had been incredibly patient in deferring justice that long. So, reward for what?

I suggest two things are in play here. On the one hand, although the Assyrians and Babylonians were Yahweh's instruments of discipline, they did not see themselves in that way. They arrogantly assumed they were able to do these things simply because they were bigger and tougher, and they carried out their attacks with no mercy and no sense of responsibility for their actions. So, the day of recompense came: the great cities of Assyria and Babylon got their due, and they are no more, while Jerusalem has existed, and sometimes even flourished, for all the intervening years.

On the other hand, not all the Israelites and Judeans who suffered the terrible tragedies of conquest and exile deserved what happened to them. They were genuinely righteous and faithful, and yet they were swept away in the maelstrom too. Nevertheless, they and their children were those who refused to say, "Oh well," and with others of their people consent to become good Assyrians and Babylonians (the purpose of exile, after all). No, they smuggled out the Scriptures; they refused to give up on Yahweh (remember Daniel?); and they dared to believe the unbelievable, that God would deliver them from the grip of great Babylon. These are the ones, many of whom never lived to see their beloved land again, for whom the reward came to another generation. These are the ones who were being repaid for a faith that would not stop.

What about us? The song says, "Let all who come behind us find us faithful." Will another generation be rewarded and recompensed for our faithfulness? May it be!

May 3

COURAGE

"Comfort, comfort my people," says your God. "Speak tenderly to Jerusalem. Tell her that her sad days are gone and her sins are pardoned. Yes, the LORD has punished her twice over for all her sins." (Isaiah 40:1–2)

Instead, you grieve because of what I've told you. But in fact, it is best for you that I go away, because if I don't, the Advocate won't come. If I do go away, then I will send him to you. (John 16:6–7)

The Judean people in exile in Babylon had every reason to be discouraged. Their nation, their capital city, and their temple were all destroyed. It looked as though their God, Yahweh, had been defeated, and worse, as though all the promises he had made were worthless. In a similar way, the disciples were discouraged. They had dared to believe that this man from Galilee, who did not meet most of the criteria for Messiah, was still the Messiah. Now, not having set up his kingdom on earth, he had said he was going to go away and leave them. Discouragement.

What is God's answer to both of these groups? "Be encouraged!" That is the meaning of the Hebrew word translated "comfort" in Isaiah 40:1 and the Greek word translated "Advocate" [KJV "Comforter"] in John 16:7. God says to the exiles, "No, I have not abandoned you; my promises have not failed. Don't give up—stand up!" To the disciples Jesus says, "I am not deserting you; I am going to send the Encourager, someone who will bring my kingdom to reality in you and in the world. Take courage!"

Someone has said, "Bravery is not the same as courage. Bravery is the act of a moment, as when a single soldier charges a machine-gun nest. But courage is a settled way of thinking, living, and acting." How easy it is to get discouraged. We look for expected results and don't see them. We look for confirmation that we are on the right road and don't find it. So, in an ancient image, we let our hands fall (see Jer 6:24). We stop trying, and worse, we stop believing.

But God, *our* God (see Isa 40:1), puts his arm around our shoulders and says, "Don't give up. Don't quit. Stay in the fight. *I have not given up on you!* I am not only with you; I am *in* you. Together, we will go forward." The Good News is that God kept his promises to the exiles and to the disciples, so we can dare to believe that he is going to keep on keeping them—through us—as we live with courage and confidence.

May 4

WALKING THE WALK

"To whom will you compare me? Who is my equal?"
asks the Holy One. (Isaiah 40:25)

Throughout the Bible, life with God is described as a walk. "Enoch walked with God," "Abraham, walk before me and be perfect." A walk—that's what you and I are called to, that's what you and I are called to live out from the beginning of our lives until the end. And that's exactly where the Hebrew people felt that it was all over. They had been so certain that they had God figured out, that they had God in their back pocket. They had his temple, they had his book, and they had his prophets. But then it was all over, their city was destroyed, their temple was destroyed, their land was destroyed, and they were in captivity in the filthy, unclean, pagan land of Babylon. Much more than that, their hopes were destroyed. But they still had their faith and they were told to walk on.

To stop walking on is to start sliding back and so God says to us, "Walk on!" There are times in our lives when we soar and times when we run, but most of the time we are called simply to walk. What is it about walking that makes this the persistent metaphor for life with God throughout the Scriptures? Well, walking is progressive. It is from here to there. If you're on a walk, you do not end up where you started. From the beginning to the end, the story of the Bible is the story of journeys. From Ur to Canaan, from Egypt to the land of promise, from Babylon to Jerusalem, from Jerusalem to Rome.

However, the Bible is about not only outward journeys but also inward journeys. From sinner to saint, from stranger to heir, from the kingdom of darkness to the kingdom of light. The biblical message says there is someplace for you to go, and it's not where you started; it's infinitely better than where you started—walk on. Walking is progressive, walking is intentional, and walking is persistent. We have a nation full of Christians who have only taken the first step—and no more. They stopped walking.

What keeps us going forward progressively? What keeps us going forward intentionally? What keeps us on the road is the character of our God, who reaches down to take us by the hand when we've fallen into the ditch again. His arms are strong enough to defeat any foe yet tender enough to hold the weakest newborn lamb.

What is the next step for you? Maybe it's something as simple as a new consistency in your devotional life. That's a continuing challenge for most people, to block out that time every day for the Lord. Maybe the Lord is challenging you to a new persistency in prayer for the world, or for your neighbors. Maybe he is calling you to new physical self-denial. Maybe you need to be saying to the Lord, "What is the next step you want me to take?" To quit reaching for more conformity to Christ and his character is to miss what the Christian life is all about. Walk on!

May 5

SONG OF MY REDEEMER

Sing a new song to the LORD! Sing his praises from the ends of the earth! Sing, all you who sail the seas, all you who live in distant coastlands. (Isaiah 42:10)

In December of 1876, Philip Paul Bliss was riding the crest of a musical career that seemed to have no limits. Aged 38, Bliss was already a well-known bass soloist and evangelistic songleader. He was also an accomplished songwriter, having published dozens of songs. Although many have now been forgotten, others are still known, including "Almost Persuaded," "Wonderful Words of Life," and "Hallelujah, What a Savior." Just a month earlier in November of 1876, he had introduced a new song for which he had written the music for words written by Horatio Spafford: "It Is Well with My Soul."

Growing up in a very poor but godly home, Bliss early learned to sing but had never heard a piano until he was ten years old. At age eleven, poverty drove him to leave home and take up work in lumber camps. At age twelve, he accepted Christ as his Savior and maintained his faith in the rough life of the camps for the next seven years. Along the way, he would pick up whatever musical training he could. Finally, he turned to farm work and there met the love of his life, Lucy Young. They were married when Philip was 21, and he spent the next year working on her father's farm. Lucy's grandmother recognized Bliss's musical talents and gave him the money for a small amount of professional training. From there he went on to become an itinerant music teacher, traveling from place to place on an old horse, carrying a sort of portable piano called a melodeon and teaching "singing schools."

Eventually he and Lucy ended up in Chicago, and not long after, he became the music director and Sunday School superintendent at First Congregational Church. In that role, he came to Dwight L. Moody's attention, and Moody urged him to trust God and go into full-time musical evangelism. Bliss did not feel he could do that at the time; however, at a prayer meeting in March of 1874, he surrendered his entire life to Christ for whatever he wanted. At that same meeting, a Civil War veteran named D. W. Whittle made a similar full surrender. The two of them formed an evangelistic team with Whittle as preacher and Bliss as musician. They ministered around the country for the next three years with unusual blessing from the Lord.

In December of 1876, Philip and Lucy were returning to Chicago by train from a Christmas visit to his parents in upstate New York. In a fierce snow storm near Ashtabula, Ohio, the train was passing over a bridge whose footings, it later turned out, had been undermined by flood waters. The bridge collapsed under the train and eleven coaches fell 75 feet into the riverbed below. Almost immediately, the overheated stoves in each of the wooden cars set the wreckage on fire. Bliss reportedly escaped, but on finding that his wife was still pinned inside the coach, he climbed back in saying that if he could not save her, he would die with her. When the wreckage finally cooled, individual bodies were not discernible.

Bliss had sent his trunk on ahead. When it was opened in Chicago, the words of a new hymn were found in it. The words of the first verse and chorus are:

> I will sing of my Redeemer and his wondrous love for me;
> on the cruel cross he suffered, from the curse to set me free.
> Sing, oh sing of my Redeemer! With his blood he purchased me;
> on the Cross he sealed my pardon, paid the debt and set me free. . .

> I will sing of my Redeemer and his heavenly love to me;
> he from death to life has brought me; Son of God, with him to be.

What an epitaph! When he wrote those words, Philip Bliss had no idea how soon—literally "brought from death to life" by the Son of God—he would be singing them in heaven. May each of us so live that in the hour of death that will be our song.

May 6
SPIRIT FILLING

The palace and the city will be deserted, and busy towns will be empty.
Wild donkeys will frolic and flocks will graze in the empty forts and
watchtowers until at last the Spirit is poured out on us from heaven.
Then the wilderness will become a fertile field, and the fertile field will
yield bountiful crops. Justice will rule in the wilderness and righteousness
in the fertile field. And this righteousness will bring peace. Yes, it
will bring quietness and confidence forever." (Isaiah 32:14–17)

And I will pour out my Spirit on your descendants, and my blessing
on your children. They will thrive like watered grass, like willows on a
riverbank. Some will proudly claim, "I belong to the LORD." Others will say,
"I am a descendant of Jacob." Some will write the LORD's name on their
hands and will take the name of Israel as their own. (Isaiah 44:3–5)

And I will give you a new heart, and I will put a new spirit in you. I will
take out your stony, stubborn heart and give you a tender, responsive
heart. And I will put my Spirit in you so that you will follow my decrees
and be careful to obey my regulations. (Ezekiel 36:26–27)

When the Spirit fills you, what can you expect? Notice what all these
texts promise in one way or another: you will have a new oneness
with God that will enable you to live his life, a life of justice, righteousness,
and wholeness (the meaning of the word translated "peace"), a life of
joyous fulfillment of his decrees and regulations. In this day and time
I think we need to emphasize that: *The Bible says that when the Spirit
comes, you will be able to live God's life. You will be able to do what he
has commanded. You will be able to live a life like his.*

Many Christians are trying to live God's life in their own ability and
wondering why they so often fail. Even when they succeed, they often find
it a "drag." It is when we allow the Spirit of God to take us over, to fill us,
that he enables you and me to live his life. Yes, we have to cooperate with
him. Yes, we have to do our part, but in the end, it's a life of rest, of settling
down in him and allowing him to do what we cannot do.

Now the Spirit comes in a marvelous variety of ways. To some, he
comes quietly; to others he comes explosively. To some, he gives special
gifts enabling them to do miraculous things for his glory, and we must
not minimize these. But let me say that the infallible mark of the Holy
Spirit's coming is not miraculous power. Those are the gifts, and they are
variable. What cannot be variable is the fruit. The infallible mark of the
Spirit's fullness is a new ability to obey his commandments from the heart.

May 7
I WILL DO A NEW THING

See, I am doing a new thing! Now it springs up; do you not perceive it? I am
making a way in the desert and streams in the wasteland. (Isaiah 43:19 NIV)

We live in a world that shouts more and more for freedom but believes
more and more in fate. We say, "This is just the way I am. I can't
help it. So you have to give me the 'freedom' to do what I can't help but
do." That's not freedom—that's bondage. We have begun to think like
pagans. To think that this world, with its endless, pointless cycles and its
relentless fate, is all there is, is to think like a pagan. We look at our broken
marriages, our wayward children, our work that is so often pointless and
unsatisfying, and it's easy to feel that whatever our dreams might have
been, whatever our hopes might have been, we're locked in permanently
to our present lives. There's no hope, there's nowhere to go. So what do we
do? We grab as much as we can along the way. The saddest bumper sticker
I've ever seen is the one that said, "He who dies with the most toys wins."
No! He who dies only having acquired toys *loses*.

The Israelites, captive in Babylon, thought that their life as a people
was over. In all the history of national exile, no captive nation had ever
gone home again. God, speaking prophetically through Isaiah, said that he
could do a new thing. He, the Creator, is not subject to fate, like the gods,
the forces of this world, are. So, he brought a whole new world empire, the
Persians, onto the scene, and the Persian emperor, Cyrus, whom Isaiah
had named in advance, said that any captive people could go home. See, a
new thing!

God can do a new thing in your life. Don't tell him what it will be, but
spend time with him and let him tell you what he wants to do. Don't tell
him your plans, but let him tell you his plans, which, I guarantee you, will
be better than yours. You are not locked in. He can set you free just as he
did for the Israelites. Believe him for a new thing in your life.

May 8
SECURITY

Thus says the LORD, the King of Israel and his Redeemer, the LORD of hosts: "I am the first and I am the last; besides me there is no god. Who is like me? Let him proclaim it. Let him declare and set it before me, since I appointed an ancient people. Let them declare what is to come, and what will happen. Fear not, nor be afraid; have I not told you from of old and declared it? And you are my witnesses! Is there a God besides me? There is no Rock; I know not any." All who fashion idols are nothing, and the things they delight in do not profit. Their witnesses neither see nor know, that they may be put to shame. Who fashions a god or casts an idol that is profitable for nothing? (Isaiah 44:6–10 ESV)

I dolatry is the manipulation of this world, this physical world, in order to ensure my security. That is why the Bible speaks out against it. There is only one way to find security in this world, and that is by releasing this world. Ever since Eden we have become more and more neurotic about security because we have been looking for it in the wrong place. Adam and Eve became insecure the moment they walked out through those flaming swords. In their anxiety they looked to this world for their security. If they were to survive, they had to have the rain, so they turned the storm into a god, a human-like being with more than human power. They did this thinking that they could control, or at least appease, such a being through sympathetic magic.

We are, of course, far too smart for that. We don't put any faces on the storm any more. But we are working just as hard to control the forces around us as any ancient pagan ever did. We are so fragile, physically, spiritually, and emotionally, and somehow we must bolster ourselves against all that threatens us. We, and our needs, are the beginning and end of everything. This is what happens when we exalt the creation—and us in it—to the place of Yahweh, the I AM. In fact, there is no security in the creation, and so long as we think there is, we will be idolaters, frantically trying to manipulate this world to give us what it never can. The only security is in the incomparable Creator, the Rock, and when we stop trying to manipulate him and his world, we will find true security in sweet rest in him and his gracious provision.

REPENTANCE

My beloved is mine, and I am his; he grazes among
the lilies. (Song of Songs 2:16 ESV)

I have blotted out your transgressions like a cloud and your sins like
mist; return to me, for I have redeemed you. (Isaiah 44:22 ESV)

My little children, I am writing these things to you so that you
may not sin. But if anyone does sin, we have an advocate with
the Father, Jesus Christ the righteous. (1 John 2:1 ESV)

A selection in a certain devotional ends with these words, "How often must we repent? Daily, for the rest of our lives." A reader commented, "How discouraging!" Precisely! Is this the best that we can expect of ourselves and the Holy Spirit: that at the end of every day we will come to our Beloved with head hanging, saying, "Well, I committed adultery again today. I'm so sorry. I won't do it again (until tomorrow). Please forgive me."? By God's grace I do not say that to my earthly beloved; why should I have to say it to my heavenly Beloved?

I think the issue here is a fundamental failure to distinguish between unintentional and intentional sin. Do I unintentionally sin against my wife? I am afraid that I do, and when I do I hope she will tell me in love and help me to do better. But even there, I do not need to come to her hang-dog each evening saying, "Well, what did I do today?" We have a love relationship, and she is not my accuser. (That's the Devil's chosen task.) If, humanly speaking, I can live day after day without intentionally breaking my wife's heart, why in the name of the One who *has* redeemed me and given me his Holy Spirit would I not live that way with my God?

To be sure, we must never forget the sins of the past and the sinful inclinations that cost our Savior his life, and there are times in the church year, such as Lent, when it is particularly appropriate to remember that and reflect on it. Equally, if we should commit an intentional sin, we need to run to our Savior and Advocate in horror and abject repentance, resolutely turning away from that thing (the meaning of the Hebrew word translated "repentance"). But every day? God forbid! Let us live in the arms of our Beloved, wholly surrendered to him.

May 10
WHEN TRAGEDY STRIKES

I create the light and make the darkness. I send good times and bad
times. I, the LORD, am the one who does these things. (Isaiah 45:7)

The verse above, especially as translated in the King James Version ("I
make peace, and create evil"), has caused a great deal of concern for
many people. Does God really cause moral evil in the world? No, he does
not. The rest of the Bible is very clear on that issue. Moral evil is in the
world because of our first mother and father's choice, and it continues to
be because all of their children choose to do it.

The possibility of making a choice for evil is in the world solely because
Yahweh permits it. We must never say that evil is caused by Satan. To do
that is to set Satan up as the equal of Yahweh. That is never the case. There
is one God alone, and all things exist as they are because of him alone.
Satan may tempt us to do evil, but he can only do that because God permits
him to do so.

So, what is this verse actually saying? When tragedy strikes, we have
to avoid two extremes. On the one hand, God never chooses a family, for
instance, and says, "Those folks have had it too good for too long. I believe
I'll send them a tragedy just to even things out." Never! But on the other
hand, neither does he say, "Oh, I wish I could prevent Satan from putting
that tragedy on those good people, but this time he is just too strong for
me. I'll get you next time, Satan!" Again, never! Whatever happens to us
comes through the hand of God alone.

In this regard it is important to think about levels of causation. Yahweh
is the ultimate cause of all things; so, if bad things are in the world, it is
because of God ("bad" is a better English equivalent of the Hebrew word
ra', because that word covers everything from moral evil to misfortune).
However, God is not the immediate cause of bad things. That is, he does
not choose to bring bad things into our lives.

So, this is what we may know: Yahweh is Sovereign in the world, and if
tragedy comes my way as a result of the fallenness of the world, it will not
come without his knowledge or his permission. He did not send it, but he
did permit it. That means that since he allowed it, he is Lord over it and can
work through it—or because of it—or in spite of it—for my greater good.
He is Lord! In that confidence we can face whatever comes, not somehow,
but triumphantly.

May 11

CARRYING THE BURDEN

Listen to me, descendants of Jacob, all you who remain in Israel. I have cared for you since you were born. Yes, I carried you before you were born. I will be your God throughout your lifetime—until your hair is white with age. I made you, and I will care for you. I will carry you along and save you. (Isaiah 46:3–4)

Yet it was our weaknesses he carried; it was our sorrows
that weighed him down. (Isaiah 53:4a)

One of my wife's and my friends works with teenaged mothers in Chicago, teenaged girls with two or three children, in some cases. In one of her letters, she told us of a seventeen-year old mother of two who tried to kill herself on what would have been her high school graduation night because her friends were graduating while she was locked in a filthy, one-room apartment with two screaming kids.

We have sensed in our friend's letters across the years a certain loss of innocence. I think when she made the decision to get into this work she thought her ministry would result in dramatic changes for these girls. In a few cases it has; some of the girls have broken out of the cycle, but a lot of them have not. In the face of that, we have sensed in her as time has passed a growing willingness to just be Jesus to these girls, just to get under the load and say, "Here, this is too big for you to carry. Put some of it on my shoulder, and we'll carry it together." She is not saying, "If you straighten up, I will help you," but just, "Let me carry it with you." She has learned that people will take advantage of you, and she has learned that her resources are limited. But she has also learned that carrying the Cross with Jesus means just giving yourself away in his strength, doing what he does, and leaving the returns in his hands.

When Morning Gilds the Skies

May 12

WHAT IS THE GOSPEL?

How beautiful upon the mountains are the feet of him who brings good
news, who publishes peace, who brings good news of happiness, who
publishes salvation, who says to Zion, "Your God reigns." (Isaiah 52:7 ESV)

And he went throughout all Galilee, teaching in their synagogues and
proclaiming the gospel of the kingdom and healing every disease
and every affliction among the people. (Matthew 4:23 ESV)

A friend asks, "What is the gospel?" The "gospel" is an announcement
of good news. The place where this first appears most obviously is
in Isaiah 52:8–12. The prophet pictures Israel, captive to her sins, as a
besieged city. The watchman sees a runner far away on the mountains
announcing that Yahweh is coming with a great army to break the power of
the siege. Good News! It can surely be no accident that Isaiah 52:13–53:12
follows immediately. How has God broken the power of sin? He has taken
the effects of our sins (i.e., death) upon himself so that he can proclaim
forgiveness for all our sins—past, present, and future—and offer us new
life. Good News!

In the New Testament the "gospel," the good news, is closely linked to
the announcement that the "kingdom" is here. This is the rule of God in our
lives. It is now going to be possible to actually live out the instructions that
God gave in his instruction manual, the *Torah*. Good News! The Israelites
were glad for forgiveness, but what about a life where sin—instead of
God—seemed to rule? Could a day come when God rules in our lives?

Jesus says that day has come. His death "cleansed the temple" of
our lives, making it possible for the Holy Spirit, who had been so long
promised, to come and take up residence in all of us, enabling us to live
God's life. Good News! This is the Bible's good news: if you will renounce
(i.e., repent of) your sins and accept God's free offer of forgiveness through
Christ, all those sins can be forgiven, and God can rule in your life through
the Holy Spirit, enabling you to be all you were meant to be, now and
forevermore. Good News!

May 13

THE DESTINY OF THE SERVANT

My servant will be successful; he will be high and lifted up; he will be greatly exalted. . . . Therefore I will assign a portion among the mighty, and he will divide the spoils with the strong. (Isaiah 52:13, 53:12a author's translation)

The fourth of the so-called "Suffering Servant Songs" begins at Isaiah 52:13 and continues on to Isaiah 53:12. When we recognize that fact, we discover a very interesting phenomenon. We are used to the descriptions of suffering, degradation, loss, and injustice that characterize the Servant in Isaiah 53:1–11, and as a result easily overlook the surprising statement in Isaiah 53:12a. However, when we recognize that the poem begins in Isaiah 52:13, and we see how it begins, we are prepared to realize the significance of that closing statement. In fact, the poem begins and ends on a note of triumph. This is the destiny of the Servant. In spite of all the tragedy and loss—no, because of the tragedy and loss, his mission will be totally successful. The Hebrew word for success has the connotations of wisdom, prudence, effectiveness (i.e., prosperity), and success. In the end, he will be in the place of the Victor.

How could Jesus leave heaven for a cow-stall? How could he lay aside the robes of divine glory and wrap himself in a towel? How could he who had been ministered to by angels take the lowest place? He could do it because he knew who he was! He could do it because he knew how the story ends! On the one hand, he lost everything—he really did. He was not merely masquerading as a limited, fragile, dying human. It was real. At the same time, he knew that he was the LORD, the Prince of Glory. He was armored against the temptation to feel sorry for himself because he knew the destiny of his servanthood.

You and I need that same sense of destiny. Why should we scrabble for position and power in this world as though this is all there is? Why should we work so hard to protect ourselves and our rights when we know the end of the story? "Blessed are you when they revile and persecute you, and say all kinds of evil against you falsely for My sake" (Matt 5:11 NKJV), for "yours is the kingdom of heaven" (Luke 6:20 NKJV). Believe it, and take the lowest place, knowing that the destiny of the servant is triumph.

May 14

HE BORE OUR GRIEFS AND OUR SORROWS

He was despised and forsaken of men,
A man of sorrows and acquainted with grief;
And like one from whom men hide their face
He was despised, and we did not esteem Him.
Surely our griefs He Himself bore,
And our sorrows he carried;
Yet we ourselves esteemed Him stricken,
Smitten of God, and afflicted. (Isaiah 53:3–4 NASB)

Notice what Jesus, according the prophet, was going to do for us when he became incarnate. He was going to "bear" our griefs and "carry" our sorrows. He was not going to stand far off and declare that we were forgiven. He was not even going to come near and say that God loves us and has a wonderful plan for our lives. On the contrary, he was going to take upon himself all the griefs and sorrows, the hatreds and the brutalities, the senseless tragedies, the pointless atrocities, all the deadly fruit of humanity's sin. This is what Jesus did, and it is what you and I must do if we are to replicate his life in ours.

I read some words of Francis Schaeffer several years ago that will always haunt me. He said, "Until I have invited that drunk into my living room, knowing full well he may vomit on my spotless rug, I do not love him. Until I have taken that young drug addict, filthy and dirty, and tucked her between the spotless sheets of my bed, I do not know the meaning of love." He bore our sins and our griefs and our sorrows. In our most horrible nightmares, we need to see pictures of ourselves as Pharisees, lifting our spotless hems lest they become sullied by the grief and the sorrows and the filth of a sinful world.

We must bear—to walk through the world and to put our shoulder under the load—as Jesus did for us, to help them carry the terrible, terrible load of their sin. Certainly, we can't carry it away as Jesus did, but we can help them carry it to the foot of the cross. And they may never go to the foot of the cross unless somebody helps them carry that load there.

May 15

LIES

We know we have rebelled and have denied the LORD. We have
turned our backs on our God. We know how unfair and oppressive
we have been, carefully planning our deceitful lies. (Isaiah 59:13)

This statement gets at the heart of the matter: "God, who 'requires
truth in the inward parts' hates all hypocrisy, falsehood, and deceit."*
Yahweh has created "what is so." This is the truth: reality that cannot be
altered. All that is "not so" is a lie. It is as simple as that.

The big lie is individual autonomy. If we take that road, then we must
build up a whole tissue of lies to support it, up to and including the final
lie: there is no God. To tell any lie is thus to partake in the Great Lie. It says
that I can distort reality to suit my own ends.

I am becoming more convinced that all sin finally comes down to
lying. If I steal something I am saying that what is not mine is mine—a lie.
If I have sex with a woman who is not my wife, I say that she belongs to
me—a lie. If I live in pride, I am saying that I am more important and more
valuable than others—a lie.

Sin begins in a lie—I can do what I want without reference to the
Creator's purposes and standards—and it ends in lie upon lie. He does
require truth in the inward parts, starting with this: you are God and I
am your creature, responsible to exercise the gift of life under your
control. Truth.

---

* G. Wilson, *The One Year Book of Prayer* (Wheaton, IL: Tyndale, 1991), 314.

When Morning Gilds the Skies

May 16

CLEAN AND UNCLEAN

We have all become like one who is unclean, and all our righteous
deeds are like a filthy cloth. We all fade like a leaf, and our
iniquities, like the wind, take us away. (Isaiah 64:6 NRSV)

Perhaps the most significant consequence of sin—as Isaiah, speaking
for the Israelites, recognizes—is that it makes us unclean in the
presence of the One who is absolutely clean. This powerful metaphor runs
throughout the Bible. Clean and unclean are opposites; the one cannot
exist in the presence of the other. If there are two surgeons operating on a
patient, and one is thoroughly clean, while the other has not taken the time
to scrub, the patient's wound will become contaminated.

Long before anyone understood the necessity for sterility in the
operating room, the biblical writers understood the contaminating power
of sin. For the pagans, "clean" and "unclean" was a matter of exorcising
evil powers so that rituals would be effective—not so in the Bible. It is the
damning power of self that makes it impossible for us creatures to coexist
with God. This explains that profound statement in Isaiah 64:6. How can
doing what is right make us filthy? Very simply, it is when we do those
right things for the wrong motives and purposes. We may give a large sum
of money to our church. That is certainly the "right" thing to do. But why
have we done it? Is it because we unselfishly love God and others? Or is
it because selfishly we want to be known to ourselves (and probably to
others) as a very generous person?

May 17

SEE MY GLORY

For I know their works and their thoughts, and the time is
coming to gather all nations and tongues. And they shall
come and shall see my glory. (Isaiah 66:18 ESV)

Father, I desire that they also, whom you have given me, may be with
me where I am, to see my glory that you have given me because you
loved me before the foundation of the world. (John 17:24 ESV)

When we glance at John 17:24, we might be a little taken aback. Doesn't it sound at least a little bit self-serving? Jesus wants all his disciples, including us, to go to heaven so we can see how good he looks or how successful he has been? No, that is not what he is saying, because "glory" in the Bible is neither fame nor outstanding success. It is reality, significance, solidity. It does have to do with reputation, but it is a solid, enduring reputation, not one that is a "glorious" flash in the pan. So, Jesus is saying that he wants his people to experience the amazing reality—the glory—of eternal life that he has purchased for us.

There is something more going on in that statement. We realize it in the Isaiah passage above, a passage that comes right at the end of Isaiah's book. It is, of course, a passage that Jesus knew very well, and it was almost certainly in Jesus's mind when he was praying this prayer. What is the goal of God in the world? It is that we, redeemed and transformed through the Spirit, may be no longer barred from the throne room of heaven by our sin and sinfulness but may bask in the reality, the glory, of his presence for all eternity. That is why Jesus could call on God at the beginning of the prayer (see John 17:1) to "glorify" him—on the Cross!—and could say that he had shared their (his and his Father's) glory with the disciples (see John 17:22). He had fulfilled what Isaiah could only dream of. He had made it possible for all the world to bask in the wondrous reality of God for all eternity.

May 18

KNOW THE LORD

But those who wish to boast should boast in this alone: that they truly
know me and understand that I am the LORD who demonstrates unfailing
love and who brings justice and righteousness to the earth, and that I
delight in these things. I, the LORD, have spoken! (Jeremiah 9:24)

"And they will not need to teach their neighbors, nor will they need to teach
their relatives, saying, 'You should know the LORD.' For everyone, from the
least to the greatest, will know me already," says the LORD. "And I will forgive
their wickedness, and I will never again remember their sins." (Jeremiah 31:34)

A book I have been reading recently says that we can never really
"know" Yahweh, the I AM. We can know something of his plans,
something of what he wants in the world, and therefore something about
him. Furthermore, we can "acknowledge" him as our God, but "know" him
in some personal way? The author says, "No."

To that idea I say, "No!" The whole purpose of the biblical revelation
is that Yahweh wants us to know him, to have a personal relationship
with him. So he has *spoken* to us. Language is the ultimate means of self-
disclosure, and that is what he has done, something the gods never do.
That author says that we can never completely know another person.
While there is some truth to that claim—all of us remain separate from
each other—to say that we cannot know another is to have missed the
whole point of marriage, which is in many ways the central metaphor of
the Bible. God wants a marriage relationship with you. He thinks you are
ravishingly beautiful and wants to give himself to you in self-denying love.
He wants to know you and wants you to know him.

Karen and I have been married a long time. When we see something
and in reaction the same words come out of both of our mouths at the
same time, we look at each other and laugh. We know one another. That's
what God wants.

May 19

HOW LIKE GOD

On July 31 of my thirtieth year, while I was with the Judean
exiles beside the Kebar River in Babylon, the heavens were
opened, and I saw visions of God. (Ezekiel 1:1)

Everything for which Ezekiel had lived was in ruins. All his life he had
been preparing for the great day when, on his thirtieth birthday, he
could enter into the profession of the priesthood, the day when he would be
consecrated for the incredible privilege of serving Yahweh, the Holy One,
the only God. Unfortunate circumstances had conspired to change all that.
In 598 BC after Nebuchadnezzar had been besieging Jerusalem for two and
a half years, the new king, the eighteen-year-old Jehoiachin, wisely decided
to surrender. In return for not destroying the city, Nebuchadnezzar took
the royal family hostage along with numbers of government officials and
priests. Ezekiel, twenty-five years old at the time, was among them.

What did this mean? It meant that Ezekiel would never serve as a
priest. Having been taken out of the holy land into a country that was
defiled, he had become defiled, and even if by some miracle he should
escape Babylon and get back home, he would be prevented from ever
serving in the Temple because of that defilement. So, his thirtieth year
would have been a bitter one, the first of many empty ones to come, and
his birthday was a dark day indeed.

However, it was in that very year, and possibly on his actual birthday
(perhaps the reason for specifying the date of this event), that God gave
him a whole new vocation, the one of prophet. How like God! In the hour
of our deepest suffering, God always finds a way to give us a love gift. He
finds a way to pull the sting out of our suffering. He finds a way to wrap
his arms around us. How like God! He does not promise sunshine all
our lives, but he promises his light every day. We have only to see it. He
does not deliver us from difficulties; expect them. Instead, he gives us his
presence and power to overcome those difficulties and actually turn them
into opportunities.

When Morning Gilds the Skies

May 20

GOD OF THE WORLD

The living beings looked like bright coals of fire or brilliant torches, and lightning seemed to flash back and forth among them. And the living beings darted to and fro like flashes of lightning. As I looked at these beings, I saw four wheels touching the ground beside them, one wheel belonging to each. The wheels sparkled as if made of beryl. All four wheels looked alike and were made the same; each wheel had a second wheel turning crosswise within it. The beings could move in any of the four directions they faced, without turning as they moved. (Ezekiel 1:13–17)

Why was Ezekiel given such a startling vision? Isaiah had a vision, but it had nothing like the color or complexity of Ezekiel's, and most of the other prophets (e.g., Jeremiah) had no vision at all. Why Ezekiel? I suggest that Ezekiel needed a revolution in his thinking. Ezekiel had trained all his life to become a priest in the gorgeous temple of Solomon in Jerusalem. Now he had been cruelly wrenched away to pagan Babylon, far from God and his house, far from legitimate worship.

Far from God? Don't believe it! Yahweh was not captive to that pretty building in Jerusalem. He is God of the world, and the representations of his glory in that hill-country town in Judea were hardly exclusive. When you begin to try to represent his beauty and wonder, the mind and the senses begin to explode with sight and sound and motion and color and—and—and—are simply breathtaking. Ezekiel, did you think worship of Yahweh was limited to that place and in those ways? Oh, my, no!

The revolution in Ezekiel's thinking was one of the things that needed to take place in order for Ezekiel to have the ministry he did. He was going to be called upon to tell the unbelieving exiles that God had no commitment to a polluted Jerusalem at all, that he could as easily burn it down as look at it. In order to declare that message, Ezekiel had to see that God's glory fills the earth. Don't believe that the ways you have learned to worship him are the only ways in which this Universal Lord can be worshipped.

May 21

FAITHFUL WATCHMEN

Son of man, I have appointed you as a watchman for Israel. Whenever you receive a message from me, warn people immediately. If I warn the wicked, saying, "You are under the penalty of death," but you fail to deliver the warning, they will die in their sins. And I will hold you responsible for their deaths. If you warn them and they refuse to repent and keep on sinning, they will die in their sins. But you will have saved yourself because you obeyed me. (Ezekiel 3:17–19)

Pastors sometimes struggle in small churches where it seems that people are not responsive; they see some of the great mega churches where every time they turn around they seem to add 1,000 people to the congregation; and they say, "What am I doing wrong?" Why doesn't God bless me?" Or maybe, more dangerously, they say, "Well, I need to learn their techniques and copy them."

There are ways of building churches, and there are ways of building churches. Some of those ways are of God, and some of those ways are not of God. God said to Isaiah, *I want you to go and preach the truth in the full knowledge that the truth will not bring these people to healing. It will harden their hearts and deafen their ears* (see Isa 6:9–10).

Will you do that? If you are pastoring a church or are a leader in a church, and you are being faithful, that's the issue. That doesn't mean that we are harsh and cruel and self-righteous. That's not faithfulness; it's just nastiness. Be faithful with a broken heart, be faithful with tears in your eyes, be faithful with love for the lost and the broken and the rebel, but be faithful.

God gave a warning to Ezekiel about watchmen. He said that if the watchman sees the enemy coming and gives the alarm and nobody listens, then it is their problem. However, if the watchman sees the enemy coming and says nothing, it is *his* problem. That's the charge that is given to all of us. Do you know the truth? Do you see the enemy coming? Do I? Am I keeping my mouth shut to those who need to hear, to be warned? May it never be! We have a responsibility to warn others. It may be that we are faced with more and more people who refuse to be warned. That was the case with Israel, and there were more than enough prophets who decided to tell the people what they wanted to hear. We dare not be among those. Let us be faithful watchmen.

May 22

JERUSALEM?

Then the Spirit lifted me up into the sky and transported me to Jerusalem in a vision from God. I was taken to the north gate of the inner courtyard of the Temple, where there is a large idol that has made the LORD very jealous. Suddenly, the glory of the God of Israel was there, just as I had seen it before in the valley. (Ezekiel 8:3–4)

If Ezekiel had to learn in the valley of Babylon that Yahweh's glory and wonder can be represented in a myriad of ways throughout the entire creation, he also had to learn that no Jerusalem is holy in itself. This is what the terrifying vision of Ezekiel 8–11 was designed to achieve. No place and no one is holy in itself. Only Yahweh is truly other, and only those who are wholly dedicated to him and share his character are holy. This is what God had said to Solomon as recorded in 1 Kings 9: He was pleased with this lovely building and would be glad to have his "name" associated with it. But, if there came a day when the worship in it no longer reflected absolute, exclusive devotion to him, he would smash and burn it in a moment.

That is what Ezekiel saw, a building given over to pagan worship in all its forms: most particularly fertility worship, from the worship of the fertility goddess at the north gate to the worship of the life-giving sun at the east gate. The filthy and sordid nature of the worship was only magnified by the presence of the Babylonian vision. Far from Jerusalem being holy and Babylon being contaminated, it was the other way around!

What about you and me? Are we going through all the forms, but God is far away? Don't deceive yourself; it is only the presence of God that sanctifies! If he is not present in his perfection, there is no holiness to be found.

May 23

YOUR MARK

And the LORD said to him, "Pass through the city, through Jerusalem,
and put a mark on the foreheads of the men who sigh and groan over
all the abominations that are committed in it." (Ezekiel 9:4 ESV)

Blessed are those who mourn, for they shall be comforted. (Matthew 5:4 ESV)

Ezekiel, exiled to Babylon along with the royal family in 598 BC, was
called to pronounce judgment on Jerusalem. Perhaps he thought
things were really not so bad back there at home, but he was given a vision
of how it really was there and why judgment was inescapable. That vision
is recorded for us in Ezekiel 8–11. As part of it, he saw a man with a scribe's
outfit, and that man was given the command seen in Ezekiel 9:4 above.
The people with the mark on their foreheads would be spared in the plague
that the prophet saw in his vision. Notice what the characteristic behavior
was: sigh and groan.

Now I don't know about you, but I am ashamed to say that it is too easy
for me to dismiss wicked people: they are wicked, they are leading others
in wickedness, just forget them! For instance, I abhor much of what is
going on in the halls of our government today—but do I genuinely mourn
over it? I'm convicted that I don't intercede enough for what's going on
there. I'm sorry that sometimes I delight when they are caught doing evil.

I need to say, "God forgive me. Give me a heart that does not condone
the tragic things that are going on there, nor yet dismisses them for their
folly, but grieves and mourns over them, still praying for everyone involved
and daring to believe that every one of them could yet be reached. Put your
mark on my forehead, God."

May 24

ONE HEART

And I shall give them one heart, and shall put a new spirit
within them. And I shall take the heart of stone out of their
flesh and give them a heart of flesh. (Ezekiel 11:19 ESV)

To grow deeper in Christ, we need to be re-programmed, and that's
what the Holy Spirit does. We have a very serious problem in terms
of the way we have been programmed to think about reality. That way of
thinking must be changed. Realistically, that change may take some time,
but it begins in a moment of faith and belief. Then, as we obey the Spirit's
prompting, it will become a full reality in us. So, how does our thinking
have to be changed ? What is it that is truly important? It is not getting
all I want to eat; it is not getting all the sleep, the entertainment, the sex,
the things, the adulation, etc. that I want. What is the important thing?
Integrity. What? Yes, integrity, to become truly one.

Still, don't seek integrity, seek God. Integrity is a by-product, the result
of having all our desires, goals, and behavior unified in service to him. That
person can be trusted. That person does not say one thing one day and
another the next. That kind of person will keep their promises even if they
were only nineteen at the time and didn't know what they were saying!
They will be more concerned about the rights of others than their own
rights. They will be the same with the weak as they are with the powerful.
Because their whole life is devoted to God, they are one.

Can God do this? Can he make our divided, conflicted hearts one? Can
he give us purity, not only in the sexual area but also in every other area
of our lives? Can he give us kindness when the whole tone of life is, "Cut
them down and hit them where it hurts?" Can God give us simplicity in our
wants? Can he give us love when everyone around us laughs at the idea of
freely giving ourselves to other people without getting anything in return?
Can God re-orient our values, can he change the way we think and act?
Can he break the heart of stone and give us a tender, responsive heart? The
Bible tells us that he can. You can claim God's promise that, by the power
of the Holy Spirit, he can make your heart one, and you will discover that
you don't have to live the American dream. You can live God's dream.

May 25

BE CAREFUL WHAT YOU ASK FOR

For any one of the house of Israel, or of the strangers who sojourn in Israel, who separates himself from me, taking his idols into his heart and putting the stumbling block of his iniquity before his face, and yet comes to a prophet to consult me through him, I the LORD will answer him myself. And I will set my face against that man; I will make him a sign and a byword and cut him off from the midst of my people, and you shall know that I am the LORD. And if the prophet is deceived and speaks a word, I, the LORD, have deceived that prophet, and I will stretch out my hand against him and will destroy him from the midst of my people Israel. (Ezekiel 14:7–9 ESV)

This passage is very frightening. In a nutshell, it says that God will give us what we ask for. The same point is made in narrative form in 1 Kings 20–21. There Ahab wanted to go to war against Syria, so his prophets gave him the message he wanted, believing and claiming they had gotten it from God. Micaiah, the true prophet, said the reason God gave it was to entice Ahab to his death.

Here the elders of the second exile to Babylon (the one that occurred in 598 BC before the third and final one in 586 BC) have come to Ezekiel wanting a good promise about Jerusalem's continuing survival. But they were not devoted to God; they were devoted to their own secret sins. So God responded, "Oh, I'll give you a message alright, but it won't be the one you want. If it *should* be the one you want, it will only be because some prophet desperately wanted to please you—maybe for cash money?—and I let him have the message he wanted."

So what's the point? Before you go asking God for some sweet promise of blessing, examine your heart. Do you want God's way or your way? Beware! If it is your way that you want, God may give you the message you are asking for, *so that the disaster you are trying to avoid will come upon you and either shock you back to him or, if you are unrecoverable like Ahab, destroy you.* Be careful what you ask for!

May 26

WHAT YOU ARE IN THE DARK

Fathers and mothers are treated with contempt. Foreigners are forced
to pay for protection. Orphans and widows are wronged and oppressed
among you. You despise my holy things and violate my Sabbath days of rest.
People accuse others falsely and send them to their death. You are filled
with idol worshipers and people who do obscene things. Men sleep with
their fathers' wives and force themselves on women who are menstruating.
Within your walls live men who commit adultery with their neighbors' wives,
who defile their daughters-in-law, or who rape their own sisters. There
are hired murderers, loan racketeers, and extortioners everywhere. They
never even think of me and my commands, says the Sovereign LORD. . . .
I looked for someone who might rebuild the wall of righteousness that
guards the land. I searched for someone to stand in the gap in the wall so I
wouldn't have to destroy the land, but I found no one. (Ezekiel 22:7–12, 30)

Josh McDowell did a survey among high school students. He asked them
a number of questions such as: "Is it okay to cheat on an exam if you
really need that grade to help your GPA so you can get into college?" "Have
you cheated on an exam within the past six months?" Of non-Christian
students, 97 percent said it is okay to cheat on an exam; 95 percent said
they had cheated in the last six months. Shockingly, among kids who
testified to being born again, 95 percent said it was okay to cheat and
91 percent said they had cheated.

So here we are, with only a few percentage points difference between
pagans and supposed Christians. That is the kind of thing Ezekiel is talking
about here. He is a captive in Babylon and telling the people back home
that Jerusalem is about to be destroyed. They are responding "No way!
We are believers here. Nothing bad can happen to us. We have a wall of
divine protection around us." But Ezekiel says there are gaps in the walls—
big gaps—and the people's behavior is not filling the gaps but making
them bigger.

He is trying to get this point across: what you are in the dark is what you
are in the light. What you are in the office is what you are in church. They
all go together; they are inseparable. Is there any measurable difference
between your behavior and that of the world around you, especially when
no one sees you? Are you a wall-builder or a wall-destroyer?

Religion is not about manipulating God to make ourselves powerful,
rich, comfortable, and satisfied. Religion is about a love affair with him
that changes the way you live in the world around you.

May 27

PROTECT YOUR HEARTS

Her sister Oholibah saw this, and she became more corrupt than her sister in her lust and in her whoring, which was worse than that of her sister. She lusted after the Assyrians, governors and commanders, warriors clothed in full armor, horsemen riding on horses, all of them desirable young men. (Ezekiel 23:11–12 ESV)

In every place of worship, I want men to pray with holy hands lifted up to God, free from anger and controversy. And I want women to be modest in their appearance. They should wear decent and appropriate clothing and not draw attention to themselves by the way they fix their hair or by wearing gold or pearls or expensive clothes. For women who claim to be devoted to God should make themselves attractive by the good things they do. (1 Timothy 2:8–10)

Many of us find Ezekiel's gross descriptions of Israel and Judah as two profligate sisters offensive. Almost certainly, that was God's intent when he inspired Ezekiel to speak in this way. The two nations' abandonment of their covenant trust in Yahweh and their turning to human nations for support is intended to arouse our disgust. But why use women as his illustration? Doesn't that betray a fundamentally low view of women?

As a matter of fact, it does not. What it does reflect is the fact that the spiritual heart of a nation is in the heart of its women. I'm not letting the men off the hook here—neither does Paul in the Timothy passage above— but there is a sense in which, just as women have the ability to be the truest Christians because of their spiritual sensitivities, they also have a greater possibility for the other kind of spirituality. Women, protect your hearts for Christ, because if you don't, the very spiritual giftedness you have can be turned into something horrifying. There is a greater capacity for spiritual insight and spiritual experience among women and that means there is also a greater capacity for corruption and tragedy.

I will never forget walking down the street in one of our great cities and coming up behind two beautifully-dressed, attractive women. As I drew nearer, admiring them, I was able to overhear their conversation. I was stunned to hear obscenities and profanities lacing everything they said. Evil behavior is not acceptable for men either, but when women do it, you know that the life of the nation is far gone.

May 28
WHAT CUP?

You will be filled with drunkenness and sorrow, a cup of horror and desolation, the cup of your sister Samaria; you shall drink it and drain it out, and gnaw its shards, and tear your breasts; for I have spoken, declares the LORD GOD. Therefore thus says the LORD GOD: Because you have forgotten me and cast me behind your back, you yourself must bear the consequences of your lewdness and whoring. (Ezekiel 23:33–35 ESV)

Thus says your LORD, the LORD, your God who pleads the cause of his people: "Behold, I have taken from your hand the cup of staggering; the bowl of my wrath you shall drink no more. (Isaiah 51:22 ESV)

And he withdrew from them about a stone's throw, and knelt down and prayed, saying, "Father, if you are willing, remove this cup from me. Nevertheless, not my will, but yours, be done." . . . And being in an agony he prayed more earnestly; and his sweat became like great drops of blood falling down to the ground. (Luke 22:41–42, 44 ESV)

Have you ever wondered about Gethsemane? Agony? Sweating like drops of blood? What was it about what Jesus was facing that would evoke such terror and revulsion? Yes, the humiliation, the beating, the death on the cross, all the things that were facing Jesus in the next twenty-four hours were terrible to contemplate, but what about all those people down through the ages who faced equally terrible deaths with a song on their lips? Why didn't Jesus "bear up" better?

The answer is in the word that is repeated in all three of the passages above, the word "cup." It is a word expressing the experience of consequences. This world that our heavenly Father has made is one of cause and effect. It is not possible to live in defiance of the way in which the world is made, whether physical or spiritual, and then escape the consequences of our actions. Oh, yes, we personally may escape them for a time, but there will be consequences, and someone will experience them. Those consequences are pictured by the Hebrew prophets as a cup filled to the brim with the most ghastly brew: all the hatred, all the tragedy, all the loss, all the missed opportunities, all the petty nastiness stemming from our determination to have our own way. We will drink it; those consequences can no more be escaped than can the loss of fingers when we unthinkingly reach across a running circular saw for something on the other side. The "cup" must be drained.

But suppose someone else—*Someone* else—were to drink it for us? The "cup" could be taken out of our hands and put into his. Now all of a sudden the agony of Gethsemane makes sense. Jesus was not agonizing over the circumstances of his own death, terrible as it was. He was agonizing over the hideous thought of having to drink the devil's brew in *our* cup, the cup of all humanity: all the hurt, all the grief, all the terror, all the evil of all time. In the end, he who is Life alone would take upon himself the Death of us all. Who in their right mind would willingly do that? Only One who was motivated by a bottomless love—a love for his Father, whom he lived to please, and a love for the poor, pitiful creatures, whom he had made for love.

May 29
HOW HIGH A PRICE?—PART ONE

Then this message came to me from the LORD: "Son of man, with one blow I will take away your dearest treasure. Yet you must not show any sorrow at her death. Do not weep; let there be no tears. Groan silently, but let there be no wailing at her grave. Do not uncover your head or take off your sandals. Do not perform the usual rituals of mourning or accept any food brought to you by consoling friends." So I proclaimed this to the people the next morning, and in the evening my wife died. The next morning I did everything I had been told to do. . . . "Ezekiel is an example for you; you will do just as he has done. And when that time comes, you will know that I am the Sovereign LORD." (Ezekiel 24:15–18, 24)

I have a question or two I'd love to ask God, and asking about the death of Ezekiel's wife would be one of them: "Wait a minute, God. Ezekiel has been faithful to you. He's been saying all these hard things; he's been acting out humiliating, demeaning things. Why would you take his wife and not even allow him to mourn publicly? It's not fair!" How might God answer my question?

First of all, notice on what day this happened. By divine inspiration, Ezekiel knew it was the day when the final siege of Jerusalem had begun. When the news of that event would finally reach the people some months later, their Babylonian captors would not allow them to mourn or show any emotion over what was happening to their beloved city. When that happened, they would look back and say in wonder, "That's what was going on with Ezekiel. God, the God who knows the future, told him, and just like we can't mourn, he couldn't mourn. Yahweh really is God!"

So, I expect God would say, "How important is it for people to have a personal relationship with me, to know me? Is it important enough that the very manner of my servants' life experiences would serve to promote that relationship, that personal knowledge. How high a price are you willing to pay to get that message through to people?" How high a price, indeed?

May 30

HOW HIGH A PRICE?—PART TWO

When he had said this, he showed them his hands and his side.
Then the disciples were glad when they saw the Lord. Jesus
said to them again, "Peace be with you. As the Father has sent
me, even so I am sending you." (John 20:20–21 ESV)

A young couple went to Papua, New Guinea, to reach a tribe of people far back in the jungle. They moved in with them and for two years they worked with them. Nothing happened. These were hard people, contemptuous of the white-skinned foreigners who seemed to know nothing about how to live.

The couple had a little boy who had been born just before they went there. After two years this little boy became ill very rapidly, and they were not able to get him out, but they prayed, "Oh God, this could be the turning point. If you'll heal our son in a dramatic way, these people will see that you are God, that you are the Lord. Heal him, God. But most of all we want you to heal him to reach these people."

The people of the village stood around and watched with implacable faces. The boy got sicker and sicker and within a matter of twenty-four hours he was dead. The couple, alone without family or friends and with these hard-faced, hard-hearted people watching them, gave their grief to the Lord. They gave their baby to the Lord, took him out, buried him, and put up a little white cross. They wept. Committing him to the Lord, entrusting his soul to the Lord, and entrusting themselves to the Lord, they went back into their hut and sat there in the darkness, silent in their grief. Both were thinking, "I guess we might as well start packing. It's over. Those people, they know our God failed us."

The next morning they were still sitting in the same place. They heard some noises outside their hut. The young missionary got up and pulled aside the curtain, and there sat the chief in front of the door and behind him sat everybody else in the village. The young man said, "Sir, what is it you want?" The chief said, "Would you teach us about your Jesus? We don't know how to die like that."

They thought they had it all figured out. God would accomplish his purposes through the healing of their son. God said, "No, I'm going to accomplish my purposes through the death of your son. Is that all right?"

How high a price are you willing to pay for God to accomplish his purposes through you?

May 31
PROFANING HIS NAME: PART ONE

I scattered them among the nations, and they were dispersed through the
countries. In accordance with their ways and their deeds I judged them.
But when they came to the nations, wherever they came, they profaned
my holy name, in that people said of them, "These are the people of the
LORD, and yet they had to go out of his land." (Ezekiel 36:19–20 ESV)

The first time I read Ezekiel 36:20, I stopped at the first half of the
verse because I was so shocked at the thought. I thought, "The Judean
people were so angry at God for sending them into exile, that they were
cursing him." Then I read the rest of the verse. Always read the rest of the
verse! How were they profaning his name? To the Babylonians it looked
like Yahweh couldn't deliver the Judeans. All the Judeans had to do to
profane God's name was to make him appear helpless!

How does that work? To understand it, we have to think about the
opposite, something that some of us pray in our churches almost every
week: "Hallowed be Thy name." What? How do we make God's name
holy? First of all, "name" in the Bible is not usually a label. Most of all, it
is your character or reputation. Second, "holy" is high, exalted, absolutely
other than a broken, fallible world. So, we are praying that God will show
himself like that—holy—in us, in our lives and in our behavior.

Then how do we profane his name? Just like the Judeans did, we
profane God's name by making it appear in our lives that he is little and
helpless, that he cannot deliver us, that he is just one more of this world's
useless gods. What do your neighbors or your co-workers think of your
God? Do they know that he can deliver you from your desires, rages, fears,
and guilts? Then you are hallowing, sanctifying, his name. Or, do they
think, like the Babylonians thought of the Judeans, that your God, like
theirs, is really helpless?

June 1

PROFANING HIS NAME: PART TWO

I will sanctify My great name, which has been profaned among
the nations, which you profaned in their midst; and the nations
will know that I *am* the LORD, says the LORD GOD, when I am
hallowed in you before their eyes. (Ezekiel 36:23 NKJV)

We pray, "Hallowed be Thy name" in the Lord's Prayer, but do we
really mean it? I suggest that we American Christians, like the
Judeans in exile, profane God's name in a variety of ways. We are not
talking about cursing or swearing here. We are talking about making it
appear that God is helpless, or that he is a petty little being who exists
for us. For instance, many preachers say in so many words, "God exists
to make us happy. He exists to answer our prayers. He exists to make us
rich." No, he does not! God is not a rabbit's foot who exists to make our
prayers come true. He is the I AM, the One on whose Being all the universe
depends. He exists in himself in his triune nature. What he wants is to
share with us the self-denying love the Trinity have for each other and to
have us share that love with one another. To suggest anything less is to
profane his holy nature—his name.

When we pray that his name should be hallowed, we are asking that
God's incomparable nature might be seen in us. We are asking that the
world might recognize that he alone is God and that he alone has the
power to deliver us from our addictions to wealth, pleasure, comfort, and
above all, to our own way. The Judeans were in exile as a result of their sin,
and that made it appear that Yahweh could not deliver them, that he was
as helpless as any other God. So, God says that he will show himself holy
through them.

Have we been delivered from old habits, old ways of thinking, old
guilts, and old hatreds, or are our lives and behaviors indistinguishable
from the lost around us? To the degree they are indistinguishable, just to
that degree, we are profaning the name of God.

June 2

REVIVE US AGAIN

I will sprinkle clean water on you, and you will be clean; I will cleanse you from all your impurities and from all your idols. I will give you a new heart and put a new spirit in you; I will remove from you your heart of stone and give you a heart of flesh. And I will put my Spirit in you and move you to follow [walk in] my decrees and be careful to keep my laws. (Ezekiel 36:25–27 NIV)

When we pray and ask God for revival, what do we have in mind? What are we visualizing a revival will look like? In most cases, I suspect that we are looking for religious ecstasy with accompanying signs of spiritual power. To be sure, the spiritual powerlessness of the contemporary church and the lifelessness of much of our devotion is an affront to God and a sign to the world that something is wrong. On the other hand, all too often revival movements that have focused on religious ecstasy have run amuck. Church history is littered with stories of heresies and sexual excess that have arisen from great revivals. Why is that, and why wasn't it the case with the revival led by John and Charles Wesley in England?

Should we try to squash the ecstasy that comes when we are face to face with God and know ourselves fully clean in his presence? Of course not—we could not if we wanted to! There was plenty of ecstasy in the Wesleyan movement, especially in the early days. John and Charles were even accused of promoting "enthusiasm," which meant "fanaticism" at that time, but that supposed "fanaticism" did not come to define the movement. Why not? The reason is because the Wesley brothers were not seeking ecstasy; they were seeking the biblical God and his character and to get rid of everything that prevented that ethical character from being reproduced in them and their people.

Notice the scripture above. What will be the result of Spirit-filling? It will be a certain kind of "walk," one whose direction and character are dictated by God's instruction manual—his *Torah*. The goal of revival for the Wesleys was nothing less than holy living. So it should be for us. Holiness should be a wedding of godly character and ecstatic experience, and if that wedding is truly done—and done right—then the joy of his presence will flood through our ethical righteousness, while the reality, consistency, and solidity of our ethical righteousness will be the anchor for our ecstasy. Revive us again!

June 3

THE THRONE OF GOD

And I heard someone speaking to me from within the Temple, while the man who had been measuring stood beside me. The LORD said to me, "Son of man, this is the place of my throne and the place where I will rest my feet. I will live here forever among the people of Israel. They and their kings will not defile my holy name any longer by their adulterous worship of other gods or by honoring the relics of their kings who have died." (Ezekiel 43:6–7)

Ezekiel first had a vision of what was really going on in the temple in Jerusalem and why God could not reside there (see Ezek 8–10). Later, he received another vision, one of a temple that was perfectly symmetrical and harmonious, out of which flowed a river of life, a temple where God could be forever enthroned (see Ezek 41–44). However, it seems clear that the language in Ezekiel is not intended to be taken literally. The throne of God is not to be in one location, in a building somewhere. The glory of God cannot be confined to a place. He is talking about something else.

In fact, you and I are the temple of God. Ever since the Garden of Eden when Yahweh was driven from his rightful throne in the hearts of Adam and Eve, he has been conspiring to come home. The tabernacle depicted it first, and then Solomon's temple, but those were only symbols of the reality. The reality of God, the glory of God, we have seen in the face of Jesus Christ, and through Jesus Christ God intends to take up his royal residence in every one of us. The harmony, symmetry, serenity, and up-welling life that Ezekiel saw are to be descriptions of us. Where God lives there is peace, life, and well-being. Everything fits together. That's what *shalom* is: wholeness. God wants to put his temple in your life and mine, the place where the glory of God can dwell and *the world can know that he is Yahweh, the Lord.*

June 4

THE MOST MISERABLE PERSON

He then brought me out through the north gate and led me around the outside to the outer gate facing east, and the water was trickling from the south side. As the man went eastward with a measuring line in his hand, he measured off a thousand cubits and then led me through water that was ankle-deep. He measured off another thousand cubits and led me through water that was knee-deep. He measured off another thousand and led me through water that was up to the waist. He measured off another thousand, but now it was a river that I could not cross, because the water had risen and was deep enough to swim in—a river that no one could cross. (Ezekiel 47:2–5 NIV)

The most miserable person in the world is a halfway Christian. That's a person who is far enough into the faith that they can't enjoy sin anymore but not far enough in to have the blessing of a fully-surrendered Christian life. It's like standing on the shore on a beautiful sunny day watching people swimming. They are obviously having a great time. They joyfully call, "Come on in, the water's great!" So you take off one shoe and sock, roll up one pant leg and gingerly stick one toe in the water and say, "Ooh, that's cold. This swimming thing is not all it's cracked up to be." That's not swimming, is it? Neither is the Christian life just a legal transaction in which we escape the fire while keeping firm control of our lives. Real freedom in the Christian life comes from diving in over your head. Why is that? It is because our retaining control is a very effective stopper on the channel of God's blessings. It is our way of saying that we will be God in our lives, to which God can only reply, "Okay, if that is the way you want it. But if you would take your hands off, and let me be God, if you'd get into water you can't cross, then all the resources of heaven could be yours."

Is your life his or yours? Do you have one toe—maybe a whole foot—in, or are you all in? What's holding you back? "Come on in, the water's great!"

June 5

TRUSTING THE NATIONS

When Ephraim saw his sickness, and Judah his wound, then
Ephraim went to Assyria, and sent to the great king. But he is
not able to cure you or heal your wound. (Hosea 5:13 ESV)

"Ah, stubborn children," declares the LORD, "who carry out a plan,
but not mine, and who make an alliance, but not of my Spirit, that
they may add sin to sin; who set out to go down to Egypt, without
asking for my direction, to take refuge in the protection of Pharaoh
and to seek shelter in the shadow of Egypt!" (Isaiah 30:1–2 ESV)

Throughout Israel's history one of the things God said over and over was, "Don't trust the nations." What was his point? And what does that have to do with you and me? He was dealing with the fundamental issue in personal relations: trust. If we are to have close personal relations with anyone, there must be trust between the two of us. If you do not trust me, you are not going to "entrust" me with yourself and all that is precious to you. So, the big question for all of us is: whom do you trust?

Yahweh said to Israel and is saying to you and to me, "Child, trust me and let me demonstrate in you all that I can be for the nations of the world." Israel, like many of us, was afraid to trust God. We cannot see him, and we cannot make him do what we want. He asks everything from us without any proof that he will truly care for us. So, what happens when we get into difficulties, which we certainly will? Where do we turn? We are deeply tempted, as Israel was, to turn to humanity for help. You see, that's what trusting the nations is all about. To "trust the nations" is to trust *human* greatness, *human* glory, *human* power. But that is foolish.

Is there evidence of Yahweh's trustworthiness? Of course there is; look at the history of Israel and of the Church. Is there evidence of human untrustworthiness, especially on the institutional level? On every hand!

So where is your trust? Are you going to put your trust in humanity, including your own, or will you trust your Creator/Redeemer God? If you trust humanity you are headed down a dead-end road and taking with you all those under your influence. On the other hand, if you will trust God, then not only will you walk out of darkness into light but also your life will show the nations the way out of their darkness.

When Morning Gilds the Skies

June 6

REFINING FIRE

Oh, how can I give you up, Israel? How can I let you go? How can I destroy you like Admah or demolish you like Zeboiim? My heart is torn within me, and my compassion overflows. No, I will not unleash my fierce anger. I will not completely destroy Israel, for I am God and not a mere mortal. I am the Holy One living among you, and I will not come to destroy. For someday the people will follow me. I, the LORD, will roar like a lion. And when I roar, my people will return trembling from the west. (Hosea 11:8–10)

The people of Israel had broken God's marriage covenant with them for a thousand years. For a thousand years they had abandoned him, their true husband, and had gone after other lovers, gods that they had made with their own hands! Finally, his patience had run out, and he was going to allow the result that he had warned them of as far back as Moses to come to reality: the good land that he had given them was going to spit them out. The fire that they had kindled was going to burst out.

God had had it, right? The covenant they had sworn to in blood specified that those who broke it would be exterminated. So, is he going to wipe them out, like an infuriated human would? No, if God lets fire come into your life, it is not because he hates you or is tired of you and wants to get rid of you. If he lets it come into your life, it is in order to purge you. He did not want to destroy his people; he wanted to refine them, and the same is true for us.

Suppose you're not rebelling against him, at least as far as you know, and something bad happens to you. Did God send that on you? I don't believe he does so directly. On the other hand, I don't believe he's just standing around watching a sinful world do bad things to us. He allows these things to happen. He could prevent them, but for some reason he has chosen not to. He has allowed it to happen, and because he's allowed it to happen, he is therefore sovereign over it and *he can work through it for blessing in your life.*

That's the real issue: it is not whether bad things will happen to you, because they will. This is a fallen world. The only question is, what will they do to me? Will they break me, or will they refine me? Will I let them drive me away from God, or will I allow him to use them to bring me closer to him?

June 7

REPENTANCE

"Don't tear your clothing in your grief, but tear your hearts instead." Return to the LORD your God, for he is merciful and compassionate, slow to get angry and filled with unfailing love. He is eager to relent and not punish. (Joel 2:13)

The words translated "repent" or "repentance" in the two testaments are very significant. In the Old Testament the idea is "to turn around," or "turn back to." In the New Testament the root idea is "to agree with." That is, we agree with God's evaluation of our thoughts and behaviors, namely that they are wrong, and we actively turn away from them and turn back to God. This is a long way from simply feeling bad about what we have done. That is remorse, not repentance. That is what happened to Judas Iscariot. He felt bad about what he had done—very bad—but he did not "repent." Perhaps you say, "Well then, why did he hang himself?" He hanged himself because he did not repent! If he had repented, he would have gone back to Jesus, thrown himself at the foot of the Cross, believing the very things that Joel knew about God to be true, and like Peter, he would have been forgiven.

Don't just feel bad about what you have done; don't just feel bad about yourself because of what you have done. Rather, turn around. Agree that it was wrong, and then consciously, willfully, turn away from it and back to God, intending to live a new life, and then receive the life-giving grace he longs to give. Perhaps you say, "But I keep doing it!" Alright, then keep on repenting. It is the Devil who says to you, "Well, you might as well just stay where you are, his patience has limits." No, it does not! I don't say this to encourage you to take advantage of that patience. God wants to empower us to be transformed, so at whatever point you are in life, "Repent, and believe!"

June 8

Applause in Worship: Part One

When the Lamb opened the seventh seal, there was silence in heaven for about half an hour. Then I saw the seven angels who stand before God, and seven trumpets were given to them. And another angel came and stood at the altar with a golden censer, and he was given much incense to offer with the prayers of all the saints on the golden altar before the throne, and the smoke of the incense, with the prayers of the saints, rose before God from the hand of the angel. (Revelation 8:1–4 ESV)

Current Christian worship practices are rooted in the rock concert. One of the consequences of that is the increasing prominence of applause in worship. I would like to suggest that applause is never appropriate to Christian worship, particularly the egregious, "Yes, let's give God a hand." Where does this instinct for applause come from? In the rock concert, at the end of a prolonged musical set, there is an extended period of applause. Why? The driving, thundering music has created such an excess of emotion in us that we must release it somehow, and applause punctuated with screams is a way to do that. We also want to express appreciation to the performers for having been able to create such pleasurable emotions in us.

So, in the sanctuary, or more likely, the "auditorium," after the prolonged musical set, we are called upon to do what? To express appreciation to God for his excellent performance in filling us with emotion? Really?! Yahweh, the I AM? Moving *us*?! Someone will say, "No, it is an expression of praise." I beg to differ. In the context, after an extended musical set, applause is an expression of appreciation, and appreciation is not praise.

Think of it this way. You are involved in a terrible auto accident just outside your parents' home. You are unconscious in the front seat, and the car is beginning to burn. Your father runs out of the house in his bathrobe, grabs the red-hot door handle and drags you out and away just before the gas tank explodes. He falls over your prostrate body, shielding you from the blazing chunks of metal that fall on his back, burning him and not you. When you come to and learn what has happened, do you "give him a hand?" Absolutely not! He has not given a thrilling public performance for your titillation. No, you fall on your knees before him, tenderly kissing those burned hands, bathing them with your tears, "lost in wonder, love, and praise." Giving our Savior "a hand," especially as a release for the pent-up emotions a performance has generated, is never appropriate.

June 9

APPLAUSE IN WORSHIP: PART TWO

But the LORD is in his holy temple; let all the earth keep
silence before him. (Habakkuk 2:20 ESV)

Not only is applause an expression of pent-up emotion, it is also a way
of expressing appreciation for some performance that we especially
appreciate, either for its excellence or because we want to encourage
someone who is making a good effort, however flawed, like children who
stand in front of the congregation, with their tiny voices all but hidden
under the sounds of some recorded group. The children may be a special
case, but otherwise, applause for some musical offering in a worship
service is not appropriate. Why not? It is because of the term I just used. It
is an "offering" to God in our presence. It is not a performance.

Suppose in ancient times a rich man brings a beautiful bull into the
Temple for sacrifice. Clearly it is a prize animal, perfect in every way. What
do we the worshippers do? Do we applaud? Do we congratulate the rich
man for going to such obvious expense? Does he graciously bow in our
direction? I hope not!

An offering is given to God, not to us, the fellow-worshippers. To be
sure, an especially precious offering may—indeed, should—move us to
deeper, more heart-felt worship. But it is an offering to God! It is not given
to us. It is not a performance for us. We should not be moved to say, "Wow,
you did a really great job. It moved me. Thank you!" If the offering moved
us to focus on the performer and the performance, then something was
wrong. A whispered "thank you," a reverent "amen," yes; applause, no.

Does all this paint me as a curmudgeon, an old man who wants to
stifle spontaneity in worship? Perhaps. But I would like to think that my
motives are a little better than that. It seems to me that applause is a way
of focusing the worship experience on us, and that way, as the old maps
say, "there be dragons."

June 10
CONTAGION

"If one of you is carrying some meat from a holy sacrifice in his robes and his robe happens to brush against some bread or stew, wine or olive oil, or any other kind of food, will it also become holy?" The priests replied, "No." Then Haggai asked, "If someone becomes ceremonially unclean by touching a dead person and then touches any of these foods, will the food be defiled?" And the priests answered, "Yes." (Haggai 2:12–13)

These two verses used to trouble me. After all, I thought, that's not right. It ought to be the other way around: you ought to be able to "catch" holiness and not "catch" sin. Recently I thought about a very simple analogy with the physical world: if you are healthy and hang around sick people, are you likely to become infected? Yes, you are. Oh, you can take special steps and maybe—maybe, I say—you can avoid getting that sickness, but the odds are, as we have seen with the recent pandemic, you're going to "catch" that disease. Suppose you are sick, and you decide to go hang around healthy people. Will you "catch" health? No. Health is not "catching." Now, maybe, by staying away from other sick people and only associating with healthy people, your sickness will go away, but it won't be because you "caught" their health.

Do you understand the analogy? It is pretty amazing. Sin is "catching." Oh, not in the sense that there is a sin bacterium, but all you have to do is to hang around sinful people and the long odds are that you will soon be just like them. On the other hand, just hanging out with Christlike people does not make you holy—Christlike. Why not? Well, it is like health. Yes, we can promote health, we can do everything possible to create healthy environments, but the truth is: *you have to choose to be healthy.* You don't just catch it. In the same way, to be holy, you have to choose it. You have to find a holy environment; you have to cultivate holy habits; you have to hang out with holy people; but most of all, you have to sell out to the Holy One. You have to liquidate every asset you have to get the Pearl of Great Price. Do you want to be like Jesus or not? It's your choice. It won't just happen.

June 11

WHY SERVE GOD?

"I have always loved you," says the LORD. But you retort, "Really? How have you loved us?" And the LORD replies, "This is how I showed my love for you: I loved your ancestor Jacob." (Malachi 1:2)

The book of Malachi asks the question, "Does it pay to serve God?" When the Judean people came back from exile in Babylon, they were excited. Against all the odds, Yahweh had fulfilled the promises of the prophets to bring them home again. So they eagerly read the prophetic books to see what other promises the prophets had made. What they found was wonderful: riches, glory, power, world-wide dominion! Wonderful! But now a century had passed, and none of those things had happened. Why should they bother to serve God if he doesn't pay off? How long did they need to keep stuffing their silver dollars into the divine slot machine until they hit the jackpot?

Do you see what the problem was? They were not serving God because they loved him but to get something from him. I am afraid that you and I are a lot like the Judeans. We demand that God show us he loves us by what he does for us. Aren't we guilty of thinking and saying, "God, if you really loved me . . . you would not have let my child die . . . you would take away my spouse's cancer . . . you would restore my health . . . you would get me this good job . . .

What if instead we said, "I know you love me; you died for me. So, I am going to let *you* choose the evidence of your love in my life." Doubt says, "I won't believe you love me till you prove it my way." That is just like the hot-blooded boy in the back seat of the car, who does not really love the girl he is propositioning; he just wants to use her. Faith says, "I don't exactly see how, but I believe you do love me, and I am going to trust you to show me in your own way."

Do you see the difference? It's an attitude shift. One approach is trying to use God for ourselves; the other is allowing God to be God, and trusting him with the outcome. Ask God to show you his evidence in his time and in his way. He will!

June 12
THE SLOT MACHINE GOD

Oh, that there were one among you who would shut the doors, that you might not kindle fire on my altar in vain! I have no pleasure in you, says the LORD of hosts, and I will not accept an offering from your hand. (Malachi 1:10 ESV)

You desire and do not have, so you murder. You covet and cannot obtain, so you fight and quarrel. You do not have because you do not ask. You ask and do not receive, because you ask wrongly, to spend it on your passions. (James 4:2–3 ESV)

How do you think like a pagan? Well, it's not very hard. It does not have to involve nasty rituals or dark occult practices. All it requires is for you to think of your God as a blessing machine. Why serve God? Simple! You serve him to get what you want. Why else would you give anything to him?

That is what had happened to the Judeans who returned to Israel from captivity in Babylon. They wanted God to make them rich and powerful. So, they tried to figure out the minimum gifts necessary to get that out of him. God had the appalling nerve to ask for their best. Not a chance! God is not worth that! So, what happened? They didn't get what they wanted. What happened next? They accused God of being unfair! That's pagan thinking.

Let's start over again. Why do we serve God? For love! He does not owe us anything, except judgment. Instead, he has given us life, both now and forever. He has given us himself in Jesus. If he were never to give us one thing more, we would still owe him everything. Does he want to bless us? Oh, yes! But we must let him choose what the blessing will look like. When we do that, knowing we deserve nothing, we suddenly find blessings all around us.

We can't tell him what to do, because that makes us God, and him the servant. Let him be God by giving him your best, gratefully thanking him for all the undeserved things in your life, and stand back! Now you're thinking like a believer.

June 13
STAINED GLASS WINDOWS

If you will not listen, if you will not lay it to heart to give glory to my name, says the LORD of hosts, then I will send the curse on you and I will curse your blessings; indeed, I have already cursed them, because you do not lay it to heart. (Malachi 2:2 NRSV)

But you are a chosen race, a royal priesthood, a holy nation, God's own people, in order that you may proclaim the mighty acts of him who called you out of darkness into his marvelous light. (1 Peter 2:9 NRSV)

The prophet Malachi accused the priests in his day of being more concerned for their own glory than for the glory of God. That is a perennial danger for professional religious people: we want people's praise for ourselves. How good it feels to hear, "You are such a wonderful minister, such a great preacher; your prayers are so touching." It's the most deadly trap in the ministry.

The role of the priest is to be a window between this world and God, so that people can look through him or her to see God clearly. That means the priest has to be completely transparent, clear glass that attracts no attention to itself. Instead, it is too easy to succumb to the temptation to become stained glass windows over which people can exclaim at our beauty. The tragedy is that God, the only hope for humanity, is completely obscured.

Before we become too comfortable in denouncing self-serving preachers, we need to remember something: *we are all called to be priests.* It is a cliché, but it is still true: the only Jesus many people will ever see is the one looking out of your eyes. Who does the world see when they look at us? Do they see the One who can transform human life into something clean and whole? Or do they see someone who covets praise? Are you free of you? Every one of us is called to be a window through whose life people can come to God. We are called to lay aside our glory so his glory can be clearly seen.

When Morning Gilds the Skies

June 14

THE REFINER'S FIRE

But who can endure the day of his coming? Who can stand when he appears? For he will be like a refiner's fire or a launderer's soap. (Malachi 3:2 NIV)

Like many in our own day, the Jews wanted justice. That is, they wanted what they were sure they deserved. They had been very religious: they had deprived themselves of things; they had disciplined their desires; they had given things to God that they could have used for themselves. And for what? Had God made them rich? No! Had he given them power over their enemies? No! Had he made them admired for their righteousness? No! So they asked, "Where is the God of Justice?"

In reply, God promised to show up. He would come to his temple and would fulfill his ancient covenant promises. But wait! What would his appearance mean? Did it mean he would pat them on the head and commend them for being good little boys and girls? It would not. For God's justice—his divine order—to prevail in this world, we must be changed from the inside out. Do you want God to manifest himself in your life? Then be prepared for "a hot time in the old town tonight." He is going to come as fire and lye soap, to burn away the dross and to eat up the dirt. Why does he do this? Is it because he hates us? No, it is because he loves us too much to leave us in that condition where our possibilities are polluted and our gifts are defiled. He longs for us to become all we were meant to be. That means we must be purified and cleansed, but that does not come easily.

It is said that a refiner knows the gold is pure when he can look into the crucible and see his face reflected there. That only happens when the fire is so hot it melts the stony ore. Do they see his face when they look at yours? Or does the dross of your self-serving desires prevent any reflection? Is the cloth of your behavior as bright and clean as if it had just come from the loom, or because you have run away from the burning lye soap, does the observer see only the deep-dyed stains of pride and self-righteousness?

Yes, come, Lord Jesus, and do your burning, searching work in my life, so that the world may see you in the right ordering—the justice—of a life and dare to believe in your ability to rightly order a world.

WHEN HE COMES

But who can endure the day of his coming? Who can stand when he appears? For he will be like a refiner's fire or a launderer's soap. (Malachi 3:2 NIV)

The people of Malachi's day, people who had returned from captivity in Babylon to a country in ruins, longed for their Covenant Lord to come and make everything right, to deliver them from the hard struggles to make a living and from their humiliating servitude to Persian overlords. Malachi assured them that the Lord was coming, but when he came, he was not going to pat them on their heads. He was not going to merely confirm them in their choices and make them rich and comfortable. He had something else in mind for them—he wanted to make them like himself!

There is something that prevented them—and prevents us—from being like him. It is our single-minded refusal to be subject to anybody, to give up control of our lives. To love as God loves, to give as God gives, to be joyful as God is joyful, that submission is exactly what has to happen. The fact is that those qualities and all the others that characterize our Savior are not created by comfort but by pain and loss, not by winning but by losing, not by getting our own way but by dying to our own way. When we are getting what we want, living our lives our way, who needs or wants to change?

Do you want to be "saved"? Oh, he will come and do it, but it will not be in the way we would like. Prepare to be refined and scrubbed, not because he wants to punish us or enjoys hurting us but because he wants the pure gold to shine forth, to see all the stains removed, to see us as we were made to be. There is no other way. If the melting gold or hurting linen could cry out, it would. "Oh, stop it," they would cry. But suppose that is the only way into God's pure, blazing presence. Will we not say, "Yes, go on."

June 16

Divorce: Part One—Devotion

You ask, "Why does he not?" Because the LORD was a witness between
you and the wife of your youth, to whom you have been faithless, though
she is your companion and your wife by covenant. Did not one God make
her? Both flesh and spirit are his. And what does the one God desire? Godly
offspring. So look to yourselves, and do not let anyone be faithless to the
wife of his youth. For I hate divorce, says the LORD, the God of Israel, and
covering one's garment with violence, says the LORD of hosts. So take
heed to yourselves and do not be faithless. (Malachi 2:14–16 NRSV)

God rejects divorce (the sense of "hated" in Hebrew). That is very clear. However, notice what the text does *not* say. It does not say that God rejects *divorcées*. If you have gone through divorce, whether of your own doing or not, God loves you and intends to work good even through that calamity if you will believe him and work with him. Still, that truth does not change the other truth: God utterly rejects the action of divorce. Why is that? This passage gives three reasons. I will deal with the first here, and the other two following.

The first reason God rejects divorce is the covenant nature of marriage. Marriage between a man and a woman was designed to be God's theological seminary in which two persons of differing temperaments and needs bind themselves to each other, and in that bond surrender themselves and their desires to one another, and in that crucible learn the meaning of a self-giving, self-denying love that is profoundly fruitful. That is the kind of relationship Yahweh wants to have with each of us. It is covenant-love in which God binds himself to us, and we bind ourselves to him.

Marriage is an earthly and visible counterpart of that divine covenant. How important is it that we keep faith with one another when the youthful fires of passion have subsided a bit? It is important enough that God is the witness to it! It does not matter whether you had a Best Man and a Maid or Matron of Honor witnessing your "undying love." God was there! To be unfaithful to those covenantal promises, especially out of selfish desire, has eternal implications. To love is not to be overcome by passion but to choose the best for another at whatever cost to ourselves. How can we be faithful to God if we will not be faithful to our wife or husband?

183

June 17

DIVORCE: PART TWO—GODLY CHILDREN

You cry out, "Why doesn't the LORD accept my worship?" I'll tell you why! Because the LORD witnessed the vows you and your wife made when you were young. But you have been unfaithful to her, though she remained your faithful partner, the wife of your marriage vows. Didn't the LORD make you one with your wife? In body and spirit you are his. And what does he want? Godly children from your union. So guard your heart; remain loyal to the wife of your youth. "For I hate divorce!" says the LORD, the God of Israel. "To divorce your wife is to overwhelm her with cruelty," says the LORD of Heaven's Armies. "So guard your heart; do not be unfaithful to your wife." (Malachi 2:14–16)

Why does God reject divorce? There are three reasons given in this passage. We discussed the first in Part One: devotion. It is that marriage is an earthly expression of the covenant between God and us humans. When we violate that earthly covenant for selfish reasons, we make a tragic statement about the covenant faithfulness of God.

The second reason is given in Malachi 2:15. The first part of the Hebrew sentence, which is represented by two sentences in the New Living Translation, is completely obscure. We know every Hebrew word, but no one is certain how they are intended to go together. The translation is different in virtually every version; for example, compare this to the New Living Translation above: "Did not one God make her? Both flesh and spirit are his" (Mal 2:15 NRSV).

The rest of the sentence is crystal clear. What is the purpose of marriage? It is godly children. Study after study shows that if children are to grow up whole, they need to see male and female models in a setting of great security. In that setting they learn law and grace, unconditional love, and so much more. In contrast, studies continue to show that when children are asked who was responsible for their parents' divorce, the large majority will say that they were. In part this is because the children often become the focus of the struggle.

I myself am testimony to this. I know now that my parents' marriage was not particularly happy. They never really understood each other, and neither ever quite measured up to the other's vision of an ideal spouse, but they were devout Christians, so divorce was never even considered. As a result, I grew up fulfilled and secure, pre-conditioned to choose a life-long commitment to Christ and to Karen. I shiver to imagine what would have become of me had my "globe" suddenly shattered, with north and south poles breaking away from each other. Thank God for marriage.

DIVORCE: PART THREE—VIOLENCE

For I hate divorce, says the LORD, the God of Israel, and covering
one's garment with violence, says the LORD of hosts. So take heed
to yourselves and do not be faithless. (Malachi 2:16 NRSV)

In Parts One and Two, I pointed out two reasons that Yahweh rejects divorce as a simple answer to marital discord. They are: the covenant nature of marriage and the importance of covenant faithfulness, and the importance of committed male and female parents to the raising up of godly children. In Part Three, I want to highlight the third reason Malachi gives, one that on the surface may seem a bit strange. He says that God rejects divorce "and covering one's garment with violence." What in the world is that about? It seems especially odd in this day of "no-fault divorce." Surely, two adults who are mature can come to a meeting of the minds about how to part ways without recrimination. Yes, perhaps so, but as a lawyer friend tells me, it is hardly ever the case. Two hurt people are almost incapable of not lashing out at the other in the desperate need to protect themselves.

I want to suggest that any divorce involves violence. What do I mean? I mean that God's mathematics of marriage are a bit strange. When he adds one and one, the answer is one! Something has taken place that can only finally be wrenched apart. Yes, the split may have been perfectly amicable on the surface, but one cannot be broken up without "collateral damage." I am saying that in marriage, whatever the couple may think or plan, there is a melding of two persons into one. I know from experience in our extended family that although the divorce may be for cause and uncontested, and even though it is followed by a happy second marriage, the first spouse cannot merely be forgotten. Thank God, there is grace to cover the situation and to enable one to live in triumph and victory. But "the two shall become one" is a reality that must be faced before a blithe decision to "split up" is taken.

June 19

WHERE IS THE GOD OF JUSTICE?

You have wearied the LORD with your words. "How have we wearied him?" you ask. You have wearied him by saying that all who do evil are good in the LORD's sight, and he is pleased with them. You have wearied him by asking, "Where is the God of justice?" "Look! I am sending my messenger, and he will prepare the way before me. Then the LORD you are seeking will suddenly come to his Temple. The messenger of the covenant, whom you look for so eagerly, is surely coming," says the LORD of Heaven's Armies. (Malachi 2:17–3:1)

The demand for justice by the Judean people returned from exile is a little ironic. At best their worship of God was apathetic. They had been giving him cheap, worthless sacrifices while withholding their tithes, and they wanted justice? I don't think so! That's often true for us, as well. We think God owes us something and are upset when we don't get it. In fact, God owes us nothing except eternal separation from him for our arrogance and self-serving.

Of course, there is injustice in this world. All of us know genuinely good, godly people whose lives seem to consist of one misfortune or outright tragedy after another. We also know people who can best be described as "rotten" whose lives seem to be the proverbial "bed of roses."

How does a good God explain this? Well, as a matter of fact, he doesn't explain it, which he probably can't in terms our tiny intelligence could grasp. What he has done is to come. He has come into this tragic, broken world as Jesus, the "messenger of the covenant." Will evil be punished? Just look at the Cross. There God took into himself all the hatred and cruelty, all the senseless tragedy of the world. We can release all the unjust things that happen to us into him. We don't have to carry them anymore. Will righteousness triumph? Just look at the empty tomb. Satan, the Death Angel, was certain he had won, but in fact, he was defeated. Jesus won! In his resurrection we have the confidence that evil *has* been defeated!

So, we can live in confidence with our unanswered questions. Wrong and injustice will *not* be the last word whatever the case may be at this moment. Where is the God of Justice? On the Cross and at the door of the Tomb. Praise his name!

June 20

A MATTER OF THE HEART

"Ever since the days of your ancestors, you have scorned my decrees and failed to obey them. Now return to me, and I will return to you," says the LORD of Heaven's Armies. "But you ask, 'How can we return when we have never gone away?'" (Malachi 3:7)

I have learned that "blessing" is a condition of the heart. I remember many years ago going to preach at a little country church "up the holler," as they say in Kentucky. When I finished, they said, "You need to go visit Granny Smith." So I said okay and asked where she lived. The response was "on up the holler." So up I went and came to a little cabin where an old lady was sitting in a rocking chair on the front porch. Her face had so many wrinkles it looked like a road map. There was a screen door with no screen in it. I could see that the wallpaper on the wall in the living room was newspapers. They had told me that Granny Smith had buried every member of her family. Yet, as she began to talk to me, it was to tell me how good God had been to her and how blessed she was. She said, "What a wonderful, loving God he is." I realized, maybe for the first time, that blessing is a matter of the heart and not at all what we hold in our hands.

That was reinforced for me years later when I was visiting with a couple from our church in a suburb of Chicago. They were DINKs (Double Income, No Kids). They lived in a half-million dollar home with two expensive cars parked in their driveway. These two stressed people spent the time telling me how hard it was just to make ends meet and how they couldn't be involved in church very much because life is really, really hard. As I looked at their furrowed brows, I suddenly thought of Granny Smith. All the "stuff" in the world is not enough without the face of God.

Are you blessed today? God will bless anyone who gives him a chance. "Return to me and I will return to you, says the LORD" (Mal 3:7). Turn around—stop living for yourself and what you can acquire—and start living to please your Savior. Then, stand back!

June 21

DREAMS

But as he considered these things, behold, an angel of the
Lord appeared to him in a dream. (Matthew 1:20 ESV)

Why did God speak to Joseph, Jesus's earthly father, in dreams? He spoke directly to Mary through Gabriel. He gave a vision to Zechariah. But he spoke to Joseph not once, but four times through dreams. Why? The Bible does not answer the question for us, but it does provide some hints.

First of all, think about that name. Is there another Joseph in the Bible? There certainly is, and he appears in the last chapters of the book of Genesis. He too is associated with dreams. His future was displayed to him in a couple of dreams. Then, Pharaoh's dreams were the means of Joseph's deliverance from prison and his elevation to second place in the kingdom. There is a further comparison between these two men: each of them was instrumental in fulfilling the work of God for his people. Joseph the first was the means whereby God could keep his promised people alive through a terrible drought and famine, stemming from fallen Nature. Joseph the second was the means whereby Jesus could be kept alive and, through him, all of us, in spite of the murderous instincts of powerful people determined to keep their power at all costs—fallen humanity.

Why dreams? First, I suggest that Joseph the second's dreams are intended precisely to call our attention to Joseph the first. This coming of Jesus is not some crazy, new idea on God's part; it is the final unfolding of the saving work that God has been about since the tragedy of Genesis 3, a work that is continually brought about through insignificant people in difficult circumstances who yet choose to live in simple obedience.

Second, dreams are an expression of the thin boundary between the visible world and the invisible one. In the coming of Jesus, that boundary is all but erased. In him the visible man and the invisible God were joined as never before, so it is entirely appropriate that his mother should be delivered from shame because of a dream, that his life be saved because of a dream, that he should return to God's land, the place of his work, because of a dream, and be delivered from one more deadly king because of a dream. God is in the deliverance business.

June 22

GOD IS WITH US

All this took place to fulfill what the Lord had spoken by the prophet: "Behold, the virgin shall conceive and bear a son, and they shall call his name Immanuel" (which means, God with us). (Matthew 1:22–23 ESV)

King Ahaz of Judah was terrified. His two northern neighbors were attacking Judah, intending to get rid of Ahaz and put their own man on the throne. Isaiah showed up and told Ahaz not to worry because Yahweh had everything under control. All Ahaz had to do was to trust God. Then Isaiah told the king that Yahweh would give him a sign that Ahaz could stand on. A little boy named "God with us" would be born.

We're not told what Ahaz's response was, but I think it might have been, "Is that all? I don't need a baby. I need a monster-man!" But there it is. A baby named "God with us." First, what does that name mean? It means that somehow, some way, God—the eternal, transcendent God—wants to share our lives. He wants to come alongside us in joy, sorrow, trouble, and excitement. He does not want to live in the lonely isolation of his holiness, watching us from far off. He wants to walk hand in hand with each of us. You are not alone.

Second, a baby? Yes, here is where Isaiah was probably speaking more than he knew. Is God's being with us just a metaphor, a figure of speech, or is it a fact? It is a fact. God entered into our human experience and took our humanness right from the outset. Like us, he entered the world as a baby. God knows every human experience, from birth to death, intimately, personally. There is nothing you can go through that he has not. You are not alone. He is with you. Walk into today with that confidence.

June 23

GOD IS IN US

Soon the world will no longer see me, but you will see me. Since I live,
you also will live. When I am raised to life again, you will know that I am
in my Father, and you are in me, and I am in you. (John 14:19–20)

This message was kept secret for centuries and generations past, but now it
has been revealed to God's people. For God wanted them to know that the
riches and glory of Christ are for you Gentiles, too. And this is the secret: Christ
lives in you. This gives you assurance of sharing his glory. (Colossians 1:26–27)

God is not only *for* us (see Ps 56:9) and *with* us (see Matt 1:22–23), but,
best of all, he is *in* us. The Apostle Paul says that this is the hidden
truth of the Old Testament. Biblical religion is not first an intellectual
system, although it is such a system. Neither is biblical religion primarily
an ethical program, although it is an ethical program. No, biblical religion
is first and foremost a participation in the divine life. It is to know God
living in you and me, reproducing his character and sharing his heart.
Jesus says this in so many words in the so-called Last Supper Discourse
(see John 13–16). Shockingly, he says that just as he is in the Father, so he
will be in us. We share the life of the Trinity!

Besides the Colossians passage above Paul expresses the thought
in other ways. In Romans 6 he says that we have died with Christ and
have been raised with him. In Galatians 3:37 he says that when we were
baptized we "put on Christ."

All this is to say that living the Christian life is not some desperate
attempt to climb up a greased rope. No, it is to allow God in Christ through
the Holy Spirit loose in us. It is to clean away those things that might
prevent him from doing his work and then to cooperate with him as he
fulfills his will in our lives. It is the difference between a rowboat and a
sailboat. Too many of us are not raising our sails, not taking advantage
of the life that is *in* us. Maybe it is pride: I want to do it myself. Maybe
it is unbelief: I really don't think this is what Christ died to do. Maybe it
is ignorance: I don't know what the Word really says. But very often it is
fear: I don't know what God might want to do with me, and I don't want
to lose control. Whatever the reason, put away the oars and raise the sail.
God is in us!

June 24

GOOD FRUIT

Don't just say to each other, "We're safe, for we are descendants of Abraham."
That means nothing, for I tell you, God can create children of Abraham from
these very stones. Even now the ax of God's judgment is poised, ready to
sever the roots of the trees. Yes, every tree that does not produce good
fruit will be chopped down and thrown into the fire. (Matthew 3:9–10)

The Pharisees and Sadducees, leaders of the Jewish religion and upright
men, had heard of the excitement surrounding the ministry of John
the Baptist and had come to watch and, probably, criticize. John's words
to them are significant. He did not say, "Repent, and get baptized." Rather,
he said, in effect, "Change your lives." What was the fruit of their lives?
Was it religious pride, judgmentalism, a critical spirit, impatience with
those less rigorous than they, superciliousness, harshness, all the while
justifying inwardly sinful thoughts and attitudes?

What might *we* say? Might we say, "I am a member of the Christian
faith, so I am safe"? If so, would John say to us, "No, no, you must repent
of your sins, accept Jesus as your Savior, and be baptized"? I don't think
so. I think he would say, "Change your lives." Now that is not going to
happen without accepting Christ, but accepting Christ is the beginning.
That means the Spirit takes up residence in us.

But then what? Are we daily cultivating the life of the Spirit so that
our life springs up in "good fruit," the fruit of love, joy, peace, patience,
kindness, goodness, faithfulness, gentleness, and self-control (see
Gal 5:22–23)? If that is not the case, are we really any different from the
Pharisees and Sadducees? And is our judgment any different from the one
John spoke in regard to them? The question is not whether you and I were
once planted in good soil with good roots. The question is whether we are
now producing the fruit of a transformed life.

FOLLOW ME: SPECTATOR FOLLOWER

One day as Jesus was walking along the shore of the Sea of Galilee, he saw two brothers—Simon, also called Peter, and Andrew—throwing a net into the water, for they fished for a living. Jesus called out to them, "Come, follow me, and I will show you how to fish for people!" And they left their nets at once and followed him. (Matthew 4:18–20)

A group of young men, undoubtedly having been out all night fishing, were cleaning up their nets, and somebody said, "There's that guy from Nazareth." Jesus walked up to them and said, "Follow me," and the rest of their lives were different. The man standing before him at the tax collector's table looked Matthew in the eye and said, "Follow me," and Matthew's life was never the same again. What does it mean to follow Jesus? There were a lot of people following him around. Why not? He was preaching good news, healing people, and passing out free lunches. It was exciting to see what he was going to do next, including telling off the high and mighty Pharisees. Who wouldn't follow around a fellow like that?

Would I be wrong to suggest that that describes the religion of all too many so-called Christians today? Are we just spectators? As Christianity becomes less of a cultural thing, there are probably fewer of those, but there are still a lot of spectators, people who are in church fairly regularly but who have never given Jesus any hold over them. They are along for the ride. When Jesus said to those men, "Follow me," there was something more going on, wasn't there? What is it to follow Jesus, really *follow* him?

June 26

FOLLOW ME: CONSUMER FOLLOWER

Then James and John, the sons of Zebedee, came over and spoke
to him. "Teacher," they said, "we want you to do us a favor." "What
is your request?" he asked. They replied, "When you sit on your
glorious throne, we want to sit in places of honor next to you, one
on your right and the other on your left." (Mark 10:35–37)

What does it mean to follow Jesus? For some it means merely to be a spectator, to be "along for the ride," merely following him around to see what he does next. I suspect that may describe too many Sunday-morning Christians: we're there, but don't ask us to put anything into the mix. COVID revealed a lot of those.

Many others would say, "No, I am committed to following Jesus, and I am willing to pay a price to follow him. I'll make financial contributions, and I may even give some time to his work." But why are we doing it? Why were the disciples into "the game"? They were not merely spectators. They had left their work and their homes. They were committed—but committed for what? They were, and we, too often, are, consumer followers. They were following Christ because of what he could do for them. The scripture above tells us they were "in the game" for what they could get out of it.

Is that true for you and me? Are we following Christ for what he can do for us? Am I following Christ to get eternal salvation? Are you following him to "get blessed"? To us, as he said to the disciples, Jesus says, "Do you know what the cost may be?" Cost? Who said anything about cost? I am willing to make a little investment of time and money in order to get a good rate of return, but possibly to drink a cup filled with bitter wine? No, I didn't sign on for that.

It has been suggested that this may account for Judas's betrayal. He was the arch consumer-follower, and he realized perhaps better than the others where this crazy man was leading them. He was not going to a throne and taking them with him; he was determined to go to a cross—and maybe taking them there, too. Well, let him go then. That's the disappointing road for the consumer-follower.

June 27

FOLLOW ME: CRUCIFIED FOLLOWER

Then Jesus said to his disciples, "If any of you wants to be
my follower, you must turn from your selfish ways, take
up your cross, and follow me." (Matthew 16:24)

We have talked about spectator followers, those who simply followed
Jesus around to see what he might do next, and consumer followers,
those who followed him for what he could do for them. This is the type of
follower that most of Jesus's disciples seem to have been in the early going.
They thought Jesus could make them important, powerful people or could
give them free food, or deliver them from political and military oppression.
But when Jesus said if you were going to follow him, you would have to
take up a cross, they began to look sideways at each other and drift away.
A cross? People died on crosses! When they gave you a cross to carry you
were on your way to your execution. Follow him to a cross? Why would
anyone do that? Well, you would do that, according to Jesus, because that
is the way to life. The way to life? Yes, because we live in an upside-down
world. The way that we think leads to life actually leads to death. The way
that we think leads up actually leads down. We think protecting yourself
at all costs leads to life, but it actually shuts you in to yourself, and there is
no life in you. It is when you die to your rights, your way, and your power
that you actually are plugged into that abundant life that begins now and
goes on forever.

Is that it? Do we submit to be crucified with Christ just because of the
payoff? No, there is something lying underneath that. That is what took
place on the shore of the Sea of Galilee. The resurrected Jesus smiled at
Peter and asked the key question, "Do you love me?" And Peter knew! Yes!
He had denied with an oath that he even knew Jesus, but that could not
change the fact: he did love him. Then Jesus put it to him: "Follow me"
(John 21:19). It is love for our blessed Savior that says, "Yes, if love took
him to the Cross, I want to go there too. If love for his lambs made him lay
down his life, then I want to go there too." So, which is it for you: spectator
follower, consumer follower, or crucified follower?

June 28

BLESSED ARE THE HUNGRY?

Blessed are you who are hungry now, for you shall be satisfied. Blessed are you who weep now, for you shall laugh. (Luke 6:21 ESV)

Blessed are those who hunger and thirst for righteousness, for they shall be satisfied. (Matthew 5:6 ESV)

Sometimes we are a little troubled by differences in the Gospels. We ask ourselves which one is right and wonder why, if both are inspired, they don't say the same thing. I would like to suggest that both are right, but that they offer differing emphases so that we can get the whole picture. A case in point is the difference between the so-called "Beatitudes" in Matthew (the better-known version) and Luke. In both of them Jesus is turning the normal understanding of blessing right on its head. What is it to be blessed? Well, it's obvious, isn't it? It is to be "fat and happy." It is to have all your earthly wants and desires to be granted. It is to be wealthy and healthy. Jesus, shockingly, says that is not the case at all. Look at Luke 6:20–22. Who is blessed? The hungry, the poor, and the mournful. What? Surely not! So we like Matthew 5:3–10 better because we think it says you can be rich but feel poor (in spirit); be fat, but feel hungry (for righteousness); etc. But this last is not what either text is saying. They go together and are making at least three points.

First, Jesus is saying that having our physical and material wants supplied must *never* be our first goal. Second, he is saying that, in fact, if you choose Jesus, expect *not* to have those wants supplied, a situation that applies in large parts of the world today. Third, he is saying that simply being physically and materially needy earns you no points. Being poor or being hungry, in themselves, are no blessing. But, if you are physically hungry *because* you are famished for Christ's character to be reproduced in you, that is to be blessed, both now and throughout eternity. Do you—do I—want to be blessed? Really?

Twenty years ago George Barna said that virtually all Christians agree that holiness is the goal of Christian life but that *virtually no* Christians are actively seeking holiness. Am I hungering and thirsting for Christ's character to be reproduced in me at the cost of my physical and material wants? Or am I in this Christian business for health and wealth?

June 29

SALT

You are the salt of the earth; but if salt has lost its taste, how can its saltiness be restored? It is no longer good for anything, but is thrown out and trampled under foot. (Matthew 5:13 NRSV)

Researchers continue to tell us that the top ten things we Christians value are no different than the top ten of the world around us. The top value for them and us is material satisfaction. That is, we, like them, think that if we just had enough things, we would be happy. Yet, we Christians continue to complain about the decline of our culture. What are we thinking? I suggest it goes something like this. "It used to be that people worked hard for what they got and gave an honest day's work for an honest day's pay. But look now, people think they can just lay around and somebody should give them what they want on a platter. Or worse yet, can you believe it, they just walk into a store and steal it! What's happening to us?" Well, what is happening to us is that we are getting smarter. If the goal of life is to have the most things, then you should get the most things the easiest way you can. Why work for it if you don't have to?

The problem is that the goal is *not* to get the most things! The Christian salt has lost its taste, and the culture around us is decaying as a result. We need to be showing the world that the goal is to be Christlike. It is to be living a life of self-denying love, of integrity for the sake of others, of undeserved kindness, of obedience to God's commands whether they pay off materially or not. We give an honest day's work to our employers not because that is the best way to get the most things but because integrity is God's way. Why obey the laws that our community has adopted? Not because the cops force us to, but because responsible and accountable behavior is God's way. Unless we let the Holy Spirit get a grip on us and change the flavor of our lives, we should not be in the least surprised to see the culture around us sliding deeper into decay. Really, what are your values? The world's or the Spirit's?

When Morning Gilds the Skies

June 30

HEAVEN IS NOT A DEMOCRACY

Don't misunderstand why I have come. I did not come to
abolish the law of Moses or the writings of the prophets. No,
I came to accomplish their purpose. (Matthew 5:17)

The story is told that in one of the World War II meetings between Franklin Roosevelt and Winston Churchill, Roosevelt was going on at length about how democracy is the finest form of government. Finally Churchill interjected, "Remember, Mr. President, the government of heaven is a monarchy." He was right, of course; the government of Heaven is not a democracy. That is very hard for us humans, especially us Americans, to accept. We don't want to believe that there is a divine Sovereign whose will is absolute, whose laws are beyond repeal. In our heart of hearts, we think heaven ought to be like this marvelous land of ours where each of us has a say in the shaping of our laws, where any law can be changed if a majority of us decide to do it. We do not want to believe that there is any power outside of ourselves that can decree how we must behave, whether we like it or not.

Like it or not, this universe is not a democracy. We do not make the laws of heaven. We do not decide today that adultery is alright, although it wasn't yesterday. We do not decide today that lying is alright, although it wasn't yesterday. Those decisions are not our prerogative. They have already been made for us. What is up to us, as Jesus makes clear, is whether we let heaven's laws accomplish their purpose or not. And what is that purpose? It is the creation of the character of the King in us. That is why Jesus came: not only so that we will be motivated to obedience out of gratitude for the King's death on our behalf but also so that the King himself may make each of us his royal residence and in doing so may reproduce his character in us as he empowers us to do his will.

July 1

NOT TO ABOLISH BUT TO ACCOMPLISH

Don't misunderstand why I have come. I did not come to abolish
the law of Moses or the writings of the prophets. No, I came to
accomplish their purpose. I tell you the truth, until heaven and
earth disappear, not even the smallest detail of God's law will
disappear until its purpose is achieved. (Matthew 5:17–18)

It is unfortunate that a great deal of Protestant theology is built upon
playing "law" and "grace" off against another. To be sure, the Pharisaic
idea that we can make ourselves good enough for God by doubling up on
every detail of the law is the way to neurosis, self-deception, and bondage.
Both Jesus and Paul have nothing but scorn for that idea, and when Luther
found it rampant in the Church, he was right to attack it. But that is not
what the Old Testament teaches.

First, as Paul says (see Rom 7:12), the law is "holy, right, and good."
One way we can help ourselves to think that way is to remember that in
Hebrew it is called "the *Torah*" that is, "the instructions." It is not a bunch
of arbitrary demands imposed by some heavenly tyrant but the instruction
manual for the human machine graciously given by the heavenly designer.
If we learn to live in the ways it instructs, we will really be achieving his
plan for us. These heavenly instructions were intended to teach us three
things: God's character, the character he wants us to share with us, and the
deadly problem that prevents us from achieving that character—self-will.
The combination of those three drive us straight to Jesus.

We love what we see of God's character, and we recognize that living
like him is the most sensible thing in the world, but we find a rock within
us saying, "But I will have my way." What to do? The blessed Cross! But
not so that Jesus can relieve us of the need to share God's character. That
would be to abolish the law and the writings. No, our desire to be like God
coupled with our inability to be like him drive us to Jesus so that his blood
can cleanse us from our sins and his Spirit can take up residence in us and
enable us to live according to the instructions! He has come "to accomplish
their purpose"!

When Morning Gilds the Skies

July 2

RECIPE FOR A SELF-CENTERED ANEMIC CHURCH

Don't misunderstand why I have come. I did not come to abolish the law of
Moses or the writings of the prophets. No, I came to accomplish their purpose.
I tell you the truth, until heaven and earth disappear, not even the smallest
detail of God's law will disappear until its purpose is achieved. So if you ignore
the least commandment and teach others to do the same, you will be called
the least in the Kingdom of Heaven. But anyone who obeys God's laws and
teaches them will be called great in the Kingdom of Heaven. (Matthew 5:17–19)

Recently a well-known evangelical preacher has stated that we need to
"unhitch" the New Testament from the Old Testament. We know how
the early church fathers would have responded to that statement: they
would have branded this man as a heretic and driven him out of the church!
We know that because that is the way they responded to the popular and
well-loved preacher Marcion, who made the same proposal in the first half
of the second century AD. Why did they react so strongly? Because they
understood correctly that the two testaments are complementary. Each
one is incomplete without the other. Who is "the God and Father of our
LORD Jesus Christ?" He is the transcendent Creator of the universe, the
all-powerful, all-wise, and all-loving King who has established the terms
of all existence. Why was it necessary for Jesus to become incarnate, die,
and rise again? Because humans, as a result of their first parents' refusal
to adhere to those terms of existence, have become estranged from their
Father and in a variety of ways have become death-dealing. Without
the Old Testament we do not know what are the questions that the New
Testament is answering. As a result, we misinterpret the answers.

A church that does not know the Old Testament—that is much of
the North American evangelical church—is likely to see God as a nice old
fellow who exists to answer our prayers, to take care of us, to make it so
we don't have to be accountable for our behavior, and to get us to heaven.
In short, our religion is about manipulating divine power in order to gain
our own ends. Friends, that is rank paganism, the worldview that the Old
Testament is at great pains to dismantle. The Old Testament idea that
God, the Holy One, has graciously satisfied his own ineradicable justice in
order to make us like himself, a process both difficult and painful, is deeply
distasteful to far too many evangelicals. If we are to correct the incipient
paganism of modern, evangelical Christianity, we do not need to "unhitch"
from the Old Testament, we need to *teach* it.

July 3

RUTHLESS WITH SIN

Then Elijah commanded, "Seize all the prophets of Baal. Don't let a single one of them escape!" So the people seized them all, and Elijah took them down to the Kishon Valley and killed them there. (1 Kings 18:40)

So if your eye—even your good eye—causes you to lust, gouge it out and throw it way. It is better for you to lose one part of your body than for your whole body to be thrown into hell. And if your hand—even your stronger hand—causes you to sin, cut it off and throw it away. It is better for you to lose one part of your body than for your whole body to be thrown into hell. (Matthew 5:29–30)

All of us are rightly troubled by the reports of mass killing in the Old Testament such as Elijah engaged in, even more with the divinely-commanded killing of the Canaanites (see Deut 20:17). There are several explanations for this behavior that can be given, but I want to focus on one here: this activity is an expression of God's passionate love for the world. Love!? Yes, love. The world has created a religion of convenience in which this world is all there is and its forces can be manipulated to provide us with that most elusive of all benefits, security. Of course, this is dead wrong (and I use "dead" advisedly). This world is not God, and manipulation of it can never make us secure. In particular, it can never deliver us from the power of evil and the death that results from it.

So what was God, the great I AM, to do? He chose a particular people to whom he could reveal himself and through whom he could provide a means of deliverance for all the world. How important was the survival of that people and their revealed faith? It was of world-shaking importance! If they were sucked down into that other way by the deliciously deceptive religions around them, the *whole world* was lost. So, as much as possible, wherever that other way of thinking was absolutely and completely ingrained in people, as in the prophets of Baal, they and the temptation they represented had to be removed—for the rest of the world's sake!

Does that mean that we followers of Christ are justified in slaughtering his enemies today? Of course not! We are not Israel. The truth has been firmly established in the Scriptures, and Christ has come. Israel and its revealed faith did survive; the hope of the world is secure.

Do these accounts then have no meaning for us? Jesus makes it perfectly clear that they are important for us. We are Israel in this sense: that it is a question whether the faith will survive in each of us. Just as Israel could not tolerate one committed Canaanite, or one committed

Baal prophet in its midst, so you and I cannot tolerate one favorite sin in our lives. We cannot make a place for it; we cannot excuse it; we cannot explain it away. How serious is this issue? Look at what Jesus says! Note that he is speaking in Semitic hyperbole. He does not mean for us to physically mutilate ourselves (in spite of what some medieval monks and nuns did to themselves). He is trying to make a point: sin cannot have a place—any place—in a Christian's life. This is what John means in his first letter when he says a Christian cannot sin (see 1 John 3:9). He is not talking about ability, unfortunately, but about nature. It is like saying a good mother could not abuse her child. Could she? Sadly, yes, but not if she is to continue to be a good mother.

So, Christian, wherever you find the "Canaanite" of wrong desire, wrong attitude, wrong ambition, etc., lurking in your life, then, by the power of the Holy Spirit, kill it, tear it out, exterminate it! Kill our enemies? No, love them. But love our sins? No, slaughter them!

July 4

NOT ON THE POWER OF GOVERNMENT

Let every person be subject to the governing authorities; for
there is no authority except from God, and those authorities that
exist have been instituted by God. (Romans 13:1 NRSV)

> "We have staked the whole future of American civilization not on
> the power of government, far from it. We have staked the future of
> all of our political institutions upon the capacity of each and all of us
> to govern ourselves according to the ten commandments of God."
> —James Madison, fourth U.S. president, primary author of the
> U.S. constitution

If a people prove themselves incapable of governing themselves from
within, which the U.S. constitution assumes to be possible, the only
alternative to chaos is state coercion. What the framers of the constitution
over-optimistically believed was that the unaided human spirit was
capable of governing itself according to biblical principles. It is not. It is
only when persons have come into a relationship with the God of the Bible
through Jesus Christ and has submitted their wills to God's will that such
a thing becomes possible through the power of the Holy Spirit.

As America more and more brazenly rejects Yahweh, along with his
instructions and resources, state coercion is becoming more and more
necessary. The problem with state coercion is that there are not enough
enforcement officers in the world to force a people to do what they don't
want to or to keep them from doing what they do want to. The Greeks
proved that philosophy cannot defeat rampant human desire; the Romans
proved that meticulous legislation cannot do it; the United States is
proving that universal education cannot do it. Tragically, democracy
cannot survive in the face of rampant desire. Thus, it is either social chaos
or state-sponsored tyranny. In the history of the world, we have oscillated
from one to the other.

What shall we believers do? Psalms 1 and 2 give us the answer. The
two psalms are framed by the Hebrew word *'ashrê*. Psalm 1 begins with
it and Psalm 2 ends with it. There is no exact English equivalent for it. It
can be translated "happy" or "blessed." It describes a person who is in a
good situation. That person refuses the counsel of the wicked and instead
delights to be guided by God's instructions (*torah*). They do not rebel
against him and his Messiah, but instead take refuge in him. There is our
chart and compass, and there is our safe harbor in the storms that are
coming. Choose happiness!

July 5

DEMOCRACY AND GOD

Let the whole world fear the LORD, and let everyone stand in awe of him. For when he spoke, the world began! It appeared at his command. The LORD frustrates the plans of the nations and thwarts all their schemes. But the LORD's plans stand firm forever; his intentions can never be shaken. What joy for the nation whose God is the LORD, whose people he has chosen as his inheritance. (Psalm 33:8–12)

I have been reading Ron Chernow's massive, Pulitzer Prize-winning biography of George Washington. I was struck by a couple of statements that Chernow makes almost as asides. Talking about Washington's very methodical approach to each day, Chernow says that he always arose early and read or did correspondence in dressing gown and slippers, and then after his private prayers, he got dressed. The second point that struck me is regarding Sunday evenings. He says Washington read to his family—often sermons. In other words, Washington was not a Christian in some formal, or nominal, sense. Rather, it was a living reality for him, a natural part of his daily life. Christian faith was simply part of his makeup, shaping his life.

This is an important point as we consider the life of our nation. However varied the religious lives of our founders may have been, there was still, even in a Jefferson, who was probably the most humanistic of them all, the conviction that there is a Creator who has established the norms of human life and that constructing one's life in accordance with those norms is the way to satisfaction and fulfillment. This is what John Adams was talking about when he said, "Our Constitution was made only for a moral and religious people. It is wholly inadequate for any other." He means that no structure of laws can make a people law-abiding and compassionate. There must be a compulsion from within, a compulsion rising from a sincere desire to serve and please our Creator, as revealed in the Bible. It is like a compass, keeping us on course.

Today, fewer and fewer of us Americans have such a compass. As a result, we have become more and more focused on self-service and self-aggrandizement, things our Constitution is completely helpless to correct. So, the challenge for those of us who believe in God and his Word is first to cultivate that inner relationship with God that will keep our own compass pointing "true north," making us the best of citizens. Let us be part of the solution, not part of the problem. Then, let us manifest that joy that comes from knowing that our God is Yahweh ("the LORD"), and let that joy be contagious.

THE BIBLE STORYLINE

But you are to be perfect, even as your Father in
heaven is perfect. (Matthew 5:48)

These words of Jesus have terrified Christians for 2,000 years. What?!
Be as perfect as God? An obvious impossibility! People have tried to
explain it away in a variety of ways, but there it is, and it won't go away.
I want to suggest another way to look at it. In the context of Matthew 5,
what Jesus is saying is that we must love as God loves, with a love that is
perfect (i.e., complete, whole) like his love is. An imperfect or incomplete
love is one that only starts if someone else loves us first; an imperfect love
will only continue if someone returns it. God's love is complete in itself,
needing no one else's to either start it or keep it going. That's what you and
I can have: a love that is a duplicate of God's.

I have come to believe that this is an expression of the Bible's
"storyline." *God wants us to be in a relationship with him that changes
our character.* That's what it meant to be an Israelite, and that's what it
means to be a Christian. The good news is that what the Israelite could not
do, we can! We *can* replicate the character of God through Jesus.

So, if you are not in a living relationship with Jesus that is changing
your character into the likeness of his character, I dare to say that you
are not a Christian. Ouch! Isn't being a Christian just to have your email
address legally changed from your.name@hell to your.name@heaven?
Well, no. You see, what Jesus is saying on the Mount of the Beatitudes is
what Moses said on Mount Sinai: you must—*you may!*—have the same
utterly glorious (i.e., holy, perfect) character that the One who loves you
(i.e., your Deliverer, your Father) has.

Why did he get the Israelites out of Egypt? So they could "walk" with
him, "walking" like he walks. Why did Jesus deliver you from the curse of
sin? So you could walk with him, walking like he walks. Are you, am I, a
Christian? What about it?

July 7

THY KINGDOM COME ON EARTH...

Our Father who is in heaven, let your name be made holy; may
your kingdom come, [that is], may your will be done on earth just
as it is in heaven . . . ." (Matthew 6:9b–10 author's translation)

When we pray The Lord's Prayer, the traditional language is "Thy
kingdom come, Thy will be done, in earth as it is in heaven." But we
tend to take a big breath between "done" and "in," and I think that misses
the point Jesus is making. It suggests that in a broad and general way we
would like to see God's will being done, and that it would be nice if it could
be done on earth—but, of course that is only a fond wish having nothing to
do with the real gospel. Wrong! Why do I say that?

Remember the Gospel message that Jesus preached (Matt 4:17) and
that he directed his disciples to preach (Luke 10:9): "Repent, for the
kingdom of God is at hand." What was he talking about? What is the
kingdom of God? It is a place where God, the Sovereign, has his way in
everything. Is that the Good News, the Gospel? Surely not! Surely the
Good News is that I don't have to worry about sinning anymore. Jesus
has died for my sins and they're all covered. To be sure, the prayer later
says, "forgive us our trespasses/debts," but then it makes that forgiveness
totally conditional on whether we forgive others—acting like God! It is not
a blanket pass to heaven.

So what are we praying when we pray The Lord's Prayer? The Greek
says, "Your kingdom come, your will be done, as in heaven so also on
earth." Why did Jesus come? He came so that God's will might be as
instantly, thoroughly, and completely done on earth as it is in heaven.
He did not come so that you and I could do our will and not have to
suffer the consequences, which is what all too much Christian preaching
suggests today.

Jesus came to make it possible through his death on the Cross and
the resulting gift of the Spirit for you and me to be able to do God's
will as thoroughly, completely, and delightedly as any angel in heaven.
Christianity will *never* transform the earth until you and I get into the
kingdom, not in heaven, but here on earth—and we can! Day after day, we
can do God's will. We can please our Father and, as his children, look just
like him. Good News!

July 8

THE GOLDEN RULE

So if you sinful people know how to give good gifts to your children, how much more will your heavenly Father give good gifts to those who ask him. Do to others whatever you would like them to do to you. This is the essence of all that is taught in the law and the prophets. (Matthew 7:11–12)

Some time ago, when I was preparing a study of Matthew 5–7, often known as "The Sermon on the Mount," I was a little nonplussed when I came to the second and third sentences in the passage above. "Really?" I thought. Jesus had clearly implied in Matthew 5:17–19 that what was going to follow was the correct interpretation of the Old Testament, the Law and the Prophets. Now at the end of that lengthy discourse, could everything he had said in the ensuing two and a half chapters be subsumed under "Do to others whatever you would like them to do to you?"

As I have thought about this question in succeeding months and years, I have come to the conclusion that the answer is, yes. What is the human problem? It is self-centeredness. That's what happened to us in the Garden. We were made to be God-centered, and thus able to be other-centered, but in that tragic hour, we turned away from God, and the result was a turning inward to ourselves. Why is that? Well, if God is truly the center of your life, you know your needs are supplied. If he is not the center, then who supplies your needs? You! You can't trust other people to do it, that's for sure. If God is your center, you can step aside for someone else to move ahead, as you hope they might do for you in a similar situation. Ah, but suppose they don't, what then? God will take care of you. If God is your center, you can give yourself away. That's what the Old Testament is all about!

We see the destruction all around us today of what was once the American spirit of generosity. What is happening is that the momentum of the great awakenings of the past in which people trusted their lives to Christ and could therefore afford to "Do unto others . . ." is fast running down. What to do? Say it again, "Lord Jesus, *you* are the supplier of my needs—not me and not them—and in the riches of your grace I am going to be a giver, not a taker." My Dad said it this way, "You gotta think about the other fella."

July 9

LORD, LORD

"Not everyone who calls me, Lord! Lord!" will enter the
kingdom of heaven. Only those who actually do the will of
my Father in heaven will enter. (Matthew 7:21)

The Bible makes it very clear elsewhere that those who call on the name
of the Lord will be saved (see Rom 10:13, quoting Joel 3:23). So what
is going on here? Is this passage saying that is not true? Well, it helps,
as it does in most cases of Bible interpretation, if we pay attention to the
context. Here the context is the Sermon on the Mount, in which Jesus is
explaining what the Sinai covenant is all about; that is, changing us on
the inside. It is not about not committing adultery but about not viewing
women as objects of desire. It is not about not murdering people but about
valuing (i.e., loving) them for themselves. Throughout the Sermon, Jesus
is saying that the purpose of God in giving the *Torah* was to show us what
kind of attitudes should shape the behavior of our lives. The tragedy of
Pharisaism is that it suggests that if we are really careful about behavior,
attitudes don't really matter.

Jesus is saying that the focus of our lives must be on cultivating
Yahweh's kingdom in our lives (i.e., doing his will, becoming transformed
from the inside out). Clearly, to him, merely doing miracles in his name
without manifesting his character is no different from a Pharisee tithing
the spices in his cupboard while contemplating foreclosing on a widow. If
my relationship to the Lord is about gaining power for external signs, as
Matthew 7:22–23 suggest, that is clear evidence that I don't know him and
have no right to call him by the name of the Old Testament God.

THY WILL BE DONE: PART ONE

Not everyone who says to me, "Lord, Lord," will enter the kingdom of
heaven, but the one who does the will of my Father who is in heaven.
On that day many will say to me, "Lord, Lord, did we not prophesy in
your name, and cast out demons in your name, and do many mighty
works in your name?" And then will I declare to them, "I never knew you;
depart from me, you workers of lawlessness." (Matthew 7:21–23 ESV)

For me, this is one of the most frightening passages in all of Scripture.
Jesus says, "There are people to whom I'm going to say in the last day,
depart from me; I never knew you." And they'll say, "But Lord, we did all
kinds of miracles in your name." And he'll say, "It's not those who call me
Lord, Lord, but those who do my will who are my children."

Sometimes we can have wonderful feelings about God, we can do
marvelous things, and yet he says, "But you never came to the point where
doing my will was absolutely the most important thing in your life." We
enjoyed doing the religious things we liked, but maybe those were not
what he wanted. The great crisis point of every human heart is right here.
Who is the King? Who calls the shots in my life? Is it me or is it God?
The cross is all about Somebody who would finally, for all eternity, say,
"Not my will but Thine be done" (Luke 22:42). That's the crisis point for
you and for me. All the religious talk, all the religious emotion, is short-
circuited if in the end I say, "Thanks a lot, Jesus, for dying for me so I can
go do what I want to do."

The question for you and me has to be, has there ever come a point in
my life where I have been willing to say, "I will let you be King in everything.
I'll let you be King in my social life, in my religious life, in my work, in my
home. You're the King."

July 11

THY WILL BE DONE: PART TWO

I take joy in doing your will, my God, for your instructions
are written on my heart. (Psalm 40:8)

Does God have a particular will for your life and mine? Does God really
have a vocation for you? Has he already chosen the right person
for you to marry? Does he have a plan for your behavior today? Is there
something that he wants you to do today? Without question, the answer
is, absolutely! God cares what you and I do today. He cares what you and I
do with our lives. He cares about who we marry. God has ultimate goals for
each of us, and in any given situation, he has a preference for what you do.

It's easy for believers to get hung up here. In many cases, perhaps
most, we are not exactly sure what he wants. He hasn't sent us any online
messages, so we get paralyzed, wavering back and forth. Well, if he wants
us to do a particular thing, why *doesn't* he send us a message? I think the
answer to that question is that he may not be so concerned about precisely
what we do as he is about what we are becoming as we learn to walk in
faith. We pray, we listen to the Word, we consult with trusted friends, we
look at the circumstances, we listen to the inner voice, and we say, "Lord,
as best I know this is what you want me to do. So I am going to step out
in faith. If this is not the way, then you must stop me!" If he doesn't stop
us, then the direction we are taking is one that is not inconsistent with his
plans and purposes. If it was not precisely what he might have liked, he is
still able, in his infinite creativity, to bring the greatest good out of it. The
most important thing is not that I do this or do that—the most important
thing is what I've *become* as I struggle to learn and to know and to do the
will of God.

July 12

GOOD, PLEASING AND PERFECT

Don't copy the behavior and customs of this world, but let God transform you into a new person by changing the way you think. Then you will learn to know God's will for you, which is good and pleasing and perfect. (Romans 12:2)

Looking at myself and then others with whom I have counseled over the years, it seems to me that we have too often focused on the *particular* will of God at the expense of his *general* will. I remember in particular one young man who quite literally agonized for several weeks whether God wanted him to propose marriage to a lovely young woman whom the fellow had been dating for several months and who was clearly quite ready to be proposed to. In the end he did propose and they have now been happily married for a number of years.

Honestly, I do not think that kind of agonizing is what Paul had in mind with the statement quoted above. We do not have to struggle over knowing God's will. His will is quite clear on about 99 percent of the issues of life. Does he want you to steal? No. Does he want you to honor your parents? Yes. Does he want you to control your physical desires? Yes. Does he want you to meet in regular fellowship with other believers? Yes. Does he want you to burst forth in rage? No. And so forth.

The crisis point lies in the fact that "the behavior and customs of this world" are largely contrary to the will of God, and it takes a transformation of our thinking to bring us to the place where we want to do God's will. Is that happening in your life? Or is "the world" subtly conditioning you to think as it does?

July 13

PERFECT REPAIR

Now the God of peace, that brought again from the dead our Lord
Jesus, that great shepherd of the sheep, through the blood of the
everlasting covenant, make you perfect in every good work to do his
will, working in you that which is wellpleasing in his sight, through Jesus
Christ; to whom be glory for ever and ever. (Hebrews 13:20–21 KJV)

May he equip you with all you need for doing his will. May he produce in you,
through the power of Jesus Christ, every good thing that is pleasing to him.
All glory to him forever and ever! Amen. (Hebrews 13:21 NLT, NIV, and ESV)

...make you complete in everything good so that you may do his will,
working among us that which is pleasing in his sight, through Jesus Christ,
to whom be the glory forever and ever. Amen. (Hebrews 13:21 NRSV)

Imagine that you and your family are about to go on an extended vacation
by car. What do you do? You take the car to an auto repair shop and tell
the mechanic, whom you trust, to check it out. Perhaps he tells you that
you need new tires, an engine tune-up, and a new fan belt. When the work
is finished and you have paid him a sizeable amount of money, you ask,
"It's okay now?" He replies, "It's in perfect working order!"

That is what the verb in this passage ("make you perfect," "equip you,"
"make you complete") is talking about. This is what James and John were
doing to their nets as reported in Mark 1:19. So what is the writer to the
Hebrews asking for in his prayer for his readers? He is asking God to put
us in a state of complete repair, perfect working order, so that we can do
those good things that God wills for us. He can do that through the power
that raised Jesus from the dead and on the basis of the covenant he sealed
with us in his blood.

I don't know about you, but I get goosebumps when I think of all that.
How far is that from "Christians aren't perfect, they're just forgiven"? Are
we perfect performers? No! Flawless skywire walkers? No! We are persons
who are all we can be, in a state of complete repair (given less-than-perfect
genes and less-than-perfect environments) for the service of God. Yes! I
believe God to do that for me. I hope you do, too.

SPIRITUAL FORMATION

Then Jesus said to his disciples, "If any of you wants to
be my follower, you must give up your own way, take up
your cross, and follow me. (Matthew 16:24)

Jesus answered, "If I glorify myself, my glory is nothing. It is my Father
who glorifies me, of whom you say, 'He is our God.'" (John 8:54 ESV)

I've made a pact with myself. I'm never, ever, going to use the term *spiritual formation* again. It is an increasingly pagan idea. I'm not interested in "spirituality"; I'm interested in Christianity! A lot of people are intrigued with the idea of becoming more "spiritual," but what that involves is acquisition. They want to enhance the "spiritual" side of themselves in order to obtain greater "inner calm" or some such. Others imagine that they can gain spiritual power so they can use that power to find greater "integration" of their fragmented lives. However, the use of spirit power to achieve my purposes is nothing other than what pagan idolatry has sought since the beginning of time.

What we must have is discipleship! I don't deny that there are programs of "spiritual formation" that are truly attempting to make disciples. In that case, why not call them what they are: discipleship training? I suspect the answer is that the term "discipleship" is a bit off-putting—and well it should be! To become a disciple, especially a disciple of Jesus, is to give up all your aims, goals, and purposes, subordinating them all to his aims, goals, and purposes. It involves a cross, and a cross is nothing other than death—to my rights, my image, my opinions, my reputation. It is not to become more "spiritual;" it is to become nothing in ourselves and everything in him, as Jesus said of himself.

July 15

TO FIND YOURSELF

Then Jesus said to his disciples, "If any of you wants to
be my follower, you must give up your own way, take up
your cross, and follow me." (Matthew 16:24)

One of the great crises in our contemporary culture is the struggle to
"find oneself." This is, of course, the tragic result of our abandonment
of the biblical doctrine of creation. In that context, it is the Creator who
defines our identity and who gives us the grace to make of that identity all
that it might possibly become. Now, thinking that all things are the result
of mindless chance, we must somehow, by force of will, choose what will
be written on the blank pages of our life.

When we bring in the biblical thought that we must surrender our
self to our Creator, the contemporary person runs away screaming. Think
of this illustration: You and I are clear glasses. Perhaps you are a crystal
goblet and I am a very ordinary juice glass. We are both filled with a clear
gas that is heavier than air and is corrosive to glass. If that gas, call it self-
centeredness, remains in you and me, it will one day eat its way through
us and destroy us. Because it is clear and we are clear, it is very difficult
to discern our actual shape from any distance. (Have you noticed how
boringly similar self-centered people are?)

Let us suppose that for some reason we cannot be picked up and
turned over so that the gas could flow out and away. Anyway, we each
think that gas is me and that without it I would be nothing. Yet it is steadily
destroying us. What is to be done? Suppose a golden elixir could be poured
into us. As the liquid slowly rises, the corrosive gas is displaced. Then,
wonder of wonders, as that golden fluid fills us, conforming to our shape,
our unique shape can be seen for all that it truly is, you as a goblet, me as a
juice glass, but in each case who we are really meant to be.

You see what I am saying: when the golden Spirit of Jesus fills us,
erasing our self-centeredness, it is then that our true, God-given self can
be seen. He does not wish to erase our self but rather to remove that self-
centeredness that is killing us, making the self he created fully visible for
the first time.

VALUES

The master was full of praise. "Well done, my good and faithful servant.
You have been faithful in handling this small amount, so now I will give you
many more responsibilities. Let's celebrate together!" (Matthew 25:21)

One hears a good deal about values these days, but the emphasis is quite regularly on "my values" or "your values" or "their values." That is, each of us chooses what is important to us, and whatever each of us chooses is just as significant and "valuable" as what anyone else might choose. That is, there are no "values" that transcend any of our own perceptions, wills, or desires.

That is, of course, what has happened in western culture since the 1960s. But the Bible tells us that there is a God who has created us on purpose to share his holy character. He made us so that we would be like him, that is, in his image. If that is true, what ought the values of every person on earth be? His! You say, "Is it that simple?" Yes, it is. What should be important for a person who recognizes that there is a God, who made us on purpose, and who holds us accountable for the resources he has given us? I believe the Bible gives us four "values":

1. *Pleasing God*—"so that you may lead lives worthy of the Lord, fully pleasing to him, as you bear fruit in every good work and as you grow in the knowledge of God." (Col 1:10 NRSV)
2. *Benefitting others*—"See that no one pays back evil for evil, but always try to do good to each other and to all people." (1 Thess 5:15)
3. *Making disciples of Jesus*—"Therefore go and make disciples of all nations, baptizing them in the name of the Father and of the Son and of the Holy Spirit, and teaching them to obey everything I have commanded you." (Matt 28:19–20a NIV)
4. *Raising up godly children*—"Has not the one God made you? You belong to him in body and spirit. And what does the one God seek? Godly offspring." (Mal 2:15a NIV)

If a person comes to the end of their life and has succeeded in doing these, the Bible says we will merit: "Well done, good and faithful servant." Are your values your Creator's values? They should be.

July 17
I COULD LOVE A GOD LIKE THAT

Then the righteous will answer him, "Lord, when did we see you hungry and feed you, or thirsty and give you something to drink? When did we see you a stranger and invite you in, or needing clothes and clothe you? When did we see you sick or in prison and go to visit you?" The King will reply, "Truly I tell you, whatever you did for one of the least of these brothers and sisters of mine, you did for me." (Matthew 25:37–40 NIV)

Bill (not his name) was a seminary student. His theology professor was world-famous, but the theology he taught was different from what Bill had been taught and believed. So Bill and the professor had several confrontations. In the middle of Bill's program, he and his wife Denise received terrible news. Their eight-year old son, Dennis, had leukemia and the doctors could not do anything for him. Some of their church friends, fumbling to say something comforting, said, "Maybe God needs another voice in the angel choir." Bill thought, "I could hate a God like that."

One afternoon Bill and Denise's doorbell rang. When Bill opened the door, he was shocked to see his theology professor. He said, "I wondered if I could play with Dennis for awhile." For a half hour the great man sat on the floor with Dennis and they played together with his toys. Then he got up and, with a smile for Dennis and one for Bill and Denise, he quietly left.

Some months later Dennis died in the hospital at four o'clock in the morning. After Bill and Denise had done what had to be done they went home. At 7:30 that morning they were sitting at the breakfast table staring at nothing. There was a knock at the back door. It was the theology professor. He said, "I wondered if I could come in and cry with you." They asked him in, and they all began to cry. After a bit the professor said, "I don't know why this has happened, but I know this: God is crying with us." Bill thought, "I could love a God like that." This is not to say that good behavior justifies poor theology. But it is to say that our grasp of the gospel must go beyond our grasp of its ideas.

July 18

IT IS FINISHED

And Jesus cried out again with a loud voice and
yielded up his spirit. (Matthew 27:50 ESV)

When Jesus had received the sour wine, he said, "It is finished," and
he bowed his head and gave up his spirit. (John 19:30 ESV)

It had happened again: Bobby Lee had defeated the Union Army of the Potomac. The men knew what would happen next: they would retreat back across the Rappahannock to their camps there, lick their wounds, renew their arms, and try again in six months or a year. But no. A group of horsemen flying the flag of the General of the Army, Ulysses S. Grant, came thundering down the road, and when they came to the fork where one way led north and the other south, without slowing they turned south. As Bruce Catton, the historian, tells it, the leading troops broke into cheers. They were going to keep going. Catton says that in that moment the outcome of the war was determined. Oh, there would yet be terrible fights and rivers of blood, but in that decision of Grant's, the victory of the Union was made inevitable. Their superiority in manpower and weaponry would not be allowed to languish.

So it was on that rocky Judean hill on a Friday afternoon 2,000 years ago. When that bleeding victim, who was not a victim at all, cried out, "It is finished," the final salvation of earth and its human race was determined. He was not saying that his life was finished, or that his earthly ministry was finished. He was saying that all that was necessary to defeat evil forever was finished! He had met death head on, and in his death, Death was forever destroyed. Is the battle over? No, there have been and will be calls for courage, fortitude, and self-sacrifice. But there is no doubt about the outcome. It is finished! Oh, Christian brother and sister, live in that assurance. It is finished!

July 19

DOUBT VERSUS QUESTION

You are blessed because you believed that the Lord
would do what he said. (Luke 1:45)

On the surface Zechariah's and Mary's responses to their respective angelic visitors do not seem that much different (see Luke 1:18, 34). Both of them were struck by the apparent impossibility of what was promised to them, Zechariah because of his and Elizabeth's age, and Mary because of her virginity, and both asked how the promise could happen. Yet Mary is commended for her "belief" whereas Zechariah is reproached for his "unbelief." What is going on?

When we look a little closer, we see the critical difference: Mary questioned, whereas Zechariah doubted. Mary only asked how the thing could happen, but Zechariah asked how he could know the thing would happen. Such a small difference, but such a big one. God is never troubled by our questions. In fact, he invites them. Question says, "I believe, help me to understand how." Doubt says, "I won't believe until you convince me with some sort of sign or with a full explanation of the means." Interestingly, Gabriel answered Mary's question (see Luke 1:35), but he did not answer Zechariah's doubt except to make him mute.

So, if you have questions about how some promise of God in the Word or in your heart is possible, that does not make you a doubter. You don't need to feel condemned or try to squash the questions. Take them to God and let him answer them in his own way and time. On the other hand, don't say, like the people of Nazareth did of Jesus, "I won't believe until he proves it on my terms." That is the surest way to tie God's hands and to shut his mouth. "And because of their unbelief, he couldn't do any miracles among them" (Mark 6:5).

A HUMBLE ESTATE

My soul magnifies the Lord, and my spirit rejoices in God my Savior, for he has looked on the humble estate of his servant. For behold, from now on all generations will call me blessed; for he who is mighty has done great things for me, and holy is his name. And his mercy is for those who fear him from generation to generation. He has shown strength with his arm; he has scattered the proud in the thoughts of their hearts; he has brought down the mighty from their thrones and exalted those of humble estate; he has filled the hungry with good things, and the rich he has sent away empty. He has helped his servant Israel, in remembrance of his mercy, as he spoke to our fathers, to Abraham and to his offspring forever. (Luke 1:46–55 ESV)

Whenever I read this passage, I think, "Somebody taught this teen-aged girl biblical theology." Boys were almost certainly taught in Synagogue schools, but who taught this young girl? I suppose it was her mother, possibly her aunts. This tells us that women were not the uneducated drones that is sometimes suggested was the case by those who look down on a supposedly male-dominated culture. What did Mary know about God and his character? She knew he is the Holy One, absolutely transcendent over his creation, but also that his special favorites are the lowly ones, not the proud, the mighty, and the rich, which is what everyone normally thinks. If they are exalted, mighty, and rich, then God obviously is blessing them, right? Not so. Why? Because the plain fact is that when we are all those things, we really don't need the transcendent God. We are doing just fine, thank you very much. It is those who know that they are desperately needy who know they must have God. It is the couple who have no children, who have no support system, who have no place to call home, who need God. What this tells us is that it is no accident that Jesus came as he did: in such humble circumstances, to such humble people. Christmas is for those who know that they have nothing and that without him they are nothing. To people like that, he delights to give himself and all the riches of heaven.

July 21

WHATEVER IT COSTS

Then Jesus turned to his disciples and said, "God blesses you who are poor, for the Kingdom of God is yours. God blesses you who are hungry now, for you will be satisfied. God blesses you who weep now, for in due time you will laugh. What blessings await you when people hate you and exclude you and mock you and curse you as evil because you follow the Son of Man. When that happens, be happy! Yes, leap for joy! For a great reward awaits you in heaven. And remember, their ancestors treated the ancient prophets that same way." (Luke 6:20–23)

When I was a child in Sunday School, we memorized "the Beatitudes," but I am sure none of us had any idea how radical the words were that we were happily committing to memory. Come on! It's the poor who are blessed, those who don't have enough to eat, those who are constantly crying, those who are laughed at and cursed? Surely not! It's just the opposite: the blessed are those with lots of money, all they want to eat, plenty of laughter, and the admiration and respect from others.

What is Jesus talking about? Well, we have ask ourselves, if all we have when they close the casket is money, food, laughter, and earthly adulation, is that blessing? No, as a matter of fact, it is not; it is eternal loss. The blessing we really need for now and all eternity is fellowship with God through Jesus Christ. That is the only blessing that really counts. And guess what? For most of the world—and most of history—to choose Christ was, and in many cases, is yet, to choose poverty, hunger, weeping, and being cursed. Jesus was saying to his disciples and to us, "Choose me! Choose me, knowing full well what it may cost. And if you do, you will really be among the blessed."

It is possible that within our lifetime—or certainly within our children's lifetimes—it will become expensive to be a Christian in America: physically expensive, materially expensive, psychologically expensive. We see signs already, and unless God graciously gives us a national revival, it will get worse. Now is the day to get our souls right with God so that we are in a position that no matter what happens we are going to stand for him. Whether it's expensive, whatever it costs, now is the day to make those decisions. Temptation never gives you a ten-minute warning. Neither will persecution. Either we're ready to stand now or we won't be ready to stand then. Blessed are the poor.

July 22

THE JOY OF THE HOLY SPIRIT

At that same time Jesus was filled with the joy of the Holy Spirit, and
he said, "O Father, Lord of heaven and earth, thank you for hiding these
things from those who think themselves wise and clever, and for revealing
them to the childlike. Yes, Father, it pleased you to do it this way. My
Father has entrusted everything to me. No one truly knows the Son
except the Father, and no one truly knows the Father except the Son
and those to whom the Son chooses to reveal him." (Luke 10:21–22)

What a fascinating phrase: "Jesus was filled with the joy of the Holy
Spirit." Another translation reads, "He rejoiced in the Holy Spirit,"
but I think the New Living Translation makes it more intelligible. What
is "the joy of the Holy Spirit"? Clearly for Jesus it was the sense that
through the Holy Spirit, his life mission was being accomplished, even
if in a rather unexpected way. One would think that the way to get the
news of the kingdom out most effectively would be to enlist the wisest
and cleverest people possible. Instead, the Father had directed Jesus to
some very unlikely people, those who were not very mature or gifted in the
world's way of thinking. They were really babies among the wolves of the
world. In his humanness, Jesus must have wondered a bit about all this.
Was it going to work? Had he maybe misheard the Father's instructions
in that all-night prayer session before he selected his disciples? But no!
The "babies" have come back jumping up and down with the news that the
kingdom of heaven was indeed breaking in—even the kingdom of hell was
acknowledging that fact. Jesus had been led by the Spirit in his choice of
those to whom he was revealing the Father.

What about you and me? What is the joy of the Holy Spirit for us?
Surely it is that same truth although on a much diminished level. It is the
sense of having "come to ourselves" like the younger son in the pigpen.
The Holy Spirit has taken up residence in us and enabled us to be all we
were meant to be, both as persons and as those filling their particular place
in the kingdom. Do you ever have that feeling "this is what I was made
for"? That is the joy of the Holy Spirit. Do you ever have that feeling "I was
able to act that way because God is in me working out his purposes"? That
is the joy of the Holy Spirit. That is what Old Testament believers longed
to know in its fullness, and that is our privilege: the joy of the Holy Spirit.

July 23

COMPARTMENTS

And behold, a lawyer stood up to put him to the test, saying, "Teacher, what shall I do to inherit eternal life?" He said to him, "What is written in the Law? How do you read it?" And he answered, "You shall love the Lord your God with all your heart and with all your soul and with all your strength and with all your mind, and your neighbor as yourself." And he said to him, "You have answered correctly; do this, and you will live." (Luke 10:25–28 ESV)

God says to us, "Children you can't compartmentalize your lives," but that is exactly what we try to do. In particular, we try to separate our religious life from the way we treat others, that is, our ethical lives. How I treat God, well, that's religion. And the rest of my life? Well, that's—life. God won't let us do that. He says to us, "Your life is a package."

The Bible illustrates that when it puts the law code into the context of a covenant with God. Elsewhere, there are religious prescriptions, and there are civil law codes, but they never come together. However, they do in the Bible; there our treatment of one another is a direct expression of obedience to our covenant Lord. Look at the Ten Commands: four about God and six about others. If we want to be his people, we must show it by the way we live in the world. God wants us to show that we love him by the way we treat the widow, by the way we tell the truth, etc. God is ethical; he doesn't lie or cheat or steal or break faith. If we are his, we can't either. If we love him, we will live his life, and he is an ethical God.

Too often we suggest that the character of our lives, while important, is not really essential to our relationship with God. What happens if you separate God from the rest of your life? It becomes very easy to slip into an idolatrous understanding of him. Why do I go to church? Why do I read the Bible? Why do I do this religious stuff? To make him bless me. That's idolatry. Having done that, because the Lord doesn't do a very good job of blessing people when they try to manipulate him, it's easy to start putting other idols into that compartment that we think will bless us more easily: money, job, house, clothes, love, power. That's what's happening in our society. But when we allow our love for God to flow through our entire life, then we know that our goal is not to be blessed but to *be* a blessing, and that changes everything.

July 24

BREAD FOR TODAY

Give us each day the food we need. (Luke 11:3)

Then he said, "I know! I'll tear down my barns and build bigger ones. Then I'll have room enough to store all my wheat and other goods. And I'll sit back and say to myself, 'My friend, you have enough stored away for years to come. Now take it easy! Eat, drink, and be merry!'" But God said to him, "You fool! You will die this very night. Then who will get everything you worked for?" Yes, a person is a fool to store up earthly wealth but not have a rich relationship with God. (Luke 12:18–21)

I wonder if, in future years, historians of the church in America will not say, "They were seduced by their wealth." Now there is nothing evil about money. It is a necessary commodity for trade and exchange. As C. S. Lewis says, God did not make anything evil. He goes on to say that the greater the good of something, the greater the possibility for perversion. That is certainly true of wealth. Unfortunately, it is rare to find a wealthy person who does not in their heart believe, "I am God. I am self-sufficient. I don't need to worry about anything. I'll just build bigger barns, and all is well."

Friends, on the world's scale, every one of us Americans is filthy rich. We really are. Perhaps you say, "I'd like to show you my checkbook. I'd show you I'm not rich." I understand. There are lots of people in this country who are a lot richer than you and I are. Still, by the world's standard, even the poorest among us are rich, and those of us in the middle class are incredibly rich. Thus, it is all too easy for us to say (without saying it, if you know what I mean), "I don't need to pray. I've got a regular salary coming in. I don't need to pray for my daily bread, I've got enough bread to last two weeks." How easy it is to become God in my life and not to be *daily* dependent upon him. Not to be *daily* recognizing, "I need God or I'm not going to make it through this day." The poor—they know they are not God. They know that if somehow, something doesn't happen from beyond their ability, from beyond their resources, they are not going to make it.

I'm not suggesting we all ought to pray to be poor, because poverty can be a grinding thing that simply absorbs your whole attention, and you don't have time for God there either. What I am saying is that you and I need to find ways to daily remind ourselves, "I need God today."

July 25

LOST

Won't he leave the ninety-nine in the wilderness and go to
search for the one that is lost until he finds it? (Luke 15:4b)

One of Satan's most effective lies is the one he told Eve in the Garden. It worked then and it has worked ever since. The lie is that God really does not care about us; rather, he cares about himself and his position, so he'll use us any way he likes to accomplish his selfish purposes. Now, Satan may really believe that, for that is *his* character. He may really believe that nobody could actually be motivated strictly by unselfish love. Whatever the reason, it is a lie. God does not care about himself; he cares for you and me. There is no more effective presentation of that truth than in Jesus's three "lost" parables: the lost sheep, the lost coin, and the lost boy.

Because the Pharisees were angry that he was associating with sinners, Jesus took the opportunity to talk about the character of God. Having grown up on a farm where we raised sheep, I have a particular fondness for the lost sheep parable. Ninety-nine of the sheep are back in the fold at the end of the day. Who cares about just one, particularly one, as I like to think, that was prone to wandering off and getting lost? Night is coming on; there are brambles and rocks, and maybe worse, out there in the dark. Let it go! Ah, no, not our Shepherd. He doesn't care about bruises, scrapes, and devouring wolves. He cares about that one sheep, paralyzed with fear, lost.

As the Shepherd stumbles through the dark, is he thinking about what he will do to that sheep when he finds it? Oh, no. When he does find it, he doesn't even make it walk home in front of him. He lays it across his shoulders and carries it. When he reaches the village, he wakes up everybody to party with him. Over one stupid sheep! That's our God. Don't believe Satan's lies; God is *for* you. He is on your side, sympathizing when you cry, grieving when you hurt, laughing delightedly when you succeed. He doesn't care about himself; he cares for you. Believe it.

PERSISTENT BELIEF

When the Son of Man comes, how many will he find
on the earth who have faith? (Luke 18:8)

I confess that I have always been troubled by the parable that precedes the verse above. It suggests that God will not do what we want him to do—or perhaps even what he ought to do?!—unless we essentially force him with a barrage of words. The fine Christian writer P. T. Forsyth has a book in which he says God will only do the right thing when we wrestle him into it. With all due respect, I do not believe that. Part of the reason I do not is because of what Jesus says elsewhere when he condemns pagans who multiply their words because they think that if they use enough, they will be heard.

So, what is Jesus talking about? I think the clue is in the verse above. This story is not so much to promote persistent praying as it is to promote persistent faith. Now persistent faith will result in persistent praying—don't misunderstand me. But it is steady unremitting faith in God that is the issue. Will my—your—faith in Jesus persist when it seems like our prayers aren't being answered? Will it persist even when we see genuine Christian faith in free fall in the West today? Will we keep praying for the lost when it seems that Generation Z is leaving God in droves?

Why is Europe, the cradle of Christian faith, largely godless today? Because Christian people did not have persistent faith. Two World Wars have seemed to prove to them that God does not answer prayer, and so they have given up their faith—and their praying. So, this parable is not designed to keep us "storming heaven" for some request we have, confident that someday we are going to wear down God's resistance and make him give us what we want. Rather, it is to address a much deeper issue: will we keep on believing in God regardless of whether he does or does not answer our specific prayers? My answer is "Yes!" When Jesus comes, I want to be found believing.

July 27

SUFFERING AND HAPPINESS

But before all this occurs, there will be a time of great persecution. You will be dragged into synagogues and prisons, and you will stand trial before kings and governors because you are my followers. (Luke 21:12)

God blesses you when people mock you and persecute you and lie about you and say all sorts of evil things against you because you are my followers. (Matthew 5:11)

Back in the "bad old days" of Christian education, before it was thought harmful to have children memorize things, we had to memorize the Beatitudes. I remember wondering what they had to do with "being at" something. I don't remember ever thinking how bizarre they are, but they are. You're blessed when you are poor? You're blessed when you are crying? You're blessed when people beat you up and throw you in a stinking dungeon because you're a Christian? Come on! What is Jesus talking about!? What he means is that when you chose Jesus then—and more and more now in many parts of the world—you were choosing to be poorer than you could be, to be continually grieved over a lost and broken world. You were—are—choosing to face misunderstanding, hatred, and loss from a world that hated and misunderstood him. So, when those things do happen to you for his sake, you can be happy? Yes, you can.

I had the great privilege of preaching in a church in Bucharest for a week in January in the early 90s. It was ten degrees Fahrenheit outside. The church held about 700, and there were easily 850 in it every night, packed to the walls. The contrast between that congregation and the American congregations I had been preaching to was startling. There were very few "beautiful people" present. Many, though not all, by any means, were old. Most were poorly dressed. Their faces were wizened and chapped with the cold. Almost all had walked through snowy streets, some for long distances, to get there. I knew that none of them were professional people—the professions were closed to any confessing Christian. If they could find any work at all, it was as a manual laborer. But the singing!—and the praying! You have never heard prayer until you have heard 850 people praying out loud—all at the same time. I stood with my eyes open watching them pray, and it struck me like a hammer: "these people are happy!" Then it struck me why that was: they had made the choice to be poor, to be harassed, to grieve, for Jesus's sake, and they knew that they had made the smart choice. My friend, choose Jesus, knowing the cost, and be happy!

July 28

Intentional and Unintentional Sin

And Judas went to the chief priests and the officers of the temple guard and discussed with them how he might betray Jesus. They were delighted and agreed to give him money. He consented and watched for an opportunity to hand Jesus over to them when no crowd was present. (Luke 22:4–6 NIV)

Then seizing him, they led him away and took him into the house of the high priest. Peter followed at a distance. But when they had kindled a fire in the middle of the courtyard and had sat down together, Peter sat down with them. A servant girl saw him seated there in the firelight. She looked closely at him and said, "This man was with him." But he denied it. "Woman, I don't know him," he said. (Luke 22:54–57 NIV)

These two passages illustrate an important point about the Bible's understanding of sin. There is intentional sin, called "sin with a high hand [raised fist]" in Numbers 15:30, and there is unintentional sin, or going astray (see Num 15:22). Judas's sin was intentional. He planned it, discussed it, and looked for an opportunity to commit it. There is no stated sacrifice in the Old Testament for this kind of sin. Can it be forgiven? Certainly. But the problem is that committing it so scars us that genuine repentance (as opposed to remorse) becomes very difficult, as it was for Judas.

Peter's sin, on the other hand, was unintentional. When he followed the mob to the High Priest's house, denying his association with Jesus was the farthest thing from his mind. However, in the moment, seeing how Jesus was being treated and fearing the consequences for himself, when he was asked to identify himself with the defendant, he said the fateful words, "I do not know him." But precisely because the sin was unintentional, when Peter recognized what he had done, he wept bitterly. This was not what he planned, not what he wanted, and he regretted it with all his heart. Jesus knew this, and weeks later, by the sea, he gently drew Peter back into the ministry that Peter had thought was forever closed to him.

Can we, through the Holy Spirit, be delivered from committing intentional sin? Yes! We can live lives that are to the very core intentionally, wholly, his. Will we ever be free from the danger of "going astray," or from the need to guard our souls diligently against such a thing? No. To be sure, we ought to have such an experience of the Holy Spirit that we are more and more sensitive to his gentle voice pointing out the danger signals, and we ought not to fall into the same pit again and again. But Jesus knows our hearts, and as he said to Peter, he has prayed for us, and like Peter, he will meet us at our seasides.

July 29

COME, TARRY, GO

He told them: "This is what is written: The Messiah will suffer and rise from the dead on the third day, and repentance for the forgiveness of sins will be preached in his name to all nations, beginning at Jerusalem. You are witnesses of these things. I am going to send you what my Father has promised; but stay in the city until you have been clothed with power from on high." (Luke 24:46–49 NIV)

In a church that Karen and I once attended, there was a very large cross-shaped window above the pulpit. In the glass the ascending Jesus was depicted with his arms outstretched. Below his feet were the words, one above the other: Come, Tarry, Go. In many ways these three words summarize the gospel. Too often, we think of the Good News simply as "Come." To be sure, it is good news. With his arms extended Jesus invites us to come to him and drop our sins, frustrations, failures, and loneliness at his feet and let him enfold us in those arms. Thank God!

Having come, something happens to us: we have become witnesses to realities that change everything, and we can't just keep quiet. As Peter said to the Jewish leaders, "We cannot but speak of what we have seen and heard" (Acts 4:20 ESV). We do not "go" because God demands it but because our experience demands it. Persons who have "come" to Christ cannot not "go" to tell about it.

But there is that third word. What about it? If the first two words are inseparable from each other as parts of the gospel, what about this one? It is the essential bridge between the two. The good news of the gospel is that we can be infused with the very life and being of Jesus. Because we have "come," this is a possibility, and as it becomes a reality, our "going" is in power and joy. However, the fullness of the Holy Spirit is not at our command. We must "wait" (see Acts 1:4) until we have come to the end of ourselves and know our absolute dependency on our Father before he can give us the gift he most wishes to give: himself.

July 30

THE WORD BECAME FLESH

In the beginning the Word already existed. The Word was with God, and the Word was God. He existed in the beginning with God. God created everything through him, and nothing was created except through him. The Word gave life to everything that was created, and his life brought light to everyone. The light shines in the darkness, and the darkness can never extinguish it. (John 1:1–5)

So the Word became human and made his home among us. He was full of unfailing love and faithfulness. And we have seen his glory, the glory of the Father's one and only Son. (John 1:14)

The words of John 1:1–18 are breathtaking in their boldness and yet exactly in concert with Matthew 1–2 and Luke 1–2. Who is this stall-born baby, the fruit of a virginal womb? He is the Creator! But what Creator? The Greeks had a way of explaining the goodness and yet the fallenness of the world by imagining that there was an almost infinite stream of beings emerging each one from the former one and each one a bit more flawed than the previous one. Thus, the being that made this world, the Logos, the Word, retained a bit of the perfection of God but was very seriously flawed.

John takes that idea and blows it to pieces. Yes, the Creator, the Word, is different from God, but at the *same time*, he *is* God. And which God is he? Uranus, Chronos, Zeus—all products of the human mind? No! He is the transcendent Yahweh of the Old Testament from whom alone streams unfailing love (i.e., grace) and absolute faithfulness (i.e., truth), which are the true light shining in darkness. This person in whom is found all that is divine became human for us. He has come and pitched his tent ("tabernacled" KJV) among us. Glory to God in the highest! Matthew and Luke convey the wonder in narrative form, while John tells the same story in the language of intellectual discourse. Glory! Mary's baby was the Creator of the Universe; God in human flesh!

July 31
JESUS'S MINISTRY

What Jesus did here in Cana of Galilee was the first of the signs
through which he revealed his glory, and his disciples believed in
him. . . . To those who sold doves, he said, "Get these out of here!
Stop making my father's house into a market!" (John 2:11, 16 NIV)

When we compare the Gospel of John to the other three Gospels,
we find a lot of differences—not a difference of emphasis or a
different understanding of Jesus's ministry, of what he was about—but a
different way of presenting him and his ministry. The differences show up
immediately: there is a different perspective on the calling of the disciples
in chapter one; then in chapter two we have a miracle not reported in the
other Gospels and the cleansing of the temple, which the other Gospels
place at the end of his ministry, in his last week on earth. What gives,
especially there in chapter two?

I suggest that John has chosen to highlight the wedding at Cana, Jesus's
first miracle, and has reported the temple cleansing out of chronological
order (one of his last actions) in order to tell us what Jesus's ministry is
all about. What happened at Cana? Transformation! The transformation
of water into wine. Jesus has not come to save us from our sins and then
leave us in them. No, he has come to transform us from the children of
the devil, trapped in our own selfishness, to children of the Father, free
to live like him. But how is such transformation possible? How can the
Spirit of God take up residence in us—hovels filled with sin? It is when the
"temples" of our hearts are *cleansed* by the blood of the Lamb! That's what
the Cross was, and is, all about. Forgiven and cleansed, we can become
the home of the Spirit—we can be transformed. In that second chapter,
John has told us what the ministry of Jesus is all about. He has told us
"the secrets of the Kingdom" (Matt 13:11). He has come to cleanse us and
transform us. Good News!

August 1

THE WATER OF LIFE

On the last day, the climax of the festival, Jesus stood and shouted to the crowds, "Anyone who is thirsty may come to me! Anyone who believes in me may come and drink! For the Scriptures declare, 'Rivers of living water will flow from his heart.'" (When he said "living water," he was speaking of the Spirit, who would be given to everyone believing in him.) (John 7:37–39a)

The Feast of Tabernacles occurred about the first of October. The harvest was over, or nearly over, and the time for fall planting was near. The dry season had prevailed throughout the summer, and now it was time for the early rains, the Fall rains, to begin. One of the great rituals of the feast was the bringing of water from the Pool of Siloam, which stood at the bottom of the city where the Hinnom Valley joined the Kidron Valley, up through the old city of David into the Temple precincts, where it was poured out to Yahweh. The Israelites understood what we all know: where there is no water, there is no life. Cosmologists, hoping to find life forms elsewhere in the universe, look for signs of water on Mars, because they know that where there is water, life might exist. Where there is no water, there is no point in looking further for life there.

It was in that context that the Galilean preacher, Jesus of Nazareth, standing in the Temple courts, cried out the words printed above. What was he saying? He was making the thoroughly shocking claim that he was the source of all that is necessary for spiritual life to exist. Really? Really! If the water of Jesus, the Holy Spirit, has flowed into you, and his presence is demonstrated by his life flowing out of you, then you are really alive. If your knowledge of Christ is only intellectual, however, or if your relationship with him is only one way—incoming—then there is real reason for concern. Life springs up where there is water flowing out. In the desert even if no water is visible, the Bedouin knows that if there are trees and bushes growing, then he can dig down and find water.

You and I have to ask: is Jesus, the water of life, so in me that living water is flowing out? If the evidence is not there, we must ask him, beg him, to pour himself into us. He longs to do it.

August 2

THE TYRANNY OF "I" — PART ONE

So Jesus said to the Jews who had believed him, "If you abide
in my word, you are truly my disciples, and you will know the
truth, and the truth will set you free." (John 8:31–32 ESV)

I write to you, not because you do not know the truth, but because
you know it, and because no lie is of the truth. (1 John 2:21 ESV)

In our American (and human) determination to know no authority other
than ourselves, we have delivered ourselves over to a tyranny that is far
worse than we imagine. Denying any reality (or truth) outside of ourselves,
we have given ourselves over to the iron grip of feelings. My thoughts aren't
necessarily real, because other people have other thoughts; my knowledge
isn't necessarily real, because other people have other knowledge; but my
feelings—ah, there is reality. Whether other people have other feelings
doesn't matter, because my feelings are real, and no one can tell me they
aren't.

So, if I feel like a woman in a man's body, the body is not reality, but
my feelings are. I need to make these physical "facts," which are actually
false, conform to the truth: my feelings. What if ten years down the road,
my feelings change, which they very well may? Shall we try to now alter the
new "facts"? That is tyranny: I am prey to whatever I feel, with no check
upon them. Are feelings not real? Of course, they are. But they are part of
reality, not the total, and they need to be tested against the rest of reality.
Pilots who are flying straight and level in clouds typically begin to feel they
are diving to the left. Unless they can check their feelings against reality
(through instruments), they will pull back on the controls, trying to correct
that false impression, until the plane is pointing straight up, loses lift, and
falls to the ground. There are realities more real than feelings.

So it is with us. We can know the Truth, Jesus, who is the ultimate
evidence of the reality of God and his Word. We can check our feelings
against the reality of his love, his care, and his design for the world he
has created. That Truth can set us free from feelings of worthlessness and
failure, from feelings of powerlessness and fear. All we have to do is to
acknowledge that he is reality (i.e., Truth), standing outside of ourselves,
and through his Spirit bring ourselves into line with reality. Freedom!

August 3

THE TYRANNY OF "I"—PART TWO

Jesus said to him, "I am the way, and the truth, and the life. No
one comes to the Father except through me. If you had known
me, you would have known my Father also. From now on you
do know him and have seen him." (John 14:6–7 ESV)

In Part One, we talked about the way in which our attempt to escape
from any authority outside of ourselves has delivered us over to the
tyranny of feelings. In this part, I want to pursue the results of that attempt
in another direction. When I am the final arbiter of what is real or not, I
doom myself to complete isolation, with the end result of emptiness and
suicide.

Why do I say that? I say it because our identity is found in relationships.
Cut me off from all relationships and I am a cypher, an empty container. In
fact, you and I are the sum total of all the relationships we have ever had.
But deep relationships are impossible without speech communication.
And what does genuine communication depend on? It depends on shared
perceptions of reality. If reality is merely a conception of my mind, there
is virtually no possibility of my communicating with you in any deep way
because your conception will necessarily be different from mine.

A number of years ago, a missionary wrote a book called *I Loved a
Woman*. In that book he talked about the difficulty of communicating
the love of God to a certain African people because the only word in their
language that could be used to translate our European concept of "love"
meant "to have sex." They simply had no conception of self-giving, self-
denying love. A new word had to be created.

In other words, we only find ourselves when we recognize that there is
a reality outside of ourselves and communicate with others who recognize
that same reality. We can only trust one another's communications if we
both agree to that reality that transcends both of us. This is what we find in
Christ. He is "Truth." That is, in him God has communicated to us that he
is utterly reliable. His love is utterly unchangeable, and it exists whether
we recognize it or not. But if we recognize it and accept it, then we can be
true. Our lives are no longer our own to fill with some vaporous conception
of our own reality. Now we can entrust our lives into the hands of the One
who is eternally True, and trusting him, we no longer have to construct
lies, untruths, to protect and project ourselves at all costs. We can be our
precious selves, wrapped in the arms of the Truth.

BREAKING THE CHAINS OF BROKENNESS

"But we are descendants of Abraham," they said. "We have never been slaves to anyone. What do you mean, 'You will be set free'?" Jesus replied, "I tell you the truth, everyone who sins is a slave of sin. A slave is not a permanent member of the family, but a son is part of the family forever. So if the Son sets you free, you are truly free." (John 8:33–36)

I get a lot of chances to talk with people about their lives, and I never cease to be amazed at the amount of brokenness there is in our world. Again and again I see someone who clearly has it all together: they are good-looking, well-groomed, confident, successful. And then I talk with them and am stunned to discover that much of what I am seeing is a façade. Behind that façade is pain, failure, broken relationships, substance abuse, and the list goes on. Sometimes I wonder, "Are there any 'normal' people left?"

Then God calls me up short. "Normal"? What's that? Some years ago, a pastor spoke to me about wanting to do a series on biblical family relationships and asking for the biblical model. As I began to think about that I was shocked to discover that there are no ideal families in the Bible. Now I suspect that Joseph and Mary had an ideal family, but there is no narrative about them. The narratives are about conflict and tension, jealousy and favoritism, murder and mayhem.

The good news is that this is the world Jesus came into. He came to make you and me able to love one another in the inescapable tensions of married life. That is, he came to make it possible to lay ourselves down, not grumpily or pouting, but easily, for that person who has given herself or himself to us. He came to enable us to be faithful to our promises, even when it is not to our advantage. He came to enable us to turn off the machine when pornographic images jump out at us. He came to make us able to forgive those who have abused us. He came to make us free to love, to serve, to be faithful, to be chaste, to lay down our lives.

This is what our world cries out for: people who can break the chain of evil. How does he do it? By supplying all our needs! If you know you are loved by God; if you know that you have eternal life; if you know that you can trust him to supply what neither you nor anyone else can, you are free! You don't have to use or abuse people; you don't have to abuse your body; you don't have to lie, or steal, or kill to get what none of these can give you anyway. He has come and you can be free!

THE GOOD SHEPHERD

I am the good shepherd. The good shepherd sacrifices his life for
the sheep. A hired hand will run when he sees a wolf coming. He will
abandon the sheep because they don't belong to him and he isn't their
shepherd. And so the wolf attacks them and scatters the flock. . . . The
Father loves me because I sacrifice my life so I may take it back again.
No one can take my life from me. I sacrifice it voluntarily. For I have
the authority to lay it down when I want to and also to take it up again.
For this is what my Father has commanded. (John 10:11–12, 17–18)

In this passage about the Good Shepherd, Jesus says three things. First,
he says that he cares what happens to the flock because he owns them.
The hired hand does not care what happens to the flock, because they are
not his. But Jesus takes responsibility for us because he has made us, and
when we ran away from him, he bought us back. If we are lost, it is a loss
to him. Beyond that, as our owner, he knows the special characteristics of
each of us and is looking out for us.

So far so good. But the second thing Jesus says seems very strange:
that he will sacrifice his life for the sheep. That doesn't make sense. Yes,
he might go to great lengths to keep his flock from being destroyed, but
give up his life for them? What good is that? After all, the flock exists for
the benefit of the shepherd, and if he is dead, what good is the flock going
to do him? He can't eat them, or wear them, or sacrifice them then. But
wait—maybe this Shepherd exists for the benefit of the flock! Maybe he
gathered them so that he could love them, so they could wear him, and eat
him, and offer him as a sacrifice. Still, how could they enjoy those benefits
if he is dead?

That's the third thing Jesus says. If he can give up his life freely, he
can take it back again freely. Our Shepherd is not dead! He is alive and can
continue to give himself to us for our benefit until that day when he leads
us through the valley of the shadow of death that he has passed through
already. Then, we are no longer sheep but now family, living with him in
his house forever, constantly pursued by his goodness and unfailing love
(see Ps 23:6).

August 6

NOTHING CAN TAKE YOU OUT OF MY HAND

I give them eternal life, and they shall never perish; no one will snatch them out of my hand. My Father, who has given them to me, is greater than all; no one can snatch them out of my Father's hand. (John 10:28–29 NIV)

For I am convinced that neither death nor life, neither angels nor demons, neither the present nor the future, nor any powers, neither height nor depth, nor anything else in all creation, will be able to separate us from the love of God that is in Christ Jesus our Lord. (Romans 8:38–39 NIV)

I have three friends all of whom have received a diagnosis of terminal cancer. One in particular is struggling with whether she has enough faith to hold on to Jesus in this difficult time—but that is the wrong perspective. It is not whether we have enough faith or not, but simply whether we want to be held or not. Jesus says that nothing can take us out of his hand, and Paul says that nothing can separate us from the love of God. Neither of those mean that we can live a life of intentional sin, offending him at every turn and still expect to go to heaven when we die. That's like saying I can sleep with every woman who will let me and still expect my wife to stay married to me. What it does mean is that our relationship to Jesus does not depend on our perfect performance as Christians or upon our ability to hang onto him. It doesn't depend on you; it depends on him. Just as long as you want to be in the palm of his hand, he will hold onto you. And that is true whether you feel it or not. He has hold of you, and *nothing* can break that hold. His love for you is unchanging, and his power is limitless.

August 7

SALVATION AND JUDGMENT

I will not judge those who hear me but don't obey me, for I have come to save the world and not to judge it. But all who reject me and my message will be judged on the day of judgment by the truth I have spoken. (John 12:47–48)

Twice Jesus tells us what his purpose was: salvation (see John 3:17 and John 12:47). He did not come to judge the world, but to save it. Yet he will judge the world; the Father has given him that authority (see the extended discussion in John 5:22–30). What is going on? Did Jesus come to judge or not? Is Jesus, the Savior, going to send us into eternal separation from God?

John 12:48 helps us here. No, Jesus's purpose in coming was not judgment, but what he has said about himself and us and the world calls for a response. What he has said is factually true, and what we do about that truth will determine our eternal destiny. It is like this. Someone says to us, "Drive around that brick wall, not into it." But we decide we know better: the shortest route to our destination is clearly through that wall. So, we floor the accelerator and smash into the wall, killing ourselves in the process. The person who gave us the good advice stands there, shaking his head, saying, "You poor fool." He is passing judgment on us, but in the end, he is not the one who killed us. It was the truth itself, and our rejection of it, that judged us. Human flesh cannot stand the sudden stop involved in a ton of metal hitting a solid brick wall. That's the truth, no matter what "Star Wars" theology might say, and we rejected it.

It will be the same on the last day. Jesus will not say to some poor, whimpering sinner, "You go to hell!" No, having rejected the truth of who he is and who we are and what we need to do, we will condemn ourselves, just as the foolish driver killed himself.

So, is Jesus your Savior, or is the truth about him your judge?

August 8

CHRIST IN YOU?

Remain in me, and I will remain in you. For a branch cannot produce fruit if it is severed from the vine, and you cannot be fruitful unless you remain in me. Yes, I am the vine; you are the branches. Those who remain in me and I in them, will produce much fruit. For apart from me you can do nothing. (John 15:4–5)

In one of his books, the mystery writer Harry Kemelman has Rabbi Small, his main character, say that the difference between Christianity and Judaism is that Christianity is a mystical religion, while Judaism is an ethical one. Unfortunately, that is not really correct. Judaism has always had a strong strand of mysticism in it, and a Christianity that has lost its ethical foundation is, in the words of Jesus, "salt that is no longer salty."

However, Kemelman's underlying point is correct: mysticism in Christianity is not just a strand, it is supposed to be at the very heart. To be a genuine Christian is to have the resurrected Christ living in you. For Paul, it is "the hope of glory" (Col 1:27), the assurance that we, too, will rise from the dead. When the second-century bishop, Ignatius, was on trial for his faith, Caesar is supposed to have asked him, "Is it true that you carry your god around in you?" Ignatius answered with a triumphant "Yes!"

What is the evidence that this wonderful mystical relationship is a reality? It is ethics! This is the "fruit" that Jesus is talking about in John 15. It is what Paul calls "the fruit of the Spirit" (Gal 5:22–26). It is obedience as a result of love—for God and others. Jesus goes so far as to say that we cannot really live out the heavenly ethic unless he is living in us and we in him. So that is the question for you and me: am I a genuinely ethical person, and is this ethical integrity a result of Christ's life in me? Yes? Hallelujah, I am a child of God!

August 9

ABIDE IN HIM

I am the vine; you are the branches. Whoever abides in me and I in him, he it is that bears much fruit, for apart from me you can do nothing. (John 15:5 ESV)

Words are very interesting things. Each one has a meaning, and you can look up that meaning in any standard dictionary. At the same time, you can only be sure what the actual meaning of a word is by looking at the context in which the word is being used. The Greek word *meno* is like that. It has the basic idea of "to remain," but in some settings it seems to mean something more like "to remain part of." In the New Living Translation committee, we debated how to translate *meno* in this part of John. Dr. Ken Taylor, father of the Living Bible, which was the base from which we were working, was very concerned for "the average reader." Would they have any idea what the now-archaic "abides" means? He argued no. Better he said, that they get some meaning rather than none. So we chose to translate the Greek word with "stays," as the NIV also has.

"Stays" is certainly not an incorrect rendering for *meno*. Yet it seems to me that Jesus is calling for something more than merely staying in him, or remaining in him. He is talking about the nature of salvation. Salvation is more than just a change of status. Oh yes, it is that, praise God! But it is *so much more* than that. It is to be living in Jesus and having Jesus living in you. It is to be an inseparable part of him as the lovely images of this verse spell out. So what English word conveys that? As far as I know only old-fashioned "abides" does it with its connotations of settling in, settling down, clinging to, connotations that "stays" does not have. If there were a better contemporary word to convey those ideas, I'd be happy to use it. I just don't know one. All that to say, yes, I do want to retain my faith in Jesus, to stay in him, no matter what life may throw at me. But, oh so much more, I want to draw my very life from him, having him enlivening me at every turn. Do you see it? Is that what you want? Oh, let's abide in him.

August 10

ASK ANYTHING IN MY NAME

In that day you will ask nothing of me. Truly, truly, I say to you,
whatever you ask of the Father in my name, he will give it to you.
Until now you have asked nothing in my name. Ask, and you will
receive, that your joy may be full. (John 16:23–24 ESV)

In John 14–16, in what is called "The Last Supper Discourse," Jesus says no fewer than five times (see John 14:13–14; 15:7, 16; and 16:23) that the disciples can ask anything in his name and they will receive it. It seems to me that there is a fine line that the Christian must walk if we are truly to live in our inheritance on this point.

First, why does Jesus make so much of this point in this, his last message before the Cross? I think it is because they are about to enter into a whole new relationship with him. He will no longer be with them as he has been. From now on, if they want to know the truth, it must come to them from the Father by the Spirit (see John 15:26, 16:12–15). Jesus says they had not had to ask in this new way before. Thus, Jesus is not talking primarily about asking for things, but for inspiration to know and live the truth. Is this where you and I live in our prayer life?

Second, to ask for something in Jesus's name is to say in effect, "Father, Jesus told me to ask for this." Can I really say, "Father, Jesus wants you to give me a new BMW"? Maybe, but I doubt it. Key here is what Jesus says in John 15:7, "If you abide in me . . . ." We can only know what Jesus wants us to ask for if we are living right in him. Then, we can ask on Jesus's behalf, confident that is what he really wants us to have.

Third, if we really want to know the Father through Jesus, and we are living "in" Jesus, we truly can ask for "anything." This is, of course, Semitic hyperbole, an overstatement to get the point across. It is rather like Jesus's statement that we cannot serve him unless we hate our parents. Of course, he does not mean that we should hate our parents but that our commitment to him must be that much stronger than even the one to them. So here, he does not mean that we can ask in his name to be instantly made a foot taller, and that it will happen. Rather, if we really want to know God and his truth—and Jesus is living and breathing through us—then "anything" that we ask in the context of that relationship is possible. To use Jesus's repeated statements here as a formula to get what we want from him, to consume it on our own desires (see Jam 4:3), is not faith but the worst sort of idolatry. What are you asking God to do in your life today? Anything is possible.

Living Outside the Trenches

In this world you will have trouble. But take heart! I
have overcome the world. (John 16:33 NIV)

If we say to people, "You ought to become a Christian because when you
do all your troubles will be over," we are not telling the truth. When you
are not a Christian, the devil doesn't care very much what you do. As long
as you keep your helmet down below the top level of the trench, nobody is
going to shoot at you. But if you stick your head up, wave a flag, and shout,
"I am for Jesus!" you ought not to be surprised if some artillery is aimed
your way. Some people will have never known real trouble until after they
become a Christian.

We ought not to be surprised at this: Jesus told us long ago that this
would be the case. So, we can live in assurance, knowing that the testing
that we are presently enduring is the proof of the reality of our faith and of
our relationship to him. Paul says in 2 Corinthians 1 that as we experience
God's power to deliver us from these troubles, we know more and more
surely that he can deliver us from death, the final enemy. Precisely as we
encounter difficulties and as God triumphs over them through us, we can
know with greater and greater assurance that when they slam the lid on
the casket, Jesus is going to be burning out the ends with a blow torch and
saying, "Welcome Home!" Don't seek trouble, but when it comes, embrace
it and look for God's deliverance, down payment on the final deliverance.

August 12

TRUTH

Sanctify them by the truth; your word is truth. (John 17:17 NIV)

We live in a world where personal convenience, personal desire, and personal comfort are everything. Faced with those realities, truth is a poor second. Why should I tell you the truth if it's not convenient? Why should I keep my promises if it doesn't serve my desires? Why wouldn't I lie if the truth would make me uncomfortable? These facts explain why 90 percent of college students in America declare there is no such thing as absolute truth. This is not a new way of thinking. It has been with us since the dawn of time. Why is that? It is because since our first mother and father, we have been seduced by a lie. That lie is that you and I and our desires are ultimate reality. That is what Adam and Eve's sin was about. If you can decide what is right and wrong for you, then you have effectively made yourself God—but that is a lie; it is not true. Build your life on that lie, and the rest of your behavior will have to be a structure of lies to support it.

If you ever admit that there is Someone outside of yourself who has your very best interests at heart, you are suddenly free to tell the truth and to be true. When you are loved by Jesus Christ to the end of eternity, you don't have to lie anymore. You don't have to impress anybody. You can keep your word because you know he will supply your needs. You can be set free to be true. He will enable you to be true, even if our culture is going to hell in a hand basket, even if people are lying about everything, even if a man's word of honor is worthless, even if it's costly to tell the truth. When you belong to Jesus, the Truth, you can afford to be true. Have you discovered a Jesus like that, One who will enable you to be true, no matter what?

August 13

CREATE IN ME A PURE HEART

Create in me a pure heart, O God, and renew a
steadfast spirit within me. (Psalm 51:10 NIV)

In this psalm David has recorded his horrified discovery of the depths of his depravity. I think before this experience he had been complacent with himself: he was basically a good man and other people could be good too if they would just apply themselves. Now this! He was a sinner! In fact, he now knows sin was in his DNA from the moment the sperm met the egg in his mother's womb.

What a great discovery that all too many of us never make! We think of our sins as unfortunate slips rather than outward expressions of a fundamentally perverse nature. But David now knows that goodness, real goodness—a heart wholly for God* and a spirit forever fixed on him—is not a matter of a simple choice. Rather, it requires radical surgery—a divine act of creation and starting over again, renewing. Without that, all his former "goodness" was just a matter of personality, as little to his credit as eye color.

Before this, was he "a man after God's own heart" (1 Sam 13:14)? Yes, I think so, but it had been simply a matter of choice. But from here on it was a reality as never before—a divine work and not a human one.

---

* The Hebrew word is *tahor*, often translated "clean." It has the connotation of being all one thing, totally unmixed.

August 14
HALLOWED BE THY NAME

Pray then like this: "Our Father in heaven, hallowed
be your name." (Matthew 6:9 ESV)

Most of us Christians make this request fairly often—some of us every day—but what do we mean? What are we asking for?

First, we are asking that something will take place regarding Yahweh's nature and reputation. That is the meaning of "name" in this setting. We are asking that his nature and reputation be perceived in the world to have a particular character and quality. What nature and quality? Holy. What is that? In the biblical context, it is to be absolutely other than anything else in the universe. There is none like him. He is absolutely one of a kind. There is none like him in his existence, which means there is none like him in his character. It means he is the One who is high and lifted up as Isaiah saw him (6:1, 52:13, 57:15). It means he is the One alone who sits on that sapphire throne as Ezekiel saw him (1:26, 10:1). It means he is not little, common, ordinary, or useful. He is the Holy One.

So we are asking, "Oh, Yahweh, Great I Am, let the world see you as you really are. Let them know you in all your holy otherness. Let whatever happens this day, or this week, or this month, cause people to say that you alone are God."

What do people say of the God you serve? What do they think of the Yahweh for whom you live? Do they see a God who can deliver from doubt, fear, temper, impatience, pettiness, and inordinate desire? If so, they are seeing a God who is holy. If not, what then?

August 15

FEAR OR LOVE

Meanwhile the church throughout Judea, Galilee, and Samaria had
peace and was built up. Living in the fear of the Lord and in the comfort
of the Holy Spirit, it increased in numbers. (Acts 9:31 NRSV)

Since we have these promises, beloved, let us cleanse ourselves
from every defilement of body and of spirit, making holiness
perfect in the fear of God. (2 Corinthians 7:1 NRSV)

Toward a correct understanding of the fear of God, I have said that
the fear of God is not the fear of punishment (what John is talking
about in 1 John 4:18) but rather a way of living. It is to live with a correct
understanding of reality and of your place in it. It is to live carefully and
responsibly, in the knowledge that your life is a gift, and that you are
accountable for what you do with it. It is really important to recognize that
this is not an Old Testament idea (e.g., obey God because you are afraid of
him) that is replaced by the New Testament idea (e.g., obey God because
you love him).

As the passages above show, the fear of God and the love of God go
together. Many of my former students remind me of something I have
frequently said in class: "If the little God who lives under your bed loves
you, that is not particularly good news; but if the God who could fry you
alive by looking at you loves you, that is good news." To have stood at
the foot of the Cross and realized what is actually taking place there—that
the Eternal, Infinite God, Life itself, is dying for us—should definitely not
diminish our awe of God and our determination not to do anything that
would hurt or displease him. Rather it should move us to a new dimension
of that determination. It should determine us, in the words of the Apostle,
to "perfect holiness in the fear of God" (2 Cor 7:1).

August 16

SINS AND SIN

But for those who are self-seeking and who reject the truth and
follow evil, there will be wrath and anger. (Romans 2:8 NIV)

We must clearly distinguish between "sins" and "Sin." "Sins" are any deviation from God's perfection, whether intentional or unintentional. They are actions as well as attitudes. But they are not the same as "Sin." "Sin" is nothing more nor less than self-will. That is why good people will go to hell—because they are good and proud of it: "Who needs God to be good? I am better than most of those people in that church anyway." Self-will, the determination to have my own way, is Sin. It is not a something; it is not a series of actions; it is a whole complex of attitudes toward self and toward others as they impinge on that self.

The Apostle Paul uses several metaphors to talk about sin, but especially "the old man" and "the flesh." When he does so, he clearly speaks about a radical change from it; death to it; putting it off. What he means is that it is possible, in a moment of radical surrender of myself (i.e., my self-will) and a radical infusion of God's grace, for that attitude to be fundamentally altered. No longer does a person live for oneself but for the love of God and others.

Does this mean that such a person can no longer commit acts of sin? Well, Adam and Eve in their perfection could! What do I mean then? What happens to the person who has died to sin? I mean that the attitudes of self-will are fundamentally altered; the person looks at the world, God, themselves, and others from a radically new perspective. No longer is it "what do I want?" From there on, it is "what does God want?" It will have a transforming effect on all their actions and attitudes. Some things will change immediately and dramatically, while others will take longer. But everything will be governed by a new outlook, perception, and disposition.

August 17

THE LAW

For no one can ever be made right with God by doing what the law commands. The law simply shows us how sinful we are. (Romans 3:20)

Well then, if we emphasize faith, does this mean that we can forget about the law? Of course not! In fact, only when we have faith do we truly fulfill the law. (Romans 3:31)

Sin is no longer your master, for you no longer live under the requirements of the law. Instead, you live under the freedom of God's grace. (Romans 6:14)

In the three passages above, the Apostle Paul makes some very telling and very important points about the Law of God. First of all, he tells us that the Law was not given so that we could earn our way into a right relationship with God by keeping it. That was the mistaken idea of the Pharisees. No, the Law had three purposes: to teach the character of God, to teach the character he would like to see in us, and to teach us that we cannot produce that character on our own.

Second, just because we cannot fulfill the Law on our own does not mean that we can forget about it, says Paul. Jesus said the same thing (see Matt 5:17). Jesus expects us to keep the Law. It is God's instruction manual for human flourishing. Moreover, he expects us not merely to keep the letter of the Law, but more than that, its underlying spirit. It is not enough not to commit adultery; don't think adulterous thoughts. Paul says the same: we can fulfill the law—reproduce the character of God—by means of faith in Christ.

But how do we do it? That is Paul's final point. We do not fulfill the Law by keeping a careful list of its requirements and matching that with a careful list of how we are keeping those requirements. That is to be under the law, and it won't work because our selfish disposition will keep defeating us. Yet we *can* defeat sin, the Apostle tells us. We do it by grace through faith. By faith we have died to ourselves and come alive to Christ. Now the Spirit of Christ graciously empowers us to live Christ's life *if we will surrender ourselves to his absolute control* (see Rom 8:1–17). That is what the Instruction Manual (the *Torah*) was all about in the first place— God's life in us. So faith does not undercut the Law; it actually establishes it.

August 18

LAW AND GRACE

What then? Are we to sin because we are not under law but under grace? By no means! Do you not know that if you present yourselves to anyone as obedient slaves, you are slaves of the one whom you obey, either of sin, which leads to death, or of obedience, which leads to righteousness? But thanks be to God, that you who were once slaves of sin have become obedient from the heart to the standard of teaching to which you were committed, and, having been set free from sin, have become slaves of righteousness. (Romans 6:15–18 ESV)

The strength of the biblical teaching on holiness is that it synthesizes the biblical teachings on law and grace without doing damage to either. You say, "What are you talking about?" In the history of the Christian church it has been very difficult to keep law and grace together. A classic example is in the Protestant Reformation with Martin Luther. Luther had struggled to be a faithful Christian, and he thought this meant keeping all the commandments of the Catholic Church and of the Bible. Trying to do this, he found himself crushed and broken. So, as he got into the Word and began to get a picture of the glory of the free grace of God, he came to see grace and law as enemies. Grace frees us from any need to try to keep God's law, he taught.

This is true, as far as it relates to coming into a saved relationship with God. Nothing we have ever done or will ever do can make us acceptable to God. It is God's free grace in Jesus that does this. The danger is that we then begin to apply this idea to the Christian life: "It doesn't matter how I live; I'm saved by grace!" If the Roman church submerged grace under legalism, the modern Protestant church has submerged the holy living that God expects of us under the cover of grace. We say, "It's alright that I don't live a life like Christ's, because I don't need to."

Perhaps you are saying, "Wait a minute! You have shifted your ground. We were talking about the law, but now you are talking about Christ-like living." Actually, I have not shifted ground. The core of the law, its ethical requirements, is nothing other than a Christ-like life. The law gives us the content of such a life. The good news that John Wesley discovered in the Bible is that it is not a matter of law or grace. Rather, as Paul says in the today's passage, grace not only brings us to God, freeing us from the wrong idea that we have to work our way into God's favor, it is also the means, through faith ("obedient from the heart"), to enable us to live the life of God before a watching world.

August 19
DON'T SIN

Well then, since God's grace has set us free from the law, does that mean we can go on sinning? Of course not! Don't you realize that you become the slave of whatever you choose to obey? You can be a slave to sin, which leads to death, or you can choose to obey God, which leads to righteous living. Thank God! Once you were slaves of sin, but now you wholeheartedly obey this teaching we have given you. Now you are free from your slavery to sin, and you have become slaves to righteous living. (Romans 6:15–18)

When we read Romans 6 we get the very clear impression that Paul intends for us to stop sinning. That is, we will stop doing the things we know Jesus, our husband, hates, the things that nailed him to a cross. Can you imagine a wife saying to her husband, "Oh, honey, you know I love you, and I know you hate it, but I just can't stop throwing cigarette butts all over the floor." Paul calls that kind of behavior slavery. He is speaking of the addictive power of sin. We are either in its grip or we are not. We are not talking about unintentional or ignorant acts and attitudes that still need the covering blood of Christ but about stuff we know full well is wrong. We have to make a choice, Paul says: we will either be a slave to sinning or a slave to doing what our Savior loves, what is right.

So, who rules your life? Who is the master whose command you cannot help but obey? Sin is addictive; it is dominating; it is destructive. You cannot be "a little bit" addicted to heroin. You are, or you aren't. "Thank God! Once you were slaves of sin. . . . Now you are free from your slavery to sin." Is it true? It ought to be!

August 20

SLAVES TO SIN OR TO RIGHTEOUSNESS?

What then? Are we to sin because we are not under law but under grace? By no means! Do you not know that if you present yourselves to anyone as obedient slaves, you are slaves of the one whom you obey, either of sin, which leads to death, or of obedience, which leads to righteousness? But thanks be to God, that you who were once slaves of sin have become obedient from the heart to the standard of teaching to which you were committed, and, having been set free from sin, have become slaves of righteousness. (Romans 6:15–18 ESV)

The Apostle Paul is unmistakably clear in his treatment of sin in Romans 6. He says in a variety of ways that there is no place for intentional sin in a believer's life. One of his arguments is seen in the passage above. Now that we don't have to worry about fulfilling the law, does grace give us permission to excuse our intentional sinning, saying "I can't help it"? Absolutely not! In fact, it is grace that makes life without intentional sin possible. He says that one of the problems with sin is that it is addictive; give it place and it will gain control of you and draw you back into its coils and chains and make you unable to live the life of Jesus Christ. If you continue in sin, he says, the lordship of your life will belong to the enemy and not to Jesus Christ. You can no more be partially sinful—we're talking about intentional sin here—than you can be partially pregnant!

Who rules your life? It is the master whose command you cannot help but obey? "God be thanked that though you were slaves of sin, yet you obeyed from the heart the form of the doctrine to which you were delivered and having been set free from sin, you became slaves to righteousness" (Rom 6:18). Notice that he does not say "set free from sin's condemnation" or "sin's guilt," but "from sin."

Perhaps someone asks, "Then what about chapter 7? Surely Paul is saying there that he is unable to stop sinning." While opinions about this differ, it doesn't make sense to me that Paul would directly contradict himself from one chapter to the next. I think he is speaking out of his experience as a Jew before his conversion, addressing a possible response of some persons to chapter 6. They would be saying, "Oh, okay, Paul, you have convinced me. I need to quit sinning and I will just go ahead and do that." To such an idea Paul is saying, "Oh no, that won't work. I tried for years to stop sinning and could not do it." In other words, he is setting us up for chapter 8. Yes, we must stop sinning (chapter 6), but we can't do it on our own (chapter 7); we can only do it by letting the Holy Spirit loose in our lives (chapter 8).

August 21

UNTO HOLINESS

Because of the weakness of your human nature, I am using the
illustration of slavery to help you understand all this. Previously, you
let yourselves be slaves to impurity and lawlessness, which led ever
deeper into sin. Now you must give yourselves to be slaves to righteous
living so that you will become holy. . . . But now you are free from the
power of sin and have become slaves of God. Now you do those things
that lead to holiness and result in eternal life. (Romans 6:19, 22)

The New Living Translation does a good job making clear what could easily be glossed over in a more literal translation of the Greek. A literal translation of Romans 6:19 says "make yourselves slaves of righteousness unto holiness." That's not very clear, is it? What is a "slave of righteousness"? And what does "unto holiness" mean? Verse 22, "Now you do those things that lead to holiness and result in eternal life," is a little clearer but still pretty opaque. What is Paul saying? He is saying five beautiful things:

1. We have changed masters. Once we were enslaved to our own desires for pleasure, possessions, power, and position. Now, we are slaves to God and are no longer ruled by desire.
2. Whereas we were once headed into deeper and deeper sin, now we are free from the power of sin.
3. We are now able to live lives that are right in God's sight, lives that conform to the pattern he had in mind for us when he created us.
4. The natural outcome of right living is godliness (God-like-ness, i.e., holiness). We can share the very character of our Creator!
5. The end result of godliness is eternal life. That makes perfect sense, of course.

What is heaven? It is the presence of God: to be with him, in him, forever. That begins now, as we share his holy character. Praise God!

Two Roads

For the wages of sin is death, but the gift of God is eternal
life in Christ Jesus our Lord. (Romans 6:23 NIV)

We have been made for God. He is the only thing—better, the only One—who can satisfy us. The devil tries to trick us by telling us, "You can be satisfied with money; you can be satisfied with fancy cars; you can be satisfied with sex; you can be satisfied with food," and on and on. It is amazing what silly things we will believe can satisfy us. The fact is, every one of those hauls us in and ties us up in knots, and then when we come to the end, we realize, "No, that's not really what I wanted." Happy is the person who finds that out before it is too late.

In the sixth chapter of Romans, Paul tells us that there are really only two roads in the world: there is the road of God-given righteousness, which leads to godly character and heaven, and there is the other road, which leads to eternal death. He sums it all up in the final verse. Usually, we quote that statement when we're talking to non-Christians, but in the structure of the book, it is clear that Romans 6 is addressed to Christians, people who have been justified by faith (see Romans 3–5). Paul is talking to believers.

He says to you and to me: "the wages of sin is death." If you and I say, "Okay, I'm a Christian. I'm going to go to heaven, and it doesn't matter if I sin a little bit; I'm just human," Paul says you are trying to walk on two roads, and that won't work. In fact, you are working for a task master who one day is going to give you a paycheck that you will have to take, like it or not. However, if you take the holiness road, the righteousness road, the Jesus road (the road he has been talking about in the whole chapter), the *gift* (not the paycheck) of God is eternal life. Do you see what he is saying? If you choose that road, the road of righteousness, your victory over sin through the Spirit doesn't earn anything. Yes, that road ends in heaven, but it is a gift—a gift! It always was and always will be. Give your life to Jesus without any reservation, take his road, the highway of holiness (see Isa 35:8), and you will never, ever, regret it.

THE NORMAL CHRISTIAN LIFE?

So the trouble is not with the law, for it is spiritual and good. The trouble is with me, for I am all too human, a slave to sin. (Romans 7:14)

A well-known preacher has said that Romans 7 describes "the normal Christian life." God forbid! If it does, then the rest of the Bible is nothing more than a carrot on a stick, inviting us to something—a life with God here on earth—that we can never actually know. Praise God, that is not true. Romans 7 does describe a "normal" life, but it is the normal life of a person who is trying to be ethical in their own strength and thereby condemned to perpetual failure. As I said earlier, Romans 7 is Paul's answer to the person who, hearing the Apostle say in such strong terms that a Christian cannot continue to live in intentional sin (see Romans 6), therefore concludes that we must defeat sin in our own strength. Paul, using his own experience as an unconverted Jew, says that effort is doomed to failure.

The evidence that Paul is not talking about the Christian life is seen in the quote above. He says that he is a "slave to sin," but in Romans 6:6, he says, "We are no longer slaves to sin." Then in Romans 8:2, we read: "And because you belong to him, the power of the life-giving spirit has freed you from the power of sin that leads to death." The "normal Christian life" is a life of freedom from the power of sin.

We might ask then why Paul uses first person pronouns in the present tense. Surely, if we took the chapter out of the context of chapters 6 and 8, we would be justified in thinking that Paul is describing his present experience. But don't take the statements out of their context! So, in that context, what is the Apostle doing? I believe he is attempting to give special poignancy to the sin problem we humans face. This is not an abstract theological discussion; it is terribly real. The "flesh" is a deadly force in us and is not going to be defeated by human effort, no matter how well-intentioned that effort may be. The only hope is to let the Spirit who is in us have absolute control. He is the only one who can defeat sin. He can! Let him!

August 24

RAISE THE SAIL

And so he condemned sin in the flesh, in order that the righteous requirement of the law might be fully met in us, who do not walk according to the flesh, but according to the Spirit. . . . You however are not in the realm of the flesh, but in the realm of the Spirit, if indeed the Spirit of God lives in you. And if anyone does not have the Spirit of Christ, they do not belong to Christ. (Romans 8:3a–4, 9 NIV)

One of the great mistakes Christians have made over the years is to read Romans 6–8 separately from each other. They must be read together. When they are, the total message is clear: First, the only way we can find God and the only way we can find God's way for us is by accepting, on faith, that what God did 2,000 years ago through his Son was for me. Then, those who have accepted this mighty work of God in Jesus Christ for themselves are done with sin (see Roman 6). They are done with it. We are not talking about shortcomings or failures, we are talking about the willful breaking of what we know to be God's purposes for human life. Next, how can I, as a Christian, live above conscious, known sin? If you are trying to use disciplined obedience to conquer sin in your life, it won't work. The law was given to show us what sin really is and to show us how sinful we really are. It was sent to lead us to the cross. It has no power to defeat our selfish desire to have our own way (i.e., "the flesh"), which must happen, according to Romans 6. That is Romans 7. So what to do? See Romans 8! In Romans 8, Paul gives us the solution. As Christians, we have the Holy Spirit in us, but he must be let loose. When that happens, and we walk (i.e., live) in his power, he will give us victory over those selfish desires (see Rom 8:4–5), and there is nothing to separate us from the loving arms of our "Pappa" (see Rom 8:15).

Imagine a person on a lake in a sailboat. It's a windy day, and he's paddling furiously, but his sail is furled on the spar. He may paddle with the best will in the world, but he's not going to get very far. Now suppose he unfurls the sail and raises it on the mast as it was intended. The wind will catch it and will take him almost effortlessly toward his goal. So it is with the Christian life. You have the Spirit of God. Christ has given him to you. Stop trying to please him in your own strength, by gritting your teeth and clenching your fists, wearing yourself out. Raise your sail; let the Holy Spirit permeate your life. It will mean letting him have the tiller, but believe me, that is a good thing.

DEEPER IN CHRIST: PART ONE

For the flesh is always hostile to God. It never did obey God's laws, and it never will. That's why those who are under the control of the flesh can never please God. (Romans 8:7–8 author's translation)

If we are to have a deeper life with Christ, we have to claim it; it doesn't come automatically. Paul says the thing that keeps us from a deeper life with Christ is "the flesh." He isn't talking about our bodies but about the desires that tend to dominate our lives in this bodily world. What keeps us from going deeper with Christ? When we live to satisfy our desires, no matter what, and we say we can take care of ourselves, no matter what, that's "the flesh" speaking. Paul says, "That will kill you." It will literally take you down. If you watch television for ten minutes, you can see that's where America is: food, sex, drink, pleasure, comfort, security, possession of things, position, power. The world says, "That's all you can get, so grab it while you can." That's "the flesh" talking. When you have given your life to getting things, to your desires and your comfort, the only thing that matters to you is getting your way. That's the flesh and that's what's killing us. That's what consistently blocks you and me from going deeper in the Lord, because there's always that voice whispering in the background, "If you really surrender your life to the Lord, you won't get all your desires satisfied, you will have to give up neat things, that stuff you spent your life getting, and, worst of all, you'll have to give up getting your own way. You don't really want to go deeper with the Lord." But I say to you, "Oh yes, you do!" There is such freedom in the deeper life in Christ, such peace and joy.

How do we go deeper with Christ? How do we bring our spirit to life? Paul says, "You have to claim what's yours." Claim God's Spirit for your life. If you are a Christian, then the Holy Spirit is in you. He's yours and mine. If you are in Christ, you are in the Spirit, and you will never get more of the Holy Spirit than you got when you accepted Christ. But the Holy Spirit needs to get more of you. Will you stop living for the flesh and let the Holy Spirit change you?

August 26

DEEPER IN CHRIST: PART TWO

For to set the mind on the flesh is death, but to set the mind
on the Spirit is life and peace. (Romans 8:6 ESV)

Tragically in American Christianity, "the flesh" has crept right into the sanctuary. Why do I serve God? To get what I want! What a tragedy! We should serve Christ because that is what we were made for! So what needs to happen? The Holy Spirit needs to fill your being with himself.

When you accepted Christ, the Holy Spirit came into you to change you. Too often, we think that means letting him have only the corners, pieces, and edges of our lives. He is not going to be content with those; he wants the very center. Will you give it to him? What is the center? It is your will. If the flesh is to be defeated in our lives, then our wills have to be re-oriented. What is it that you want? Power, possessions, status, security, comfort? No, what we want is all we were meant to be. It's written in a well-known hymn, "Take my will and make it Thine, it shall be no longer mine. Take my heart—it is Thine own, it shall be Thy royal throne."

That's where Jesus was in the Garden of Gethsemane the night before his crucifixion. Might that cost you some pain, might that cost you some difficulty? Absolutely! If it cost Jesus, why wouldn't it cost his followers? But that pain, that suffering, is as nothing compared to the pain and suffering that keeping the flesh in some place of influence in your life will cost you. When we do that, Paul says, we have linked our spirits to a body that is dying. When the body dies, it will drag us down to eternal death (see Rom 8:10–11).

Claim the promise that the Holy Spirit who is in you, if you're a Christian, can fill you and re-orient your will and give you his will and give you *joy* in doing his will. Have you ever consciously turned over the center of your life to the Holy Spirit and claimed his fullness? If you haven't, that's the next step to going deeper with the Lord, the next step in becoming truly like him.

August 27

LIFE IN THE SPIRIT

For if you live according to the flesh you will die, but if by the Spirit you put to death the deeds of the body, you will live. For all who are led by the Spirit of God are sons of God. For you did not receive the spirit of slavery to fall back into fear, but you have received the Spirit of adoption as sons, by whom we cry, "Abba! Father!" The Spirit himself bears witness with our spirit that we are children of God, and if children, then heirs— heirs of God and fellow heirs with Christ, provided we suffer with him in order that we may also be glorified with him. (Romans 8:13–17 ESV)

If through the Spirit's power we put to death a life of satisfying our own desires, what may we expect? Above all, it is life! The way of desire is death. All our desires decline to death.

I remember my father as he neared 100 years of age saying, "I just don't have any appetite anymore." Likewise, the empires we have built to satisfy our desires for worth and significance all crumble to dust. The Spirit gives life! What we give away of ourselves to others multiplies and grows, never ending. But where does life come from? It comes from another, whether physical or spiritual. We did not choose the hour of our birth, it came from two others who, if all was well, loved one another. So it is spiritually. Our life comes from our Father, our "Pappa." We do not have to give ourselves worth in a frantic search for pleasure, possessions, position, and power. We are alive because our Father has gathered us into his arms in a laughing bear-hug, an embrace made possible because we have allowed him to put to death our foolish idea that life was to be found in our satisfaction of our desires.

But notice the last part of the last sentence above: "provided we suffer with him." What? No, I surrendered my desires to him so as not to suffer! Foolish thought! In this world we will suffer. That is a fact of life. Much of our praying is to avoid suffering, but what the Spirit gives us is the ability to triumph through suffering. A recent article says that the catastrophic rise in teen suicides is because of a lack of "emotional resilience." They don't know how to face suffering. But we do! The Spirit promises that our suffering is "with him." There is the key! Will we suffer? Yes. And perhaps more because we have chosen Christ. However, if we have surrendered to the Spirit, then we know four things for certain: our suffering is not a punishment, he is with us in the suffering, suffering cannot defeat us, and *life* wins!

August 28
GLORIFIED WITH HIM

The Spirit himself bears witness with our spirit that we are
children of God, and if children, then heirs—heirs of God and
fellow heirs with Christ, provided we suffer with him in order that
we may also be glorified with him. (Romans 8:16–17 ESV)

When Jesus had spoken these words, he lifted up his eyes to
heaven, and said, "Father, the hour has come; glorify your
Son that the Son may glorify you." (John 17:1 ESV)

In a good deal of the preaching of recent years, there has been an emphasis upon the great good news that we are children of God, the King, and thus his heirs. A good deal of attention has been given to all the good things that means for us. For instance, we can expect to be healed of all our diseases—unless, unfortunately, we do not have enough faith in our Father. Furthermore, we can expect that all the wealth of heaven should be ours here on earth—if we have enough faith to claim it. In short, as "King's Kids" our lives should be of endless physical and material blessings.

This "gospel" has been transported overseas, and, it must be admitted, is responsible for a good deal of the explosive growth of Christianity outside of North America these days. But this vision of the Christian faith is strangely selective in the reading of its texts. All the apostles make the same argument that Paul does in the verses from Romans printed above: we are the children of God *provided* we suffer with him. In other words, there is a conditionality about our inheritance. If we do not share in Christ's sufferings for the world—which I take to include self-denial for the world's sake, persecution and deprivation because of the world's hostility to Christ, and physical suffering as a result of the world's bondage to sin— *we have no part in his glory*, either here or hereafter.

There is a remarkable expression of this in the Lord Jesus's High Priestly Prayer for his people in John 17. Jesus asks the Father to "glorify" him in the "hour" that is now come upon him. What does he mean by such a statement? Among other things it must mean that as Jesus dies upon the Cross on the next day, the true reality and greatness—the meaning of "glory" in the Bible—of his life and ministry will be displayed. A horrible, gruesome death is glory? Yes, and so it is for us. The true glory of our life and faith is most clearly seen when we suffer with grace, confidence, and victory. Being a "King's Kid" does not mean we won't suffer; it means we *will* suffer but that we can do so "gloriously," as our Lord did.

257

August 29

BONDAGE TO DECAY

For the creation was subjected to frustration, not by its own choice,
but by the will of the one who subjected it, in hope that the creation
itself will be liberated from its bondage to decay and brought into the
freedom and glory of the children of God. (Romans 8:20–21 NIV)

What a pungent phrase: "bondage to decay"! But it is absolutely correct. Everything in creation is decaying. This was brought home to me recently when I got a message from Apple on my phone, speaking of "battery aging" and ways to slow it. It made me realize that the scientists' talk of isolating the "aging gene" in us humans and stopping it is futile. Does the battery have an aging gene? No, it does not. It just gets to the point where it cannot be charged any more. It has decayed! Everything in nature, including us, is decaying, running down, running out, dying.

Something in us humans whispers, "No." I remember my Dad when he was in his nineties saying, "I look in the mirror and wonder who that old man is in there. I don't feel old. I don't really feel any older than I did when I was eighteen." Being forty-five at the time, I chuckled at the idea. Being a lot closer to my nineties now, I realize he was right. My spirit, the essential me, has not aged! Oh yes, it has changed—at least some for the better, I hope. For sure, I have added some wisdom that I did not have at eighteen, but it is still the same "me" in this running-down body.

What does that mean? It means God has made us for eternity! Elizabeth Goudge, a British novelist and a Christian, says it this way:

> When you don't expect to be happy, there is suddenly Easter in your soul, though it be midwinter. Something, you do not know what, has broken the seal upon that door in the depth of your being that opens upon eternity. It is not yet time for you yourself to go out of it but what is beyond comes in and passes into you and through you.

That's it! Though our bodies age and die, God had decreed that our selves will live forever, either in joy or in sorrow, and nature's hope is that it too will one day join us in joy, forever freed from the bondage to decay.

August 30

VICTIMS OF FEELINGS

As it is written: For your sake we face death all day long; we are considered as sheep to be slaughtered. No, in all these things we are more than conquerors through him who loved us. (Romans 8:36–37 NIV)

One of the great dangers of our society is that it can very easily make us feel that we are victims of any number things: persons, forces, situations, you name it. When we feel like that, there are two results: we feel sorry for ourselves, and we feel helpless. So, we feel that we have a right to indulge ourselves and that no one can justly expect anything of us.

Did you notice the key word in that paragraph? It is "feel." We have become controlled by our emotions. If you "feel" that something is so, then it is so. Not so! The Holy Spirit wants to enable us to take control of our feelings and to make something of our lives.

We see this so clearly in Joseph. If there was ever anybody who had the right to feel victimized, it was he. He was a victim of his father's parental favoritism, of his brothers' jealous cruelty, of his brother Reuben's failed good intentions, of his mistress's lies, of his master's refusal to believe him, and of the butler's forgetfulness. I am sure that, being human, he had his dark days in that long thirteen years, but it is clear that he never let his emotions rule him. Why not? It was because he knew that God, not the victimizers, was in control of his life and that God's purposes are good. Because God never gave up on Joseph, Joseph never gave up on God. The result? Joseph did not fall prey to the temptation to self-indulgence. Instead, and he took it upon himself to act responsibly. His circumstances did not rule Joseph; Joseph took charge of his circumstances.

What you can do may seem very small. That doesn't matter; let the Holy Spirit fill you, and do it, whatever it is. Do it with the Spirit's energy and the Spirit's integrity. You may never see the results this side of eternity, but you will make a difference—in your own life, if nowhere else. We are not victims; we are conquerors, more than conquerors!

August 31
A LIVING SACRIFICE

Offer your bodies as living sacrifices, holy and pleasing to God—
this is your true and proper worship. (Romans 12:1 NIV)

Although many Christians believe it, the Christian life is not an effort to earn God's praise or favor. The Christian life is a glad, joyous response to what he has done for us. That is what the Apostle is talking about in Romans 12–15. How do you demonstrate that you have received his forgiveness, that you are filled with the Holy Spirit, that your heart is right with God? It is by the way you live. That is what is going on in the passage above.

There are a couple of surprises here. In the first place, we might expect that Paul would, in the light of everything he had said in Romans 1–11, beg his readers to offer their spirits or their hearts. That is where the real work of transformation has to happen, isn't it? But he does not. Why? Because the only evidence of real spiritual transformation is in what we do with our bodies. If I use my body in a way that is clearly contrary to the way God made us, it says everything you need to know about the state of my heart. The Apostle makes a similar point in 1 Corinthians 6:20: "For you have been bought with a price; therefore glorify God in your body" (NASB).

Then he asks for a "living sacrifice." That is an oxymoron. By definition an animal that is sacrificed has to die. Here I suggest that he is thinking along the lines of his own words: "I die daily," or "I am crucified with Christ, yet I live." Yes, there is a once-for-all sacrifice of our lives to Christ, but it is a sacrifice that must be renewed and worked out anew every day of our lives.

Then he wraps it up with a conundrum: to offer yourself in this way is "logical worship." Surely to worship is to be carried out of yourself in praise and ecstasy. It is not to be reduced to cold logic. Paul's point is that if you want to praise God in the way that is the most appropriate to who he is and what he has done, then you do it by throwing your body on his altar every day. That is what truly "spiritual" (as NAS, ESV, and others translate the word) worship would look like.

September 1

MARKS OF A SURRENDERED CHRISTIAN: NEW ATTITUDE TOWARD SELF

Do not think of yourself more highly than you ought, but rather think of yourself with sober judgment, in accordance with the measure of faith God has given you. (Romans 12:3 NIV)

Four new attitudes mark the surrendered Christian, the person who is being transformed by the spirit of God: a new attitude about themselves, a new attitude about others, a new attitude about obedience, and a new attitude toward the commandments.

What is the central problem of the human race? It is self-centeredness. Self-centeredness is just as controlling for those with low self-esteem as it is for those with high self-esteem. It's simply that your whole life focuses upon you: "I am the center of everything." How do you avoid that? By seeing yourself as a contributing part of the body of Christ. You have a part to play and if you don't play your part, either from arrogance or from false modesty, the body of Christ is not going to function as it should. The world says, "You are just a cog in a machine; you are all you've got, so you'd better play it to the hilt." The Word says, "You are a priceless contributor to the whole of what God is doing and if you don't make your contribution, what God is doing for the world is going to be hurt."

Think of a room full of people. As they came into the room, each one of them was given a funny-shaped little piece of cardboard. There are colors on the pieces, and some of the people begin to compare their piece to other people's pieces. They discover that some pieces fit with others, and they begin to see a pattern emerging. But some of the people find their piece dull and plain, and they just sit by the wall, feeling mistreated. Others, observing that when pieces are fitted together the distinctive shapes of individual pieces are no longer obvious, refuse to allow theirs to be joined. What happens? The height of frustration is spending hours on a jigsaw puzzle and then finding that there are pieces missing. The puzzle is not complete. All you see is those missing funny-shaped holes.

Your piece of the puzzle is vital. Put that piece God has given you into the whole picture. Be transformed in your attitude about yourself. See yourself as holy, God-chosen, a key piece in the puzzle of those who need you.

September 2

MARKS OF A SURRENDERED CHRISTIAN: NEW ATTITUDE TOWARD OTHERS

Then make me truly happy by agreeing wholeheartedly with each other, loving one another, and working together with one mind and purpose. Don't be selfish; don't try to impress others. Be humble, thinking of others as better than yourselves. Don't look out [only]* for your own interests, but take an interest in others, too. (Philippians 2:2–4)

In Romans 12:21, Paul concludes a line of thought that began in verse three of that chapter by saying, "Don't be conquered by evil, but conquer evil by doing good." How do we do that? Many of us attempt to do it with a greater emphasis on ourselves: focusing more on spiritual values, overcoming bad habits, having devotions, attending church more often. Those are all good, but they are not what Paul has been talking about. He has been talking about the way we treat others. According to him, the way you conquer evil is in your relationships to other persons. We do it by being loving to others, honorable to others, diligent with regard to others, by being a joyous person in our relationship to others, patient with others, and humble in relationship to others.

John Wesley said it this way: "There is no holiness but social holiness." He meant there is no holiness unless you live it out in your relationships with other people. The transformation that Christ wants to perform in us is one that will take place in our relationships with other people. Yes, it's wonderful to discipline ourselves, to deepen our spiritual lives, to do what we ought to do in our own persons, but that's not God's ultimate program. His ultimate program is to change how we relate to others.

The fruits of the spirit listed in Galatians all have to do with relationships. It is as we experience the love of Christ in our relationships that evil is conquered. It is as those relationships fail and break down that evil wins a battle. Let Jesus transform you in your relationships to others—you don't do it by your own effort!—and become a key factor in God's defeat of evil in this world.

---

* "Only" is not actually in the Greek text. Almost all English versions include it because of the "too," or "also" in the next line, but Paul's admonition seems stronger than that.

September 3

MARKS OF A SURRENDERED CHRISTIAN: NEW ATTITUDE ABOUT OBEDIENCE

Let every person be subject to the governing authorities; for there is no authority except from God, and those authorities that exist have been instituted by God. (Romans 13:1 NRSV)

Be transformed in your attitude toward yourself, toward others, toward obedience, and toward the commandments. Paul says that a good indicator of our attitude toward obedience is seen in the way we relate to government. There are two pitfalls to be avoided. One side says, "I am a Christian, so I don't have to obey mere human governments. Human laws don't have any bearing on me. I live by grace. If the law says so and so, I don't have to do that. I'm a Christian." The other side says, "Since God instituted government, I have to do whatever it says, even if it's wrong."

Paul says, "Be obedient to human government as unto God." What does he mean? He means that it is very easy to kid ourselves that we are obedient to God when we can't see him. Your real attitude toward obedience will be seen in how you respond to human authority, as represented in all levels of government. God established government. He gave it to us. Why? Because humans need to practice obedience. We have to surrender our Adam-born rebelliousness. If I am living in defiance of my human government, it's foolishness to say I am obeying God. What about civil disobedience? If indeed the human government calls me to do things that God tells me not to do, then my allegiance is clear. It must be to God. Paul is calling us to see the government not as a threat but as an opportunity to practice the kind of obedience that is typical of joyous Christians. Obey the government because government is God's design for teaching us obedience. See obedience to government as an opportunity to practice obedience to God.

A young Russian man told me how impressed he was when he visited America with how law-abiding Americans are. I told him there is one simple reason for that. It is because of our long Christian heritage. I also told him that it is disappearing as we speak. When we run red lights, when we speed, when we cheat on our income tax, etc., those are an infallible measure of our attitude toward obedience, and, Paul says, toward God.

September 4

MARKS OF A SURRENDERED CHRISTIAN: NEW ATTITUDE TOWARD COMMANDMENTS

Owe nothing to anyone—except for your obligation to love one another. If you love your neighbor, you will fulfill the requirements of God's law. For the commandments say, "You must not commit adultery. You must not murder. You must not steal. You must not covet." These—and other such commandments—are summed up in this one commandment: "Love your neighbor as yourself." Love does no wrong to others, so love fulfills the requirements of God's law. (Romans 13:8–10)

This is the fourth and last of our series on the Apostle Paul's marks of a surrendered (and transformed) Christian in Romans 12 and 13. In some ways this is a "follow-on" from the previous mark: obedience. There, Paul used our response to government to talk about the necessity of an obedient spirit. Here, he goes further, talking about the necessity of being transformed in our attitude toward the commandments.

There are two wrong attitudes toward commandments in the Bible. One attitude says, "I'd better do this or God is going to get me." The other wrong attitude says, "Because I'm a Christian I can live as I wish. I am forgiven by grace not on account of my obedience." The first attitude asks, "How little obedience can I give to satisfy the minimums?" The result is a cold, calculating, heartless, minimal obedience. The second attitude explains away the most obvious disobedience as being acceptable because God in his grace wants me to be happy.

What is the transformed attitude toward the commandments? Paul says, "Do it for love." Why don't I steal? Because I love that person, and I'm not going to take what belongs to them. Why don't I commit adultery? Because I love that woman too much to do that with her. It's not love that makes you commit adultery, it's lack of love. If you really love that woman, you won't go to bed with her. She's too precious to be used in that way. Be transformed. It is for love that you do not lie, steal, covet, etc.

What about the first four commandments about God? It's because you love God that you make him first in your life, it's because you love God that you refuse to make an idol of him, it's because you love God that you don't just throw his name around in cheap and dirty ways. It's because you love God that you give a seventh of your time to him. One of the most loving things you can do for your neighbor is to love God.

So "don't be conformed to this world" which says, "Only obey as many of the commandments as you are forced to." See obedience to the commandments as an act of love for others.

September 5

SUBMIT TO AUTHORITY

Everyone must submit to governing authorities. For all authority comes
from God, and those in positions of authority have been placed there
by God. So anyone who rebels against authority is rebelling against
what God has instituted, and they will be punished. (Romans 13:1–2)

This passage has created a lot of heartburn over the centuries. First,
it seems out of place in its setting in Romans. In chapter twelve Paul
is talking about how love enables us to overcome evil with good. Then in
Romans 13:8 he goes back to love, saying that we fulfill the requirements of
the *Torah* when we love our neighbors. Second, this passage has been used
by governments across the centuries to justify oppression. Evil people, like
the Nazis, have demanded that Christians do whatever the government
says because their God commands them to. Third, it doesn't seem that
Paul himself obeyed it. Reliable tradition tells us that Paul was killed by
the Roman authorities because he refused to submit to them when they
required him to say that Caesar was God.

So what's going on? Better scholars than I have puzzled over this, but
let me make a suggestion. Paul's emphasis on free forgiveness through
faith in Christ that issues in love has an implicit danger. That danger is
this: "Oh, I am free to do what I want as long as I can say that it is really
the loving thing." Do you see where this can lead? Who defines what the
loving thing is? Me? The problem with that is that our capacity for self-
deception in the service of our own ends is almost limitless. So Paul, I
believe, pulls in a very practical check on that kind of anarchy. We need to
learn submission. Our desires and our ways have to be brought under the
control of something outside ourselves. Of course, that is first of all to God,
and then to his Word. But even there, the power of the self to justify what
it wants to do is frightening. So Paul brings in something very concrete:
I learn submission by submitting to earthly authority, which is a proxy
for God's authority. Christianity does not make me a worse citizen but a
better one.

However, there is a caveat that Paul, in the interest of making his
point, does not bring up. When government, instead of *exercising* God-
given authority, *usurps* that authority, then God must be obeyed. Can
we criticize the government? Yes. Might there be a time when we must
defy the government? Yes. But in the meantime, let's learn submission by
obeying authority, as represented by the government.

September 6

MEMBERS OF ONE ANOTHER

For as in one body we have many members, and the members do not
all have the same function, so we, though many, are one body in Christ,
and individually members one of another. (Romans 12:4–5 ESV)

Therefore, having put away falsehood, let each one of you speak the truth
with his neighbor, for we are members one of another. (Ephesians 4:25 ESV)

The Bible is responsible for four great pillars of civilization: individual worth, liberation, rationality, and historical progress. Yet if we try to dispense with the God who makes them all possible and absolutize them, they are deadly. Take individual worth, for example: the Bible tells us that each one of us is in the image of God and that he knows us by name. What a blessing! Take God out of the equation, however, and we are left with individualism, the conviction that I and my desires are the only things that matter in the world.

That attitude can creep into our faith. We can come to feel that we are Christian individuals who do not need anyone else and are not responsible to anyone else for what we do. So, you cannot tell me that what I am doing is wrong, and if it is, it's my problem, not yours, so "butt out." The Bible tells us that we are all a part of the body of Christ. So, if I fall into sin, it's your business because I weaken you. If you fall into sin, it's my business because together our life in Christ is damaged. If I become a materialist and live for all I can get, it's your problem too. If I am mastered by greed, it's your problem.

So, as you and I make choices and decisions about our walk with God, we need to make them with each other in mind. This is why I am committed to fostering long-term small groups where we can learn to love and trust one another. When we submit ourselves to one another, encouraging, loving, and helping one another to see what we might not see ourselves, we are living as and strengthening the body of Christ. If you are not in a group now, I encourage you to find one, or start one. We are of individual worth, but we are also the body of Christ.

September 7

THE CHRISTIAN MESSAGE

Love does no wrong to others, so love fulfills the requirements of
God's law. This is all the more urgent, for you know how late it is;
time is running out. Wake up, for our salvation is nearer now than
when we first believed. The night is almost gone; the day of salvation
will soon be here. So remove your dark deeds like dirty clothes, and
put on the shining armor of right living. (Romans 13:10–12)

What is the Christian message? The book of Romans gives us the most complete summary. First, all of us were made to live in a dependent relationship with God. But none of us can do that. None of us can forge a relationship with God on our own. None of us can find true life on our own. Something in us demands to be God, and that selfish attitude separates us from him and results in behaviors that are destructive to our lives and the lives of those around us.

God has come across the barrier to us in Jesus. He has taken the consequences of our rebellion—death—upon himself. If we believe what God says about Jesus, "He's my Son and he gave his life for the sins of the world," and accept that sacrifice on our behalf, we can have that life-giving relationship we were made for. We can be re-united with God.

Just as the rebellion manifested itself in certain behaviors, so the re-union must also. Accepting Christ's offer of eternal life is not merely a legal transaction. It is to invite the life of God into ourselves through Christ. That must necessarily entail a radical transformation of our attitudes toward ourselves and toward others and toward what life is about. At its most basic, that transformation will involve a change of viewpoint from inward to outward. Do something that would hurt my Savior? Oh, never! Live as though other humans—my brothers and sisters—those for whom he died—are merely objects for my use? God forbid!

It is all possible—it is *only* possible—through the Holy Spirit of God who comes in and transforms us from lost to saved, from self-centered to other-centered, from sinner to saint. Praise God he has come, the Savior, the Comforter, the Deliverer, our Father, has come.

WHAT ABOUT MY RIGHTS?

In the same way, some think one day is more holy than another day, while others think every day is alike. You should each be fully convinced that whichever day you choose is acceptable. Those who worship the Lord on a special day do it to honor him. Those who eat any kind of food do so to honor the Lord, since they give thanks to God before eating. And those who refuse to eat certain foods also want to please the Lord and give thanks to God. For we don't live for ourselves or die for ourselves. If we live, it's to honor the Lord. And if we die, it's to honor the Lord. So whether we live or die, we belong to the Lord. (Romans 14:5–8)

One of the things that we as humans, and especially as Christians, struggle with is ethical decisions. Of course, for believers in scripture some things are clearly right and wrong. They are right or they are wrong, and our choices make no difference. But there are other things where the grayness is terribly frustrating. We wonder, "Is this right or is that right? Should I do this or do that? God, just tell me!" But God has chosen not to give an absolutely clear word. How do we work that out?

In Romans, Paul tells us to ask ourselves two questions, "How will my decision affect others?" and, "Will this honor the Lord?" The questions he does not leave room for are: "Do I have a right to do this?" and, "Can I get away with it?" Notice two things here. First, rights never enter into the gospel discussion, and that's hard for us twenty-first-century Americans to believe, because the only thing we know about ethics is rights. Rights have nothing to do with the gospel, and we would do well to remember that. Second, notice the differences in the questions. The first set does not include me, while the second set is only about me. There is the issue: If I am to make good ethical decisions, God has to do something in my life to take the focus off me. If I do this thing, will I injure the conscience of a brother or sister? Then I cannot do it. Can this activity be done in the Lord's honor? Then do it with joy.

How do I decide that? Well, what about recreational activities on the Lord's Day? Do they promote rest and creativity? Or do they promote more stress, competition, and large expenditures, so that we have to have Monday "to rest up"? Again, the question ought not to be, "Can I do this and not injure my faith?" but, "How will this express and enhance my faith?"

September 9

ACCEPT ONE ANOTHER

Accept one another, then, just as Christ accepted you, in order to bring praise to God. For I tell you that Christ has become a servant of the Jews on behalf of God's truth, so that the promises made to the patriarchs might be confirmed and, moreover, that the Gentiles might glorify God for his mercy. As it is written: "Therefore I will praise you among the Gentiles; I will sing the praises of your name." (Romans 15:7–9 NIV)

In Romans 12:3–15:15 Paul is speaking about the behavior of those persons who are not conformed to this world but have been transformed through a divine reconstruction of their ways of thinking (see Rom 12:1–2). How does this transformed way of thinking manifest itself in regard to ethnic and religious differences? Paul tells us to look at the example of Jesus, but it is very easy to gloss over the radical implications of what he says. When you take out all the intervening independent clauses, Paul says that Jesus became a servant to Jews for the sake of Gentiles. Jesus subjected himself to the Jewish lifestyle: he was circumcised, he didn't eat unclean food, and he observed the Jewish festivals. Why did he do those things? Not just to win the Jews. He became subject to those customs as a means of winning the Gentiles. It was through what God had revealed to the Jews that Gentiles would have the chance of salvation. That is a radical thought!

The transformed mind says, "I want you to have every opportunity to know Jesus, and if my conforming to a certain lifestyle will help in that, I will do it. On the other hand, if my giving up a lifestyle that is comfortable to me will help in that, I will gladly give it up." I have never forgotten a story a missionary told. He said that when they arrived in the host country, the barrels that held all their belongings were held up in customs for six months. They had to live from hand to mouth, but their ministry proceeded in a wonderful way. Then, the barrels were released and they finally had their stuff. He said that all the inroads they had made into the community seemed to disappear. Slowly he began to understand. For the first six months, they had been living in poverty just like the people. Now, from the people's perspective, all that American wealth had come to stand in the way.

The transformed mind does not say, "You must conform to me," but rather, "How can I conform to you?"

September 10

WOULD SAINT PAUL HAVE WORN A MASK?

Don't just pretend to love others. Really love them. Hate what is wrong. Hold tightly to what is good. Love each other with genuine affection and take delight in honoring each other. (Romans 12:9–10)

Everyone must submit to government authorities. For all authority comes from God and those in positions of authority have been placed there by God. So any one who rebels against authority is rebelling against what God has instituted, and they will be punished. (Romans 13:1–2)

I think the answer to the question posed above is: certainly. There was a single principle that flowed through Paul's ministry. That principle was the Cross and what the Cross is all about: submission. Here it is submission to government authority in that it represents God's authority and submission to others in the sense that we love them just as unselfishly as our Savior loved them. This thing of submission is very hard for us individualistic Americans, who are so used to having the freedom to control most if not all the aspects of our lives.

A young boy of my acquaintance said to his father, "I'm going to move out into the backyard and live in a tent where I won't have to obey any of your rules." His father replied that that would be fine, but he did wonder what his son would eat and suggested that as long as he was eating his father's food, all the rules would still apply. The boy was crestfallen.

There it is. Some government official says, "You must wear a mask during the present pandemic," and the knee-jerk response of many of us is, "Not me!" Why not? "Because nobody tells me what to do, and anyway, it's uncomfortable." Maybe a non-Christian can say that, but I don't see how a Christian can. The way of the Cross says, "I will not give space in any way to a rebellious attitude. My attitude to duly constituted authority will always be submission." (Of course, as the early church demonstrated, when that authority was exercised in the face of God, that was another issue. But that does not apply here or in most of life's issues.)

Not only would Paul gladly submit to government authority whenever possible as unto God, he would also submit his "rights" to the best interests of those around him. If a mask would keep him from breathing potentially harmful germs on others, he would gladly experience the minor discomforts a mask entails in order to protect them. To be walking with God in a redeemed relationship through Christ is to see others as he sees them: persons of infinite worth who are deserving of every good he (and we, his children) can give them.

When Morning Gilds the Skies

September 11
DO NOT JUDGE

Or do you not know that the Lord's people will judge the world?
And if you are to judge the world are you not competent to judge
trivial cases? Do you not know that we will judge angels? How
much more the things of this life? (1 Corinthians 6:2–3 NIV)

In this so-called "post-modern" age, even more than previously, it seems that everyone's favorite Bible verse is, "Judge not that you be not judged" (Matt 7:1) That is because now more than ever we insist that whatever we want to believe about life and the way to live it is up to each of us alone, that no one may dare tell us that what we want is wrong. Yet in the passage of Scripture where the above verses are found (1 Cor 5:1–6:20), Paul is shocked that the Corinthians have not passed judgment on one of their members for committing a flagrant case of incest.

Is Paul contradicting Jesus? To use Pauline language, "By no means!" As always in the Bible, context is everything. When Jesus told his hearers not to judge, he meant that they were not to judge others to make themselves look better. They were not to judge others in order to deflect attention from themselves. They were not to judge others so that they could avoid dying to their own passions and desires. He did not mean that we have no responsibility to each other to challenge one another to the best and highest character. He did not mean that there are no standards of behavior for Christian believers, and he did not mean that we should allow our own imperfect performance to rob us of our voices.

The issue is, "Why am I doing this?" Paul passed judgment on this case of sinful behavior and called for the Corinthians to carry out his judgment for two reasons. The first was for the sake of the Church, "the fellowship." The second reason was for the sake of the sinful person himself. Paul clearly wished the man to repent and be restored to the fellowship.

As in every issue in the Christian faith, the key is love. Do I love the Church enough to speak, to act? Do I love the person enough to speak, to act? If passing judgment can be a selfish act, so can not passing judgment be a selfish act. In the end, the question is always, whom do I love?

September 12

THE INSIDIOUS NATURE OF TEMPTATION

If you think you are standing strong, be careful not to fall. The temptations in your life are no different from what others experience. And God is faithful. He will not allow the temptation to be more than you can stand. When you are tempted, he will show you a way out so that you can endure. (1 Corinthians 10:12–13)

We need to recognize the insidious nature of temptation. In his book *A Plain Account of Christian Perfection*, John Wesley makes an interesting statement. He says words to this effect, "I used to say that a sanctified [made holy] person never felt temptation. I don't say that anymore." Experience is a great teacher, isn't it? So what is temptation anyway? I offer what follows very tentatively, but I think it rings true in my own life, and I suspect it is what Wesley was talking about.

I suggest that oftentimes the internal feeling we have in response to some external event is actually the temptation, not the external event itself. Suppose someone makes a left turn in front of me when I have the right of way, and I am in a hurry to get somewhere because I have to preach a sermon on holiness, and I have a reaction of irritation. Well, doesn't that mean I should turn around and go home? Surely people who are being made holy don't have reactions like that, do they? I am not so sure. I think that reaction may in and of itself be the temptation and that the issue is not to try to deny that feeling but to determine what to do with it. Shall I nurture it, cuddle it, enjoy it? Shall I scream at the other driver, try to cut him off, or spend the rest of my trip mentally rehearsing how unfair it was? Or can we live in the place Charles Wesley talked about in his hymn: "I want a principle within of watchful, godly fear, a sensibility to sin, a pain to feel it near." Are we in that relationship with the Holy Spirit where he can say, "Hey, John, you don't really want to hang on to that irritation, do you?" Then, we can respond, "Oh, no," and find a wonderful divinely-given ability to let it go and be as pure as the driven snow.

I think many of us have beaten ourselves up for a long time and become privatistic, legalistic, and over-introspective because we have such feelings. Would it be good to get to a point where nothing that happened externally could arouse in me any kind of wrong feeling? Possibly so, but that might be to be physically dead! Let me suggest that having the feeling itself in and of itself is not wrong. That is the temptation. What we do with the temptation is the issue.

September 13

DOES IT MATTER?

And if there is no resurrection of the dead, then Christ has not been
raised. And if Christ has not been raised, then your faith is useless
and you are still guilty of your sins. (1 Corinthians 15:16–17)

For the last century and a half, Bible scholars, in Europe first and then in the United States, have argued that the biblical narrative could not have occurred as it stands. Their reasons for this, although they start with a basic hostility to miracles, are still not without some basis, enough so that many students feel compelled to accept at least some of the arguments. One writes recently, "If I accept that Moses did not write the Pentateuch and that what is reported to have happened there did not happen, how does that affect my understanding of the rest of the Bible?" Here is my answer. Basically, the question is this: why did the Israelites create an entirely fictional history for themselves (with a literary genre—historical narrative—that no one else of that time ever used for this purpose) in order to convey their religious ideas, while at the same time obscuring how those ideas actually arose?

For the secularist, the answer is of no real importance. But if we believe what the Bible says about God and the meaning of life, the answer is all-important. Why should we believe their theological insights are true when they lie to us about how those insights came to them? It will not do to say, "Well, they really did not think of themselves as lying. They were just using literary conventions of the day." Where are those "literary conventions" outside of Israel? They do not exist. No other nation anywhere before or during Bible times attempted to express their religion through a connected narrative of human historical persons and events. That does not mean that Moses sat down to write a history in our modern sense. No, he was telling how Israel had come to know God through God's actions and words *in certain aspects of Israel's historical experience*. So, although we should not use this narrative to reconstruct a complete account of Israel's history, we can say that what is reported is an accurate account of what happened. That means we cannot separate the authenticity of what is derived from these experiences (i.e., the theology) from the authenticity of the report itself. These things happened!

September 14
DEATH, WHERE IS YOUR STING?

"O death, where is your victory? O death, where is your sting?" For sin
is the sting that results in death, and the law gives sin its power. But
thank God! He gives us victory over sin and death through our Lord
Jesus Christ. So, my dear brothers and sisters, be strong and immovable.
Always work enthusiastically for the Lord, for you know that nothing
you do for the Lord is ever useless. (1 Corinthians 15:55–58)

There are two experiences common to every human being on earth, no matter their ethnicity, economic status, culture, or location: birth and death. For much of the world in most of human history, both have been an accepted feature of daily life. Babies were being born almost every day, and almost every day, someone was dying, often one of the recently-born babies. In 1637, during the Thirty-Years War, when battles between Protestants and Catholics were devastating Germany, plague and famine came to the refugee-filled city of Eilenberg. In that year Pastor Martin Rinkart buried 5,000 people, including his wife. Death was a present reality that people had to come to terms with in some way.

In modern Western society, we have succeeded in hiding death away. We have put it in hospitals and nursing homes where only the minimum have to see it. We have made health a fetish, acting as though if we just work hard at it, life can go on indefinitely. The result is the panic that runs through a society faced with a pandemic. This is not to suggest that due caution should not be taken, particularly so as not to infect others, but it is to say that unless Jesus comes back first, we all will die, and that fact should not come as a surprise.

So how do you face death? If all you know is this life, you try to deny death—or forget about it or cover it up with finery. When you can do none of those, you despair, admitting that it has won in the end—or not. Martin Rinkart wrote these words, "Now thank we all our God with heart and hand and voices, who wondrous things hath done, in whom this world rejoices." What? Is the man delusional? No, he is not. He knows that death, whenever and however it comes, is not the winner. It is Satan's biggest gun, and it has failed. Our God, Father, Son, and Holy Spirit, has defeated death. If this disease, or some other, marks the end of this earthly life for any of us, God's children, it is not the end of life but only the entry-way into the rest of life. Thanks be to God! Let us live these days in the victory of the resurrection.

September 15

BE ON GUARD

Be on guard. Stand firm in the faith. Be courageous. Be strong.
And do everything with love. (1 Corinthians 16:13–14)

It is really hard to improve on these brief instructions for the Christian life. They are terse, to the point, and comprehensive. If we do these consistently, we will be faithful to the end. Friends, there is no guarantee of that. I have been crushed recently to learn that a man who has been in the ministry for many years, whose ministry I have admired and been blessed by has lost his ministerial credentials because of sexual misconduct. So if that can happen to someone like that, it can happen to any of us. The collapse doesn't have to be as visible as that; it can be any of a number of other things; but the good news is that it does not have to happen! We can run the race and win the prize, and it is as simple as Paul's simple words.

The first challenge is to know that we have an enemy who is out to destroy us: *be on guard!* That doesn't mean we need to live in constant tension. "Greater is he that is in us than he that is in the world." But we have to recognize the threats in order to utilize our wonderful resources.

Then, *stand firm in the faith.* All around us we see people who are compromising. Can you keep a personal faith while undercutting the intellectual roots of that faith? Yes, for awhile, but there is an end to it. There comes a day we will have gone too far: when we open the drawer to draw on our faith, we will find the drawer empty.

In it all, we must *be courageous.* In stories about battle, courage is often simply the willingness to take action. We think that "bravery" is some special quality that a person manifests all the time, but that is hardly ever the case. A squad of men is pinned down by enemy fire, and suddenly one of them, perhaps the least likely one, jumps up and rushes the enemy emplacement and destroys it—courage. Our Enemy tells us, "You can't do anything; you'll fail; it's too much." So sure enough, we do nothing. Instead, let's be courageous and act.

Finally, do it all *in love.* Yes! What is this faith all about? Oh, it's about me—me being on guard, me keeping the faith, me acting with courage. No! It's not about me. It's about God and others. The Devil does not really care how he gets me to focus on me. If he succeeds in that, he has won. Why do all this? For love—love of the One who has loved me to the end, love of those for whom my Lover has given everything. Follow these simple instructions, day after day, and the prize is ours.

September 16

A SWEET FRAGRANCE

But thank God! He has made us his captives and continues to lead us
along in Christ's triumphal procession. Now he uses us to spread the
knowledge of Christ everywhere, like a sweet perfume. Our lives are
a Christ-like fragrance rising up to God. But this fragrance is perceived
differently by those who are being saved and by those who are perishing.
To those who are perishing, we are a dreadful smell of death and doom.
But to those who are being saved, we are a life-giving perfume. And
who is adequate for such a task as this? (2 Corinthians 2:14–16)

What does it mean to be in covenant with God, to belong to him and have him belong to us? How do I show that I'm in a relationship with God? By loving my neighbor enough not to steal from him. By loving him enough not to lie to him or commit adultery with his wife, etc. God is profoundly ethical, and those who know him are as well. However, it is not merely a matter of being ethical; it is, like him, treating people ethically because we love them. The Apostle Paul says the whole Law is summed up in one word—love (see Gal 5:14)! This is not a warm, fuzzy kind of love but a hard-edged love in the sense that I die to myself for the love of you.

You can believe God for a love that overflows. You can believe God for a supernatural control of your desires. You can believe God for a disciplined life. You can believe God for the ability not to cut your leaders into shreds, for a spirit that rises up in gratitude, for a spirit that prostrates itself before the living God twenty-four hours a day and as a result has the ability to find good in the most unlikely people.

I've been involved in Christian organizations my entire professional life and what breaks my heart is our tendency to assign bad motives to one another, to assume the worst in each other. Oh, the *sweet fragrance* of the lives of those who look at people around them and believe the best of them and look for understanding of why they act as they do, those who extend grace and mercy to everyone they come in contact with. This is to know God.

September 17
ENVY AND JEALOUSY

For I fear that perhaps when I come I may find you not as I wish, and that you may find me not as you wish—that perhaps there may be quarreling, jealousy, anger, hostility, slander, gossip, conceit, and disorder. (2 Corinthians 12:20 ESV)

It is striking that in the Epistles, when there is a catalog of sins, envy and jealousy seem to appear in every one. By my count they appear some dozen times. Why so common? I suggest that it is because the underlying problem they reflect is so common. That problem is an unsurrendered ego. If I have to protect myself and project myself in every situation, then the accomplishments and attainments of others will always be a threat. I will never be able to truly rejoice with them.

Most of the time, as in the passage above, envy and jealousy are associated with quarreling and strife. So it is that often "church fights" are borne out of envy and jealousy. When somebody is being spoken well of, it hurts us, and we have to find a way to diminish them, even to the point of blowing some issue completely out of proportion so that it becomes a pretext for bringing them down. Someone is getting ahead of us, and we cannot stand it.

What is the cure? I think it has three parts. First, we need to let God love us. When we know that we are really loved and valued by God, we don't have to bring anyone else down to lift ourselves up. Second, we need to give ourselves to God without a limit or a rival. We are his and what happens to us is his business. Third, we need to see others not as competitors but as brothers and sisters. When these three are in place, the command to love one another is not an impossible challenge but a real possibility.

Murder is terrible. Lying, cheating and stealing are awful. But deeper than all of those are envy and jealousy. They are among the truly deadly sins. Oh God, guard our hearts against them.

September 18

DISPOSITION AND PERFORMANCE

But we pray to God that you may not do anything wrong—not that we may appear to have met the test, but that you may do what is right, though we may seem to have failed. For we cannot do anything against the truth, but only for the truth. For we rejoice when we are weak and you are strong. This is what we pray for, that you may become perfect. (2 Corinthians 13:7–9 NRSV)

Today many people shy away from any use of the word "perfect" in relation to Christian living. It is easy to understand why we would do that. "Perfect" means "flawless." A perfect diamond is one without a single flaw, but we will all agree that no human is flawless. Yet, the Bible, both in Greek and Hebrew, uses terms that would be best translated into English with "perfect," as above. What does the text have in mind? Is it really possible for a human Christian to be "perfect"?

Well, yes, it is. As the contemporary chorus says, "God can make a perfect heart." However, it is absolutely essential that we distinguish between disposition and performance. None of us will ever perform flawlessly. Many times people have expected that if they surrendered their will to God and believed the Holy Spirit to fill them, they would have no more behavior problems. When that did not happen, they became discouraged and gave up. In other cases, insisting that God had done his promised work, people have denied that their behavior problems existed.

Changed behavior is a matter of growth in holiness. That being said, real growth in those areas is only possible after God has changed our disposition. The unsanctified, or unholy, disposition is what Ezekiel called "the stony heart" (Ezek 11:18–21, 36:24–28). It insists on its own way. That condition can only be dealt with in a crisis moment of faith. God cleanses us of that perverted, self-centered will and gives us a new disposition. Ezekiel calls it a "heart of flesh," one that is completely responsive to God. Your disposition is perfected, made completely his. Whereas before there was a tendency to say, "I'll do what you want if it's what I want," now the response is a glad, "Whatever you want!" We will sometimes struggle to know exactly what he wants, but when we know it, there will be a yes! Our disposition has been made whole, complete, for God.

September 19

IT'S NOT ABOUT PERFORMANCE

My old self has been crucified with Christ. It is no longer I who live, but Christ lives in me. So I live in this earthly body by trusting in the Son of God, who loved me and gave himself for me. (Galatians 2:20)

One of the deadliest traps for those who seek to live holy lives is the performance trap. We measure our relationship with God by how well we are doing in achieving certain standards. But our performance is not our work; it is the Lord's. This is what Paul means when he says in today's verse, "It is no longer I who live, but Christ lives in me." It is also what he is talking about in Philippians 2:9 when he says he does not want his own righteousness achieved by obeying the law but God's righteousness that comes by faith.

Some have thought he was talking about God's merely declaring him righteous when in fact he was not. That is not what Paul is saying; he expects himself and other Christians to live righteous lives. The issue is how. Shall it be by our efforts? Then we will always live in condemnation, knowing we fall short.

Instead, we live out God's life and character by faith. This is what Paul was trying to get the Galatians to understand when he asked them if they, having come into a relationship with God by grace through faith, now thought that they could live out that life through effort (see Gal 3:3).

It is the same for us. The Christian life is not a tightrope walk before admiring, or critical, crowds. It is a walk in a garden with our Father, who, as we let go of our pride and our fear, enables us to walk like he does.

September 20

CALLED TO LIVE IN FREEDOM

For you have been called to live in freedom, my brothers and sisters.
But don't use your freedom to satisfy your sinful nature. Instead, use
your freedom to serve one another in love. For the whole law can be
summed up in this one command, "Love your neighbor as yourself." But
if you are always biting and devouring one another, watch out! Beware
of destroying one another. So let the Holy Spirit guide your lives. Then
you won't be doing what your sinful nature craves. (Galatians 5:13–16)

Paul goes Jesus one better, doesn't he? Jesus said the whole law could
be summed up in two commands (see Matt 22:37–40), and here Paul
says it can be summed up in one! I suspect that Paul means that if we truly
love God, we will be able to love others, and that *that* is the goal of the
whole thing, but whether we say one or two, is that right? Is the law about
love?

Most of us don't think so. For most of us, the law is about a whole
bunch of demands. It certainly has nothing to do with love. The gospel,
on the other hand, is about love, and the gospel has set us free from the
demands of the law. That means we are free to do what we want, confident
that we will be forgiven.

That is exactly where Paul will not go. The apostle is thinking along
these lines: if we try to use God's commands as a way to make ourselves
good enough for God, our sinful determination to have our own way (i.e.,
"the sinful nature," or "the flesh") will always defeat us. We will be in
bondage, always trying and always falling short. The Cross tells us we don't
have to make ourselves good enough for God; he has already forgiven us
in self-sacrificing love. We are free! Free to do what? Run amok? Live like
the devil? Never!

Now, having received the Holy Spirit through the Cross, and thus
being filled with the love of God, we are free to fulfill the purpose of the
law in the first place: giving ourselves away for others in self-sacrificing
love. Why do we not dishonor our parents, murder, steal, slander, commit
adultery, and lust after the possessions of others? Because God will get us
if we do? No! It is because we cherish our parents' reputation; we cherish
the possessions, the life, the reputation, and the sexual integrity of those
around us. Spirit-filled believers have been set free from their demand
to have their own way and are enabled to care more about others than
themselves. They are now free to fulfill the true purpose of the law: love.

September 21
THE FREEDOMS OF THE CHRISTIAN

*For you were called to freedom, brothers and sisters; only do not
use your freedom as an opportunity for self-indulgence, but through
love become slaves to one another. (Galatians 5:13 NRSV)*

I saw a T-shirt today with the slogan "Don't Mess with My Freedom."
What was the wearer wanting to communicate about freedom? I am
quite sure he was thinking, as so many Americans are today, of his right to
do anything he wanted. Freedom in this day and time has come to mean
freedom from constraint of any sort, including the constraints of duty,
responsibility, the common good, or whatever. "I must do my own thing at
whatever cost to anybody else" has become the common line. What's gone
wrong to make us think like that? We have lost hope.

Above everything else America's dream was founded upon hope—the
sturdy conviction that with good will, faithfulness, and hard work it was
possible to achieve anything. Having lost that hope, we have fallen into
the pit of self-indulgence, and if someone or something dares to limit that
right of self-indulgence, they are in serious trouble. That is not freedom. It
is merely another kind of bondage.

Thank God for the freedom that comes to us in Christ Jesus—freedom
to love when we are not loved in return, freedom to serve without keeping
a record of who is serving us, freedom to take that lower place without
martyrdom or bitterness, freedom to find contentment where it meets us
instead of lunging at it and missing it, freedom to be pure, freedom from
deceit or malice, freedom from self-consciousness, from jealous ambition,
from arrogant pride, and from the passion to possess. Freedom.

We hope for heaven with him one day, but better than that, we may
know today what it is to be like him in his grace, to be like him in his
power, and to be like him in his freedom. There is the assurance that you
and I, through the indwelling Spirit, may turn every constraint into an
opportunity and in so doing, be free. Freedom in Christ today, tomorrow,
and forever—that's true freedom.

September 21

GOD IS LOVE

For you have been called to live in freedom, my brothers and sisters. But don't use your freedom to satisfy your sinful nature. Instead, use your freedom to serve one another in love. For the whole law can be summed up in this one command: "Love your neighbor as yourself." (Galatians 5:13–14)

When we Christians say God is holy, what do we mean? Well, holiness is differentness, otherness. So, we mean that he is utterly unlike any other thing in the universe. He is holy. But how is he different? What truly sets him apart? If you could distill his holiness down to a single characteristic, what would it be? It is self-giving love. This is what makes God different from every other being in the universe, including us humans.

Yes, once in a while you and I are self-giving, maybe to our children, maybe to a close friend, but God is love. He is self-giving all the time, everywhere, every way, anyhow—that is who he is. In the Old Covenant God was saying, "Do you want to my know ways (see Ex 33:13)? My ways are to give myself away." That was so evident in the Golden Calf incident, and ever after; from that point on, the only covenant obligation Yahweh had to the people of Israel was to destroy them. They had sworn in blood, "Make us like those dead bulls if we ever break our covenant with you" (see Ex 24:1–8). Then, they turned right around and broke their promises. God, as covenant lord, should have been obligated to fulfill their oath. Instead, for a thousand years and more, he kept on giving himself away to them.

What kind of a God is this? One who will keep giving himself away when, legally speaking, there is no more reason to do it? One who gives when there is no likelihood he is going to get anything back? Yes! And that is different! That is *Holy*.

The message of the New Testament is nothing more than the fulfillment of all that was revealed in the Old Testament. How far will he go to keep his covenant? To the Cross—all the way to the Cross. He will give himself away in the almost certain assurance that ninety percent of the people he gives himself to will spit on him. That is what his holiness is about. God is Holy; God is Love.

September 22
GODLINESS OPTIONAL

For you have been called to live in freedom, my brothers and sisters. But don't use your freedom to satisfy your sinful nature. Instead use your freedom to serve one another in love. . . . The sinful nature wants to do evil, which is the opposite of what the Spirit wants. And the Spirit gives us desires that are the opposite of what the sinful nature desires. These two forces are constantly fighting each other, so you are not free to carry out your good intentions. But when you are directed by the Spirit you are no under obligation to the law of Moses. (Galatians 5:13, 17–18)

In all his letters, but especially his early ones, Paul is walking a tightrope. He wants to demolish a mistaken interpretation of the Old Testament without demolishing what the Old Testament reveals about God's intentions for life. The mistaken interpretation is that of the Judaism that emerged after the return from the Babylonian exile. This idea was that the way we make ourselves acceptable to God is by scrupulously keeping every injunction of the Mosaic law, especially the ceremonial ones like circumcision and Sabbath.

But that is wrong. Nobody in the Old Testament was ever accepted by God because of their perfect law-keeping. The reason, as Paul clearly saw, was that nobody could keep the real injunctions of the law: loving God with all your heart, soul, and strength, and your neighbor as yourself, because their sinful nature (i.e., self-serving desire) would always defeat their good Spirit-given intentions (see Gal 5:16–17). The Good News of Christ, clearly foreshadowed in the Old Testament, is that God accepts us for free. That is possible because of the sacrifice of Christ. Paul trumpeted that Good News everywhere he went!

That left him with a new problem. What people tended to hear was: because God accepts us for free, we can "live like hell" (i.e., "satisfy our sinful nature") and still have eternal life (see Gal 5:13). "No!" says Paul, emphatically. God's intention that we should share his life and character as revealed in the Old Testament has not changed at all. What has changed is the apparent motive. Whereas Judaism was saying that we had to try to be godly in order to be accepted by God, Paul shows us that we are now enabled to be godly because we have been accepted by God. God wants us to be and do what he does—his goal from the beginning—but now it need no longer be a battle where we try—unsuccessfully—to fulfill an obligation. Now it is to be a natural result of our cooperation with the Spirit who lives in us and fills us with himself. We are now free to become what God intended for us before time began.

September 23

HOLY TO THE LORD

Even before he made the world, God loved us and chose us in
Christ to be holy and without fault in his eyes. (Ephesians 1:4)

What is God's goal for human life? It is holiness and completeness.
That is what Ephesians 1:4 tells us, and that is in confirmation
of Genesis 17:1, where God says to Abram, "Walk before me and be
complete."* It is interesting to see how that thought is developed in the
Bible. It really starts with the revelation to Moses that God is so holy that
the very dirt where he appears is holy (see Ex 3:5; confirmed again to
Joshua in Josh 5:15). It then is fleshed out in Exodus 19:5–6, where God
says Israel will be a holy nation. The point here is that whatever belongs
to God takes on his exclusive character. That is emphasized by the gold
medallion on the front of the High Priest's turban on which was inscribed,
"Holy to the Lord" (Ex 28:36).

This is a key point. Holy does not mean "set apart" with no ethical
implications, as you sometimes hear said. Holy means partaking of the
character of what you have been dedicated to. For Yahweh that character
is good, true, right, just, pure, and unfailing love. That is God's goal for all
of us, not just the priests.

You get the clue to that at the end of the Old Testament. Zechariah tells
us that in the last day, even the cooking pots will be holy, and the horses'
harness bells will be inscribed with "Holy to the Lord." Joel 3:17 says,
"My holy mountain Jerusalem will be holy forever." Yahweh means for
everything and especially everybody to be his alone, sharing his character.
This thought is sealed by the very last words in the Bible, Revelation 22:21:
"The grace of the Lord Jesus be with all the holy people" (see the NLT and
NRSV). That's the goal. God wants us to be like him; he wants us to share
his character. He began in the most general and representative ways and
brought it down to all people through his gracious provision in Jesus.

---

* The typical modern translation of the Greek and Hebrew words for "wholeness"
or "completion" is "blameless" (for example, see the NIV). This might give the
impression that while something is quite defective it is still considered to be
without blame. That impression is quite false.

September 24

SALVATION BY WORKS?

For he chose us in him before the creation of the world to be
holy and blameless in his sight. In love he predestined us for
adoption to sonship through Jesus Christ, in accordance with his
pleasure and will—to the praise of his glorious grace, which he has
freely given us in the One he loves. (Ephesians 1:4–6 NIV)

For it is by grace you have been saved, through faith—and this is not from
yourselves, it is the gift of God—not by works, so that no one can boast.
For we are God's handiwork, created in Christ Jesus to do good works,
which God prepared in advance for us to do. (Ephesians 2:8–10 NIV)

The Bible teaches that forgiveness of sins is not the final purpose of the
Cross. To be sure, the first purpose of the Cross is forgiveness of sins,
resulting in a right standing before God, something even the most rigorous
obedience of the *Torah*, as summarized in the Ten Commandments,
cannot do. We are given a right standing before God through faith in
Jesus Christ, nothing else. But innocence before him is not God's desired
end; his desired end is our holiness (see Eph 1:4). What is holiness? Is it
positional or behavioral?

Many Protestants, concerned that any emphasis on Christian behavior
will dilute our insistence on "grace alone," deny that holiness has anything
to do with behavior, but that position is simply not scriptural. It is clear
from Ephesians 2:8–10 that grace through faith is supposed to issue
in "good works." Is a holy life (i.e., "good works," or fulfilling the Ten
Commandments) a requirement to be forgiven, to become "saved"? No.
However, if we have received divine grace to be forgiven, we have *also*
received divine grace through the Holy Spirit to live holy (i.e., God-like)
lives, as conveniently summarized by the Ten Commandments. There is
good reason to doubt the faith of someone who claims to be a Christian
while living a life that is ruled by desire and thus indistinguishable from
that of the world (i.e., God-less).

September 25

GRACE

God saved you by his grace when you believed. And you can't take
credit for this; it is a gift from God. Salvation is not a reward for the
good things we have done, so none of us can boast about it. For we are
God's masterpiece. He has created us anew in Christ Jesus, so we can
do the good things he planned for us long ago. (Ephesians 2:8–10)

In every great religion there is a word that sums up what that religion is about. The classic example is Islam: the Arabic word *islam* means "submit"—submit to Allah or be crushed. For Buddhism the word is "deny." Deny the reality of pain, deny your own reality. What about Christianity? It is "grace"! Our coming into a right relationship with God is none of our work, it is all of his grace. Thank God! To find God is not to climb up a greased slide toward heaven, slipping back, crawling forward. To find God is to allow his arms to enfold us and lift us to his bosom. Grace.

No other world religion teaches salvation by grace. Every other one teaches that we must make ourselves acceptable to God by some effort on our part. Not Christianity. All we have to do is receive the promise of God that Christ has died to deliver us from the consequences of sin and has risen again to deliver us from the power of sin.

Here is the final feature that distinguishes Christianity from all the rest: our Founder is alive! Muhammad is dead, Buddha is dead, Confucius is dead, but Jesus Christ is alive! The miracle of Christianity is that it is not a doctrinal system. *The miracle of Christianity is the miracle of the exchanged life.* Christ in you. Here is the pinnacle of grace. God gives us his very life in Jesus.

When Morning Gilds the Skies

September 26

MORE THAN A BUS TICKET

For it is by grace you have been saved, through faith—and this not of
yourselves, it is the gift of God—not by works, so that no one can boast.
For we are God's handiwork, created in Christ Jesus to do good works,
which God prepared in advance for us to do. (Ephesians 2:8–10 NIV)

What was Jesus's purpose in coming? It was to make it possible for the
Old Testament promise to be realized. Yes, he came to die for our
sins, but that isn't the end purpose for which Jesus came. A great deal of
the tragedy of the evangelical church in America today is because we have
missed that point. Today it is largely impossible to distinguish believers
from non-believers on the basis of the quality and character of their lives.
Why is this? We think that Jesus is a bus ticket to heaven: you come to the
altar, buy a ticket, and wait for the bus to come. No! Jesus came so that the
Holy Spirit as promised in the Old Testament could come upon his people
and enable them to live holy lives (see Ezek 36:24–26).

The Spirit cannot take up residence in a filthy temple. So, Jesus came
to be the perfect sacrifice whereby our sins could be forgiven, the temple be
made clean, and the end result of the whole thing could happen—the Holy
Spirit could come into our lives and take up residence and we could share
his character (see Matt 13:42–45 about what happens when the temple is
left empty). This end result is the point being made in Ephesians 2:8–10.
Many of us have memorized the first sentence and paid no attention to the
second. That is exactly what has happened in the church. We are saved by
grace, not by any good thing we have ever done.

So, while it is good to do good things, they don't really matter! No!
Read the second sentence. The reason God created us is to do good works:
that is, to share his character, to be holy. That was his plan from the
creation of the world (see Eph 1:4). Jesus is not a bus ticket! In the Spirit
he is the living, breathing presence in us, enabling us to live God's life in
the present world and forever more.

September 27
COMPLETING THE REFORMATION: PART ONE

God saved you by his grace when you believed. And you can't take
credit for this; it is a gift from God. Salvation is not a reward for the
good things we have done, so none of us can boast about it. For we are
God's masterpiece. He has created us anew in Christ Jesus, so we can
do the good things he planned for us long ago. (Ephesians 2:8–10)

In many ways Martin Luther did not complete the Reformation that he
began. Perhaps he could not because of the road on which he had to come
in order to recover salvation by faith. Luther, child of Roman Catholicism,
had been trying to make himself acceptable to God by killing "the flesh"
and by holy living. He was trying his best to fulfill the command, "Be holy,
as I am holy." Unfortunately, nobody can do that on their own, as the first
three chapters of Romans makes very clear. So Luther was lost in despair.
Then he discovered the great good news of the first half of Galatians and
Romans 3–5: It is not our holy behavior that atones for our sin and gives
us fellowship with God. God himself has made us acceptable to him by
grace alone through faith alone. Holy behavior is not necessary to enter
a relationship with God. If we think that is so, holy behavior can be an
absolute hindrance.

So Luther stopped short (which, by the way, is why he found the book
of James so distasteful). In the light of his earlier frustration and failure,
he thought that holy behavior in this life was neither possible nor really
necessary to a relationship with God. That's unfortunate because holy
behavior clearly is a vital component in a relationship with God, as the rest
of both Galatians and Romans spells out.

It remained for John Wesley to complete what Luther had begun. Holy
behavior *is* both expected and possible in this life *on exactly the same basis
as initial salvation—grace alone through faith alone.* Here is the totality,
the fullness, of salvation: we can be welcomed into a walk with God in
which past sins are all forgiven, and we are enabled to please him with
behavior just like his—all through grace! That is the true Reformation!

September 28

COMPLETING THE REFORMATION: PART TWO

That is not the way you learned Christ! For surely you have heard about him and were taught in him, as truth is in Jesus. You were taught to put away your former way of life, your old self, corrupt and deluded by its lusts, and to be renewed in the spirit of your minds, and to clothe yourselves with the new self, created according to the likeness of God in true righteousness and holiness. (Ephesians 4:20–24 NRSV)

My teacher, Dr. Dennis F. Kinlaw, recently gone to glory, liked to tell the story of something one of his teachers at Princeton University, Professor Emile Caillet, had said. As Dr. Kinlaw told it, Caillet, a French Protestant, said that Luther only recovered half of the gospel in the Reformation. Yes, he did recover the truth that we are justified (i.e., declared innocent before God) by grace through faith alone. That was a huge step forward—by going back!—but it wasn't far enough. According to Caillet, the second half of the gospel had to wait 200 years after Luther to be recovered through the ministry of John Wesley. That great evangelist came to realize that we are not only brought into a redeemed relationship with God by grace through faith but also are enabled to live righteous lives by grace through faith. As Caillet saw it, Luther only took his rediscovery of the power of grace halfway to the truth.

Caillet was right: to say that we can have a redeemed relationship with God but that God cannot enable us to live his life in the world is not very good news. However, it is great good news that the grace of God is able to "save to the uttermost." This is what the hymn writer was talking about when he wrote, "Be of sin the double cure: save from wrath and make me pure." Salvation involves both deliverance from condemnation and empowerment to live God's life from day to day. This is why I prefer not to use the older language of "saved and sanctified." That language suggests that being "saved" (i.e., justified) is all that is really necessary but that some super-Christians might wish to take a further step. No! To genuinely experience God's "salvation" is to be brought into such a clean relationship with God that his Holy Spirit can reproduce God's character in us. That is salvation: not a state but a "walk," a new "way of life."

TOUCHDOWN

This will continue until we all come to such unity in our faith and knowledge of God's Son that we will be mature [KJV "perfect"] in the Lord, measuring up to the full and complete standard of Christ. (Ephesians 4:13)

St. Paul used the analogy of the footrace several times to talk about the nature of the Christian life. I want to suggest another one: the American game of football. In order to achieve the goal in the game of football, it is necessary to gain possession of the ball. It might be through regaining a fumble, a pass interception, or receiving a punt or kick-off, but you must have possession of the ball. I suggest this is analogous to conversion. In order to achieve God's goal for his people, you have to be "in Christ" (2 Cor 5:17), whether the result of a prayer at a mother's knee, at the altar of a church, or as with C. S. Lewis, on the back of his brother's motorcycle. Without that saving relationship with him, we are the victims of our sin, constantly on the defense against deceitful self-worship and voracious desire. In the end, the winners at football are those who kept possession of the ball, and the losers are those who did not.

Possession of the ball is not what the game is *finally* about. Yes, possession is absolutely necessary. Without the ball nothing can be accomplished. But if, possessing the ball for 7/8ths of the game, we only move it back and forth at midfield, we miss the point and perhaps at the end of the day will lose the game. The goal is to move the ball down the field and eventually push it across the line at the end of the field. That line is called "the goal line" for a reason.

What is the goal of the Christian life? It is to grow up into the full character and nature of God in Jesus (see Eph 4:13). That's why he saves us from the captivity of our sin: to make us like himself. He intends to make us all we were ever meant to be. That's the goal line! We don't have to wait for death to see the referee's raised arms. Why not today?

So where are you? Does he have you first and ten on the opponent's 20-yard line! Or are you fiddling around on your own 20-yard line? Personally, I want to hear, "Touchdown!"

September 30

A MOMENT OR A MILE

Then we will no longer be immature like children. We won't be tossed and blown about by every wind of new teaching. We will not be influenced when people try to trick us with lies so clever they sound like the truth. Instead, we will speak the truth in love, growing in every way more and more like Christ, who is the head of his body, the church. (Ephesians 4:14–15)

Do not lie to one another, seeing that you have stripped off the old self with its practices and have clothed yourselves with the new self, which is being renewed in knowledge according to the image of its creator. In that renewal there is no longer Greek and Jew, circumcised and uncircumcised, barbarian, Scythian, slave and free; but Christ is all and in all! As God's chosen ones, holy and beloved, clothe yourselves with compassion, kindness, humility, meekness, and patience. (Colossians 3:9–12 NRSV)

There can be no question that as Christians, we are expected to be Christ-like. Christian faith is not first of all a set of ideas that we accept. It is first of all a relationship in which Jesus Christ comes, by grace through faith alone, to inhabit us. So Paul can say, "Christ in you, the hope of glory" (Col 1:27). Our hope to share the glory of God is as a result of Christ's life lived in us.

How is that Christlikeness achieved? Is it the work of a moment, "you have stripped off the old self," or is it only as the end of a long mile of self-denial and the steady putting on of new clothes, "growing in every way more and more like Christ"? I think the answer to the question is, "yes." That is, both are necessary, and whenever the Church has limited itself to one answer or the other, it has become anemic.

Many today find the Christlike life a struggle, a "will-o-the-wisp" that we must continually try to lay hold of but never quite achieve. The reason for that is that they are trying to put on new clothes without having been stripped of the old clothes. They have not had that moment when by faith they have allowed Christ to strip them of their self-esteem (otherwise called pride) and their continual self-focus and have been set free from their blindness to follow him (see Mark 10:46–52). Then, and then alone, is real growth into Christlikeness possible. The moment only accomplished the stripping off, but it is a moment without which the reclothing is impossible.

On the other hand, to be merely stripped is hardly to have reached the goal. It is now possible to become clothed in the character of Christ, and that is the work of a lifetime. A moment or a mile? Yes! The question for us then is: have I ever truly allowed Christ to bring me to that moment, and if I have, how am I allowing him to work it out in my daily walk?

October 1
SAINTLY DISCIPLES

Then we will no longer be immature like children. We won't be tossed and blown about by every wind of new teaching. We will not be influenced when people try to trick us with lies so clever they sound like the truth. Instead, we will speak the truth in love, growing in every way more and more like Christ, who is the head of his body, the church. (Ephesians 4:14–15)

In his book *Of God and Men*, A. W. Tozer makes this telling statement:

> The fact is that we are not producing saints. We are making converts to an effete type of Christianity that bears little resemblance to that of the New Testament. The average Bible-Christian in our times is but a wretched parody of true sainthood.

When I read those words, a truism occurred to me: holiness and discipleship are inseparable. What ought to be the goal of our discipleship programs? Saints. It is impossible to be a true disciple without being made holy, that is, like God. Likewise, to be holy—cleansed of self-interest—must issue in discipleship. Sadly, the two concepts are often treated, and thought of, in hermetically sealed compartments.

What does Jesus mean when he says, "Go into all the world and make disciples" (Matt 28:19)? He means that we should make people holy, peoples whose desires, affections, goals, and focus is to be like Jesus, to act as he does, do what he does, and want what he wants. Is that possible unless we allow the Holy Spirit to make our divided wills one? Of course not! Discipleship without holiness is an impossibility. Similarly, holiness must be the Spirit-enabled reproduction of the nature, character, and behavior of Jesus in a person, in short, a disciple. Is the goal of our churches to create saints? It should be.

GOD'S PATTERN

Since you have heard about Jesus and have learned the truth that
comes from him, throw off your old sinful nature and your former way
of life, which is corrupted by lust and deception. Instead, let the Spirit
renew your thoughts and attitudes. Put on your new nature, created
to be like God—truly righteous and holy. (Ephesians 4:21–24)

There is a pattern in the way God acts and that pattern can be followed right through the Old Testament and into the New Testament. There are four phases in it. First, we are brought into a relationship with God by grace. That's the basis of it all. Abraham came into a relationship with God strictly by God's grace. The Hebrew people were delivered from Egypt by grace. God wants a relationship with us, and the only way that is possible is by grace. He has to come to us; we can never work our way to him.

Second, the kind of relationship he wants is for him to live in our midst: in the midst of the camp for the Hebrews, and the midst of our selves for us. He can only do that if we share his character. We must "walk" as he "walks," live like he lives, do what he does, and be what he is. You can't have a relationship between two people who are pulling in opposite directions. If you're going to be in a relationship with him, you've got to learn how to walk with him.

Third, we can't walk like he walks! It took the Hebrew people 1,000 years to finally get that into their heads. We are sure in our pride that with just a little more effort, a little more shaping up, we can do this! But we can't. So, we are tempted to give up, concluding that God really doesn't expect us to be godly people.

Fourth, he does! The Hebrew people saw some folks in whom a different spirit, a holy spirit, was at work, and they said, "God, why can't you do that for all of us? Why can't you empower us with your Holy Spirit to live your life here on earth." And he said, "I'm going to! But first your filthy temple has to be cleansed. Once that is done by my Son, my Spirit will come into every person who believes in my Son, and he will enable them to walk as I walk."

That's the pattern. There's only one catch: just because you have the Spirit, doesn't mean the Spirit has you. If you know Christ but are not able to live God's life, there is one likely cause: you've never actually given your control panel, your heart, completely to him. Do it now.

October 3

AMERICAN GREATNESS

Put on your new nature, created to be like God—truly righteous and holy.
So stop telling lies. Let us tell our neighbors the truth, for we are all parts of
the same body. . . . Don't use foul or abusive language. Let everything you
say be good and helpful, so that your words will be an encouragement to
those who hear them. And do not bring sorrow to God's Holy Spirit by the
way you live. Remember, he has identified you as his own, guaranteeing
that you will be saved on the day of redemption. Get rid of all bitterness,
rage, anger, harsh words, and slander, as well as all types of evil behavior.
Instead, be kind to each other, tenderhearted, forgiving one another, just
as God through Christ has forgiven you. (Ephesians 4:24–25, 29–32)

All over the ancient world, from Sumer to Rome, it was understood that virtue—upright ethical behavior—is a necessity for human life to flourish. So, there were strict law codes in every culture to try to enforce that kind of behavior. It was ethics by coercion, and it didn't work very well.

What did not happen in those cultures was any real connection between virtue and religion. There was little connection because religion is a way to manipulate the gods into giving you what you want, and upright ethical behavior does not go very far toward making the spirits do that. Part of the reason for that is that the gods themselves are not virtuous. They are just like us, only bigger.

Then along came Israel. Their God, Yahweh, seems to value virtue above everything because, wonder of wonders, he is virtuous. Suddenly, being virtuous was the way to please him, the One who had freely delivered you from Egyptian bondage. That carried right over into Christianity, as the passage above clearly shows. Virtue is the expression of your new life in Christ.

Fast forward to America. For over 200 years Americans have been incredibly honest, generous, and faithful. Why? Because our ancestors loved the Lord. So, whether it paid or not, they didn't lie. They were charitable and generous because they knew a Lord who was charitable and generous and because they knew their needs were in his hands. Today that's mostly gone. We're back in the pagan place where ethics have nothing to do with religion. America has lost *its motive for ethical behavior!* A visitor from England in the 1830s, Andrew Reed, wrote, "America will be great if America is good. If not, her greatness will vanish away like a morning cloud." For over 200 years America's greatness lay in that ethical behavior that sprang from the love of God. Oh, for people to be like that again.

October 4

BE FILLED WITH THE HOLY SPIRIT

Don't act thoughtlessly, but understand what the Lord wants you to do. Don't be drunk with wine, because that will ruin your life. Instead, be filled with the Holy Spirit, singing psalms and hymns and spiritual songs among yourselves and making music to the Lord in your hearts. And give thanks for everything to God the Father in the name of our Lord Jesus Christ. (Ephesians 5:17–20)

We tend to get caught in the extremes on so many of the great issues in the Christian life. This is especially true in regards to the Holy Spirit. Is the Holy Spirit in all born-again Christians? Yes! Do we, as born-again Christians, need to be filled with the Holy Spirit sometime after we are born again? Yes! Wait a minute, aren't those two responses contradictory? If you have the Holy Spirit, you surely don't need to get him again—that's one extreme. Or if you do need to get him after conversion, then obviously you did not get him in conversion—that's the other extreme.

Well, as in all forms of expression, words are important. Notice the word I used in the second question: "filled." If you have accepted Christ as your Savior, having acknowledged your sins and consciously turned away from them (i.e., repented), then the Holy Spirit is in you (see Rom 8:9). He is "regenerating" you, giving you new desires and new behavior. You can't be a Christian at all unless he is working out the relationship and the character in you.

However, for the Spirit to be in you does not mean he is filling you. Water can be in a glass, yet not be filling it. That is the case with all too many Christians. The Holy Spirit is in us but not filling us. What is the evidence of that? We see this illustrated in the Apostle Paul's description in Romans 7. The believer no longer wants to sin and indeed sees it as something to be avoided, yet finds himself or herself often defeated by it.*

So, what is to be done? We need to allow the Holy Spirit to fill us completely. To change the metaphor, he needs to go from being the honored guest in our house to being its owner. This is what Paul is talking about in the Ephesians passage quoted above. What does the Lord want? That we should be filled with the Spirit.

---

* I use Romans 7 here for illustration only. Romans 7 does not describe "the normal Christian life" as some have labeled it. The person there described is "a slave to sin" (Rom 7:14), something Paul says cannot be true of the Christian (Rom 6:6–7). That person is trying to defeat the power of sin in their life through effort, and it is not possible.

October 5

THE HOLY SPIRIT: PURITY, POWER *AND* LOVE

Don't be drunk with wine, for that is debauchery. Instead, you all should be continually filled with the Holy Spirit. (Ephesians 5:18 author's translation)

If we are filled with the Holy Spirit, what can we expect to be the evidence of that fact? Is it a one-time event subsequent to conversion? Is it something that after conversion has to be continually renewed? I would argue that it is the latter that most adequately captures New Testament teaching on the subject. I think the passage for today encapsulates this thought. But even if we agree on that point, what does the fullness of the Holy Spirit entail? For many, focusing on the teachings on the gifts of the Spirit in 1 Corinthians, the primary evidence of the Spirit's fullness is spiritual power, manifested in miracles. Others would point to the context of Ephesians 5:18, especially Ephesians 5:3–18, and would say that the expected evidence is moral purity.

However, that argument is double-edged, because the introduction to this context is the call to be imitators of God who "walk in love, as Christ also has loved us and given himself for us" (Eph 5:1–2). In short, moral impurity is a lack of love, and we live a life of moral purity for love's sake. Any other kind of morality is only another expression of sinful self-serving.

The problem with the heading for this devotion is the "or." The work of the Holy Spirit in his fullness is purity, power, *and* love, with purity and power existing for and as an expression of love. If we debate about purity and power and forget love, or even if we include love as only another feature, we have missed the point. The Holy Spirit fills us so that we may manifest the multi-dimensional love of Jesus to a lost world (see Eph 3:14–19). We do so both in purity and power but all for love's sake.

October 6

Courtesy, Kindness and the Christian Life

Make my joy complete: be of the same mind, having the same love, being in full accord and of one mind. Do nothing from selfish ambition or conceit, but in humility regard others as better than yourselves. Let each of you look not to your own interests, but to the interests of others. Let the same mind be in you that was in Christ Jesus. (Philippians 2:2–5 NRSV)

I suppose it is a sign of advancing age, but it seems that I remember more often these days some of the things my father said. One of them is, "You gotta think about the other fella." How simple, and how increasingly absent from our common life these days. We are harried, stressed, anxious, and running late, and other people are just in our way. "I don't have time to be kind! Some other day!" We often think of courtesy and kindness as simple, common things that we could pick up and do whenever we wish, but I don't think that is true at all.

Notice the word that is repeated three times in the passage quoted above: "mind," which means attitude, or way of thinking, and in this case, a way of thinking about ourselves. This "mind" is to put the concerns and needs of others before your own. That is the attitude of Jesus. He did not think about his own divine rights; he thought about our desperate need. Such an attitude is far from normal to us humans, and it is not something that can be packaged up as a nice, neat New Year's resolution: "I am going to be kind to one person—who doesn't deserve it!—every day." Well, that's not a bad idea, but like most good resolutions it won't last without something deeper having taken place first.

This kind of undeserved grace to others, this kind of incredible self-forgetfulness, is only possible to those who, like Jesus, have died to their rights. Have you, have I? Have I ever, in a moment of utter submission, died to my way and come alive to his, and am I daily allowing him to pronounce the death sentence over my "own interests"? That is what it will take for most of us to introduce courtesy and kindness back into the public square. Let it happen.

HUMILIATION ON PURPOSE

Who, being in very nature God, did not consider equality with God something
to be used to his own advantage; rather, he made himself nothing by
taking the very nature of a servant, being made in human likeness. And
being found in appearance as a man, he humbled himself by becoming
obedient to death—even death on a cross! (Philippians 2:6–8 NIV)

One of the special features of God's revelation is its use of illustrations.
In one sense, the whole story of Israel is one grand illustration of
our desperate condition and the lengths to which our Creator-Redeemer
is willing to go to deliver us from that condition and its consequences.
Jesus's life, death, and resurrection is another one of these illustrations.
As Paul says, he is the very image of the invisible God. God did the same
thing through his prophets. They were called to act out the truth about
the people and God. Here is the point: again and again, what they had to
act out was humiliating and demeaning. So, Isaiah had to walk around
naked (maybe he had a loin cloth?) for three years to symbolize the way
the people would be when going into exile because of their sins. Hosea was
required to marry a woman who was known to be a prostitute, which is
what Israel was in God's eyes. Ezekiel's calling may have been the toughest
of all: again and again we see him having to act out disgusting things,
tragic things.

Seeing all this we tend to say, "God why would you do that to your
chosen ones?" The simple answer is, *the only hope for the human race
is in the destruction of pride.* That's what it cost Jesus. Jesus, the Son of
God, was demeaned and humiliated. So God said to his prophets, "You are
the forerunners of The Prophet. If you are going to confront the evil of the
world don't expect to be thanked. Don't expect to be exalted and glorified.
If you are going to confront the evil of the world, if you are going to bear
the sufferings and the sorrows and the shame of the world, just expect it;
you are going to be demeaned and humiliated." If you serve God in this
world, humiliation is much more to be expected than exaltation.

October 8

I SURRENDER ALL?

Yes, everything else is worthless when compared with the infinite value of knowing Christ Jesus my Lord. For his sake I have discarded everything else, counting it all as garbage, so that I could gain Christ. (Philippians 3:8)

Judson Van DeVenter's gospel song "I Surrender All" is often sung as an invitation hymn at the end of evangelistic services, but what does it mean? Sometimes people say to me, "What is my all? I'm not sure what God is asking for, so I don't know whether I can say that or not." Years ago, I heard an illustration from the missionary-evangelist J. T. Seamands that was a great help to me at the time and has been since. He said, "God is coming to you with a sheet of paper. At the top it says, 'I give to God everything listed below.' At the bottom is a place for you to sign. Probably there will be one thing filled in on the page, but the rest is blank. During the rest of your life, God will return to you from time to time with something else filled in. If you feel a hesitation, all you need to do is to look at the signature at the bottom." You don't need to know everything at the moment of your surrender, but that surrender shapes every decision thereafter, and God will help you at each new step.

Why do we have to take such a step? It is in the nature of the love relationship. Love requires an exclusive belonging. The connection between full surrender to God and the marriage vows is not accidental. God will never be satisfied with a part of your affection, just as I am not satisfied with a part of Karen's affection, nor she with only a part of mine. Belonging to each other completely, we can trust each other, and love is rooted in trust. Love cannot bloom in an air where the commitment is partial and variable. God wants all of us because he loves us and wants his love to come to full bloom in our lives. Did Karen and I know what full surrender of our lives to each other might require in the coming years? No, we did not, but we knew enough to know that we wanted to belong completely to each other so that our love would have a chance to send down roots deep enough to withstand whatever might come—and it has.

That's what God wants—all of you. Have you signed the sheet of paper? If you have, all God's resources of love are yours. If not, why not?

October 9
A PASSION TO BE LIKE HIM

Indeed, I count everything as loss because of the surpassing worth of knowing
Christ Jesus my Lord. For his sake I have suffered the loss of all things and
count them as rubbish, in order that I may gain Christ and be found in him, not
having a righteousness of my own that comes from the law, but that which
comes through faith in Christ, the righteousness from God that depends on
faith—that I may know him and the power of his resurrection, and may share
his sufferings, becoming like him in his death. (Philippians 3:8–10 ESV)

As we seek to be holy people, the primary need is to exalt Jesus. All too
often we have suggested that holiness is an "it," that God does "it" in
my life. So, we ask, "Have you got 'it'?" Has God done this process, this
thing? Have you had "the crisis"?

Really the question is: is Jesus the sole, only, reigning Lord of my
life? Is Jesus's mind being recreated in me? Is Jesus being glorified by my
behavior? Are people being drawn to Jesus because of my life? Is Jesus
becoming more beautiful, more desirable, because of what he is doing in
my life? Any movement that focuses on Jesus, that calls attention to Jesus,
or that glorifies Jesus can't go very far wrong.

If we make our emphasis on us, our performance, behavior, or actions,
we are walking on the edge of the cliff. Sanctification is Jesus. It is not an
"it." It is a *him* and if we will focus on Jesus, if we will put Jesus at the
absolute center of our lives and deny his place to anything else, holiness is
going to follow like morning follows night.

Exalt Jesus, focus on Jesus, focus on the reality. Holiness is a passion,
not a performance. It is a passion for Jesus, a passion to know his ways, a
passion to know his life, a passion to be like him.

October 10

RIGHTEOUSNESS, OR RIGHTEOUSNESS?

. . . not having a righteousness of my own that comes from the law,
but that which is through faith in Christ—the righteousness that
comes from God on the basis of faith. (Philippians 3:9 NIV)

In 2017 we celebrated the 500th anniversary of the Protestant Reformation, beginning with Martin Luther's nailing of his 95 theses to the door of the Wittenberg Cathedral. In many ways, that whole movement has centered around the question of righteousness. Is our acceptance by God dependent upon our righteous behavior, or not?

Luther, as so many others before and since, was in despair over his inability to find peace with God although he did everything he knew to live according to every standard of righteousness the Church set forth. Then he came to grips with verses like the one quoted above: righteousness is not the result of our efforts but the result of faith! What a relief! He could stop struggling to be good enough for God and simply trust God through Christ for his righteousness. This is good news. When our behavior not only falls short of what others expect of us but more than that, of what we expect of ourselves, we can rest in the sufficiency of God's grace. Ahh!

Is our "righteousness" simply a matter of judicial record? Does God simply account us as righteous because of Christ so that our actual behavior is of little or no importance? This is where a good deal of Protestant thinking has gone in recent years. Surely the truth, as is the case in so many instances, is between the two extremes. Does our acceptance by God depend on how righteous we are? No. But are people in whom the Holy Spirit dwells expected to live righteous lives? Yes!

The issue is: how do I live a Christlike (i.e., righteous) life? Do I do it through my own effort? That can only produce pride and bitterness. Or is it the result of dependence on (i.e., faith in) Jesus? In that case the result is humility and gratitude. The whole issue is the one of relationship. Righteousness is not the goal—intimacy with Jesus is—and righteous behavior is the happy, and maybe even inevitable, by-product.

October 11

PERFECT?

Not that I have already obtained this or am already perfect, but I press on to make it my own, because Christ Jesus has made me his own. Brothers, I do not consider that I have made it my own. But one thing I do: forgetting what lies behind and straining forward to what lies ahead, I press on toward the goal for the prize of the upward call of God in Christ Jesus. Let those of us who are mature think this way, and if in anything you think otherwise, God will reveal that also to you. (Philippians 3:12–15 ESV)

In Philippians 3:12 Paul says, "I am not yet already perfect, I have not attained." That gives us a lot of comfort: "Whew," we say, "that lets me out. I don't need to worry about how I live. Because if Paul, of all people, wasn't perfect, my goodness, why should I worry?" Then in the fifteenth verse, after he has talked about what is true of him, he says, "Everyone who is perfect ought to have the same attitude that I have." "Now wait a minute," you say. "He didn't say 'perfect,' he said 'mature.'" Well, as a matter of fact, he did say "perfect," both in verses 12 and 15 (check out the King James Version). So what has happened? Modern translators, reflecting modern culture, cannot stomach any idea of human perfection.

If that is true, then what is Paul saying? It looks like he is saying he is not perfect but that everybody who is perfect ought to be like him! That makes no sense! So, what is he saying? He is using the word, purposely, I think, in two "perfectly" good, but different, ways. On the one hand, he is saying that God is not done with him: "I don't know Jesus yet like I plan to know him, like I believe I am going to know him. I don't know yet the full power of his resurrection in all that it could do in me. I don't know yet the fellowship of his sufferings, the likeness to his death, in all the possibilities that it has for me. No, I am not finally perfected." However, he then says, "I will tell you what God has done for me. He has perfected me in this sense. He has made my heart one; he has made my desires one; he has made my goals one; he has made me one. He has put before me the vision of what I may be in Christ, and he has imprinted it so much on my mind that everything in my life is subordinated to that vision, and in this sense, I am perfect, and you should be too."

Brothers and sisters, that can be true for us. Done, finished, nothing more to be done? Of course not—not this side of heaven. But—one? Yes! "All for Jesus, all for Jesus, all my being's ransomed powers; all for Jesus, all for Jesus, all my days and all my hours." That perfection we can know—now.

October 12

THE KINGDOM OF LIGHT: PART ONE

We continually ask God to fill you with the knowledge of his will through all the wisdom and understanding that the Spirit gives, so that you may live a life worthy of the Lord and please him in every way: bearing fruit in every good work, growing in the knowledge of God, being strengthened with all power according to his glorious might so that you may have great endurance and patience, and giving joyful thanks to the Father, who has qualified you to share in the inheritance of his holy people in the kingdom of light. For he has rescued us from the dominion of darkness and brought us into the kingdom of the Son he loves, in whom we have redemption, the forgiveness of sins. (Colossians 1:9–14 NIV)

This is a tremendous prayer. In these words, we see the Apostle Paul's conception of the Christian life. Let me misquote him so that you can see more clearly what he is saying: "I pray that you will struggle against sin all the time, and although you are doomed to fail, I pray that you will nonetheless be encouraged by the knowledge that all those sins you can't help committing are under the blood."

Is that what Paul says? No! He is not talking about forgiven sinners who will continue to be defeated by sin but will just experience continuing forgiveness. That is to continue in what Paul calls the kingdom of darkness. We, as believers in Christ, have been transferred to a new kingdom, the kingdom of light. We are no longer subject to the Prince of Darkness. We can live "a life worthy of the Lord and please him in every way." Isn't that wonderful good news?!

October 13

THE KINGDOM OF LIGHT: PART TWO

We continually ask God to fill you with the knowledge of his will through
all the wisdom and understanding that the Spirit gives, so that you may
live a life worthy of the Lord and please him in every way: bearing fruit in
every good work, growing in the knowledge of God, being strengthened
with all power according to his glorious might so that you may have
great endurance and patience, and giving joyful thanks to the Father,
who has qualified you to share in the inheritance of his holy people
in the kingdom of light. For he has rescued us from the dominion of
darkness and brought us into the kingdom of the Son he loves, in whom
we have redemption, the forgiveness of sins. (Colossians 1:9–14 NIV)

I want to look with you at the incredible offer that Jesus makes when he
invites us to become a subject of his in his Kingdom of Light. Yes, I did
say "become a subject of his." There is the rub. We want to be forgiven;
we want our broken lives to be put back together; we want to be delivered
from the fear of death; but give up the right to do what we want with our
lives? Wait a minute. Yes, there it is. He does offer forgiveness—there it is
in verse 14—but it is the result of receiving him as our King.

Look what he offers: wisdom and understanding of the way the world
is made so that we will be able to receive every blessing that the Creator
intended for us: lives that just naturally bear good, sweet fruit in all our
relationships; coming to know our Creator, our Savior, our Life-giver
better and better; having the power to face the difficulties that a fallen
world will inevitably bring down upon us with endurance and patience,
and yes, even gratitude (as we see how our King has made us more than
conquerors).

In view of all this, why would we cling to the right to run our own lives?
If we will give him the deed to our little hovel, he will turn it into a palace.
Instead, we say we would rather just be forgiven and still retain ownership
of our hovel, failing to understand that what Jesus has come to give us is
infinitely more than mere forgiveness.

Don't live in defeat; live in victory. Live in all that he has promised. Is
it costly? Yes, it will cost you everything. But, in return for your all, he'll
give you his all. Can you beat that deal?

October 14

IDENTIFIED WITH CHRIST

See to it that no one takes you captive through hollow and deceptive philosophy, which depends on human tradition and the elemental spiritual forces of this world rather than on Christ. For in Christ all the fullness of the Deity lives in bodily form, and in Christ you have been brought to fullness. He is the head over every power and authority. In him you were also circumcised with a circumcision not performed by human hands. Your whole self ruled by the flesh was put off when you were circumcised by Christ, having been buried with him in baptism, in which you were also raised with him through your faith in the working of God, who raised him from the dead. (Colossians 2:8–12 NIV)

In the book of Colossians, the Apostle Paul is being asked whether it is what you know or what you do that makes you a Christian. His answer is surprising: "Neither! It is who you are in Christ that makes you a Christian." He says: you were "buried with him in baptism, in which you were also raised with him through your faith . . . ."

As Christians we must be careful not to measure our Christian life by externals, what Paul calls "human tradition and the elemental spiritual forces of this world"—how often we go to church, how we dress, our spiritual education, etc. We cannot measure our relationship to Christ by worldly things. Neither can we measure it by what we know. I've often thought there should be a warning sign above the administration buildings of the seminaries around the country that states, "It's not what you know that makes you a Christian—it's Who you know."

As important as knowledge is and as important as Christian works are, if we let them obscure our living identification with Christ, we are in real trouble. Focusing on and living for the externals cuts us off from the very source of our life: Jesus Christ. How easily we can substitute knowledge *about* Christ for knowledge *of* him. How easily we can substitute Christian behavior for Christian living. It is who we are in Christ Jesus that makes us a Christian. It is who we are as he lives his life through us in knowledge, obedience, and love. What are you doing to cultivate that Life within you?

October 15

THE TRAITS OF HOLINESS

Therefore as God's chosen people, holy and dearly loved,
clothe yourselves with compassion, kindness, humility,
gentleness and patience. (Colossians 3:12 NIV)

In Colossians 2 and 3, Paul describes the life that can be ours—a holy life—if we will allow ourselves to be completely identified with Christ. In Colossians 3:12–14 he begins his conclusion by identifying the qualities of the holy life. Notice that none of them can be practiced in isolation. Holiness that can only be practiced in a closet is not holiness at all. In verse 12 he names compassion, kindness, humility, meekness, and patience:

- Compassion is the ability to feel what the other person is feeling. That's why we need holiness in our lives—so we can forget about ourselves and think of others.

- Kindness is just simple, ordinary thoughtfulness. It's thinking of what we can do for other people and not what they can do for us.

- Humility—I'm reminded of a poster I saw once. It said, "Humility is not thinking little of yourself, it's not thinking of yourself at all." It is to lift others up, not yourself.

- Meekness—there's a word that has fallen on hard times. Nobody wants to be meek. That's the character in a children's book: Lowly Worm. But that's not what Paul meant in Colossians. To be meek—and remember, it is they who will inherit the earth—is not to be weak. It is someone who is not self-assertive, someone who does not have to be aggressive to get his or her own way.

- Patience means putting up with people, accepting and loving them in spite of all their foibles, over and over again.

How is all this possible? It is possible for those who have gratefully taken their needs off their own backs and laid them onto Jesus. If we won't do that, then those around us had better watch out. But if we will, our friends, family, and neighbors will all be blessed. That is holiness.

October 16

THE GRACE OF HOLINESS

Therefore, as God's chosen people, holy and dearly loved, clothe yourselves with compassion, kindness, humility, gentleness and patience. Bear with each other and forgive one another if any of you has a grievance against someone. Forgive as the Lord forgave you. And over all these virtues put on love, which binds them all together in perfect unity. Let the peace of Christ rule in your hearts, since as members of one body you were called to peace. And be thankful. (Colossians 3:12–15 NIV)

If you love me, keep my commands. And I will ask the Father, and he will give you another advocate to help you and be with you forever—the Spirit of truth. The world cannot accept him, because it neither sees him nor knows him. But you know him, for he lives with you and will be in you. I will not leave you as orphans; I will come to you. (John 14:15–18 NIV)

God has called his people to live holy lives—lives which manifest his character, especially in our relationships with one another. But whenever we try to do that, we seem to fail. Then does God call us to something that he knows we can't do? Oh no. God calls us to something for which he supplies the energy, motivation, life, love. The Comforter has come—and through him Jesus himself has come (see John 14:15–21)!

Holiness is nothing other than the work of the Holy Spirit as he reveals in us the character of the Living God:

- Love when we are not loved in return.

- Purity in a world that is increasingly deceptive and immoral.

- Self-forgetfulness in a world that says, "Take care of yourself, baby, for you're all you've got. If you don't protect yourself, you've lost everything."

But Jesus says, "Whoever saves his life will lose it. But whoever loses his life for my sake will find it" (Matt 10:39). We are called to holiness and empowered in holiness by the Holy Spirit coming upon our lives. God grant it!

October 17

A Second ___?___ of Grace: Part One

We pray most earnestly night and day that we may see you face to face
and supply what is lacking in your faith. . . . so that he may establish your
hearts blameless in holiness before our God and Father, at the coming
of our Lord Jesus with all his saints. (1 Thessalonians 3:10, 13 ESV)

When we Wesleyans talk about the need for a second work of grace in a person's life if he or she is going to be able to live a consistently Christ-like life, a lot of our non-Wesleyan friends part company with us. They say, "There is only one work of grace in the Bible. It is the Cross. When we put our faith in Christ and his redeeming grace, we are delivered from the guilt and condemnation of sin, and that is that."

I am very sympathetic to that point of view, and I totally agree that there is no grace outside of the Cross. But I just want to ask, is deliverance from the guilt and condemnation of sin all the Cross is good for? Is that all the Cross is intended to accomplish? The answer to both those questions is no. I say that for two reasons. First, the thrust of the Old Testament is all about living God's life in a fallen world. That is, it is about *overcoming* sin and living a life that is a mirror of God's life. Second, the New Testament letters are all written to believers, and in every one of them, the apostles are telling their readers that now that they are saved from the guilt and condemnation of sin by grace through faith, they have got to quit sinning. How do we do that? By trying really hard? "No," say the apostles with one voice, "that won't work!"

So, what are we supposed to conclude? Are we supposed to quit sinning when we can't?! In a variety of ways, the apostles tell us that we *can* quit intentional sinning but that it takes a further act of faith (see 1 Thess 3:9–13), a further application of the grace of the Cross for that to happen. Why is that necessary? Because you cannot exercise faith for what you don't know you need. When we accept Christ, we assume that there will be no problem in living for him. It is only after we have tried to live for him and been defeated by a devilishly stubborn self-will that we realize we need to believe God for the grace of the Cross to defeat that will and deliver us from it so that our will is one with God's.

So, what shall we call this? A second application of grace? A further application of grace? The exchanged life? The transformed life? I honestly don't care what you call it. I only want to know, is that where you are living? If not, why not?

A Second ___?___ of Grace: Part Two

As we pray most earnestly night and day that we may see you face to face and supply what is lacking in your faith. (1 Thessalonians 3:10 ESV)

I recently read in a dictionary article on holiness the unequivocal statement that there is no such thing as a second work of grace. I understand why an author might say such a thing. "Second work of grace" could imply that what Christ did on the Cross was not sufficient, that God must do something more subsequent to that. Whatever anyone who used the phrase might have thought, that is surely not a correct understanding. Everything necessary for salvation up to and including glorification was accomplished in one work of grace on the Cross.

But is it normal to expect a second crisis in the Christian life? Yes, it is. You only have to read Christian biography to know that is the case. Whether you are talking about missionaries like C. T. Studd or J. Hudson Taylor or pastors like Harold John Ockenga, each of them at some point subsequent to their conversion came to a place where they had to make a full surrender (i.e., consecration?) of themselves and to exercise faith— exactly as Paul was wanting the Thessalonians to do—for God to make their divided hearts one for God.

Perhaps we might say there needs to be a second appropriation by faith of *all* that Christ did on the Cross so that we can live fully Christlike lives. The reason the evangelical church has made so little impact on our society is that too many believers have stopped short of that appropriation. We do not want to surrender our stubborn wills to God, and we do not believe he can make us one for him. But he can! That is what he died to do! He doesn't just want us to go to heaven. He wants us to walk like Christ walks—now—not just in eternity.

How important is this? Paul *was praying night and day* for the opportunity to share with the Thessalonians that although their faith was talked about all over the Mediterranean world, *there was more to believe for.*

What about you? Have you believed Christ to crucify your hell-inclined will and to bring you into a level of life in which you are all his, without a limit and without a rival? You can! Do it!

October 19

WHAT CAN WE EXPECT?

Now may the God of peace make you holy in every way, and
may your whole spirit and soul and body be kept blameless until
our Lord Jesus Christ comes again. (1 Thessalonians 5:23)

For the past several days, I have been inviting you to make a full appropriation of what Christ did for you on the Cross and allow him to give you an undivided heart. Maybe you say, "Well, I have done that, and it didn't work." I understand that and want to say that you are not alone.

So what is going on? First, you may be expecting the wrong things. Were you expecting a great emotional surge? Were you expecting to have no more personality problems? Were you expecting to have no more temptations? This experience, whatever you call it, The Exchanged Life, The Deeper Life, Entire Sanctification, or whatever, does not guarantee any of those.

A second thing you need to consider is that genuinely surrendering your self-centeredness may take more than a simple decision to do so. It is not uncommon for persons to struggle with this for weeks or even months. It is not that Jesus cannot do this for you in a moment but that you may have to allow him to dredge up some things that you are not in fact really ready to surrender, and that may take some time. Don't give up! Allow him to do his work!

What can you—ought you—to expect as a result of this crisis of faith? You can expect a new victory over temptation, a new desire for prayer and the Word, a new boldness in testimony, a new ability to love the unlovely, a new compassion for the least and the lost, and a new hatred of sin in all its manifestations. Then, expect to grow in holiness. Jesus is not done with you—now he can really get started! What will this require? Cooperation with the Spirit! What he asks, do. Where he sends, go.

Run, don't walk, from sin. But if you fall into it, call a spade a spade. Don't hide it or try to explain it away. Confess it—right now—and be clean. The same is true with faults, like being bossy or opinionated. When the Spirit points out that stuff—and he will—don't argue; surrender it. I used to think he would get to the bottom of all that with me, but he hasn't yet, and you may find that to be true for you. Don't fight it, love it. That's the way to Christlikeness.

October 20
Sexuality

For this is the will of God, your sanctification: that you abstain from fornication; that each one of you know how to control your own body in holiness and honor, not with lustful passion, like the Gentiles who do not know God; that no one wrong or exploit a brother or sister in this matter, because the Lord is an avenger in all these things, just as we have already told you beforehand and solemnly warned you. For God did not call us to impurity but in holiness. (1 Thessalonians 4:3–7 NRSV)

The tragedy that is engulfing a major evangelical denomination today reminds us that the area of sexuality is one of the main areas in which the Enemy targets God's servants. The larger collapse of our society in regard to sexual identity and expression only underlines the problem.

What is going on is the collapse of biblical ethics in the general decline of the West into a pagan worldview. What is that worldview? That this psycho-socio-physical cosmos is all there is to reality. If you believe that, several things follow, chief among which for this discussion is that life is purposeless and without any ethical absolutes. In short, "Nobody tells me what to do with my life."

That being so, desires rule, and chief among them is sexual desire. We might debate why sexual desire is so powerful. One possibility is that the genetic need to propagate humanity drives us, with the complex gratifications that sexual expression provides undergirding it. So, like every pagan society that has ever existed, we become more and more sex-obsessed. The result is that even those who would say they adhere to the biblical worldview, that the transcendent Creator has an explicit way for us to live, find themselves sucked into the vortex.

Is there a solution? Certainly there is. It is in your devotional life, both private and public. Oh, it is not in merely adhering to routine, although that matters. It is in what the routine is in aid of. Are you passionate about pleasing your Savior, your lover? If you are, then you will not allow *anything,* such as the increasingly filthy TV shows and movies, let alone pornography, infect your vision of who he is and what he has designed our behavior to be. Perhaps you say, "Oh, Oswalt, don't be a prude!" Why not? If that's what it takes to protect my relationship with Jesus, and with Karen, and with my children, and with women to whom I minister, then I will gladly be a prude. How about you?

October 21

THE BLUES

Rejoice always, pray continually, give thanks in all circumstances; for this
is God's will for you in Christ Jesus. (1 Thessalonians 5:16–18 NIV)

In 1949 the British author Dorothy Sayers made a typically profound
observation that is even more relevant today than it was seventy-three
years ago. She said that if a person insisted on denying reality and continued
to believe that the universe exists to supply his or her needs, they would
soon begin to conceive that the universe bears an implacable hostility
toward them and their needs. The result would be a generally disgruntled
attitude and a sense that life is not fair. Such people, she said, are always
going around with a bad case of "the blues." She further says that to choose
to remain in this state is to choose to enter into the experience of hell.

When I read these words, I immediately thought how well they
describe the situation in our society today. We are surrounded by masses
of disgruntled people who are angry because things are not going their
way. They are not getting what they want, and they *are going to get it, or
know the reason why!*

Sadly, I find too many Christians in this same state. After all, *we* are in
the right, and it is just wrong that the society should hold us in contempt.
Furthermore, we *know* what is right, and we are going to *make* the society
conform to it. To all of this, the Apostle Paul has three words: "Rejoice
always, pray constantly, give thanks in everything." That is the prescription
for victorious living. We don't get what we deserve? Give thanks! What we
deserve is the back of God's hand! *Anything* good we receive from him is
undeserved. Treated with contempt or worse? Take it to God, unload it on
him, and be free. Dark and difficult days? Rejoice in the face of the Father
shining on you with love. *In everything* there is reason to give thanks, if
we will. The old line says it well: "I complained that I had no shoes until I
met a man who had no feet." Which do we choose? Gratitude for what we
have, or anger for what we don't have? Heaven or Hell?

October 22
PRAYER
Never stop praying. (1 Thessalonians 5:17)

When I was a seminary student, one of my classes visited a nearby Trappist monastery. The Trappist rule is very severe. They all take a vow of silence and self-denial. They sleep in tiny cubicles in a large, unheated room and eat very sparingly. The guest master who was given a special dispensation to talk to us said that he usually lost 20 pounds every Lent which it took him the rest of the year to regain. As we went around with the guest master, a question was forming in all of our minds: "What is this guy doing here?" We were thinking that because he was so impressive. He was tall, blond and good-looking, with the build of a footballer that he said he had been in college. On top of all that, he had a very winning personality. Finally, one of us got up the courage to ask the question. He smiled. Obviously, this was not the first time he had been asked. He said, "When I finished college, I wanted to do something to make a difference in the world. I finally decided that the best thing I could do for the world was to pray for it." Ouch! What can you say to that? Will you say, "Well, it's all very well to pray, but, hey, you can get too much of a good thing." Or, "Prayer is well and good, but it's more important to do things." Or will you finally get right down to it and say, "Actually, I don't think prayer is that effective."

I am not suggesting that we all "quit our day-jobs" and move into monasteries or nunneries, but every time I think about that incident I wonder again what my prayer practices are saying about what I really think of prayer. Is it really possible to change the course of events through prayer? Does my praying somehow cooperate with the intentions of God to bring about good in the lives of people I am praying for that would not happen, or at least would not happen in the same way, if I did not pray? When I pray, am I touching the heart of God? My answer to every one of those is "Yes!" Then the Voice says, "Then wouldn't you like to do it more intensely, more intentionally, more joyfully, and more frequently?" Yes, Lord, yes.

October 23

Transforming a Weakness

Once we, too, were foolish and disobedient. We were misled and became slaves to many lusts and pleasures. Our lives were full of evil and envy, and we hated each other. But—When God our Savior revealed his kindness and love, he saved us, not because of the righteous things we had done, but because of his mercy. He washed away our sins, giving us a new birth and new life through the Holy Spirit. He generously poured out the Spirit upon us through Jesus Christ our Savior. (Titus 3:3–6)

My father was forty-five when I was born, and I may have broken the pattern, but at least up until this point, Oswalt men never showed emotion. That was my Dad. I know now that I was the apple of his eye, but I'll tell you, he squelched that emotion more effectively than I could ever imagine. As far as I knew, I was an inconvenience to him. He was very effective at telling me what I did not do right. Now don't misunderstand me, he was a good father. I'm so grateful to God for giving me a father with the integrity, the sense of responsibility, and all the good characteristics he had, but I grew up with a positive lust for affirmation.

I didn't realize this for a long time. All I knew was that as a Christian seeking to live God's life, I was plagued with envy. Somebody would get an honor, and I would be eaten up with envy. I didn't deserve it, hadn't earned it, and wasn't in the running, but I wanted it. For many years, I beat myself with the assistance of my enemy whispering in my ear, "And you call yourself sanctified. You call yourself filled with the Holy Spirit and you go around with all that stuff." I would pray earnestly, "Lord, Lord, take away these feelings." The Lord began to help me, and what he said to me was, "John, I put you in that family. I put you in a situation where that lust for affirmation would indeed arise. Now do you want me to destroy you and make somebody else?" I said, "No, probably not."

He began to help me understand that to be John Oswalt is to have that particular weakness. For the first time in my life, I stopped saying, "If I would be entirely sanctified, I would quit being me," and began to say, "If I were entirely sanctified, I would be me, *but set free.*" So, when someone would get an honor, and the feeling would begin to rise, instead of trying to beat it down or deny it, I began to say, "Here, Holy Spirit. This is ugly. I don't want this." Then, I began to experience consistent victory. He did not change my tendency, but he helped me to understand where it came from and to accept that origin. If today I have any degree of sensitivity to the need of other persons for affirmation, it's because of that. The Lord didn't take the weakness away, but I think *he's transformed me in it.*

When Morning Gilds the Skies

October 24

LEARNING OBEDIENCE

Even though Jesus was God's Son, he learned obedience
from the things he suffered. (Hebrews 5:8)

This must be one of the most surprising, if not most shocking, statements in Scripture. Jesus learned obedience? What can that mean? Surely the Second Person of the Holy Trinity did not need to learn obedience! Jesus says in the Gospel of John that he always does his Father's will (see 4:34, 5:30, 6:38–39). What does suffering have to do with it anyway? What can the writer of Hebrews possibly mean?

Because commentators vary widely in their interpretation of this statement, I need to be cautious. Nevertheless, I want to suggest a possibility, and one that has direct relevance to us. I suggest that before he became a human, the Second Person—the Son—never had to confront the necessity of choosing to obey the First Person—the Father. It had never been a question before. The three-personed God knew what he wanted to do and all three Persons did it as a matter of course together. But now, as a human, Jesus encountered the possibility all of us humans have been given by God: disobedience. I don't know what would have happened had Jesus actually disobeyed the Father; I suppose the universe would have flown to pieces. In any case, obedience now required a choice, and, praise his Name, Jesus gladly embraced it: he learned obedience.

He learned obedience from the things he suffered? Yes, obedience always comes at a price. The minimum price is admitting that somebody else—anybody else—has the right to tell us what to do. The price goes up steeply when what somebody else wants us to do hurts. Would Jesus still obey God when to do so meant that he could not use his power to feed himself when he was hungry? Would he still obey God when saying what he was supposed to say drove the crowds away? Would he still obey God when his own people unjustly executed him? Yes, yes, and yes! Suffering is the truest evidence of what we really believe and what we are really committed to. Jesus passed every test, and we may live forever because of it.

October 25

SUFFERING EQUALS GLORY

But we see him who for a little while was made lower than the angels, namely Jesus, crowned with glory and honor because of the suffering of death, so that by the grace of God he might taste death for everyone. (Hebrews 2:9 ESV)

They wondered what time or situation the Spirit of Christ within
them was talking about when he told them in advance about
Christ's suffering and his great glory afterward. (1 Peter 1:11)

Five times in the New Testament, the equation is made between Christ's suffering and his glory: Romans 8:18, Hebrews 2:9, 1 Peter 1:11, 1 Peter 4:13, and 1 Peter 5:1. Although the causal connection between the two is implied in the first, third, fourth, and fifth times, it is made entirely explicit in the Hebrews passage: Jesus was glorified for one reason— because he suffered! The point being made in all those passages and the surrounding ones that depend on them is that the road to glory for us is likewise through suffering.

Such an idea is alien to everything we think and to a great deal of the preaching of the gospel around the world today. It has to be said that one reason for the explosion of the Church in much of the so-called "Majority World" in the last forty years is because a gospel has been preached that promised power, wealth, and good health to all who have the faith to seize them.

But that is not what the Book says! The Bible says that for Jesus to confront the evil of the world and to "de-fang" it, he had to suffer. That kind of suffering was exactly what the early church was experiencing, and they were asking their teachers, "Is this right?" Their teachers were responding, "Why are you surprised? If Jesus had to suffer to 'bring many sons to glory,' why do you think you're going to get off scot-free?" Jesus himself had said as much (see John 15:20).

In fact, it is through suffering that our character is refined, just as fire tempers steel and purifies gold. We could even say that until we have met suffering and overcome it, we have not really grown up. Of course, only a neurotic seeks pain, but when pain comes, we need neither think we are being punished nor that God has somehow forgotten us. Rather, we can accept the fact that in a fallen world, physical suffering is a given that can be made a tool for Christian growth, and that the pain of undeserved persecution is evidence that we really do belong to the Savior in his painful battle with evil.

When Morning Gilds the Skies

October 26

A PLACE OF REST—A ROOST

So then, there remains a Sabbath rest for the people of God, for
whoever has entered God's rest has also rested from his works as God
did from his. Let us therefore strive to enter that rest, so that no one
may fall by the same sort of disobedience. (Hebrews 4:9–11 ESV)

So there remains a Sabbath rest for the people of God. For the one who has
entered his rest has himself also rested from his works, as God did from his.
Therefore let us be diligent to enter that rest, so that no one will fall, through
following the same example of disobedience. (Hebrews 4:9–11 NASB)

What is Canaan a symbol of? In many of our hymnals it is heaven, and
the Jordan is death. I don't want to dismiss that too easily, because
there is a certain correctness there, but I'm not sure we really understand
what the connection is between Canaan and heaven: it is *rest*. More than
100 times Canaan is said to be the place of rest. In fact, the Hebrew word
is closely related to "roost." Noah knew when the dove did not return that
it had found a place to rest—roost. Naomi said to Ruth that she had a
responsibility to find a place of rest—a roost—for her widowed daughter-
in-law.

What is a roost? It is a place where a bird can land and settle in for
the night or from the storm. The Hebrew people had been enslaved and
oppressed, then they had wandered in the desert for forty years, prey to
every kind of uncertainty. Now God was bringing them into a place where
they could land and settle, and if they would be obedient, they could
be secure.

But the writer to the Hebrews says that the Hebrews *did not* enter their
rest. They didn't? Oh, yes, they entered the physical land alright. However,
they never, or only rarely, experienced the rest the land was supposed
to make possible. Why not? Because they would not give up their futile
attempts to take care of themselves. They could not give up their fruitless
trying to manipulate the forces of nature to make themselves secure.

Oh, Christian, have you entered your rest? Like a bird settling down
on a branch, have you given up your attempts to make your life work?
Have you given over control of your life to your Lover? Have you stopped
fluttering around from place to place and thing to thing? That's why Jesus
saved you, to bring you to that blessed place of rest in him. Heaven is
nothing other than the culmination of the rest we are intended to enjoy
now. Don't miss it!

Do We Need the Old Testament?

For the word of God [Old Testament] is living and active and
sharper than any two-edged sword, piercing as far as the division
of soul and spirit, of both joints and marrow, and able to judge the
thoughts and intentions of the heart. (Hebrews 4:12 NASB)

Do we need the Old Testament? Many people today, including some
prominent preachers, say no, but they are wrong. We do need the Old
Testament. Why? The answer is pretty simple: we need the Old Testament
to understand the New Testament correctly. The two testaments
complement each other. Each one is incomplete without the other. For
instance, it is very easy to make the God of the New Testament just a
kindly grandfather who will let you get away with anything. On the other
hand, it is very easy to make the Old Testament God a terrifying ogre who
will strike you dead if you cross him. Neither view is correct.

The perfectly pure God of the Old Testament loves you all the way to
his own death on the Cross, and the gracious God of the New Testament
is the righteous Judge who will send you to hell. We need both testaments
to get an adequate picture of God. Here's another example: the Cross
is the answer, but what is the question? Why did Jesus die? If you only
know the New Testament, you may well say that it is: how can our sins
be forgiven so we can go to heaven? But that is wrong. The question the
Cross is answering is the Old Testament one: how can a holy God take up
residence in a sinful person? Does God want to forgive our sins? Of course.
But that is the beginning of the story of redemption, not the end, as so
many Christians tragically see it. He wants to forgive us so his Spirit can
fill us and transform us into a holy temple for him to live in.

The Old Testament is a book of unanswered questions, but the New
Testament is a book of pointless answers. Together, they are the full-
orbed, exciting Word of God. The Old Testament is a tough read, but if you
will apply yourself to it, you will become a real Christian.

October 28
OBSOLETE?

By calling this covenant "new," he has made the first one obsolete; and what is obsolete and outdated will soon disappear. (Hebrews 8:13 NIV)

The law is only a shadow of the good things that are coming—not the realities themselves. For this reason it can never, by the same sacrifices repeated endlessly year after year, make perfect those who draw near to worship. (Hebrews 10:1 NIV)

This is the covenant I will make with them after that time, says the Lord. I will put my laws in their hearts, and I will write them on their minds. (Hebrews 10:16 NIV)

What is the place of Old Testament ethical teachings in a Christian's life? Some who read passages like those reproduced above would say, "None! We are Christians, not Jews. Everything we need by way of ethical instruction can be found in the New Testament." However, that conclusion is wrong because it misreads what these passages are talking about. The writer is confronting an opposite fallacy: the commandments of the Old Covenant, the law, were given to us so that we could make ourselves good enough for God—complete, whole, perfect. So, we Christians have to keep obeying all those commands, including the sacrificial system. Not true, the writer says. The sacrificial system could not make us right with God; those practices were only pointers, teachers, showing us God's true method: the Lord Jesus. So, because the reality has come, there is no need to—in fact, we must not—continue to revere the pointers.

What about the ethical commands? They are also teachers, teaching us that there is something terribly wrong with us. We cannot do those things, even when we narrow them down to just the externals. So because I can't use those ethical commands in the old, obsolete way (i.e., to save myself), shall I just forget them? No! They are the heart of a New Covenant, one that God, through the Holy Spirit and by virtue of the blood of Christ, graciously writes on my heart. This is the thrust of Jesus's Sermon on the Mount—he wants to make internal and achievable what had been only external and unachievable. So, are you living in the full inheritance that Jesus died to give you? You can share the character of God. Are you?

WHAT DID HE DO?

Though he was God, he did not think of equality with God as something
to cling to. Instead, he gave up his divine privileges; he took the
humble position of a slave and was born as a human being. When
he appeared in human form, he humbled himself in obedience to
God and died a criminal's death on a cross. (Philippians 2:6–8)

A thought struck me as I read this passage: the very things that God
promised to Abraham, Jesus gave up. God gave Abraham a place to
call his own, progeny, and reputation, but Jesus had none of those. What's
happening? Is desire wrong? Was God just accommodating himself to
an Abraham who was a "babe" in faith? No, God knows and honors our
deepest desires, and he proves his trustworthiness by giving them to the
man who will (finally) resist the desire to get them for himself. The lesson
there is that desire is dangerous and that to master it we have to surrender
its fulfillment into God's hands. In short, we have to die to it.

That is what Jesus is showing us. He died every day of his earthly
life. He died to a place of his own; he died to sexual love and children;
he died to his reputation. He began all that in the very way he came to
earth, and because he was the master of his desires—killing them, as it
were—he was really, truly, alive. Dietrich Bonhoeffer, in his book *The Cost
of Discipleship*, says that we can only own something that we can honestly
consider ourselves as being better off without. Otherwise, he says, it owns
you. The same thing applies to desire. If I must have it, I am in deep trouble.

No, our desires are not bad. Jesus clearly enjoyed life, but he
demonstrates to us that we must be masters of our desires at all costs. In
some cases that will go to the lengths of refusing to fulfill those desires.
C. S. Lewis says that to be fully human is to have your desires under the
control of your will and your will under the control of God.

October 30
GOD'S PROVISION: PART ONE

He did not enter by means of the blood of goats and calves; but he entered the Most Holy Place once for all by his own blood, thus obtaining eternal redemption. The blood of goats and bulls and the ashes of a heifer sprinkled on those who are ceremonially unclean sanctify them so that they are outwardly clean. How much more, then, will the blood of Christ, who through the eternal Spirit offered himself unblemished to God, cleanse our consciences from acts that lead to death, so that we may serve the living God! (Hebrews 9:12–14 NIV)

Have you ever thought about the significance of the placement of the sacrificial system in the revelation at Sinai? Is the system given in order to make the people acceptable to God, so that they can enter into a relationship with him? No. They are already in a relationship with him, they are already delivered from Egyptian bondage, they have already accepted God's covenant with him, and they have already experienced his presence among them in the Tabernacle. Only after all that, in Leviticus 1–9, do we find the instructions for making sacrifices. Why?

In this placement God is making a very profound statement about the radically different meaning of sacrifice in the biblical understanding of reality. In a pagan view sacrifices are a way of manipulating God—getting him to do what I want—whether forgiveness, blessing, or whatever. The God of the Bible cannot be manipulated. He forgives, delivers, reveals, and abides simply out of his own grace. God did not deliver the Hebrews from Egypt because they offered sacrifices to him. He delivered them for love.

Here is the difference between biblical faith and the religions of the world. In biblical faith God is reaching out to us, attempting to change us, while the religions of the world are reaching out to the gods, attempting to change them. The Israelites were constantly forgetting this and slipping back into the pagan use of sacrifices, one that frankly nauseates God. We Christians are all too prone to the same kind of thinking: "What has Jesus done for me lately, and how can I get him to be more responsive to my wants?"

So why sacrifices at all? They were object lessons to teach us the nature and the cost of sin. How could God extend the grace of forgiveness without upsetting the whole cause and effect world he made? The person who sins *shall* die. There it is—no ifs, ands, or buts. So, what has he done? He has taken our death upon himself! The blood that drenched the altar day after day, month after month, year after year, was meant to drive that point home. Oh, the blood of Jesus!

October 31

GOD'S PROVISION: PART TWO

For his unfailing love toward those who fear him is as great as the height
of the heavens above the earth. He has removed our sins as far from
us as the east is from the west. The LORD is like a father to his children,
tender and compassionate to those who fear him. For he knows how
weak we are; he remembers we are only dust. (Psalm 103:11–14)

In Part One, I pointed out that the instructions for the sacrificial system
come only at the beginning of Leviticus, after the deliverance from
Egypt, the sealing of the covenant, and the directions for the building of
the Tabernacle. I said that this placement was designed to show that we do
not get into a relationship with God by manipulating him in some magical
fashion. Rather, it is God who brings us to himself only because of his own
grace.

This placement of the sacrificial system says something more. Exodus
is unmistakably clear: to be in a saved condition is to be living the life of
God in covenant obedience. We are joyfully walking with our Father. Just
as sacrificial love made it possible to be in this relationship, sacrificial love
makes it possible to remain there. God did not give the system of sacrifices
for those who wanted to sin and still get to heaven. That becomes strikingly
clear when we discover that the whole system was for *unintended* sins. If
you sinned intentionally, as David understood, there was no prescribed
sacrifice for that (see Ps 51:16–17). It had to be dealt with on a case-by-case
basis. Yahweh's sacrificial forgiveness is for those who want to live with
him and yet in human weakness and ignorance will necessarily fall short of
perfect performance. As the psalmist says, he knows our weaknesses and
has made a means whereby these need not forever separate us from him.

Bottom line: you and I may never use the blood of Christ as a fire
escape, allowing us to do what we want and get away with it. We may never
suppose it simply gives God Jesus-colored glasses so that he never sees
what the real character of our lives is. Rather, blood-bought and blood-
sealed, we may walk with him in unblemished fellowship secure in the
knowledge that if in ignorance or weakness we unintentionally fall short
in some way, there is grace for all.

November 1

FLYING ON INSTRUMENTS

But we are not like those who turn away from God to their
own destruction. We are the faithful ones, whose souls will
be saved. Faith shows the reality of what we hope for; it is the
evidence of things we cannot see. (Hebrews 10:39–11:1)

Some years ago, a friend of mine was renewing his instrument flying license, and he asked me if I would like to go along. Enjoying flying as I do, I jumped at the chance. It was a lovely sunny day, and the instructor and I, looking out the windows, could enjoy it. But my friend could see none of that, because he was wearing a large dark visor that completely blocked his vision of anything but the instrument panel of the plane, as would be the case if he were flying at night or in clouds.

As I recall, the instructor flew for the take-off and then turned the controls over to Bill (not his real name). At this point, I was really hoping that Bill had learned his lessons well, because we were completely dependent on his ability to follow the instruments. It is essential that the pilot follow them, because when we humans have no external point of reference, our senses are completely unreliable.

After we had flown awhile, with Bill responding to the instructor's instructions about compass heading, turning, and climbing or descending, the instructor said we were ready to head back and called the airport tower for directions. Looking out, I could see the airport far away on our right. As the flight controller gave Bill his directions about heading, attitude, and altitude, I watched us move around and slowly begin to line up on the runway. If we drifted a little right or left, the controller's calm voice would guide Bill back again. By the time we reached 500 feet and Bill could lift the visor and land us visually, we were lined up perfectly. As I watched this all from the back seat, I thought this must be how it is for the angels looking on at us. They can see our destination perfectly and see whether we are headed in the right direction with the right attitude and at the right height. We can't see it at all, and unless we can find some external reference points, some instruments, as it were, we are lost. Thank God, we do have an all-sufficient instrument, the Bible, the Word of God, and we have the voice of the Flight Controller, the Holy Spirit, sounding in our ear, telling us how to read that instrument. What a day it will be when the Controller says, "Okay, you can lift the visor and come on in."

November 2

THE CROSS AND UKRAINE

Because of the joy awaiting him, he endured the cross, disregarding its shame. Now he is seated in the place of honor beside God's throne. (Hebrews 12:2b)

He was destined before the foundation of the world, but was revealed at the end of the ages for your sake. (1 Peter 1:20 NRSV)

All of us who have seen the carnage in Ukraine whether in print or on the screen have been broken-hearted. The picture of an elderly woman kneeling in the street wailing for her dead husband is imprinted on my mind, as is that of a younger woman looking emptily at the bodies of her husband, brother, and brother-in-law in the court in front of her house. What are we to make of such horrors? We are told many younger people are leaving the church because they cannot put the idea of a good, providential, all-powerful God together with the kind of a world depicted in scenes like these. How could a good God who can do anything allow such senseless tragedy, and so much of it?

It seems to me that what we see here is a failure in Christian education. Where is a good God in the terrible things that are happening not only in Ukraine but also in Myanmar and a host of other unnamed places? *He is on the Cross!*

Could God have made a world where it was impossible to deviate from his good will? Of course, he could have, but that would be a world where self-giving, self-denying love was also impossible. So, he chose to make a world where refusal to do his will was a possibility. Suppose humans would, in utter foolishness, take up that latter option? What then? We could turn the good creation into an ongoing train wreck, as we have done. What then? Could he stop it? Not without destroying all the sons and daughters of Adam. So, what then? He would *enter into the suffering* resulting from that wreck. He would take it all into himself. He would kneel in the street with that elderly woman or in front of her house with that younger woman, and if they would let him, he would enfold them in his arms. He chose to do that, if necessary, before the world began.

That is why we are Easter Christians. We do not celebrate the unselfish martyrdom of a good man. No, we celebrate God taking *all* the horror, *all* the petty, senseless cruelty, *all* the accidental deaths, *all* of it into himself, giving back endless love. *That* is what the Cross is about. Embrace it for yourself and know that God is good.

November 3

SOLDIERS OF THE CROSS

Live such good lives among the pagans that, though they accuse you
of doing wrong, they may see your good deeds and glorify God on the
day he visits us. Submit yourselves for the Lord's sake to every human
authority: whether to the emperor, as the supreme authority, or to
governors, who are sent by him to punish those who do wrong and to
commend those who do right. For it is God's will that by doing good you
should silence the ignorant talk of foolish people. (1 Peter 2:12–15 NIV)

It will not be news to anyone that, as Christians in North America, we
feel beleaguered. It seems that every other religion gets treated with
respect except ours, which is treated with contempt. It seems as though the
customs, practices, and values that are dear to us, practices and values that
we believe are essential to human flourishing, are those that are reserved
for special attack.

How do we respond? There is a real danger here. The fact is that
Christian ideas and values have been privileged in this country, and now
when that is no longer the case, we are tempted to react out of outrage.
How dare our fellow citizens take away our privileged status, especially
when *we know* that to do so is to eat away at the very fabric of our country?
We are confusing our status and the good of the country. Are we really
motivated for the country or for ourselves?

The greatest danger, it seems to me, is to try to enforce our values
through political means. Does anyone remember the eighteenth
amendment? It prohibited the manufacture, sale, and transportation of
beverage alcohol in this country. It was accomplished by Carrie Nation
and the Women's Christian Temperance Union. It was a Christian political
victory. Was it a good thing? Almost certainly. Did it accomplish good?
No. Its primary effect, which is still with us, was the institutionalization of
organized crime.

Why did it fail? Because the majority of the people did not accept it. It
was a political victory only. Any attempt by Christians to force unbelievers
to accept Christian values by political means, including abortion, dare
I say, *will fail*. We either convince people of the truth of Christian faith
and values by living submissive, loving, transformed lives, or we do
nothing at all. Romanian believers said it, "The weapon of the Lamb is the
bared throat."

November 4

THE WAY

Without holiness no one will see the Lord. (Hebrews 12:14b NIV)

Too often we have given the impression that salvation is a change of state accomplished through a judicial transaction. While that is not untrue, it is, unfortunately, to miss almost all that God is about with us. A reasonably careful reading of the Bible makes this point very clear: God wants to make us over into the image of Christ. To be saved is to experience a change of character that is accomplished through a life-long cultivation of the gift of the Holy Spirit made possible through the death and resurrection of Jesus.

The book of 1 John illustrates this point very clearly. The book is answering the question, "What is it to be a Christian?" Our standard evangelical answer is: repent of your sins, believe that Jesus Christ died to forgive you of your sins, and accept him as your Savior. In short, believe. John underlines the importance of right belief, but only as the third in a series of things. First—*first*, I say—a Christian exhibits the moral character of God. Second, a Christian exhibits the relational character of God. Third, a Christian believes that Jesus is divine and human, the fulfillment of the Old Testament promises of a genuinely unselfish Deliverer.

So, to be a Christian is to obey, love, and believe. If you truly believe, it *must* change the way you live. Your way of living is going to be shaped by a passion to do what God does, to be what God is, to walk like God walks, and that is love. If your belief doesn't issue in an obedience that brings you to self-giving love, something is missing in your Christian experience.

To be a Christian is to be in a relationship with God that changes your character. That change of character begins to happen in the moment of conversion, but if it is to continue, there must come a moment when we face the deep self-centeredness that dominates our lives and invite the Holy Spirit to displace that self-centeredness by filling us with himself. Through the fullness of the Holy Spirit, it is possible to fulfill God's dream of our sharing his character with him as we live in lifelong, intimate fellowship with him. This is what "you must be holy, for I am holy" is all about. To be holy is to be saved (see Ex 31:13; Lev 22:32).

November 5

HOLY AWE

Therefore, since we are receiving a kingdom that cannot be shaken
let us be thankful, and so worship God acceptably with reverence and
awe, for our God is a consuming fire. (Hebrews 12:28–29 NIV)

A holy life grows out of a wholesome awe. There are two reasons for
that awe. One is the impartial judgment of the perfect God; the
other, the imperishable salvation of the perfect Savior. When you and I
kneel at the cross, when we realize what it cost God to save us, when we
realize how carefully it was planned from the foundations of the universe,
when we realize the wonder of the plan, there ought to be an awe in us:
"Oh God. All this for me? All of the wonderful plans? All of the careful
provisions? Yourself, for me? Oh God, don't let me do anything that would
bring disgrace upon your name. Don't let me do anything that would make
the world think less of this incredible salvation that you have given for
me. Oh God, give me a fear of bringing disgrace on that wonderful gospel.
Put in my heart a fear of offending your righteousness. Put in my heart a
fear of bringing disgrace upon the wonderful work of salvation. Make me
like yourself so that I won't bring shame on your wonderful name. Let the
fire of your holiness burn up everything in me that has the potential for
making you look small, weak, and helpless. Let everything I am say 'What
a great God and what a great salvation!'"

November 6

TAMING DESIRES

Then, after desire has conceived, it gives birth to sin; and sin,
when it is full-grown, gives birth to death. (James 1:15 NIV)

Buddhism and Christianity have at least one thing in common, and that is their conviction that desire is at the root of the problems of the human race. Buddhism says that the solution is to extinguish desire. When that is fully accomplished we will reach Nirvana, which is nothingness. Personally, I don't find the Buddhist solution very attractive, but I must admit that when I was a young man struggling with my sexuality, there were times when I unwittingly thought that was the right route. I said to myself, "Oh, if I could just get to the point where I saw an attractive woman and did not feel sexual attraction for her, then I would be a real Christian."

I was sharing these feelings with a wise person one day and he said, "John, if you get to the place where you see a beautiful woman and no longer feel sexual attraction for her, you will not be a Christian, you will be dead!" The issue is not, how do we get rid of our desires, but how do we take them captive for Christ's sake (see 2 Cor 10:5)? The issue is not, Lord, take my desires away so I won't have to struggle with them anymore. It is, how can I harness these desires for your purposes in me? That is where love comes in.

Men, if you are attracted to a woman, pray for her that God will bless her. It is hard to see her as the object of your desire after that. In the same way, when someone has mistreated you and your first desire is to retaliate, offer a prayer for that person. It may not be exactly what the Psalmist meant by "a sacrifice of the lips," but I guarantee that it will be a sacrifice! You don't feel like it? Love is not something you feel but something you do. This is the love of God poured out in you for them.

November 7

FIRE INSURANCE

So you see, we are shown to be right with God by
what we do, not by faith alone. (James 2:24)

On the surface, the statement above is pretty shocking to most of us Protestants. Our forefather, Martin Luther, made a very strong case that we are saved from our sins "by grace alone, through faith alone." For that reason, he called the letter of James "a right strawy epistle," referring to Paul's statements in 1 Corinthians 3:12–15 about building with precious metals and stones or with hay and straw. We can understand Luther's concerns because the church of his day had largely neglected the truth that we can only become acceptable to God by grace through faith. However, in recovering that truth, it is very possible to go into the opposite ditch, and it seems to me that is what has happened to much of the evangelical church in North America. We have come to view salvation as a kind of fire insurance. We don't want to burn in Hell, and we learn that Jesus has paid the insurance premium for us, and further, that all we have to do to accept the policy from God is to swear allegiance to him. If we never go back on that oath of allegiance, the policy is eternally in force.

Then what happens? All too often we ask, "How far from Jesus can I live and still keep the policy in force?" In our world today, with its more and more ambiguous definitions of sin, it appears you can really live a long way from him. But that's the wrong question. The question is, "How much like my Savior can I be?"—because that is why he saved us from sin: so that we can be made over in the image of Christ. What does that image look like? It looks like the Old Testament law as interpreted by Jesus. Too many say, "I'm not saved by keeping the law; I'm saved by grace. I didn't do anything to get saved, and I don't have to do anything to keep saved." That's dead wrong.

Jesus makes it plain that the principles established in the Law are forever (see Matt 5:18). They are certainly not the *way* to God, and if we try to make them that, they can only condemn us. But when we have come to God through faith in Christ, those principles define the *walk* with God. Through the Holy Spirit, they can become internalized, and true godliness—God-like-ness—the purpose of salvation, can be ours. Don't ask how far you can live from Jesus, but how close to him. That's why he died.

November 8

OUR INHERITANCE

Praise be to the God and Father of our Lord Jesus Christ! In his great mercy he has given us new birth into a living hope through the resurrection of Jesus Christ from the dead, and into an inheritance that can never perish, spoil or fade . . . kept in heaven for you. (1 Peter 1:3–4 NIV)

It is so interesting to me that the rich young ruler, when he came running up to Jesus, said, "Good Master, what good thing shall I do, that I may have eternal life?" (Matt 19:16 KJV). That is not a very smart question. There is no good thing you have to do to inherit eternal life. You just have to be born into the right family. Have you been born into the right family? You have been breaking your back for forty, fifty, sixty years, trying to be good enough. It won't work. It is an inheritance. All you have to do is to be born to a living hope. To "an inheritance that can never perish, spoil or fade."

My children never have to worry about having a big inheritance. If you are born into the family of a Methodist preacher, you don't have to worry about that. I am rather glad about it. I don't know anything more sickening than brothers and sisters squabbling over an inheritance. It's ugly, defiled, corrupted. Peter says there will be no squabbling over this inheritance, for every one of us will get the full share. Isn't that great? I don't know whether you knew it or not, but I am going to inherit all of heaven! If the rest of you want to come along, that's alright with me, but I get it all. The wonderful truth is, you get it all too! Every one of us gets the whole inheritance!

This inheritance is not something passing away to squabble over. It won't defile you or corrupt you; it will set you free. It is reserved. Isn't that great? There is a reservation there with your name on it. You know where your name is written: it is written in the reservation book, on the hand of Jesus Christ. My name is written on his hand.

Is your name written on the hand of Jesus today? Is it written in the nail-scarred hand? If it is, you are part of the family. You are an heir—we are joint heirs with Christ (see Rom 8:17; Gal 3:29, 4:7).

November 9

GLORY AND SUFFERING

In all this you greatly rejoice, though now for little while you may have had to suffer grief in all kinds of trials. These have come so that the proven genuineness of your faith—of greater worth than gold, which perishes even though refined by fire—may result in praise, glory, and honor when Jesus Christ is revealed. (1 Peter 1:6–7 NIV)

One of the surprising things we find in the book of 1 Peter is the way he connects suffering with glory. What he says is that suffering presents us with an opportunity to demonstrate the true glory of living for Jesus. If you can maintain an even temper, a kindly smile, and a quiet spirit when your stomach is full and the sun is shining, that is nice, but it hardly proves anything, does it? It is when the world has fallen in on us that we discover what we really believe.

The glory of living for Jesus is that he enables us to take terrible, hard things in life and not be broken by them but victors over them. That, as Peter says in the verses above, counts for something. Not to lash out when everything is wrong, to smile through the tears, to be gentle and thoughtful when screaming is called for, that counts for something.

But counts for what? Is Peter merely talking about stoicism: "grin and bear it"? No, not at all. He is talking about a faith that enables us not to deny the pain, but to embrace it—in the confidence that Christ can use it for good in our lives and the lives of those around us, that it can be a refining fire that will free us of that frilly, sentimental faith that "King's Kids" never get hurt, that it can strip us to the bare bones of real faith, which can endure all the way home. It is the survivors to whom the victory wreaths will be given.

November 10

THE GIFT OF GRACE

Therefore, preparing your minds for action, and being sober-minded, set your hope fully on the grace that will be brought to you at the revelation of Jesus Christ. As obedient children, do not be conformed to the passions of your former ignorance, but as he who called you is holy, you also be holy in all your conduct, since it is written, "You shall be holy, for I am holy." (1 Peter 1:13–16 ESV)

Why is it that you and I are not more holy? It is because we really don't believe the grace of God. It is because we really have not come to that place where we know how deep his love for us, how immense his resources are that he wants to pour out on us. If we really knew that, if we really felt it, if we really thought through the implications of grace, we would not be saying, "How little like God can I be and still go to heaven?" No, we would be saying, "O my gracious Father, how much like you can I be?"

We say we believe in grace, but many of us are really still trying to work our way into the favor of the heavenly Judge, and that is hard work, and we don't feel like we are getting anywhere. So, we often settle for the minimums and live our sloppy lives, hoping that it will get us by. What's the problem? We have never really surrendered to his grace. We have never really let him love us with all the immensity of his love.

If we can ever get one glimpse of how precious we are to him and how delighted he is in us, if we can ever feel the wonder of that, then the passion of our hearts will be how much like him we can become. Grace doesn't bring God down to our level; grace raises us to his level. It makes it possible for us to live in his presence and, out of pure hearts, reflect his shining face. Rest your hope fully on the grace that is to be brought to you at the revelation of Christ Jesus. If you really rest on grace, you will want to be like the One who is giving his grace.

November 11

As Obedient Children

As obedient children, do not conform to the evil desires you had when you lived in ignorance. But just as he who called you is holy, so be holy in all you do; for it is written, "Be holy, because I am holy." (1 Peter 1:14–16 NIV)

May God himself, the God of wholeness, make you completely holy. May your whole spirit, soul, and body be completely whole until the coming of our Lord Jesus Christ. He who calls you is faithful, and he will do it. (1 Thessalonians 5:23–25 author's translation)

There are three thoughts that capture my attention when I look at 1 Peter 14–16, but let's look at them in reverse order. First, "it is written." Peter is quoting from the Old Testament book of Leviticus where the command appears in these words four different times (Lev 11:44–45; 19:2; 20:7, 26). Yahweh is speaking in the context of the Covenant: if you are going to be in a covenant with a great king, you do what he says. But this is more than merely doing what he says; it is being what he is and doing what he does. That's pretty shocking.

Second, I notice "be holy in all you do." Some contemporary Christian teachers tell us that holiness is not a particular kind of behavior but merely a condition: you belong to God and are set apart for his use, like a vessel in the temple. Yet Peter says holiness is a way of acting. That corresponds perfectly with Leviticus 19, which begins with the command for us to be holy. The rest of the chapter, beginning with a command to honor our parents, is a whole series of commands to do or not do certain things.

What is it about these commands that is particularly holy? Why does God have to command us to be holy? Why is it not something we do ordinarily? It is because of "evil desires," but what are those? The issue becomes clear when we look at the commands of Leviticus 19. What do they all have in common? They are all other-oriented!

To be holy is to be focused on the good of others, just as our God is supremely focused. Unfortunately, our "evil desires" and the desires of the world in which we live are focused squarely in the opposite direction: on ourselves. God wants to change our orientation. What a thought! This is not something we can do for ourselves. It has to happen through the power of the Spirit of Christ living in us. What we do have to do—and this is where the command comes in—is to give him permission to do this—that's not necessarily an easy decision to make—and we have to believe him to do it. If we do our part, then, as Paul says, he is absolutely faithful to do his part (see 2 Tim 2:11–13).

November 12

A PURE HEART

Now that you have purified yourselves by obeying the truth
so that you have sincere love for your brothers, love one
another deeply, from the heart. (1 Peter 1:22 NIV)

What does that mean: "purified yourselves by obeying the truth"? If I were to say to you that I have lump of pure gold in my hand, what would I mean? I would mean that it was all gold, not part platinum or part silver; it is all gold. This comes right out of the Old Testament. David was a man who loved God with a whole heart (see Ps 101:2), not with part of his heart, but with his whole heart.

When we hear the truth that Christ has died for us so that we might share his divine nature (see 2 Pet 1:4) and then obey his command to be filled with his Spirit (see Acts 1:4–8; Eph 5:18), our hearts, the core of our personality, are made one. We are pure. I am not talking about something mystical or ritualistic. The Holy Spirit just takes our divided heart and makes it one. We are altogether for Jesus, undivided in our love for the Father, the Son, and the Spirit. When that happens, Peter says, we are able to love one another sincerely, genuinely, purely.

Can God do something like that for people like you and me, where we can love one another, not with part of our heart, not with part of our intentions, not with part of our dreams, but with all of our hearts? Oh yes, when you have gotten yourself off your hands, then you don't need to pretend any more. When it no longer matters what they think, but only what God thinks; when you no longer have to prove something to yourself, and to the world because you have gotten yourself off your hand; then you can love other people, and you can love them with a whole heart, a pure heart.

When our hearts are not one for God, we sometimes act in loving ways because that is what is expected, and, burdened with the weight of ourselves, we want others to think that we are loving. But Peter says, "No, that is not what we are talking about. We are talking about love that gives itself away whether it is understood or expected or accepted or not." The King James Version says it is "unfeigned love," un-pretended love. It is pure love from a pure heart.

November 13

IMAGE: NAILED TO THE CROSS

Therefore, rid yourselves of all malice and all deceit, hypocrisy,
envy, and slander of every kind. (1 Peter 2:1 NIV)

What motivates deceit in our lives? Image. Image. Image. I want to look good. You want to look good, and we are afraid that if somebody really knew us, they wouldn't like what they saw. Deceit and hypocrisy grow out of the corrupting power of the need to impress people and make ourselves look good at all costs. Peter says, "if you want to know what it means to love people, your image has got to be nailed to the cross. Lay it aside. You will never love so long as your life is ruled by your image. Instead of worrying about the image of Christ in you, instead of longing for the image of Christ to be born in others, all you are caring about is your image."

Then he says, "Lay aside envy." My victory, my image, my honor. I want people to think I am worth something, and they won't think I am worth anything if you are worth more than I am. I am driven by a lust to be seen as having achieved something, whether I actually have or not! Driven by my image, I don't want you to be honored, I want me to be honored.

This is to have a heart that is divided. We are talking about a heart, part of which wants the best for other people—it really does—and part of which wants the best for me. Peter says, "You will never be able to love people purely, you will never be able to love them without pretense and deceit, until there is a cross at the center of your life, and your victory and your image and your honor are nailed to it."

November 14

CHOSEN

But you are a chosen people, a royal priesthood, a holy nation, God's special possession, that you may declare the praises of him who called you out of darkness into his wonderful light. (1 Peter 2:9 NIV)

For he chose us in him before the creation of the world to be holy and blameless in his sight. In love he predestined us for the adoption of sonship through Jesus Christ in accordance with his pleasure and will. (Ephesians 1:4–5 NIV)

I have always been a lousy baseball player. I think the reason is that I am both left-handed and left-eyed; therefore, the ball is always somewhere it wasn't supposed to be. What a feeling it was when my best friend was one of the captains when we were choosing up sides, and the first person he chose was me. He knew that I couldn't hit a ball. He knew that I kept losing the ball in the sun on cloudy days, but he chose me anyhow. What a feeling! The fact is, every one of us has been specifically chosen by God.

That is the miracle of election. It is not that he chose some and rejected others. No, he has chosen us all. You say, "Well that means that none of us are special." No, that means all of us are special. Every one of us, because he is God, has been chosen first. What a wonder! He chose me, he chose you. He looked at you and said, "Oh, she's my number one choice." He looked at you and said, "Ah, he is the one I choose first." Every one of us, chosen by the Father. Chosen by means of the sanctifying Spirit.

How did we get to be in a relationship with God the Father? Through the Holy Spirit, for there's no other way. What kind of a Spirit is it, which has brought us to Christ? He is the Spirit of holiness. If you are a Christian today, it is because the Spirit has made you Christian and keeps you a Christian, and who is he? He is the Spirit of holiness, and he has chosen you, his child, to be just like him, your Daddy.

November 15

SELF-WILL: THE BASIS OF SIN

He personally carried our sins in his body on the cross so that we can be dead to sin and live for what is right. By his wounds you are healed. (1 Peter 2:24)

We must continually clarify and explain the nature and meaning of sin. Virtually all of us think of sin as bad actions. That is true enough, but where do those bad actions come from? They come from one source: self-will. Now what is that? It is the determination to have my own way at all costs. People who don't do obviously bad things can be just as ruled by self-will as those who do bad things. So, what is so bad about self-will? It is simply 180 degrees off from the way God made us to live. He made us to find our delight in allowing him to be God in our lives, doing what he says, walking in all his ways. Self-will says, "I am the most important person in my life. I will determine what is right and wrong for me. I will have my own way at whatever cost." That is why good people will go to hell. It is because they are good, and proud of it: "Who needs God to be good? I am better than most of those people in that church anyway."

Self-will is Sin. It is not a something, not a series of acts, but a whole complex of attitudes toward self and toward others as they impinge on that self. This is what the Apostle Peter means when he talks about dying to sin. He does not mean that it will become impossible for a person to commit a wrong act that they will need to repent of. What he does mean is that in a moment of a radical surrender of one's self-will and an infusion of God's grace, those attitudes of self-will can be fundamentally altered (see also Col 3:5–17). The first question is no longer "What do I want?" Now, it is "What does God want?" That changes everything.

Are we talking about a "personality transplant"? No, but there has been a fundamental alteration in the way the person looks at the world, at God, and at themselves. There has been a fundamental change in outlook, perception, and disposition—they have died to sin. Will the implications of that change have to be worked out in life for a lifetime? Oh yes. Will the evidences of the change be more immediate and obvious in some than in others? Oh yes. But none of that can alter the one great truth: God had changed the disposition of the heart from inward to outward.

November 16

WIVES, BE WHAT?

Wives, in the same way be submissive to your husbands so that, if any of
them do not believe the word, they may be won over without words by
the behavior of their wives, when they see the purity and reverence of
your lives. Your beauty should not come from outward adornment, such
as elaborate hairstyles and the wearing of gold jewelry and fine clothes.
Rather, it should be that of your inner self, the unfading beauty of a gentle
and quiet spirit, which is of great worth in God's sight. (1 Peter 3:1–4 NIV)

It's a text that has caused many a preacher to sweat and many
parishioners to sit on the edge of their seats: "Wives be submissive to
your husbands . . . ." Let me start by telling you what this verse is *not*
saying. It is *not* saying that wives are to be doormats. It is *not* saying that
our marriages should be oppressive. It is *not* giving husbands license to
abuse their wives. What it is saying is that the best way for a wife to witness
to her husband is to say through her example of submissiveness, "I love
you more than myself."

I believe there is a difference between men and women, and now
you are thinking, "Wow, what penetrating insight!" What I mean is that
our sinful tendencies are different. I think the sinful tendency of men
is to think of people (e.g., women) as objects, things to be used in order
to achieve their goals. They forget about people as people who are to be
loved. That's a man's sin. So, what is the sin of women? I think it is to want
to manipulate people (e.g., men), to want to run their lives, to "help" them
get organized, to "help" straighten them out.

I think what this passage is trying to do is to encourage women to look
upon their marriage as a tool for producing in themselves that beauty that
will last when the anti-aging lotions and potions have finally given up. It
means that as you find the grace to make his goal more important than
your goal, you will find the truest good in your own life.

November 17

HOME

And the God of all grace, who called you to his eternal glory in
Christ, after you have suffered a little while, will himself restore you
and make you strong, firm and steadfast. (1 Peter 5:10 NIV)

On my desk I have a plaque that I treasure. It show a fully-rigged sailing
ship coasting in on a calm sea with a beautiful sunset behind it. On it
is this message: "Life is not a journey into a foreign country; it is a journey
home." My wife and I were recently on an auto trip. The last day we were
on the road for about eleven hours, almost all of it in the rain, with hard,
driving rain for about four hours on an interstate highway heavy with
trucks.

When we finally arrived home, it was quite dark. I cannot quite
describe the feeling when we pulled into the garage, and then opened the
door into the house—our own house—filled with familiar things. Peace,
rest, relief, ease? Yes, and several other emotions that I cannot quite name.

The next morning during my devotional time, it struck me forcibly,
"That's what it will be like to reach heaven!" Home. Yes, the last part of the
journey may be very hard, with lots of stress, uncertainty, and difficulty.
But what a moment it will be to open that door and be home!

That's the promise, and that is our eager expectation. So if you cannot
see the road in front of you very clearly and there is a monster eighteen-
wheeler bearing down on you from behind, just plug faithfully ahead.
Home is waiting.

November 18

A STORY FOR MY GRANDCHILDREN

That which was from the beginning, which we have heard, which we
have seen with our eyes, which we looked upon and have touched with
our hands, concerning the word of life—the life was made manifest, and
we have seen it, and testify to it and proclaim to you the eternal life,
which was with the Father and was made manifest to us—that which
we have seen and heard we proclaim also to you. (1 John 1–3a ESV)

You ask me when I, the Apostle John,* first knew he was God? I can tell
you the day and the hour. It was in the Spring of that third year. We
were in Perea, across the Jordan, on our way to Jerusalem. We had begged
him not to go, but he just looked at us, and said, "You still don't understand,
do you?" and then he turned around and walked on. What could we do?
He was the Messiah after all, odd as that seemed on the surface, and we,
ragtag bunch that we were, were going to be his government officials. We
would show those Jerusalem bigwigs something—maybe.

About the third watch of the night, I heard him get up. He was doing
that a lot in those days. He told us he was praying, and I thought I would
follow him and try to find out what he was praying about. The next thing I
knew, my eyes popped open, and the sun was just about to come up over
those eastern hills. I looked up and there he was, sitting on the little knoll
just above where we had stretched out to sleep.

I got up as quietly as I could and crept up the hill until I could lay behind
a bush off to his side and see him in profile and maybe hear whatever he
was saying. But he wasn't saying anything. He was just sitting there. Then
I became aware of a little bird hopping along the ground, going from bush
to bush, until finally it was right at his feet. He looked down at it, and
a little smile crossed his lips. Then he held out his forefinger to it, and
quick as a flash, the little bird hopped up onto it. It looked at him for a
moment, and then opened its beak wider than seemed possible and began
to sing at the top of its voice. It wasn't a very melodious song; the little
thing didn't have the greatest voice, but as it sang the smile on Jesus's face
got wider. Finally, the song ended and the two just looked at each other. I
was too far away, of course, to actually see the look in the bird's eyes, but
I knew without any doubt at all that it was a look of absolute adoration,
the adoration of a creature for its Creator. Then Jesus slowly lifted his
hand with the bird still perched on his outstretched finger, and raising his
eyebrows, nodded. I knew he was saying, "Thank you, now go do what I

---

* In this devotional, I pretend to be the Apostle John telling a story.

made you for. Go and fly!" Slowly, almost reluctantly, the little bird raised its wings. Then it leapt into the air and soared away, singing as it went.

Without looking at me, Jesus said, "Good morning, John." He knew I had been there all along! I got to my knees and looked up, and there on his face was the same little smile that had greeted the bird. I fell on my face, thinking, "Dear God, this rather ordinary-looking man, who spoke in the country accents of Galilee, with whom I had talked and laughed, from whose dirty, dusty feet I had sometimes untied sandals, whom I had seen tired, frustrated, crying—was God!"

Then I felt a hand on my shoulder, and he said quietly, "Get up, my son." As I rose to my feet I saw that smile again and on either side of it outstretched arms. I threw myself into his embrace, and in that moment felt the arms of Life about me, and more than that, the arms of Love— Eternal Love. Oh yes, I knew.

November 19

FOR FELLOWSHIP

We proclaim to you what we ourselves have actually seen and
heard so that you may have fellowship with us. And our fellowship
is with the Father and with his Son, Jesus Christ. (1 John 1:3)

So we are lying if we say we have fellowship with God but go on living
in spiritual darkness; we are not practicing the truth. (1 John 1:6)

So you must remain faithful to what you have been taught from the beginning.
If you do, you will remain in fellowship with the Son and with the Father. And
in this fellowship we enjoy the eternal life he promised us. (1 John 2:24–25)

I know you have had the same experience I have had in reading the
Bible: a passage you have read a hundred times suddenly catches your
attention in a way it had not before. First John 1:3 did that for me recently.
The only reason John is telling people about his experience with Jesus
is so that they can have fellowship with the disciples, who happen to be
in fellowship with God? Is that all? Well of course that is not all, but the
problem was not in the Bible but in my shallow understanding of the word
"fellowship."

What is fellowship? Well, it is talking together with Christian friends
after church or perhaps in a little more extended way at a church supper.
As a matter of fact, while we need not dismiss those experiences, fellowship
as John and the rest of the New Testament uses it is much more than that.
The New Living Translation effectively captures that when it translates the
older version's, "abide" (e.g., 1 John 2:24–25) with "remain in fellowship."

Salvation is not finally about having our sins forgiven and going to
heaven. It is about coming to be "in" God: to live in him, to experience him
through the real presence of the Holy Spirit in our lives and, as a result, to
be bound in the same way to Christian brothers and sisters. We will go to
heaven together or not at all.

To "abide" in God, then, is to have a living relationship with him that
changes everything. John wants us to have the eternal life that Jesus's
Cross and Resurrection makes possible. Eternal life is found in no longer
living in lonely selfish isolation but in coming to be "joined at the hip" with
God. *That* is fellowship. Do you have that?

November 20

HOLINESS IS FOR OTHERS

We proclaim to you what we ourselves have actually seen and
heard so that you may have fellowship with us. And our fellowship
is with the Father and with his Son, Jesus Christ. We are writing
these things so that you man fully share our joy. (1 John 1:3–4)

Why do we seek to share the holy life of God? The subtle temptation is
to seek it for myself, but that is wrong. Holiness is not my possession
to be enjoyed by me, to be flaunted as an example of my achievement. That
might be the case if a holy life could ever be achieved by human effort, a
trap the Galatian Christians had fallen into, but that is never the case. Any
holiness that we achieve through effort is only another form of that self-
righteousness that is to God bloody rags (see Isa 64:6).

We are only able to share the holy character of God as a gift of his grace.
There is nothing there for us to boast about. So why does God give us this
wonderful gift? He gives it to us for the sake of others! John's statement
quoted above is always something of a shock. Why is he writing? Surely,
it is so that my sins can be forgiven and I can be assured of heaven—but
that is not what he says. He says that he is writing so that we can have
fellowship with the other believers, whose fellowship is with the Father
and with Jesus.

The curse of sin is alienation—from God and from one another. God's
passionate desire is that we may be delivered from that lonely isolation
and be restored to fellowship with others and himself. That happens when
you and I are graciously delivered from a life of self-reference and self-
serving. Then, you are more important to me than I am. Then, we have
begun to taste the fellowship that the Trinity have with each other and long
to have with the world. *That* is holiness.

November 21

STEP INTO THE LIGHT

This is the message we heard from Jesus and now declare to you: God is light, and there is no darkness in him at all. So we are lying if we say we have fellowship with God but go on living in spiritual darkness; we are not practicing the truth. But if we are living in the light, as God is in the light, then we have fellowship with each other, and the blood of Jesus, his Son, cleanses us from all sin. If we claim we have no sin, we are only fooling ourselves and not living in the truth. (1 John 1:5–8)

Have you had the experience as I have had when reading the testimony of a really saintly person and finding them lamenting the depth of their sin? When you see that, if you are like me, you ask, "How can this be? This person is not living in sin. They are not practicing sinful behavior. What's going on?" They are living in the Light. We never see the depth of our sinfulness, we never see how twisted and corrupt we have been—and could be again—until we come into the Light. Physically speaking, if I can look at myself in a mirror with a dim light, the dimmer the better, I look pretty good. Turn the light up bright and, oh dear, a blotch here, a flaw there, and a shiny bald head on top of it all.

That's what the Apostle John is talking about. As Christians, too many of us are living far from the Light, and we feel pretty good about ourselves. But come into the Light, the Light that shines out of the Word, and we will see how desperate our need is and how tragically we have hurt him and misrepresented him to the world. Before we come into the Light, we can easily think we are better than 90 percent of the people in the world. And maybe by the world's standards that is nearly true. That's because we aren't in the Light.

The world's light is nothing but a guttering candle. Get into the Light, see what you are apart from his continual grace. Then let that Light flood into you. In your own eyes you will see how truly miserable you are in yourself, but in the world's eyes you will be what you are—a miracle of grace.

BOMBARDED BY THE WORLD

Do not love the world or the things in the world. If anyone loves the world, the love of the Father is not in him. For all that is in the world—the desires of the flesh and the desires of the eyes and pride of life—is not from the Father but is from the world. And the world is passing away along with its desires, but whoever does the will of God abides forever. (1 John 2:15–17 ESV)

We are bombarded by the world. The thing that television and the Internet has done more than anything else is, it has made it almost impossible for us to isolate ourselves from the world's mentality. How does it think? "This is all there is, baby! You only go around once, so get all you can while you can." What is it we should get? Pleasure, possessions, comfort, security, and power.

As with the singer Peggy Lee, when we have gotten them all, we cry out, "Is that all there is?" Because this world is an awful joke. In itself, it is meaningless. We can't think about meaning when there is none. What is the good of all that grasping when Death stands there grinning, about to strip us of everything? Some, in their craze for drugs or alcohol, understand quite well: just drown yourself in forgetfulness.

To all of us John says, "For God's sake, we have lived that way long enough, that all there is to live for is pleasure and possessions and power." All that is passing away! Do we want security? God has given us the greatest security of all, the knowledge that this world is not the end but only the beginning. He has given us an eternal Word, in which we meet the eternal God, who speaks the eternal Truth. If we surrender our foolish desires to his blessed purposes, we too will live forever and ever.

We live in fallen, broken, unjust world, but we need not be broken by it. We must armor ourselves in every way we can from thinking like the world thinks. We have to spend time in his book, hanging out with his people, doing his work, and living his life. Don't think like the world thinks! It's deadly.

November 23

To Do My Master's Will

Do not love the world or anything in the world. If anyone loves the world, love for the Father is not in them. For everything in the world—the lust of the flesh, the lust of the eyes, and the pride of life—comes not from the Father but from the world. The world and its desires pass away, but whoever does the will of God lives forever. (1 John 2:15–17 NIV)

There is a line in a hymn that says: "Oh may it all my powers engage to do my Master's will."* I heard an account in a funeral service recently that illustrated this thought to me in a powerful way. In the deceased man's papers was this report.

This man had lived alone with his beloved dog, a retriever. Better than anything else in the world, the dog loved to go with his master to a nearby lake, there to retrieve sticks that his master would throw out into the water. He would come back, dripping wet, holding the stick in his mouth with that particular doggy grin on his face, and drop the stick at his master's feet, dancing with anticipation to do it all again.

One day, for whatever reason, the dog could not find the stick. Perhaps a wayward current had gotten it, or maybe it was waterlogged and sank before he could get to it. At any rate, he could not find it. He swam in circles, looking and looking. His master called him to come back in, but that dog had been sent to do a job, and he was going to do it. He kept swimming in larger and larger circles, and it began to become clear that he was exhausting himself. The owner was becoming anxious that he was going to lose his dog. Finally, he hit on the idea of throwing another stick, trying to get it as near to the failing dog as possible. He succeeded, and the dog got it and came to shore. Dropping the stick at his master's feet, though panting, he signaled that he was ready to go again. He delighted to do his master's will. As I heard that story, I wondered if I have anything like that same determination, a determination to do my Master's will, at all costs—all costs. Oh, may it be.

---

* "A Charge to Keep I Have" by Charles Wesley.

November 24

CHRISTIANS, DO NOT SIN: PART ONE

Dear friends, we are already God's children, but he has not yet shown us what we will be like when Christ appears. But we do know that we will be like him, for we will see him as he really is. And all who have this eager expectation will keep themselves pure, just as he is pure. Everyone who sins is breaking God's law, for all sin is contrary to the law of God. And you know that Jesus came to take away our sins, and there is no sin in him. Anyone who continues to live in him will not sin. But anyone who keeps on sinning does not know him or understand who he is. (1 John 3:2–6)

What is the key to victory over sin in our lives? Make no mistake, we can have—indeed, must have—that victory. John is unmistakably clear on that subject in his first letter. There are three conditions for that victory. The first one is: don't make victory over sin your focus. That is to work on a negation. Can you empty a glass of its air by turning it upside down and shaking it? Not a chance. What can you do? Fill it with water! It is the same here. Focus on filling your life with Jesus! That's what John means when he says that when we know that one day we will be absolutely Christlike, it motivates us to do everything we can now to enjoy as much of that reality as we can. Make your relation to Jesus the focus of your life. Make him number one, front and center. That's what John is talking about when he says "anyone who continues to live in him."

Is your life centered in Christ? Are you focused on pleasing him? Are you pursuing him and his will with everything you have? Then you know what Scottish pastor Thomas Chalmers called "the expulsive power of a new affection." There is simply no room for sin in a life filled to the brim with love for Jesus. Does Jesus have first place? Or are you trying to have a little of him and a little of the world at the same time? Perhaps you say, "Well, I think he is first, but I don't really know." Take an inventory of your life: where is your time spent, where are your interests, what do you have to have and can't live without? Have you ever consciously given him your whole life? If there is any question at all, do it now, and victory will follow.

November 25

Christians, Do Not Sin: Part Two

But when people keep on sinning, it shows that they belong to the devil, who has been sinning since the beginning. But the Son of God came to destroy the works of the devil. Those who have been born into God's family do not make a practice of sinning, because God's life is in them. So they can't keep on sinning, because they are children of God. So now we can tell who are children of God and who are children of the devil. Anyone who does not live righteously and does not love other believers does not belong to God. This is the message you have heard from the beginning: We should love one another. (1 John 3:8–11)

John, in his argument against "sinning religion," ties together several thoughts. The first, as here, is that we are, through conversion, born of God and therefore can—and will want to—manifest the qualities of our Father, God, and our brother, Jesus. That is, we do not so much focus on not sinning as we do on sharing our Savior's life and character.

The second thought is also seen in the passage above: we don't sin because we are motivated by love. On the surface, it seems a little odd that John concludes his paragraph on not being a child of the devil with the command to love one another. In fact, it is not odd at all. Again, John is emphasizing the positive. Trying not to sin is a bit like trying not to think about pink elephants; the harder we try, the more focused we get on the thing. "No," John says, "focus on others, especially Christian brothers and sisters, and what is best for them." As we focus on others and what is best for them, the focus necessarily shifts away from us, and from our performance. At bottom, sin is self-centeredness, so freedom from sin is to become refocused on our Savior and then on our brothers and sisters. To be free from sin is to be delivered from ourselves—from our desires, our stuff, our image—and set free to give ourselves away for others.

So the question for us is not, "Was what I just did, or thought, or said, sinful?" Rather, it should be, "What can I do to help them, serve them, encourage them, challenge them, for the love of Jesus?" That is what "born into the family of God" means.

When Morning Gilds the Skies

November 26

CHRISTIANS, DO NOT SIN: PART THREE

You know that he appeared in order to take away sins, and in
him there is no sin. No one who abides in him keeps on sinning;
no one who keeps on sinning has either seen him or known
him. Little children, let no one deceive you. Whoever practices
righteousness is righteous, as he is righteous. (1 John 3:5–7 ESV)

Whoever keeps his commandments abides in God, and
God in him. And by this we know that he abides in us, by
the Spirit whom he has given us. (1 John 3:24 ESV)

The third reason that John gives for why Christians cannot make a
place for sin in their lives is this: it is a violation of what Jesus came to
earth to do. Here John is perfectly "in synch" with the Apostle Paul. Both
of them agree on this point, and it is one that I don't think most Christians
think of when they explore the reason for Jesus's coming. I think we would
say that he came to forgive sin, or perhaps that he came to give us eternal
life. Neither of those answers is wrong, and both Paul and John use them
in other places, but here and in Romans 6:1–10, the reason they give is
that Jesus came to destroy sin. That is pretty strong language, isn't it? He
did not only come to remove sin's effects—the guilt, the condemnation—
but he came to "do away with sin" and the second death it results in. He
came to get rid of it altogether! Sin died in him! Really? Yes, really. If we
only think the Cross procured our forgiveness, we think far too little of it.
The Cross destroys sin. That is power.

Think of it this way. You have cancer and the surgeon removes it, but
then he tells you that it has gone into the lymph system and that there is
nothing he can do about that. Good news? Hardly! But that is what we are
saying when we limit the power of the Cross to forgiveness.

How is this thing possible? What does the Cross do for us that makes
a life of victory over sin possible? What the Cross does is to clean out our
"temple" so that the promised Holy Spirit can come to live in us, or "abide"
in us, to use John's language. If you will let the Holy Spirit, who is already
in you through Christ, take control of your life, you will find not only a new
resistance to sinful desires but also a positive hatred for what nailed your
Savior to the Cross. You can live a life where every motive of your heart is
to please him. Let the Holy Spirit do his work and destroy sin in your life.
The world needs you.

November 27

Don't Miss the Target

Everyone who sins is breaking God's law, for all sin
is contrary to the law of God. (1 John 3:4)

Unlike their neighbors, the Israelites knew that fellowship with God
depended on how well they followed his instructions. Thus, they had
nearly a dozen terms to express the various aspects of failure to do that.
Three occur most frequently: sin, iniquity, and transgression. I want to
talk about each of these in three successive devotions.

The word translated "sin" (Hebrew, *ḥaṭa'*) is the most frequent and
the most general. The original idea of the word was "to miss a target." The
corresponding Greek term (*hamartia*) has the same origin. "Sin" can refer
to intentional thoughts, motives, and actions as well as unintentional ones.
It refers to any deviation from God's wishes, expectations, and norms.

It is one of the great errors of word study to assume that every use of a
word carries with it the original idea, and I do not want to suggest that when
I think with you about "sin." However, that idea still offers a useful visual
aid when we try to understand the nature of sin. So what is it to sin? It is
to miss God's target for your life, whether intentionally or unintentionally.
For instance, one of God's targets is for me to be exclusively faithful to my
wife, and adultery, whether it is the result of seduction or intention, is to
miss that target. The result is that the arrow of my life goes off somewhere
into the weeds, losing its purpose, direction, and ultimately, even its value.

Here's the point: Yahweh has a very specific pattern for human life.
Accept that pattern, aim at it, train your spiritual muscles, practice hitting
it, and keep practicing hitting it, and you will have fellowship with God.
Choose some other target, or just let your muscles get flabby so that even
if you might like to hit God's target, you can't, and God is not going to be
there. Don't miss the target!

November 28
JUST GET OVER IT?

Therefore, thus says the Holy One of Israel, "Because you despise this word and trust in oppression and perverseness and rely on them, therefore this iniquity shall be to you like a breach in a high wall, bulging out and about to collapse, whose breaking comes suddenly, in an instant." (Isaiah 30:12–13 ESV)

The second of the three most frequently used words in the Old Testament to describe human deviation from Yahweh's expectations for us is "iniquity" (Hebrew *'awon*). It is the most difficult to define precisely. Perhaps that is one of the reasons the English equivalent has almost completely disappeared from contemporary usage.

English dictionaries define "iniquity" as "a grossly immoral act." According to the Oxford English Dictionary, it first appeared in English in 1275 AD in a psalter, where it was simply a transliteration of the Latin *iniquitas*, which can be translated as "injustice." When we look at how the word is used in the Old Testament, it seems to define the objective results of sin. That is, when we sin, something comes into existence that cannot be simply ignored. The effects have to be dealt with. Thus, it can be defined in some cases as "guilt." Have you ever had someone say to you when they have abused you in some way, "Oh, I didn't mean anything by that. I'm sorry; just get over it." It's not that simple, is it?

In the passage above, oppression and perverseness have brought a situation into existence that cannot be just overlooked. It must be treated in some way. It is as though water has seeped into a wall, dissolving the mortar, with the result that the stones are beginning to bulge outward. Unless something is done to repair that situation very quickly, the wall is going to fall. So it is with sin in all its manifestations. It is not merely "on paper." It alters relationships; it sets in motion a chain of events that must be addressed; it brings into being a new reality.

This is where the death of Christ comes into the picture. He is the "repairer of the breaches" (Amos 9:11). He comes to heal the wounds, to take into himself the objective results of what we have done. Do not believe that when we deviate from God's plans and goals for us, that is just an internal, subjective matter. It is not. It is a tear in the fabric of existence, a tear that requires blood to mend it.

November 29
DON'T FENCE ME IN

Transgression speaks to the wicked deep in his heart; there
is no fear of God before his eyes. (Psalm 36:1 ESV)

Have mercy on me, O God, according to your steadfast love; according
to your abundant mercy blot out my transgressions. (Psalm 51:1 ESV)

The third of the three most common Hebrew words for an offense
against God is "transgression." If sin is sometimes unintentional,
transgression is always intentional. It is the expression of that attitude
in us that, in the words of the old Western song, says, "I can't stand
fences!" It is the outworking of that spirit that Paul bemoans in
Romans 7:9–11 (paraphrased): "I didn't want to do wrong until the law
forbade it, then I just had to do it!"

There is something in the human heart that is determined to deny any
limits on its freedom. So, when we are informed of a limit, there is nothing
for it but to go over it. Our loving, heavenly Father says, "Here is the way
I designed you to live," and something is us, something stemming right
back to Genesis 3, says, "*I* will determine what is right and wrong for me."
This is what the songwriter calls "the bent to sinning." Others have called
it "original sin." Whatever you call it, it issues in transgression.

This is where the Cross comes to its greatest glory. Yes, the blood of
Christ can cleanse us from all "sin"–all those times when we have, for
whatever reason, missed God's target for our living. Yes, the blood of
Christ can wash away our "iniquity," the reality of what we have done that
has stained the garment of life right down into the warp and woof of the
fabric. But what about our innate rebelliousness, our determination to
have our own way, our refusal to accept God-created limits, something
that seems "engraved with a diamond point on the tablet of [the] heart"
(Jer 17:1)? Can the cross do anything about *that*? Oh, yes, it can! The blood
of Jesus can "blot out our transgressions" and with it, God can create in us
a clean heart. Believe him! He can do that in your life.

November 30

ALL HIS

We know how much God loves us, and we have put our trust in his love. God is love, and all who live in love live in God, and God lives in them. And as we live in God, our love grow more perfect. . . . Such love has no fear because perfect love expels all fear. . . ." (1 John 4:16–17a, 18a)

C. S. Lewis, in a sermon entitled "A Slip of the Tongue," speaks powerfully of the necessity of our yielding every area of our lives to God. If we do not, he says, it is like going to the seaside, and instead of diving in and giving ourselves completely to the sea, we simply wade a bit. This will not do, he says, because God, the passionate Lover, will not be content with only a part of us.

I fully agree with that sentiment. How could I not as it is so thoroughly biblical? To do otherwise is to miss the full meaning and benefit of our salvation. Why do we hang back? It is for fear—that such a surrender to God would take us to places we do not want to go, would require of us things we do not want to do, would ask of us things we do not want to give. John says, total love does away with fear. God really does love us totally: he is *for* us and *always* wants the best for us. If we will let go of all our other loves and will love him completely, we will no longer be afraid of his will. Once we know for certain what it is, that is the very thing we too want.

But we need to go one step further than Lewis takes us. He says that this surrender to love must be renewed every day—right—but then he says the reason we must do that is because the invader cannot be driven out of our territory until death. Using the image of occupied France, he calls upon us to be part of the Resistance, and not of Vichy. Oh, the Good News of the Bible is better than that! We can be like England, where the Enemy controls no part of us! Is he a threat to be guarded against every moment? Yes. Are there forces within us that are responsive to his temptations? Yes. Will his attacks lose none of their fierceness until death? Yes. But he does not live here! He owns no part of us! This is Jesus-territory! Dear friends, that is our birthright. We can belong wholly to the Lord of Life. Why settle for anything less than that?

December 1
THE HIGH GROUND

There is no fear in love. But perfect love drives out fear,
because fear has to do with punishment. The one who
fears is not made perfect in love. (1 John 4:18 NIV)

Perfect love is the high ground of Christian life and experience. What do I mean by that? When armies are in conflict, each army tries to get to the highest ground—the position of strength. Perfect love is the high ground in Christian theology. We can say that for two reasons. The first is biblical. None can doubt that love like God's is the biblical goal. It is here in 1 John; it is in Matthew 5:48; it is in Ephesians 5:1–2; and it is the clear implication of many other passages. We may try to explain it away, to make it meaningless with a hundred qualifications, but there it is.

The second reason is experience. None can dispute that this is this world's need. Many years ago, a secular song writer said it very well, "What the world needs now, is love, sweet love." The child of the world knows that as well as the child of the Word. None can deny that perfect love is the need and the goal. Over and over again we are called to love. So, the high ground—the ground that is most easily defended and that the enemy must somehow drive us away from—is the idea that in some real sense perfect love is a real experience that may be achieved.

The problem is in two wrong conceptions. In the first case we see love like God's as an impossible demand, a horrible, heavy requirement that we are supposed to achieve but which we know we never can. The second problem is that we interpret "perfect" in a different way than the Bible means. God does not ask for a flawless love. Rather, he asks for a love of the same quality as his: one that does not need another's love to start it or another's return of love to keep it going. It is a love that is complete in itself. Today, stop struggling to love in some flawless way (like God does). Instead, rely on his promise to love through you and let his love, not yours, set you free.

December 2

THIS IS HE WHO CAME

This is he who came by water and blood—Jesus Christ, not by water
only but by the water and the blood. And the Spirit is the one who
testifies, because the Spirit is the truth. (1 John 5:6 ESV)

The boy's father was a small-town lawyer. Normally he never touched
alcohol, but on the evening of December 31, he would take a bottle of
whiskey and a glass, go into his home study, and not reappear until late on
the morning of January 1, showing the effects of the night. When the boy
got old enough to sense what was happening, he asked his mother about
it. She said, "He just has to stop himself from adding up the failures of the
old year and the uncertainties of the new one. Otherwise, they would just
be too much for him."

Maybe some of us find ourselves in a place like that: the failures of the
past and the uncertainties of the future weigh pretty heavily. I would like
to offer another antidote than whiskey. It is suggested by the phrase in the
verse above: the water and the blood. Have there been failures in the year
past, even cause for bitter regret? Very probably. Put them under the blood;
that is why Jesus came to be born in a stable: to shed his life-blood for our
sins. His gracious blood "can cleanse each spot" as the songwriter says.
Lay out your ugly spots one by one if you need to, and then consciously let
his blood wash over each one. They are gone!

What about the year ahead, with all of its unknowns, some rather
frightening? It is the water—the water of the outpoured Spirit—that gives
us the courage to go forward confidently. If you know Christ, then his
Spirit is in you. This assurance gives us the willingness to dare, knowing
that what we begin, living in his will, he can and will complete. We do not
know the future, but he who is in us does. He can take all our flawed efforts
and turn them to good. The water and the blood are ours!

December 3

LIES ABOUT SIN

This is the message we heard from Jesus and now declare to you:
God is light, and there is no darkness in him at all. So we are lying
if we say we have fellowship with God but go on living in spiritual
darkness; we are not practicing the truth. (1 John 1:5–6)

There are lies that everyone, and especially every Christian, should
know:

1. Lie # 1: Because you have been a good person from the time you
   were born, you do not need forgiveness or for Christ to come into
   your life. (see 1 John 1:10)
2. Lie # 2: You can be in a relationship with God who is light and go
   on sinning, which is darkness. (see 1 John 1:6)
3. Lie # 3: You can come to the place where you cannot sin. (see
   1 John 1:8).

The point John is trying to make is this: sin is a reality that separates
us from God; it is moral darkness. Furthermore, it is a moral darkness
that infects every person who has ever lived. It is not a matter of relative
goodness. It is a matter of each of us setting ourselves up as God. If it were
a matter of goodness, they we would have to be as good as God. The only
person who has ever done that, truly lived in the light, is Jesus. Thus, the
only source of light in this dark world is Christ, the Second Person of the
Trinity. You need him, and I need him if we are to exist in God's presence.
That means that if we have come into the light through Christ, we simply
cannot make a place in our lives where darkness still reigns.

Clearly, John is trying to convince us, his readers, that a Christian
cannot sin (see 1 John 3:9). We cannot bring the light into our lives and
then expect a little darkness to coexist with it. Can you imagine a lighted
room where there is blob of darkness floating around?!

But "cannot" is not talking about impossibility. It is talking about
permission or expectation. Christian, you cannot expect to sin any more
than I can expect to commit adultery against my wife. I cannot! Ah, but we
never come to the place where sin is not a possibility. If we allow ourselves
to drift away from the light, darkness is inevitable. We, like the moon, do
not produce the light; we reflect it. So, stay in the light! Does a Christian
have to sin? Absolutely not. Can they sin? Oh, yes, but the good news is
that if they confess and repent the Light will come back into their lives, and
they can shine without a speck of darkness.

December 4
REALISTIC ABOUT SIN

We know that those who are born of God do not sin, but
the one who was born of God protects them, and the evil
one does not touch them. (1 John 5:18 NRSV)

We need to be realistic about sin. To be a human is to have the sin condition. None of us can say we are without sin. Likewise, none of us can say we have never sinned. If we are real about those facts, let's be real about another one: Christians do not sin! Several times John makes that point in 1 John. Most modern translations will say something like "Christians do not continue to sin." This is fair; it reflects the Greek verb form, which speaks of continuing action. This reflects the truth that John is not saying it is *impossible* for a Christian to sin. Rather, he is saying that a Christian has gotten out of the sin business, that a Christian makes no room for sin in his/her life. A Christian says, "Father, I delight to do what pleases you; I'm not asking how far I can live from you and still make it into heaven."

The defeat of sin cost Jesus his life. Will I make a place for it in *my* life? Never! Will I supinely say, "Well, I am just human, so I can't help re-crucifying Jesus every day?" How could I? No, I want to know what pleases him, what glorifies him, what shows how holy he is. Now, to be sure, being human, sin is always a *possibility* for us. John knows that, so he tells us if we should sin, we have an advocate in Christ Jesus. Thank God! But that is an emergency position, not permission to live filthy lives. Likewise, when Solomon says that there is no one who does not sin (see 1 Kgs 8:46), he is not saying that we all sin all the time. He is simply stating the fact, as John does, that *everybody* needs forgiveness.

A Christian is marked by a certain attitude toward the commands of God and that attitude is, "God, there will be no place for sin in my life. I expect not to sin." This is not our work but the work of the Holy Spirit whom Jesus's death and resurrection have made available to us. We do not live above sin by trying really hard but by surrendering our lives to him and allowing his wind to fill the sails of our tiny craft. Christians do not have to sin. That is not an onerous demand but a glorious promise! Are you living there?

December 5

THEY REFUSED TO REPENT: PART ONE

But the people who did not die in these plagues still refused to repent of their evil deeds and turn to God. They continued to worship demons and idols made of gold, silver, bronze, stone, and wood—idols that can neither see nor hear nor walk! And they did not repent of their murders or their witchcraft or their sexual immorality or their thefts. (Revelation 9:20–21)

The cataclysms described in such bizarre figures in Revelation 9 seem more plausible than ever before: a great meteorite striking the earth; in the chaos after that, nations fighting each other with armored helicopter gunships; and finally, someone in the region of Iraq and Iran setting off an atomic war. Well, whether those kinds of things are what the chapter is talking about or not—and if you meet anybody who says they know what Revelation is predicting, keep a tight hold on your billfold!—the final two verses are crystal clear: there is nothing that can make a person repent. Nothing? Yes, nothing.

We sometimes imagine that after death, people confronted with heaven or hell will of course repent, but that a furious God will say, "No, you had your chance and you missed it. Now go to hell!" I think that is a very wrong picture, and these verses confirm such a position. Nothing can *make* us repent. Why not?

First, you cannot repent without a Spirit-given conviction that you are wrong and need to change. Such a conviction is a gift, and it is not available to us on our demand. When it comes to you, don't put it off! Do it then; it may not come your way again.

Second, the price of repentance is too high. You have to give up control of your life and give that control over to God, whom your "friend" Satan assures you is out to ruin your life and make you just a nameless gear in his cosmic machine. That price is simply too high for most folks. If heaven requires that I must give up my right to do what I want with my life, I don't want heaven. As John Milton has Satan say, "Better to rule in hell, than serve in heaven." This is why there are so few death-bed conversions. So, if you feel a tug in your heart to turn away from something you are doing, from your rights, your way, your self, turn! Turn now! Or there may come a day when you will feel no such inclination at all.

December 6

THEY REFUSED TO REPENT: PART TWO

The rest of mankind who were not killed by these plagues still did not repent of the work of their hands; they did not stop worshiping demons, and idols of gold, silver, bronze, stone and wood—idols that cannot see or hear or walk. Nor did they repent of their murders, their magic arts, their sexual immorality or their thefts. (Revelation 9:20–21 NIV)

We said in Part One that there is nothing that can make a person repent. Why not? Because the price is too high. The text says that they will not "repent of the works of their hands" and then begins to speak of the practice of idolatry. Idolatry is an attempt to manipulate this world to supply my needs. It puts my needs, and my capacity to meet my needs through "my hands," in the forefront of life. When that happens, people who get in my way have to be removed, "murdered," in one way or another. When that happens, indulging my desires in any way I can is "natural." When that happens, I have a "right" to any stuff I really want. If I were to repent, to turn around from that way of life, what would I have left? The Enemy adroitly whispers, "Nothing!" Of course, that's a lie, but people who have lived this way all their lives are more than ready to believe it.

The truth is that lifelong choices finally become so ingrained within us that nothing can make us change. So, the word for you and me is, repent now! Don't imagine that you can take care of yourself. Don't make your needs primary. Surrender your life to your Creator, who loves you, who knows your needs better than you do, and who can meet them better than you can. Don't make your life the sum total of "the works of your hands." Make your life "the work of *his* hands." Then, if there is anything to repent of in the last days, you won't have any trouble doing it.

December 7

STRETCH OUT YOUR HAND

Then Jesus went over to their synagogue where he noticed a man
with a deformed hand. . . . Then he said to the man, "Stretch
out your hand." So the man stretched out his hand, and it was
restored, just like the other one. (Matthew 12:9–10a, 13)

Have you noticed that there are several cases like the one above, where
Jesus asks a person to do something that is impossible before they
are healed? Here Jesus asks the man to move a hand that is evidently
paralyzed. In John 5, he tells the man who has been paralyzed for 38 years
to get up! In Mark 10, he tells a blind man to come to him through a great
crowd. And in Luke 17, he tells the ten lepers to go and show themselves
to the priest—a necessary step for restoration to the community—while
they are still lepers. In short, in these cases, Jesus calls the person to make
some move in anticipation of what he is going to do for them, and in the
first three cases, it was something that the person was literally incapable
of doing.

What is the lesson here? In asking this question, I am not trying to
set up some iron-clad pattern that God always has to follow. Whenever
we make a box for God, the only result we can be sure will follow is a
broken box. God is the Creator; he will not be put into boxes. But there is
a principle here that seems often to apply to life with God. That principle
is that faith sometimes has to be put into practice *before* we have any hard
evidence that what we are believing for will happen. I think of the woman
whose husband had left her who heard God say to her that he would come
back to her and that she would bear his child. She went out and bought
some baby furniture, and indeed, it happened as God had said it would.

Note that this must never be a way of twisting God's arm for what
we want. Rather, if God directs us to believe for something or undertake
something that seems a frank impossibility, then it may well be necessary
for us to take a first step into the unknown so that he can then come
alongside and supply the resources within and without to carry the thing
through to the end. That step will be hard, if not impossible, humanly
speaking, but if that is what God directs and we do it, we will find his
promise fulfilled as we are on the way.

LAW AND GOSPEL

I tell you the truth, until heaven and earth disappear, not even the smallest detail of God's law will disappear until its purpose is achieved. So if you ignore the least commandment and teach others to do the same, you will be called the least in the Kingdom of Heaven. But anyone who obeys God's laws and teaches them will be called great in the Kingdom of Heaven. (Matthew 5:18–19)

In Matthew 5:18 Jesus says that not the smallest letter nor the tiniest dot will disappear from the *Torah* (law) until everything it was intended to do is accomplished. We might think that the Cross would be that accomplishment, but from the way Jesus follows up his comment, that doesn't seem to be the case. Rather, he seems to be saying the purpose of the *Torah* will be fulfilled when its instructions have become internalized.

In the book of Galatians the Apostle Paul seems to take a different view. There, he seems to be saying in no uncertain terms that the only purpose of the Law (*torah*) was to restrain our baser passions until the Spirit could be poured out upon us. When that happened as a result of the Cross, we would be free of all the requirements of the Law (*torah*). See Galatians 3:23–39.

Is Paul really saying that it no longer matters how we live now that we have the Spirit? He is not! He in fact is saying the same thing Jesus said: before the Cross made the Spirit available, we only did what God wanted on the basis of "must." Now, in the Kingdom of the Spirit, we do what God wants for love. What is not clear is the distinction Paul is assuming between the externals of the law (e.g., days, times; see Gal 4:10), and the character renovation (e.g., fruit; see Gal 5:22–6:10) that the law (*torah*) is aiming for.

So the issue is not law (*torah*) versus gospel (no *torah*) but between an external system of godliness focused on external actions, such as circumcision, observance of holy days, etc., and enforced by coercion and an internal system focused on attitudes towards others and motivated by love for the Savior. In truth, the purpose of the gospel is to make possible the fulfillment of God's instructions for life (the *Torah*).

December 9

Christ Is the Reality: Part One

He canceled the record of the charges against us and took it away by
nailing it to the cross. In this way, he disarmed the spiritual rulers and
authorities. He shamed them publicly by his victory over them on the
cross. So don't let anyone condemn you for what you eat or drink,
or for not celebrating certain holy days or new moon ceremonies
or Sabbaths. For these rules are only shadows of the reality yet to
come. And Christ himself is that reality. (Colossians 2:14–17)

In the nineteen verses between Colossians 2:8 and Colossians 3:4,
references to Jesus appear sixteen times, eleven by title (Christ) and five
more times in the pronoun ("with him," "in him"). Sixteen references in
nineteen verses. What is going on?

From the surrounding content and from what we know through the
book of Acts, it appears that the early Church, among all the problems
it faced, had two that were perennially troublesome: Gnosticism and
Judaizing. They were two opposing views of what it meant to be a Christian,
both wrong, and Paul is confronting them head on. In somewhat altered
form, both views are still with us, and both are still wrong.

The Gnostics (see Col 2:8–15) said that it was what you knew that
made you a Christian. According to them, Christ, one of several divine
mediators, had come to make special secret knowledge available to "the
elect," the chosen. While we today might not think of the knowledge being
so secret, there is still with us the common idea that Jesus was one of many
great teachers whose divinely-inspired mission was to teach really smart
people how life and society should operate.

In contrast, the Judaizers (see Col 2:16–23) said that it was not
what you knew but what you did that made you a Christian. To be really
Christian, you had to accept Christ as your sacrifice, but you also had to
fulfill all the Jewish requirements, including circumcision and observance
of all the Jewish holy days. Again, we may not have those particular "hang-
ups," but there is still the belief among many of us that we are Christian
because we do certain things but not certain other things.

In this passage, Paul says both of those ideas are wrong. They make
us captive to systems and practices and cannot deliver us from the deepest
bondage of all, the bondage to desire (see Col 2:23).

December 10

CHRIST IS THE REALITY: PART TWO

For in Christ lives all the fullness of God in a human body. So you also are complete through your union with Christ, who is the head over every ruler and authority. When you came to Christ, you were "circumcised," but not by a physical procedure. Christ performed a spiritual circumcision— the cutting away of your sinful nature. (Colossians 2:9–11)

P aul says that it is neither what you know nor what you do that makes you a Christian but who you are in Christ. Of course, he is making his point in the strongest of contrasts. Correct Christian thinking (i.e., doctrine) is very important. Likewise, a Christianity that does not result in transformed behavior is not Christianity at all. Paul makes those points clearly elsewhere in his writings. But he is trying to drive home his chief point here: unless you have a living relationship with Christ, unless his life is being reproduced in you, unless his Spirit is putting to death your "sinful nature [i.e., flesh]," what you know and what you do are of no consequence.

There it is. If your Christianity is merely an intellectual or an ethical system, it is not what Christ came to do. It is not faith. Christian faith is an intellectual/ethical system that is shaped and empowered by a "new birth." That is, something has happened within you as a result of faith in Jesus that has transformed your way of thinking and that has revolutionized your way of acting. This faith will hold you in the midst of the worst shocks of life in ways that a brilliant grasp of doctrine or a highly disciplined religious life never can (see Col 2:23). You have died to yourself and your ability to make sense of your life and have come alive to Christ in all his glory.

Is the living Christ alive in you today? Is he the reality of your faith?

December 11

SUBMISSION

But my people did not listen to my voice; Israel would
not submit to me. (Psalm 81:11 ESV)

For the mind that is set on the flesh is hostile to God, for it does
not submit to God's law; indeed, it cannot. (Romans 8:7 ESV)

Obey your leaders and submit to them, for they are keeping
watch over your souls, as those who will have to give an account.
Let them do this with joy and not with groaning, for that
would be of no advantage to you. (Hebrews 13:17 ESV)

In his classic devotional book, *The Imitation of Christ,* Thomas à Kempis
makes the striking observation that our flesh will not submit to us if
we will not submit to those in authority over us. This is reminiscent of
the comment of C. S. Lewis, who suggests that before the Fall, nature was
submissive to Adam and Eve. That first pair were able to decide when they
would sleep and when they would not, when they would eat and when they
would not, etc. But this was only true because they submitted to the Lord
of nature. In the Fall, they imagined that they could still rule nature if they
refused their submission to God, but it was not so and has never been so
since.

If our bodies, our flesh, still dictates to us when we eat and sleep, our
"flesh," our wills, can be brought into submission to our true selves, our
souls, if we will learn to bring ourselves into submission. How hateful
submission is to us! I find it very interesting how carefully we have to
tread over those passages in Paul where he commends the submission
of wives to husbands. I understand that in our fallen state to submit to
another suggests to us that the other must be of greater value than the one
submitting, but that is not the case in the biblical world. We are all of equal
value. The issue is the fallen will. Somehow that stubborn refusal to bow
must be broken, and every opportunity to bring the will into line ought
to be taken, whether in the home or the office or the school. To practice
joyful submission to those who in the hierarchies of life are "over" us is to
experience a mastery over ourselves that is the key to the Christlike—the
holy—life.

December 12

TESTING

These trials will show that your faith is genuine. It is being tested as fire tests and purifies gold—though your faith is far more precious than mere gold. So when your faith remains strong through many trials, it will bring you much praise and glory and honor on the day when Jesus Christ is revealed to the whole world. (1 Peter 1:7)

Peter says, "When our faith is tested, that is the moment of great joy." That's not usually the way we see it, though, is it? We don't want the testing that comes in our life. It's painful. But there is no pure metal without refining, and our faith, likewise, must be refined. How badly do you want your faith to shine purely when Jesus is revealed? Bad enough for it to be tested?

Faith that is not tested is no faith at all. If you believe because everything is going well in your life, what does that prove? It is when you believe in spite of the difficulties, in spite of the troubles, that you know you have faith. In fact, it is because of the difficulties and because of the troubles that you can be confident that you are really in the faith. Trouble doesn't prove God hates you—trouble proves you're on the right side.

In too many cases we preachers mislead people. We tell them to accept Christ so all their problems can be solved, but the opposite may well be the case. When you're not a Christian, the devil doesn't care much what you do. As long as you keep your helmet below the top of the trench, nobody's going to shoot at you. But if you stick your head up and say, "I'm for the Lord," you ought not to be surprised if some hand grenades come flying in your direction. Testing!

Live in the knowledge that the testing that you are presently enduring is the proof of the reality of your faith and of your relationship to him—an incorruptible inheritance. In fact, rejoice in the opportunity this test gives you to drive the stake of your faith down deeper and to raise its flag that much higher.

December 13

A SABBATH REST

So there is a special [Sabbath] rest still waiting for the people of God. For all who have entered into God's rest have rested from their labors, just as God did after creating the world. So let us do our best to enter that rest. But if we disobey God, as the people of Israel did, we will fall. (Hebrews 4:9–11)

What kind of rest is the writer to the Hebrews talking about in verses 3:7–4:13? I suggest that he is talking about a spiritual condition that is the result of believing Jesus's promises. He begins by arguing that because Jesus is a better messenger and High Priest than Moses ever was (see Heb 3:1–6, resumed in 4:14ff), there is all the more reason that we should not react to Jesus as the first generation of Hebrews to leave Egypt reacted to Moses. They refused to believe that God could actually give them rest in Canaan. So, in contrast, we should have confidence that Jesus can give us rest. What rest? That is the question.

One possibility is to continue the analogy: Canaan is analogous to life after death. If we continue our faith in Jesus through death, we will enter into eternal rest. That is certainly possible. The most serious objection to that position is the reference to "today" in the quotation of Psalm 95 (see Heb 3:15, 4:7). Apparently, we do not need to wait for death but can experience that rest now. This suggests that he is talking about a spiritual condition that can be experienced in the present. That impression is strengthened when we read that the entry into Canaan did not exhaust the meaning of the promise (see Heb 4:8) but that God continues it into the present.

So what rest are we talking about? I think the passage above (Heb 4:9–11) explains it. We are called to enter a rest from our need to save ourselves, to be good enough for God, to somehow defeat sin in our lives. By giving ourselves away completely to him in confidence and hope, we will find his power fully able. Resting in him we can know victory, serenity, and wholeness (i.e., *shalom*). The author refers to it as a "Sabbath" or "stopping" rest, one like God's.

Today, you can rest in Christ's finished work for you. Do you believe that? Do!

December 14

SOLITUDE

Then Jesus, full of the Holy Spirit, returned from the Jordan
River. He was led by the Spirit in the wilderness. (Luke 4:1)

We live in days of endless noise. I don't mean the noise of the wind in the trees, a rushing brook, or excited birds in the morning. No, I mean the noise of Facebook, CNN, Fox, and YouTube. I see people walking down a sidewalk totally oblivious to a glorious, blue-skied, balmy-breezed day because their face is buried in the "noise" emanating from a glowing screen held in their hands. It is no wonder that we are keyed-up, worked-up, emotionally fragmented people who know nothing of serenity, moderation, and peace. It is no wonder that we are prey to the latest electronically-produced demagogue and are so easily led astray by them.

It is no accident that Jesus began his ministry with forty days of solitude. He needed to get away from the noise of his world. He needed to focus on reality. He needed to face reality in the form of the enemy tempting him to go about his ministry in self-serving ways.

Where will you find solitude during this Lenten season? What about this: remove all electronic media of any sort on each Sunday. Radical? Perhaps. But maybe life-giving, maybe life-renewing.

December 15

SOLITUDE AND PRAYER

But when you pray, go away by yourself, shut the door behind you, and
pray to your Father in private. Then your Father, who sees everything,
will reward you. When you pray, don't babble on and on as the Gentiles
do. They think their prayers are answered merely by repeating their
words again and again. Don't be like them, for your Father knows
exactly what you need even before you ask him! (Matthew 6:6–8)

Before daybreak the next morning, Jesus got up and went
out to an isolated place to pray. (Mark 1:35)

Jesus makes a very great point in the Sermon on the Mount about
praying in solitude. Go into your closet and shut the door. His primary
point in that section of the sermon is that we should not practice our
religion to be seen, whether it be giving, fasting, or praying. You will notice
that Jesus practiced this as well. When he prayed, he went off away from
people. Why did he do that? I am convinced that it was because he did not
want to be distracted.

We are so distractible. It seems that it is especially true in prayer.
Wesley counseled that you should keep a pad of paper in your prayer
closet, so you can write down the distracting thought and move on. We
are least distracted in a quiet and lonely place. There we can focus on
God, ultimate reality. The world and the Devil will fight against you and
your solitary prayer time with everything it has, because they know that
if they lose their grip on you in this particular realm, their whole chance
of maintaining some foothold is you is shaken right down to the ground.
If you don't practice solitude in this way, it is very likely that you will not
pray at all.

In this season of the year, it is almost laughable to speak of time to pray
in solitude. We are rushing from place to place doing this and that. But is
that not precisely the reason we should be doing it? Refocusing ourselves
on what the season is about: God with us?

December 16

SOLITUDE AND PRIORITIES

After sending them home, he went up into the hills by himself to
pray. Night fell while he was there alone. (Matthew 14:23)

One of our Enemy's great strategies is to keep us running. Someone has
spoken of "the tyranny of the urgent." We rush from this thing that
has to be done to that thing that has to be done to the next thing that has
to be done. All too often, the really important things that ought to be done,
although not right at this moment, never get done at all. If we *stop* and
walk away from all that stuff, if we go off alone with God, it is amazing how
he can reorder our priorities.

I believe that is what Jesus was doing during that forty days in the
Judean wastelands. He was letting God show him what he needed to do
and did not need to do in his ministry. His Father was showing him what
mattered and what didn't matter. Jesus was taking a deep breath and a
long view. I wonder if he was also giving himself time to grieve over what
had happened to John the Baptist (see Matt 14:10–13).

Is that something you need to do during this season? Perhaps you are
sacrificing your children or your spouse on the altar of your busy-ness,
and God wants to point that out to you. Maybe you are overlooking a great
opportunity that is right in front of your face but is obscured by all those
little things clamoring to be done. Maybe there is some reflecting that you
need to do but have not done. Solitude with God is the place to have your
eyes opened.

December 17

WAIT IN HOPE

My mercy and justice are coming soon. My salvation is on the way.
My strong arm will bring justice to the nations. All distant lands will
look to me and wait in hope for my powerful arm. (Isaiah 51:5)

In Isaiah 49–55 the prophet is talking about how it is that Yahweh can use sinful Israel as his chosen and beloved servants to be the evidence of sole Godhood—as he had said he would in chapters 41–48. The answer to the question is God's mighty arm, which will wipe clean the record of their sins. He will save them and redeem them. They will be able to live transformed lives that testify to Yahweh's world-shaking power. So God challenges them to wait in confident hope for that arm to be revealed. It is not only Israel that waits; it is the entire world. What God is going to do for Israel has worldwide implications and impact.

When that arm was actually revealed (see Isa 53:1), it was a terrible shock. It was not some mighty weight-lifter's arm. Rather, it was a little spindly thing that hardly had enough strength to lift itself, let alone defeat the mighty power of sin. People were tempted to say, "Surely this is not what we hoped for." But, yes, it is. Our hope is in that mighty power that was revealed in the weakness of the stable and the humiliation of the Cross. The power of God is his ability to take into himself all that sin could deal out and to give back love. That is our hope. Out of death comes resurrection.

Dear Lord Jesus, thank you that your weakness is power, and that your death is life. We have waited and you have come. Praise you! Let the weakness of your self-denial and the death of your right to your own way come to reality in us this Christmas. Amen.

December 18

A SPECIAL POSSESSION

Give these instructions to the Israelites: When you come into the land of Canaan, which I am giving you as your special possession, these will be the boundaries. (Numbers 34:2)

Remember that the LORD rescued you from the iron-smelting furnace of Egypt in order to make you his very own people and his special possession, which is what you are today. (Deuteronomy 4:20)

But you are not like that, for you are a chosen people. You are royal priests, a holy nation, God's very own possession. As a result, you can show others the goodness of God, for he called you out of the darkness into his wonderful light. (1 Peter 2:9)

When God makes out his Christmas wish list, what is the first item on it? You and me! We are what God wants as his "special possession." That Hebrew word, *nahala*, is usually translated "inheritance" (following the KJV), especially when referring to Israel's land, but today that meaning is far too restrictive, having come to mean something received from a dead parent. The New Living Translation, as above, has the better rendering: "special possession."

Yes, God's gift to Israel was the land of Canaan, a place where they could belong and prosper. But the gift *he* wanted was *them*! That is still true: God delights to give us good gifts of life, health, prosperity, and the ultimate gift of eternal life, but what he wants is us. He wants to live in your heart and mine, and he wants us to live in his heart. Ultimately, that is what eternal life is: living in the embrace of God.

How easily we focus on God's gifts to us, including his special gift of Jesus. But why does he give us gifts, including the Gift? It is because he wants what is to him the only thing worth having: our hearts. Christina Rosetti said it well: "What shall I give him, poor as I am? If I were a shepherd, I would give a lamb. If I were a wise man, I would do my part. Yet what I can I give him, give him my heart." All God wants for Christmas is *you*.

December 19

SIGNS: PART ONE

But Moses said to God, "Who am I that I should go to Pharaoh and bring the children of Israel out of Egypt?" He said, "But I will be with you, and this shall be the sign for you, that I have sent you: when you have brought the people out of Egypt, you shall serve God on this mountain." (Exodus 3:11–12 ESV)

This will be the sign for you, Hezekiah: "This year you will eat what grows by itself, and the second year what springs from that. But in the third year sow and reap, plant vineyards and eat their fruit." (2 Kings 19:29 NIV)

Do you ever feel like you need a sign, something that will prove to you that you are doing the right thing? Hezekiah was like that, and hundreds of years before him, Moses was too. God was asking each of these men to take a very big risk, one that could have fatal results if it went wrong. With Moses he was directing an old man to go back to Egypt, where there was a death sentence hanging over his head, and Hezekiah was being encouraged to thumb his nose at the Assyrian emperor's demand that he surrender. So, each of these men received a sign that they could trust God in taking this big risk.

What signs are these? To Moses, Yahweh said that one day Moses would lead his delivered people in worship on this very mountain (see Ex 3:12), and he gave Hezekiah the—dare I say it, crazy—sign quoted above: just wait three years and the Assyrian army that was presently devastating the land would be gone. Wait three years?! Yes, that is what God calls us to. To be sure, sometimes he gives us something immediately, as he did with Gideon in Judges 6:36–40. But that is not usually the case. Usually, he tells us about something that is going to happen in the future.

Why does God do this? It is for the same reason that he gave prophecy, not so that we can know the future but so that we will be encouraged to live faithfully now, daring to believe that he has the future in charge. Then, when the sign, or the prophecy, is fulfilled in the future, the vindication of our faith will encourage us to believe him still more fully.

What a day it must have been for Moses there on Sinai, as he recalled Yahweh's words. Likewise, what a day it was for Hezekiah as he watched his people sowing their fields in peace. Trust is always trust; that is, it is always a risk, because we must always come to the end of ourselves before God can do anything for us. Only then, when he can do anything he wants with us, can he save us.

Sure, go ahead and ask for a sign, but don't expect it to be fulfilled today! What you need to do is trust him.

December 20

SIGNS: PART TWO

As the crowd pressed in on Jesus, he said, "This evil generation
keeps asking me to show them a miraculous sign. But the only
sign I will give them is the sign of Jonah." (Luke 11:29)

Here, Jesus is doing the same thing we talked about in Part One. When the people demanded a sign that he really was the Messiah, he said the only sign he would give them was the sign of Jonah (see Luke 11:29), which with hindsight we know was his resurrection after spending parts of three days in the grave.

Again, I ask, what is the point of a sign like that? It is precisely about faith. Faith is about launching out into the unknown on the basis of a promise. That is what Abraham did, and it is what every spiritual child of Abraham has had to do ever since. But faith is not merely about launching into the unknown. That is not faith but stupidity. The sign is the promise: there is something to aim at, something to believe for. We dare to believe that the One making the promise is trustworthy, and we stake our lives on it, frame the shape of those lives on it. That is what biblical faith is about.

God does not usually give us unmistakable evidence before the fact to provoke us to action, but he does give us something to believe for. For us, the sign is that we will be raised from the dead, like Jesus. What a day that will be! Are you getting ready?

December 21
SIGNS: PART THREE

Hear this, House of David! Isn't it enough for you to wear out the people
that now you have to wear out my God as well? Therefore the Sovereign
will give you a sign: the maiden has conceived and is about to give birth to a
son; she will name him "God With Us." (Isaiah 7:13–14 author's translation)

King Ahaz was terrified. His two northern neighbors, Israel and Syria,
had attacked Judah, bent on deposing him and putting somebody else
on the throne. While he is checking his defenses, here comes Isaiah. (Why
is it, when you least want religious advice, some pious soul shows up!)

"Good news, Ahaz! You can trust Yahweh!" (Oh, sure.)

"Ask him for a sign, as high as heaven or as deep as hell." (What to do?
You don't want to appear a total atheist. Oh, I know!)

"I wouldn't think of testing God like that." (Piety is a wonderful cover-
up for unbelief.)

"Ahaz, isn't it enough that you wear out the people that now you have
to wear out my God, too? Well, you're going to get a sign anyhow, like it or
not. The maiden has conceived and is about to give birth to a baby boy. She
is going to name her baby 'God With Us.' And before God With Us is three
years old, the two nations you're so frightened of are going to be gone!"
(Oh, great! What happens to me in those three years? This is just like God.
Why can't he show me something right now that will *make* me believe
he can be trusted? Wait a minute—did he say the *maiden* has conceived?
What's that about?)

"Isaiah, did you just say a woman has conceived? A maiden is still
a virgin."

"I don't know, Ahaz. But that's what God told me to say. Maybe this
sign *is* as high as heaven or as deep as hell. Maybe this isn't just about
God being with you and me in this crisis. Maybe it is about God *actually—
physically*—coming to be with us through a virgin! Wouldn't that be great,
Ahaz?" (Good grief! Now I've not only got a religious fanatic on my hands,
but a certifiable nut!)

"Oh yes, Isaiah, that is indeed a wonderful thought. I am *so* glad you
shared it with me." (Now go away and leave me alone.)

Yes, indeed, it is a sign as high as heaven and as deep as hell. It took
700 years for the sign to come to its full fruition, but it has "come to pass."
Praise the Lord! Some, like Ahaz, dismissed it as foolishness, but the
saints, daring to believe what they could not see, trusted the God whose
promises never fail. May we be like them this Christmas.

December 22

SIGNS: PART FOUR

For unto you is born this day in the city of David a Savior, who is Christ
the Lord. And this will be a sign for you: you will find a baby wrapped
in swaddling cloths and lying in a manger. (Luke 2:11–12 ESV)

Here we are again with another of God's strange signs. Alright, we have
seen a startling apparition: angels, yes, and singing, too. That doesn't
happen every night. And a stunning message: the Messiah, the One we've
been waiting for all these years has been born tonight. Yesss!

But wait. Born where? Here, in little, nondescript Bethlehem? Not
Jerusalem? How are we supposed to recognize him? He'll be lying in a
hay trough, wrapped in rags? What? And we're supposed to leave our
flocks out here unguarded and go from door to door, waking people up
and asking if they have a baby in one of their hay troughs? Then, if we find
something one, *that* will be the proof that we didn't just drink too much
cheap wine tonight?

Well, I suppose if I had had an angelic vision like that, I might have
been moved to take a walk like that. But really, a baby wrapped in rags
lying in a hay-trough, *that* is the evidence that God can be believed? Yes, it
is, and somehow that is just what the shepherds found, and that convinced
them that what they had heard out of the sky was exactly right—the
Messiah had come!

This is all so like our God. He calls us to do crazy things, acting on what
is sometimes the flimsiest of evidence, daring to believe that somewhere
down the road will come the confirmation that will demonstrate we
really weren't crazy to trust him. And what about that confirmation—a
baby wrapped in rags lying in a hay trough? Yes, our God is anything but
conventional!

But what's the point? Oh, surely the point is what all that the world
looks to for significance and worth—glory, that is—things like wealth,
status, money, and possessions. No, they are all empty trinkets without
him. *With* him, rags and a hay-trough are heaven.

Is he to be found this Christmas? Oh yes! Just be sure you're looking
in the right place.

December 23

SIGNS: PART FIVE

Then Simeon blessed them, and he said to Mary, the baby's mother, "This child is destined to cause many in Israel to fall, but he will be a joy to many others. He has been sent as a sign from God, but many will oppose him." (Luke 2:34)

We have seen that God's signs are somewhat strange. Sometimes the sign is an immediate confirmation of the validity of what has been said (for instance, the splitting of Jeroboam's altar as confirmation of the prediction that a Davidic king named Josiah would one day desecrate that altar [see 1 Kgs 13:5]). However, much more commonly, the sign itself is a future promise whose fulfillment will confirm the faith of the one who acts upon the promise.

It begins with Abraham, for whom the promise is a land that he never possessed. Because of his act of faith, though, his descendants did indeed possess that land. The culmination of all of those signs is Jesus Christ, as Simeon recognized. What an act of faith it was—and is—to recognize him!

What about the Wise Men? They were looking for a king; what was it about a little boy in the modest home of a refugee couple that made them say, "This is him!"? Faith. What made Simeon, who had read the same Scriptures that had led others to look for a heaven-sent mighty man, to joyfully embrace this baby of a couple so poor that the only circumcision offering they could afford was a couple of pigeons, and instantly proclaim, "This is he!"? Faith.

Yes, the Savior of the world, the One who by reason of dying for the world, will have supreme authority over the world in the end is this One, who "has no comeliness that we should desire him" (Isa 53:2). How like God! *This* is the evidence upon which we are to stake our eternal destiny? *This* is the reason why we should surrender the shape and direction of our lives to God's will? A quiet, homely man telling stories in a country accent? Yes, he was able to do some startling miracles, but that was not enough to counteract all the contrary evidence. So they cried, "Give us a sign!" And he replied, "The only sign I will give you is the sign of Jonah" (Luke 11:29). Exactly.

Believe in him now because at some future point, he will rise from the dead. What kind of a sign is that? It is a God sign. Yet even that, when it was fulfilled, was not enough to produce faith in an unbeliever. Today, for you and me, Jesus is the sign that there is a God, a God of infinite, undeserved love.

December 24

MY PEACE I LEAVE WITH YOU

But the Helper, the Holy Spirit, whom the Father will send in my
name, he will teach you all things and bring to your remembrance
all that I have said to you. Peace I leave with you; my peace I give
to you. Not as the world gives do I give to you. Let not your hearts
be troubled, neither let them be afraid. (John 14:26–27 ESV)

At this Christmas season, one of the recurring themes related to the coming of Christ is that of peace. On the night of his birth the angels sang, "Peace on earth." That seems entirely appropriate as Isaiah tells us he is the Prince of Peace and of his kingdom and peace there will be no end (see Isa 9:7). Yet he himself said he did not come to bring peace to the world, but a sword (see Matt 10:34). What are we to make of this, especially in the light of the verses above? Is Jesus confused, or what?

He is not confused, but these verses are talking about three different things: the ultimate impact of Christ's ministry in the world, the short-term impact in the world, and the means by which Christ intends to achieve his goal. Intimately connected with all that is the biblical concept that we translate with the English word "peace." The English word primarily connotes the absence of conflict. While the biblical terms, rooted in the Hebrew words having the consonants *sh*, *l*, and *m*, can connote that idea, they go much deeper. They speak of making something whole and complete. One of the words is used for paying a debt. That is, as long as the debt is not paid, the arrangement is incomplete, it is not "at peace." But when we pay off the debt, we make the transaction whole.

So, God's ultimate goal for his cosmos through his Son is that all wrongs will have been righted, all sins atoned for, and nothing left unsettled or undone: peace. What a day, the day of his Second Coming! But what of the immediate impact of Jesus's ministry, the day of his First Coming? Did it put things together for the Jews? Far from it! It forced them to make difficult decisions. Was this itinerant preacher from Nazareth the Messiah? And more than that, was he the Son of God? As Jesus said, he brought a sword that would divide families and nations into warring factions. His stupendous claims could do nothing else in a world where sin holds so many in its iron grip.

But what about this period between the two comings? Are we simply to resign ourselves to a hopeful anticipation of that last day, all the while echoing the words of Longfellow's hymn: "there is no peace on earth"? No! That is the beauty of what Jesus said in John 14. He can give a peace about which the world knows nothing. He can make each of us whole, complete. He does not offer absence of conflict, calm, shining days where trouble is far away. No, he told us that in this world, before his Second Coming, we will have trouble.

Instead, he offers a "peace" that the world cannot give! He can take our divided hearts, partly his and partly our own, and make them one for him. That is peace, the peace that Christmas has made possible, here and now. That is my Christmas wish for you, that you have or you will allow the Holy Spirit to take all the strands of your life and make them all his. Merry Christmas indeed!

December 25

WHO COMES TO CHRISTMAS?

For unto us a child is born, unto us a son is given. (Isaiah 9:6 KJV)

H ave you ever thought about the cast of characters in the Christmas accounts? When you do, I think you will be impressed at the breadth. For instance, there is the *young*. Mary was most certainly a teenager, and perhaps a young teenager (see Matt 2:18). Christmas has about it all the freshness and anticipation of youth. Then, there are the *old*. Anna and Simeon are near the end of their lives, which have been lived with expectation and hope (see Luke 2:25, 34, 36). Christmas is about the fulfillment of life, the final resolution of all the hopes and dreams, fears and despairs, successes and failures. Christmas means life ends in triumph, not with a sigh.

There are *females*: young Mary and old Anna. Christmas is for women. Although for centuries oppressed and imprisoned in their own homes, lusted after, and feared by their men, God's choice to come into a virgin's womb and be welcomed by an aged widow in Christmas tells us that he values women for and in themselves. Of course, there are *males*. The primary one is Joseph, a man characterized above all by sensitivity to God and instant obedience. (see Matt 1:19–25). He is not a "macho-man," a "wild one." He is decisive, to be sure, but in a quiet and unassuming way that is always shaped by his responsibilities for his wife and child. The "macho-man" is Herod, the child-murderer (see Matt 2:16). Christmas is for real men.

There are *intellectuals*: the magi (see Matt 2:1, 7, 16). Christmas in all its wonder and profundity can engage the sharpest minds available anywhere. There are also the *illiterate*: the shepherds (see Luke 2:8, 15, 18, 20). It is not necessary to have an advanced degree to appreciate the wondrous simplicity of what God has done in laying aside all his prerogatives to become the child of a refugee couple.

There are the *rich*: people bearing gifts of gold, frankincense, and myrrh (see Matt 2:11). And at the other end of the social spectrum, there are the *outcasts of society*, good for nothing except wandering around after sheep, trying to keep them out of trouble.

Christmas is for all of us: young, old; female, male; educated, illiterate; rich, poor—all of us. Christ came to earth for every one of us no matter where we find ourselves. The Baby in the manger lifts his arms to each of us and invites us to join him in his crying over a broken world and in his laughter over a world redeemed.

December 26
WHO DOESN'T COME TO CHRISTMAS?

"Where is the newborn king of the Jews? We saw his star as it rose, and we have come to worship him." King Herod was deeply disturbed when he heard this, as was everyone in Jerusalem. He called a meeting of the leading priests and teachers of religious law and asked, "Where is the Messiah supposed to be born?" "In Bethlehem in Judea," they said, "for this is what the prophet wrote: 'And you, O Bethlehem in the land of Judah, are not least among the ruling cities of Judah, for a ruler will come from you who will be the shepherd for my people Israel.'" (Matthew 2:2–6)

We have thought of who came to Christmas and concluded that the world knelt before the newborn King, but who didn't come? The politically and religiously powerful: Herod and the priests and the teachers of religious law. Why didn't they come? Perhaps Herod's absence is the easier to explain. This Bethlehem baby posed a challenge to the personal position that Herod had so carefully built up through genius, intrigue, and murder over the past thirty years. No matter who that baby was, he was not going to supplant Herod! Oh, but that is what Jesus does. He comes to take us off the throne of our lives so that we can have fellowship with the Lifegiver. Are you willing to come to Christmas, "Herod"?

What about the priests and the Bible scholars? Shouldn't they have gotten out their chariots and "hot-footed" it to Bethlehem to see this great event which the Bible—no wandering star—is so clear about? Why didn't they? I would suggest that they had become so familiar with religious things that they had forgotten what the religion is all about—a living relationship with the living God. The priests were concerned with keeping the customs and traditions and rituals just right, and the Bible scholars wanted to be sure they got the citations of the famous rabbis of the past just right. The Messiah? In Bethlehem? Oh yeah, maybe so, but we've got other things to think about.

Is that you and me? Do we love the Christian religion or Jesus? Are we willing to come to Christmas?

December 27
REJOICE!

Shout to the LORD, all the earth; break out in praise and sing for
joy! Sing your praise to the LORD with the harp, with the harp and
melodious song, with trumpets and the sound of the ram's horn. Make
a joyful symphony before the LORD, the King! (Psalm 98:4–6)

One of my professors once said that you can tell a lot about a people
on the basis of their vocabulary. The more important something is
to them, the more words they have to express the various connotations.
Thus, it is said, the Eskimos have seven different words for snow.

This is an especially important point in the Hebrew language, because
it has a very small general vocabulary. That means that for some important
words, there will be several different, though-related, English ideas
expressed by one single Hebrew word. So, when we find several Hebrew
words used for a single idea, it means that idea is really important.

For concepts related to sin there are at least eight different Hebrew
words, but the same thing is true with the idea of singing joyfully. In
Psalm 99 no fewer than five different words for musical rejoicing appear,
four of them in verse four alone. Why would this be the case? Why wouldn't
one all-purpose word, like "sing," for instance, be enough?

Clearly it is not enough because the Israelites need more ways than
just one of expressing the wonder they have found in Yahweh, their God.
He is the Creator, the Savior, the Wonder-worker, the Deliverer, the One
who made the world in order, and who, praise his name, is coming to set it
in order—the meaning of the word often translated "judge"—again. He is
Love, he is Truth, he is Power.

This is why Christmas is a musical season. He has come! One carol is
not enough. We need every one in the repertoire, and we need some new
ones. But it is not just about the Baby; it is about the fact that the Creator-
Savior-Wonder-worker-Deliverer-Reorderer has come! Our God is cause
for rejoicing. If you are not singing for joy these days, maybe you need to
reflect a little more deeply on the wonder of our God.

December 28

THE KINGDOM OF THE CHILD

*In that day the wolf and the lamb will live together; the leopard will
lie down with the baby goat. The calf and the yearling will be safe
with the lion, and a little child will lead them all. (Isaiah 11:6)*

*Then he said, "I tell you the truth, unless you turn from your sins
and become like little children, you will never get into the Kingdom
of Heaven. So anyone who becomes as humble as this little child
is the greatest in the Kingdom of Heaven." (Matthew 18:3–4)*

In Isaiah 7–12 there is a very interesting feature: the prominence of
children. It is especially interesting because of the historical context
of these chapters. Judah's northern neighbors, Israel and Syria, were
attacking Judah and were going to take King Ahaz off the throne—
probably by killing him!—and make another man king, almost certainly
not someone descended from David. You can understand that Ahaz was
terrified, as was the whole Davidic family.

Isaiah's answer was with children. There was his son "Only a Remnant
will Return" and his other son "The Spoil Speeds, the Prey hastes." Then
there was "God With Us" and the poor little kid with four names, the
first of which was "Wonderful Counselor." The last child, referred to in
Isaiah 11:6, has no name, but he is filled with the Spirit of God. What is
going on?

Judah doesn't need children; they need some sort of a WWF wrestler
who can crush the enemy! What is it with all these children? To answer
that question we need to reflect a moment on the source of all the violence
and hatred in the world. That source is nothing other than pride—pride
multiplied exponentially, expanded to worldwide dimensions. So what
is the solution? More violence spurred by pride? Hardly! We need less
pride. This is where children come in. I used to think Jesus used them as
examples because children are innocent. Then Karen and I had some!

Matthew 18:4 explains the exemplary quality in children. They are
humble; that is, they are not self-conscious. Can children do bad and cruel
things? Of course they can, but they are remarkably free of pride. This is
the gift the Holy Spirit makes available to us adults: glad self-forgetfulness.

Let us receive this gift at Christmas and take it with us into the new
year. To receive the gift, we will have to surrender our pride, but the
exchange is worth everything.

December 29

WHY HE CAME

He has been merciful to our ancestors by remembering his sacred
covenant—the covenant he swore with an oath to our ancestor Abraham.
We have been rescued from our enemies so we can serve God without
fear, in holiness and righteousness for as long as we live. (Luke 1:72–75)

Why did Jesus come? It is common to assert that the reason many
of the Jews rejected Jesus as the Messiah was because he did not
fulfill their expectations of the Messiah. He was not a royal figure who did
signs and wonders on a national scale to deliver them from their enemies
so that they, God's people, could live in power and abundance. While that
may have been true for some, even many, notice what Zechariah, John
the Baptist's father, expects the Messiah to do. Yes, he will deliver his
people from their enemies, and I suppose that might have been a military
deliverance in Zechariah's imagination, but look what the deliverance is an
expression of and look what he expects it to achieve.

First, it is a fulfillment of the Abrahamic (not the Davidic) covenant.
That promise was of progeny, a homeland, and a blessing to the nations;
that is, of endurance, security, and mission. The Messiah's coming was the
evidence that these promises would not fail.

Second, what would the Messiah's coming make possible? Would it
mean comfort, security, pleasure, and power for God's people (something
very little different from the expectation of modern Christians of their
Christ)? No, it would mean freedom to serve God without fear, a service
marked by a quality of life indistinguishable from God's own life.

Why has Jesus come? He has come to make it possible for God's
original intent to be realized, and Zechariah knew that! As we look to the
new year, let us anticipate with joy the courageous service of our God,
living lives that are a mirror of his. It is for this that Christ came. He did not
come so that we could live for ourselves, confident of our spot in heaven
after awhile. He came so that the Holy Spirit could take up residence in
clean temples, out of which could shine the very light of God in a dark and
darkening world.

December 30

ALL THINGS NEW

Look! I am creating new heavens and a new earth, and no one will even think about the old ones anymore. (Isaiah 65:17)

This means that anyone who belongs to Christ has become a new person. The old life is gone; a new life has begun! (2 Corinthians 5:17)

And the one sitting on the throne said, "Look, I am making everything new!" And then he said to me, "Write this down, for what I tell you is trustworthy and true." (Revelation 21:5)

Why do we speak of a "new" year? Are we going to have June as the first month followed by April as the second? Is Spring going to precede Winter? Of course not. This year is going to be just the same as last year, with the same months, the same seasons, following one another in the same sequence as they always have. This isn't a new year, it is just the old one starting over. The "Preacher" says it well, "There is nothing new under the sun" (Eccl 1:9 and about a dozen times more). The key term there is "under the sun." Yes, if that is our only vantage point, there is nothing new and no possibility of anything genuinely new ever occurring. That is so because the world is incapable of altering itself. Differences, yes, but something absolutely new? Never. So, can you and I ever transcend our conditioning and environment? No. The best we can hope for is self-realization.

However, Yahweh, the I Am, who exists in himself, is the Creator, existing apart from what he has created. Having brought it into existence, he can alter that creation in any way he chooses. So, he can do a new thing, such as taking a people home from captivity when no one has ever gone home from captivity before. In the same way, Yahweh can take a life that has been locked in a recurring cycle of despair and do a new thing. Through his power, we *can* transcend our conditioning and environment and become a new person. Of course, he is working with the same basic stuff of our personality, but he can come up with radically new results. He can *save* us, and it can be a new year!

December 31
PROGRESS

But forget all that—it is nothing compared to what I am going to do.
For I am about I to do something new. See, I have already begun!
Do you not see it? I will make a pathway through the wilderness.
I will create rivers in the dry wasteland. (Isaiah 43:18–19)

As we look into another year, I wonder if we are aware of how much we owe the Bible for our Western way of thinking and how tenuous that way of thinking is as our ignorance of the biblical way of thinking grows exponentially. In pagan thought there is constant change but no progress. This life is an endless cycle coming from nowhere and going nowhere. In that cycle nothing is permanent, but the endless changes accomplish nothing.

So, where did our Western idea of progress come from? It comes straight from the Bible, where there is a God who, unlike the gods, is not captive to the unchanging system. He is outside the cosmos and can enter it and alter it in any way he wishes. More than this, unlike the gods, our God has plans, good plans. So, when he makes promises to an old, landless, childless immigrant couple, he points to a future unlike anything they have known before. It is not merely change he offers but progress.

Then, as we think of the year ahead, we can confidently expect that the end of the year will not only find us different but better. We are not prisoners of maddening, meaningless change but pilgrims on our way to the heavenly kingdom.

INDEX

Scripture References

OLD TESTAMENT

When Morning Gilds the Skies

Topics/Personas

A

B

C

rejoice 10, 16, 18, 70, 78, 91, 101,
    103, 106, 120, 125, 169, 189,
    191, 203, 220, 227, 254–255,
    258, 268, 312, 365, 381, 383

repent 64, 108, 144, 147, 174, 191,
    205, 271, 326, 337, 356,
    358–359

resentment 16–17

resurrection 61, 67, 113, 118, 186,
    274, 298, 302, 326, 342,
    357, 370, 373

revival 83, 116, 169, 219

righteousness 79, 106, 141, 169,
    181, 186, 195, 249–251, 279,
    301, 327, 343

rights 11, 148, 159, 194, 212, 268,
    270, 297, 358

Rinkert, Martin 274

Roosevelt, Franklin 197

Rosetti, Christina 371

Roy, Olivier 112

S

Sabbath 283, 366

sacrifice 17, 26, 37, 52, 99, 176,
    216, 226, 234, 260, 267, 283,
    287, 321–322, 328, 362

salvation 15, 27, 30, 33, 36, 39, 46,
    80, 101, 115, 127, 193, 216,
    236, 238, 269, 285–286,
    288–289, 309, 326–327,
    329, 342, 353

sanctification 106

Satan 12, 33, 106, 145, 186, 223,
    274, 358

Schaeffer, Francis 149

Seamands, J. T. 299

Second Coming, The 377–378

security 40, 60, 88, 112, 143, 184,
    200, 254–255, 345, 383

self
    absorption 17
    assertive 306
    centeredness 206, 213, 261,
        310, 326, 348
    conscious 13, 63, 382
    denial 138, 153, 168, 183,
        196, 232, 257, 291, 313,
        324, 370
    doubt 47
    esteem 261, 291
    forgetfulness 78, 297, 382
    giving 98, 121, 183, 232,
        282, 324, 326
    indulgent 54, 259
    inflation 47
    interest 110, 291–292
    justification 17
    pity 17
    realization 384
    righteousness 106, 181, 343
    serving 26, 54, 110, 134, 152,
        180–181, 186, 283, 296,
        343, 367
    will 198, 245, 308, 337
    worship 290

Sermon on the Mount 206–207,
    319, 368

servant 117, 148, 179, 214, 269

sexuality 11, 38, 159, 169, 275,
    280, 311, 320, 328

Shaeffer, Francis 119

shame 124, 188, 298, 327

signs 169, 207, 219, 230, 372–376,
    383

sin 16–18, 20, 25, 30, 33, 37, 42,
    46, 53, 64, 76, 85, 87–88,
    92, 99, 107, 125, 134, 144,
    147, 149–152, 168, 171, 177,
    201, 204, 229, 241, 246,
    250–251, 253, 257, 266, 272,
    286, 288–290, 295, 303,

Made in the USA
Columbia, SC
05 November 2023

25011064R00222